Israel's National Security Law

Terror attacks on Western civilian targets have stimulated interest in the dilemmas faced by liberal societies when combating threats to national security. Combining the perspectives of political science and law, this book addresses that discourse, asking how democracies seek to harmonize the protection of individual liberties with the defence of state interests.

The book focuses on the experience of Israel, a country whose commitment to democratic values has continuously been challenged by multiple threats to national survival. It examines the legal, legislative and institutional methods employed to resolve the dilemmas generated by that situation, and thus provides a unique interpretation of Israeli national security behavior. Policy-making and policy-implementation in this sphere, it shows, have reflected not just external constraints but also shifts in the domestic balance of power between the executive, the legislature and the judiciary. The book concludes with an agenda of the measures that each branch of government needs to implement in order to repair the flaws that have developed in this system over time.

Based on a close reading of legislative and court proceedings, the book proposes a new taxonomy for the analysis of national security legal frameworks, both in Israel and elsewhere in the democratic world. As such it will be of great interest to students and scholars of political science, national security law, Israeli history and civil–military relations.

Amichai Cohen teaches International Law at the Faculty of Law, Ono Academic College, Israel, and is a researcher at the Israel Democracy Institute. His research interests are International Humanitarian Law, and the interaction between International Law and Domestic Law.

Stuart A. Cohen teaches Political Studies at Bar-Ilan University, Israel, where he is also senior research associate of the BESA (Begin–Sadat) Center for Strategic Studies. He is the author of *Israel and its Army* (Routledge 2008) and edited *The New Citizen Armies: Israel's armed forces in comparative perspective* (Routledge 2010).

Israeli history, politics and society
Series Editor: Efraim Karsh
King's College London

This series provides a multidisciplinary examination of all aspects of Israeli history, politics and society, and serves as a means of communication between the various communities interested in Israel: academics, policy-makers; practitioners; journalists and the informed public.

1 **Peace in the Middle East**
 The challenge for Israel
 Edited by Efraim Karsh

2 **The Shaping of Israeli Identity**
 Myth, memory and trauma
 Edited by Robert Wistrich and David Ohana

3 **Between War and Peace**
 Dilemmas of Israeli security
 Edited by Efraim Karsh

4 **US–Israeli Relations at the Crossroads**
 Edited by Gabriel Sheffer

5 **Revisiting the Yom Kippur War**
 Edited by P R Kumaraswamy

6 **Israel**
 The dynamics of change and continuity
 Edited by David Levi-Faur, Gabriel Sheffer and David Vogel

7 **In Search of Identity**
 Jewish aspects in Israeli culture
 Edited by Dan Urian and Efraim Karsh

8 **Israel at the Polls, 1996**
 Edited by Daniel J Elazar and Shmuel Sandler

9 **From Rabin to Netanyahu**
 Israel's troubled agenda
 Edited by Efraim Karsh

10 **Fabricating Israeli History**
 The 'New Historians', second revised edition
 Efraim Karsh

11 **Divided against Zion**
 Anti-Zionist opposition in Britain to a Jewish state in Palestine, 1945–1948
 Rory Miller

12 **Peacemaking in a Divided Society**
 Israel after Rabin
 Edited by Sasson Sofer

13 **A Twenty-Year Retrospective of Egyptian–Israeli Relations**
Peace in spite of everything
Ephraim Dowek

14 **Global Politics**
Essays in honor of David Vital
Edited by Abraham Ben-Zvi and Aharon Klieman

15 **Parties, Elections and Cleavages**
Israel in comparative and theoretical perspective
Edited by Reuven Y. Hazan and Moshe Maor

16 **Israel and the Polls 1999**
Edited by Daniel J. Elazar and M. Ben Mollov

17 **Public Policy in Israel**
Edited by David Nachmias and Gila Menahem

18 **Developments in Israeli Public Administration**
Edited by Moshe Maor

19 **Israeli Diplomacy and the Quest for Peace**
Mordechai Gazit

20 **Israeli-Romanian Relations at the End of Ceaucescu's Era**
Yosef Govrin

21 **John F Kennedy and the Politics of Arms Sales to Israel**
Abraham Ben-Zvi

22 **Green Crescent over Nazareth**
The displacement of Christians by Muslims in the Holy Land
Raphael Israeli

23 **Jerusalem Divided**
The Armistice region, 1947–1967
Raphael Israeli

24 **Decision on Palestine Deferred**
America, Britain and wartime diplomacy, 1939–1945
Monty Noam Penkower

25 **A Dissenting Democracy**
The case of 'Peace Now', an Israeli peace movement
Magnus Norell

26 **British, Israel and Anglo-Jewry 1947–1957**
Natan Aridan

27 **Israeli Identity**
In search of a successor to the pioneer, Tsabar and Settler
Lilly Weissbrod

28 **The Israeli Palestinians**
An Arab minority in the Jewish state
Edited by Alexander Bligh

29 **Israel, the Hashemites and the Palestinians**
The fateful triangle
Edited by Efraim Karsh and P. R. Kumaraswamy

30 **Last Days in Israel**
Abraham Diskin

31 **War in Palestine, 1948**
Strategy and diplomacy
David Tal

32 **Rethinking the Middle East**
Efraim Karsh

33 **Ben-Gurion against the Knesset**
Giora Goldberg

34 **Trapped Fools**
Thirty years of Israeli policy in the territories
Schlomo Gazit

35 **Israel's Quest for Recognition and Acceptance in Asia**
Garrison state diplomacy
Jacob Abadi

36 **The Harp and Shield of David**
Ireland, Zionism and the state of Israel, 1937–1963
Eliash Shulamit

37 **H V Evatt and the Establishment of Israel**
The undercover Zionist
Daniel Mandel

38 **Navigating Perilous Waters**
An Israeli strategy for peace and security
Ephraim Sneh

39 **Lyndon B Johnson and the Politics of Arms Sales to Israel**
In the shadow of the hawk
Abraham Ben-Zvi

40 **Israel at the Polls 2003**
Edited by Shmeul Sandler, Ben M. Mollov and Jonathan Rynhold

41 **Between Capital and Land**
The Jewish national fund's finances and land-purchase priorities in Palestine, 1939–1945
Eric Engel Tuten

42 **Israeli Democracy at Crossroads**
Raphael Cohen-Almagor

43 **Israeli Institutions at Crossroads**
Raphael Cohen-Almagor

44 **The Israeli-Palestine Peace Process Negotiations, 1999–2001**
Within reach
Gilead Sher

45 **Ben-Gurion's Political Struggles, 1963–67**
A lion in winter
Zaki Shalom

46 **Ben-Gurion, Zionism and American Jewry**
1948–1963
Ariel Feldestein

47 **The Origins of the American–Israeli Alliance**
The Jordanian factor
Abraham Ben-Zvi

48 **The Harp and the Shield of David**
Ireland, Zionism and the state of Israel
Shulamit Eliash

49 **Israel's National Security**
Issues and challenges since the Yom Kippur War
Efraim Inbar

50 **The Rise of Israel**
A history of a revolutionary state
Jonathan Adelman

51 **Israel and the Family of Nations**
The Jewish nation-state and human rights
Alexander Yakobson and Amnon Rubinstein

52 **Secularism and Religion in Jewish-Israeli Politics**
Traditionists and modernity
Yaacov Yadgar

53 **Israel's National Security Law**
Political dynamics and historical development
Amichai Cohen and Stuart A. Cohen

Israel: The First Hundred Years (Mini Series)
Edited by Efraim Karsh

1 **Israel's Transition from Community to State**
Edited by Efraim Karsh

2 **From War to Peace?**
Edited by Efraim Karsh

3 **Politics and Society since 1948**
Edited by Efraim Karsh

4 **Israel in the International Arena**
Edited by Efraim Karsh

5 **Israel in the next Century**
Edited by Efraim Karsh

Israel's National Security Law

Political dynamics and historical development

Amichai Cohen and Stuart A. Cohen

LONDON AND NEW YORK

First published 2012
by Routledge
2 Park Square, Milton Park, Abingdon, Oxfordshire OX14 4RN

Simultaneously published in the USA and Canada
by Routledge
711 Third Avenue, New York, NY 10017

First issued in paperback 2014

Routledge is an imprint of the Taylor & Francis Group, an informa company

© 2012 Amichai Cohen and Stuart A. Cohen

The right of Amichai Cohen and Stuart A. Cohen to be identified as authors of this work has been asserted by them in accordance with sections 77 and 78 of the Copyright, Designs and Patents Act 1988.

All rights reserved. No part of this book may be reprinted or reproduced or utilized in any form or by any electronic, mechanical, or other means, now known or hereafter invented, including photocopying and recording, or in any information storage or retrieval system, without permission in writing from the publishers.

Trademark notice: Product or corporate names may be trademarks or registered trademarks, and are used only for identification and explanation without intent to infringe.

British Library Cataloguing in Publication Data
A catalogue record for this book is available from the British Library

Library of Congress Cataloging in Publication Data
Cohen, Amichai.
  Israel's national security law: political dynamics and historical development/Amichai Cohen and Stuart A. Cohen.
  p. cm. – (Israeli history, politics and society)
  Includes bibliographical references and index.
  1. National security–Law and legislation–Israel. I. Cohen, Stuart, 1946– II. Title.
  KMK3350.C64 2011
  343.5694′01–dc22

2011007332

ISBN 13: 978-0-415-54914-1 (hbk)
ISBN 13: 978-1-138-78873-2 (pbk)

Typeset in Baskerville
By Wearset Ltd, Boldon, Tyne and Wear

To our families
Psalms 128:5–6

Contents

Acknowledgments	xii
Abbreviations	xiii
Introduction	1

PART I
Foundations — 9

1	Frameworks of analysis	11
2	Cultural contexts	30

PART II
Development — 49

3	Centralization, 1948–1963	51
4	Diffusion, 1963–1977	78
5	Realignment, 1977–1995	106
6	Legalization, 1995–2008	143

PART III
Perspectives and prescriptions — 175

7	Diagnosis: Israel's hybrid national security legal framework	177
8	Prognosis: modes of reform	208

Notes	242
Bibliography	252
Index	275

Acknowledgments

In more senses than one, the writing of this book has been a family enterprise. Our first and deepest debt of gratitude, therefore, is to the members of our families, joint and separate, who have supported us in ways too numerous to specify. We dedicate this book to them with love, and with the prayer that they will continue to display similarly remarkable virtues of tolerance, support and understanding in all walks of life.

Sincere thanks are also due to other individuals, without whose assistance and encouragement we would never have embarked on this project, let alone seen it through. Primary amongst these are the chairpersons of our individual academic homes in Israel, respectively Dean Dudi Schwarz of the Faculty of Law at Ono Academic College and Professor Amikam Nachmani of the Department of Political Studies at Bar-Ilan University. In addition to creating an ambience particularly conducive to research and academic discourse, both persons also generously granted us sabbatical leave, which enabled us to focus on this project. Indeed, many of the concepts developed in this book were conceived and thrashed out during the course of 2009–2010, which we both spent in Washington, DC: Amichai at the Washington College of Law, the American University and Stuart at the Center for Peace and Security Studies, Georgetown University. Both institutions provided a remarkably hospitable environment, and it is, therefore, a pleasure as well as a duty to express our gratitude to, respectively, Dean Claudio Grossman and Professor Daniel Byman, who did more than we could ever have expected to make our stays enjoyable as well as productive.

Special thanks are also due to Professor Efraim Karsh, the editor of the series in which this book appears, who from the first expressed confidence in our project and interest in its progress.

Ultimately, however, it is the publisher who enables the manuscript to see the light of day. Not for the first time, working with Routledge has proven to be a delight. The forbearance and professionalism exhibited at every stage of the commissioning and production process have been exemplary and are much appreciated.

Abbreviations

CGS	Chief of the General Staff
CO	Commanding Officer
DER	Defense (Emergency) Regulations
FADC	Foreign Affairs and Defense Committee of the *knesset*
GSS	General Security Services (*shabak*)
ICC	International Criminal Court
ICJ	International Court of Justice
IDF	Israel Defense Force
IHL	International Humanitarian Law
ISC	Israel Supreme Court
HCJ	High Court of Justice
MAG	(Chief) Military Advocate General
MCSA	Ministerial Committee on Security Affairs
MK	Member of the *knesset*
NSC	National Security Council
NSS	National Security Staff

Introduction

Academic enquiries into the formulation and implementation of Israel's national security policies advanced a significant stage in 1995, when Dr Yehuda Ben-Meir published his seminal and authoritative study of *Civil–Military Relations in Israel* (Ben-Meir 1995). Ben-Meir possessed the unique advantage of combining a broad theoretical understanding of the subject with an unprecedented wealth of empirical data, much of it gleaned during a long political career that had included a spell as Israel's deputy minister for foreign affairs, 1981–1984. He also displayed particular sensitivity to the changing substance of the issues affecting Israel's national security discourse. Not least was this evident in his decision to devote the initial pages of his study to a description of the government of Israel's response to the rising incidence of terrorist activity in the early 1990s, and especially to the kidnap and murder of an Israeli policeman in December 1992. On the day the body of the victim was discovered, Prime Minister Yitzchak Rabin gave instructions that the Israel Defense Forces (IDF) be ordered to intern more than 400 Palestinian residents of the West Bank, who were known to be active members of the Hamas organization, and deport them across Israel's northern border into Lebanese territory.

This was not the first occasion since 1967 that Israel had resorted to deportation. Hitherto, however, the measure had been employed infrequently and the numbers involved on any single occasion had been very small. Clearly, therefore, Rabin's decision cannot be explained away as a continuation of past policies. It must be considered a new departure. Searching for the reasons for the change, Ben-Meir places responsibility firmly on the shoulders of Israel's defense establishment, whose power and influence over decision-making he considers the entire episode to encapsulate. In his account, the person most strongly in favor of a large-scale deportation was the chief of the IDF's general staff (CGS), General Ehud Barak, who had long advocated such measures. Once Barak had secured Rabin's acquiescence, which the most recent terrorist outrage made forthcoming, the government was bound to adopt the course the two men proposed. No forum in the country could withstand the pressure exerted by the coalition of an adamant CGS with a prime minister who had campaigned in the recent elections as 'Mr. Security', a reputation built upon Rabin's own tenure as CGS during the late 1960s and enhanced during his extended service as Minister of Defense, 1986–1990. The cabinet's approval of the deportation was indeed almost a formality.

Without in any way disputing the validity of Ben-Meir's overall analysis of the imbalance in relations in Israel between politicians and generals, retired as well as active, the present study starts from the premise that those are not the only actors directly involved in the formulation and implementation of Israel's national security policy. Much of that policy has in fact evolved within the context of a discourse that is as much legal as pragmatic, and hence can usefully be analyzed from the perspectives of the input provided by both legislators and the judiciary. Re-examination of the 1992 Hamas deportation episode provides evidence of the extent to which that is so.

As a political tool, deportations had always been problematic. One reason was substantive: they were based on the debatable idea that Palestinian violence in the regions conquered by Israeli forces during the course of the Six Days War of 1967 ('the Territories') was a minority phenomenon; it could be contained by identifying its perpetrators and deporting them to a neighboring Arab country. By and large, it was assumed, Palestinian resistance to Israeli rule would be passive, or even non-existent. The decision to deport 400 Hamas activists undermined that entire thesis. It implied that terrorism and support for terrorism was much more widespread than had earlier been assumed. It also constituted an admission that the Palestinian *intifada* ('uprising'), which had been raging since December 1987, could not be brought to a halt simply by deporting isolated troublemakers.

Then there was the legal predicament. The details need not detain us here (they are discussed at length in subsequent chapters), but at least some experts in international law maintained that deportations were strictly forbidden by Article 49 of the fourth Geneva Convention of 1949, which in some form or other they considered applicable to Israel's control over the Territories. True, Justice Meir Shamgar, the president of the Israel Supreme Court (ISC), which functions as both the country's supreme appeal court and high court of justice, had some years previously ruled that specific deportations based on security concerns did not violate the Convention – a judgment that was castigated in some quarters of the legal community and ridiculed in others. Even so, judicial accommodation with executive wishes was bound to have its limits. The ISC could hardly be expected to provide the same sanction when large numbers of deportees were involved.

Against that background, the process that led to the decision to deport the alleged Hamas activists exudes an air of near negligence. Prudence alone would seem to have required so major a break with previous policy to have been thoroughly prepared and thought through. But Rabin issued his deportation order without once consulting all of his cabinet or discussing his options with a relevant parliamentary committee. The only opinions he canvassed in the immediate aftermath of the policeman's murder were those of his immediate coterie of personal aides. Immediately prior to presenting his deportation proposal to the cabinet he did go through the motions of consulting the Minister of Justice and the Attorney General. But he did not give them the time they required to offer a considered opinion. Like the CGS, Rabin was a man in a hurry. To delay Israel's response to the murder, he argued, was to run the risk of encouraging additional outrages.

The deportation process, too, was something of a shambles. Four hundred and eighty-seven persons were named on the initial list of deportees. During the night of 16 December 1992, 418 of them were interned (or taken from the locations in which they had already been interned), handcuffed, put on buses, and transported to the Lebanese border. Meanwhile, rumors of the impending operation and its size began to spread, and were soon picked up by various non-Government organizations (NGOs) specializing in the defense of Palestinian human rights. Their lawyers immediately rushed appeals against the implementation of the deportations to the chambers of Justice Aharon Barak, who happened to be the ISC 'emergency judge' on duty that night. From the Government's point of view, this was an unfortunate coincidence. Aharon Barak had always been less tolerant of deportations than Shamgar, and was accordingly far more likely to accede to petitions that the deportations be delayed. This was especially so when it became apparent that the leading petitioner was The Association for Human Rights in Israel, Israel's largest and most influential human rights NGO. The appearance of this body as the first named appellant transformed the deportees issue from a personal case into one of public interest. Quick to appreciate the implications of the scenario that had begun to unfold, Justice Barak did indeed order the deportations halted, pending a discussion at the Supreme Court scheduled for early the following day.

Ensuing developments followed a course worthy of a vintage Hollywood legal drama. At 5 am the next morning, 17 December, three justices of the ISC (Shamgar, Aharon Barak and Menachem Elon) duly convened to discuss the case. Not unexpectedly, they were unable to reach a consensus. Indeed, the only point on which they all agreed was that this particular potato was too hot to be handled by just the three of them. It had best be referred to an enlarged quorum, which would consist of four more of their colleagues. Rabin fumed at the postponement, and bullied the clerk of the court into bringing forward by an hour the sitting of the panel of seven justices, originally scheduled for 11 am that day. The CGS was even more pro-active. Ignoring all other commitments in his diary, General Ehud Barak took the unconventional step of requesting that the justices allow him to appear before them in person. Granted permission to do so, he duly turned up at the court, in full military regalia, and in the course of a lengthy presentation persuasively argued that the deportations constituted a national security priority.

All this while, the Hamas detainees were sitting handcuffed on the buses, which overnight had reached the Israeli–Lebanese border. There, they became targets of intense media scrutiny and international attention, which increased even more when the government of the Lebanon announced its refusal to allow the deportees to enter Lebanese territory. At the ISC the wheels turned more slowly, mainly because the forum of seven justices, like its predecessor, split into two camps, led respectively by justices Shamgar and Aharon Barak. Ultimately, it took a private consultation between these two protagonists to hammer out a compromise that enabled the ISC to present a united face. At 7 pm that evening, the justices finally announced that, notwithstanding their misgivings about the procedure and the numbers involved, they had rejected all appeals to issue a temporary injunction blocking the deportations, which were thereby sanctioned.

By that time, however, Israel had forfeited the element of surprise and, it soon transpired, been placed at a diplomatic disadvantage too. The deportees, who had been summarily dumped in a 'no-man's-land' area between Israel and the Lebanon, and provided with only makeshift accommodation in wintry conditions, had become objects of sympathy the world over. Israel, by contrast, was cast in the role of persecutor and bungler – an image exacerbated when Israeli government spokesmen admitted that in the rush to round up Hamas operatives, bureaucrats had allowed several 'mistakes' to creep into the names of those deported. Within a matter of days, Rabin and his ministers felt constrained to bow to US pressure, and halved the original term of deportation.

There remained one final act. Two weeks after the deportation operation commenced, the ISC unanimously decided to sanction the deportations, provided that the deportees would subsequently be allowed some kind of hearing. In practical terms, this decision was very much a dead letter, since the deportees refused to take any advantage of the right thus granted. Indeed, the substance of the decision has been much debated and widely criticized. Nevertheless, in retrospect it also deserves recognition as a watershed in the policies adopted by the ISC in matters affecting state security. Under the intellectual leadership of Justice Aharon Barak, who was to succeed Shamgar as president of the ISC in 1995, the highest court in the land would henceforth display a far greater readiness to intervene in such matters than ever before. Indeed, after December 1992 the entire sphere of national security was deemed to be as 'justiciable' as any other area of public life.

Even thus compressed, the events of December 1992 clearly tell a story considerably more complex than that contained in Ben-Meir's account. In addition to providing a cameo portrait of the balance of power between the defense establishment and civilian echelons in Israel's government, the episode also reveals the extent to which other actors, and especially members of the judiciary, had proved themselves capable of playing a role in the decision-making process that was influential and potentially decisive.

This book traces the sources and consequences of that development. In so doing, it also examines on a broader canvass the interactions between the legal framework of national security conduct and the practical and political circumstances to which national security action responds. That nexus, we argue, is not altogether intuitive. In no country, and least of all in Israel, is national security law the product of a scientific model of how to arrive at national security decisions. Rather, the legal framework reflects the relative power and standing of multiple decision-making institutions, not all of which are conventionally thought to exert an influence on the national security realm. Within that category come the legislature, NGOs and above all, the courts, the institutions to which democracy has traditionally entrusted the task of interpreting and implementing the law. Democratic societies depend upon the courts to balance the needs of national security against other values, primary amongst which are human freedoms. How they accomplish that mission, and the provisions that they make in order to ensure that other institutions of the state behave in an appropriate fashion when exercising their legitimate powers, are questions that touch upon the very essence of democratic government.

While political scientists have long analyzed decision-making in general and in areas associated with the defense of national security in particular, lawyers have been considerably slower off the mark. The field did not gain recognition as a legitimate area of legal study until the publication in 1990 of Harold Koh's ground-breaking work, *The National Security Constitution* (Koh 1990). Interest certainly grew in the aftermath of the 9/11 attacks, which generated an exponential rise in writings about what measures governments in liberal societies were, and were not, entitled to take in self-defense. Nevertheless, a decade after that seismic event, scholars in this emerging discipline still lack a common tradition and *lingua franca* of discourse. Even those who recognize national security law to be a reflection and determinant of wider political conflict cannot pinpoint precisely how the intersections operate and find expression.

We suggest that the clusters of definitions, terms and analytical tools presented in the present work can, with necessary modifications, be applied universally and thus contribute to the general advancement of the field. Our own focus here, however, is specifically on the 'case' of Israel, and on the dynamics that can be seen to have underpinned the development of its national security legal framework. In part, therefore, the book presents a historical narrative. It aims to demonstrate the manner in which that framework has evolved and to identify the circumstances and personalities who enabled (sometimes compelled) it to do so. At the same time, however, the study also possesses an explanatory dimension. At this level, its purpose is to complement an analysis of what happened with a study of the impulses that, in the various dimensions of the national security framework, helped to determine outcomes at different stages of the story. Based on those findings, we conclude the work with an agenda of the reforms that we consider require implementation in order to correct the imbalances and distortions in the system that have emerged over time.

In undertaking this analysis we have adopted an interdisciplinary perspective, which is based on the premise that law is not abstract and disconnected from the views and ideologies of specific judges and other actors (Leiter 1998). Because we consider law and politics to be mutually constitutive, intertwined and not independent, we seek to merge insights derived from political studies with those garnered from legal theory. To the best of our knowledge, no similar enterprise of this scope has previously been undertaken. True, the political science literature presents an exceptionally rich body of studies that examine national security decision-making from various perspectives. But even those classics in the field that do refer to the legal context of the subject (e.g., Hermann 1987; Hillsman 1992; Allison and Zelikow 1999; Halperin and Clapp 2006), consign the lawyers and jurists to the outer margins. In this respect, the legal literature has proven more useful. Indeed, entire 'schools' of scholarship have for some time been marrying the study of law to the social sciences, with the 'legal process school' of jurisprudence being especially prominent in this regard. Although in recent years criticized and, to some extent, replaced by the dominant theories of law, economics (or 'public choice') and 'critical legal studies', the basic themes of 'legal process' are still considered viable (Rubin 1996) and two have proved to be especially relevant to our work. The first is the notion that the separation of powers is important. Different institutions possess different capacities and authorities and their independence must therefore be preserved (Young 2005). The second assumption of 'legal process' is that courts perform a specific function in protecting the separation of powers and in guarding human rights (Fallon 1994).

Whilst the notion that institutions matter and that law relates to political power sharing and struggles is almost universally accepted, scholars still debate the reasons for the emergence of law. Adherents to 'critical' schools (such as feminists and Marxists) claim that law and institutions are a tool, used by hegemonic elites in order to secure and maintain dominance over minorities or weaker groups (MacKinnon 1987). By contrast, some 'public choice' scholars claim that public institutions and law are a reflection of the marketplace of politics, a forum in which interest groups and politicians trade in law, power and money, and generally advance their own interests (Mashaw 1997). Neither of the latter approaches has found full expression in Israeli scholarship. Feminist legal scholarship, although relatively the more developed of the two, tends to focus on the traditional areas of criminal law, labor law and family law (Barak-Erez 2007a). Other forms of interest group analysis are almost entirely undeveloped. Asaf Meydani and Shlomo Mizrachi, who have analyzed the role of the Supreme Court from this perspective (Meydani and Mizrachi 2006; Mizrachi and Meydani 2006) are the exception that proves the rule. The resultant paucity of critical analyses is especially marked where national security law is concerned. Only Barak-Erez and Meydani have been brave enough to attempt occasional forays into the minefield that traces connections between national security issues and critical legal theory (Barak-Erez 2007b) or interest group theory (Meydani 2007). Otherwise, that terrain remains *terra incognita.*

This book is designed as an initial effort to repair some of those conceptual deficiencies. It opens, therefore, with two chapters that lay out both the frameworks of analysis that we employ in the body of the work and with a brief introduction to the unique characteristics of the cultural context out of which we consider Israel's national security legal framework to have emerged. The following four chapters offer a chronological account of the evolution of that framework, positing a periodization determined by consecutive milestones in the history of Israel's confrontation with national security threats and prospects. Finally, the work concludes with two chapters that seek to distil the lessons derived from the historical record. The first ('diagnosis') adapts a tripartite taxonomy of executive behavior originally posited by professors Oren Gross and Fionnaula Ni Aolain (Gross and Aolain 2006) in order to account for what we term the hybrid character of Israel's national security legal framework. The second ('prognosis') offers some suggestions for its reform.

Part I
Foundations

1 Frameworks of analysis

Ever since its foundation as an independent state in 1948, Israel has habitually been depicted as 'a nation in arms'. Of the several circumstances justifying that description, undoubtedly the most conspicuous is the pervasiveness of armed conflict in the national narrative and consciousness. Born into battle, Israel has, throughout its history, been almost continuously engaged in some form of violent military confrontation with one or more of its neighbors. War has been central, as much to the formation of the collective identity of most Israelis as to their state's consolidation. Conscription and mandatory reserve duty have buttressed war's effects. Indeed, one of the hallmarks of the Israel Defense Force (IDF) is its status as a 'people's army', service in which is nominally compulsory for all citizens, women as well as men.

Principally as a result of those circumstances, issues related to national security intrude on almost every aspect of Israeli life, private as well as public, to a degree far greater than in most other countries. They figure especially prominently in Israel's national security legal discourse, which in large part has been shaped by attempts to find suitable ways of harmonizing the defense of the country with the preservation of the civil liberties that Israel's Declaration of Independence guarantees to all its inhabitants. Remarkably, nevertheless, Israel possesses no integrated body of laws defining the practices and procedures whereby state agencies can both authorize the resort to military force and ensure adequate supervision over its use. Like the United Kingdom, Israel has never formulated a written constitution (albeit for different reasons). Neither have Israel's jurists and legislators ever committed to writing an internally consistent set of principles in accordance with which the rules and standards governing national security activity might be extrapolated, step by legal step, from fundamental postulates concerning the purposes of Israeli society and its ideals. Instead, the *knesset*, Israel's parliament, has from time to time enacted 'Basic Laws' (thus far, 11) that supposedly embody the foundations of the country's legal principles and hence could, at some future date, conceivably comprise the building blocks out of which an integrated and internally consistent constitutional text could be fashioned. That status is signified by the fact that some (but not all) of the Basic Laws are 'entrenched' in the sense that they contain clauses specifying that any changes to them will require the support of at least 61 of the 120 *knesset* members. A 'regular' majority of those who participate in the vote will not suffice (Navot 2007:19–21, 35–42).

But 'entrenched' or not, Basic Laws affect only specific sections of the overall corpus of the national security framework with which this book is concerned. For the most part, to talk of Israel's national security legal framework is to refer to a far less formalized cluster of unwritten conventions and accepted legal practices and principles. Indeed in this area, perhaps more than any other, Israel's constitutional style has tended to be overwhelmingly oral and pragmatic, reflecting an approach that eschews broad and theoretically grounded formulations. As a result, national security legislation in Israel has been sporadic and piecemeal. Such as it is, the existing corpus comprises individual responses to here-and-now exigencies rather than logical extensions of an explicitly architectured way of thinking about the ways in which national security legislation ought to be devised and implemented.

Academic discussions of the subject evince similar patchwork traits. Certainly, and as references throughout the following pages will demonstrate, several political scientists have analyzed national security decision-making at the apex of Israel's civil–military dialogue, in the process providing both diagnoses of the manner in which Israel's senior politicians and soldiers have operated in this sphere in the past and prescriptions specifying the ways in which they ought to do so in the future. Legal scholars, whose works are also cited below, likewise address many of the specific tensions between the needs of state security and the protection of human rights that over the years have been generated in Israel by the experience of protracted armed conflict and, more particularly still, by the prolonged occupation of the territories conquered by the IDF in the course of the Six Days War of 1967. Still lacking, nevertheless, is a synoptic review of the numerous issues that warrant inclusion as components of Israel's national security law and – even more glaringly – a comprehensive analysis of the ways in which they have been addressed. The present study aims to repair both lacunae and thus to facilitate comparisons of the dynamics and substance of Israel's national security legal framework with those that have been identified in other countries.

The changing meaning of 'national security'

One possible explanation for the absence of a comprehensive survey of international security legal framework lies in the chameleon-like attributes of the phenomenon under review. 'National security', after all, has always been a notoriously imprecise term, meaning different things to different people (Wolfers 1962). Even in its classic sense, when it referred primarily to the circumstances warranting the state's exercise of military force, national security embraced an exceptionally wide variety of interests, needs and priorities, not all of which were equally amenable to legislation and many of which proved, even in the most advanced of liberal democracies, to be stubbornly resistant to judicial review. In recent years, especially, the analytical problems thus raised have been exacerbated by the increasing elasticity of the term. Even at the zenith of the Cold War some scholars in the West proposed broadening the concept of 'security' to include threats to the quality of life emanating from state and non-state actors alike (Ullman 1983; Mathews 1989). Subsequent changes in the political and intellectual climate have further accelerated the search for new paradigms. Global developments, it is now argued, suggest that the traditional focus of national security on strictly military threats that emanate from identified enemy forces located outside a state's borders is out-dated. Partly, this is because in many countries the primary threats to the physical well-being of most individual citizens are currently not military at all, but stem from other sources: resource scarcities; global climate change; disease pandemics; trans-boundary pollution; drug trafficking; and computer viruses and hacking. More blatantly violent threats, too, have assumed new forms, and are now more likely to emanate from trans-national networks of criminals and ideologically inspired terrorists than from conventional armed forces (*The Human Security Report* 2005). Since problems of that scale defy solution at the national level, even in the most powerful of states, many observers advocate that old concepts of 'national security' be replaced by a multi-layered network of 'international security' paradigms, more in tune with the realities of increased interdependence in world affairs (Katzenstein 1996; Miller 2001; Caldwell and Williams 2006:1–15).

To an extent far greater than is often acknowledged by analysts who emphasize Israel's multi-faceted and allegedly inveterate 'militarism' (e.g., Kimmerling 1993), echoes of some of the new meanings attached to national security have begun to permeate the Israeli public and academic discourse on military-related matters too. Indeed, so much is this so that the IDF's failure to crush recurrent Palestinian insurgencies since 1987 has been traced to Israeli society's squeamishness, manifested in its adoption of precisely the same self-denying ordinances with respect to the use of force that, in this view, are also responsible for the abysmal counterinsurgency record of other liberal democracies (Merom 2003; Gat and Merom 2010). Be that as it may, indications of a current realignment of national security priorities are certainly numerous. Recent years have witnessed a substantial growth in the number of environmentalist groups prepared to vocalize opposition to the depredations caused to Israel's coastline and countryside by IDF bases and exercises, all established in the name of national security (Perez and Rosenblum 2007). On occasions, politicians have likewise advocated a revision in traditional priorities. Thus, the argument that 'security' involves more than military might is enlisted with almost ritual regularity whenever there is a need to justify additions to social welfare and education budgets at the expense of cuts in financial allocations to the IDF. Allied themes have also become central planks in the platform of persons, some in government others in opposition, who advocate that Israel stands to gain more 'security' from concluding peace agreements with her neighbors than from continuing to maintain her military bases and civilian settlements in the territories that she conquered from them in 1967. And last – but certainly not least in terms of influence and impact on the substance of Israel's national security legal framework – justices of Israel's Supreme Court (ISC) have, ever since the early 1980s, persistently denied to 'security', as narrowly defined, the deference that it traditionally enjoyed. Justice Aharon Barak encapsulated the shift when declaring in 1989: 'Security is not an end in itself, but a means. The end is democratic government, i.e., a government of the people which guarantees individual freedoms' (Bracha 1991:99).

To attribute such changes simply to swings of mood in 'the marketplace of ideas' (Merom 2003) is, it seems, to mistake their true cause. They have also been fuelled by more concrete transformations in the character of the military confrontations for which the country has had to gird itself (S. Cohen 2008:37–41). Prior to the 1980s, at the core of Israel's security concerns lay the danger of cross-border invasions by the conventional armies of her immediate Arab neighbors, on the lines of those carried out in 1948 and 1973 and threatened in 1967. Thanks largely to the peace treaties concluded with Egypt in 1979 and with Jordan in 1994, fears that the 'confrontation states' might launch further cross-border assaults of that sort thereafter very much receded. Overall, however, a general sense of insecurity persisted (Arian 1995).

Two circumstances account for that apparent paradox. One was the realization that Israel's cities and hinterland were becoming increasingly vulnerable to attack by long-range missiles, which could be launched by 'distant' enemies who had once been thought to lay 'beyond the horizon' of the IDF's immediate strategic concern. In a fairly mild form, that danger materialized in 1991, when Israel was targeted by 39 Iraqi 'Scud' missiles, all armed with conventional warheads, during the course of the first Gulf War. In subsequent decades, Iran's increasingly hostile rhetoric, especially when broadcast as an accompaniment to her suspected drive to attain nuclear capabilities, touched even more sensitive nerves, generating fears of a new version of the Holocaust that had engulfed six million Jews just two generations ago. Existing capabilities were clearly inadequate to deal with this new dimension of threat to Israel's national security. Amongst other things, it required the IDF to establish an entirely new 'Rear Command' (*pikud oref*) responsible for what in the United States was subsequently to be labeled 'homeland security'.

The second reason for the persistence of Israel's sense of fragility lay in processes under way at the opposite pole of the force spectrum, in the sphere of sub-conventional threats. Here too the experiences of the 1980s proved pivotal. Thereto, 'low intensity' and terror attacks on the lives and property of civilians and soldiers, although frequently bloody, had generally been relegated to the sidelines of Israeli security concerns. By the end of the twentieth century, by contrast, they were dominating the IDF's operational agenda. Israeli forces were heavily committed to countering the threat posed by Hizbollah irregulars operating out of Lebanon, initially by attempting to maintain a 'security zone' north of the Israeli border (an enterprise that was somewhat ignominiously abandoned in 2000) and in 2006 by launching a full-scale – but almost equally unsuccessful – assault on the Hizbollah infrastructure in the region. Still more onerous were the strains imposed by the need to suppress the threat to Israel's security emanating from within the Territories. In those areas, the relevant watersheds were the first Palestinian *intifada* ('uprising') in 1987, the even more violent round of fighting, (the 'second *intifada*'), which erupted in 2000, and the attacks that various terrorist groups subsequently launched against Israel's southern townships from bases in the Gaza Strip, which persisted even after Israeli forces were unilaterally withdrawn from the region in 2005. Combined, these convulsions too mandated a re-definition of the term 'national security'. It now had to incorporate the provision of protection not just to the collectivity but also to individual Israeli citizens – on both sides of the 'Green Line'. At the same time, and as Justice Barak never tired of pointing out, it also had to be broadened to ensure that the treatment accorded to Palestinians, convicted terrorists as well as non-combatants, would not negate the liberal and democratic values which the State of Israel is committed to uphold.

Periodization

This book traces the manner in which Israel's national security legal framework has been shaped by those multiple changes, and in turn has responded to them. Its underlying structure, accordingly, is chronological and is designed to reflect the rhythm dictated by periodic realignments in the focus and form of Israel's national security behavior. Specifically, we divide Israel's history since 1948 into four almost equal phases of time, each of which witnessed shifts in the ways in which representatives of the constituent branches of Israeli government formulated, implemented and monitored the national security policies for which they were (or claimed to be) responsible. Hence, each of the historical chapters that make up the body of this book opens with a brief characterization of the major security challenges of the relevant period and of the domestic environment that affected their interpretation by government officials. Against that background, each chapter then goes on to discuss the steps taken in the national security sphere, and concludes with an assessment of their impact on both the substance and form of the legal framework bequeathed to the succeeding period.

Distinctions between the four periods lend themselves to two levels of analysis. The first, and most straightforward, examines changes in the influence exerted on Israel's national security legal framework – broadly defined – by each of the three constituent arms of Israeli government: executive, legislature, and judiciary. In that scheme of things, the following picture emerges.

- The first period, which spans the years 1948–1963, was clearly one of executive dominance and is hence designated an era of 'centralization'. Dominated by the towering figure of David Ben-Gurion – who, other than for a short interval in 1954, throughout those years functioned both as Prime Minister and Minister of Defense – this period was characterized by the hegemony of the government over all aspects of the formulation and implementation of national security legislation and action. Parliamentary input in these spheres was marginal; judicial deference was almost total.
- Ben-Gurion's retirement in 1963 ushered in our second period, during which the national security framework steadily became more diffuse – a process very much stimulated by the wars of 1967 and 1973 and, even more so, by the IDF's 'administration' of the Territories. It was during this period that executive power ceased to be concentrated in a single pair of hands; that the *knesset* for the first time passed legislation that sought to define constitutional direction over the armed forces (Basic Law: The Army, 1974); and that the ISC evinced an incipient willingness to accept petitions from Palestinian residents of the Territories, thereby foreshadowing the possibility of some judicial control over military action there. Hence, this period is termed one of 'diffusion'.
- Menachem Begin's victory in the general elections of 1977 heralded the onset of the third era (here designated 'realignment'), which lasted for almost two decades. Altogether these were years of substantial political, social, geo-strategic, military and economic flux, whose fissiparous effects were felt in numerous areas of Israeli public life. The impact on the national security legal framework, which prior to 1977 had appeared to be advancing towards equilibrium, was especially profound. Increasingly, both the legislature and the judiciary sought to play more assertive roles in an expanding span of security-related affairs, and utilized a wide range of newer mechanisms in order to do so. Hence, the activities undertaken by these branches of government were not restricted to the conventional tools of legislation and judicial decision, respectively. In order to exercise greater control over executive actions, the *knesset* also made more extensive use of its Foreign Affairs and Defense Committee (FADC). Likewise, the period also saw a proliferation of judicial commissions of enquiry.

- Our final period, which extends from 1995 until the present, is here termed 'legalization', a designation that reflects the increasingly profound influence now exerted by the judiciary on Israel's national security legal framework. This phenomenon is by no means exclusive to Israel. Largely in an effort to prevent an erosion in the scope for judicial review precipitated by a rapidly expanding international regulatory apparatus, in democracies throughout the world, national courts have likewise gradually reversed their traditional policy of deference to their executive branches in the field of foreign and security policy. Since 2001, especially, they have begun more aggressively to engage in the interpretation and application of relevant international law (Benvenisti and Downs 2009). What nevertheless remains distinctive about the Israeli example, however, is the wide variety of expressions that this strategy assumed, especially as orchestrated by Justice Aharon Barak, who presided over the ISC between 1995 and 2000. Under Barak's stewardship, the court did not restrict its modes of intervention, where national security issues were concerned, to the traditional tools of the enforcement of existing laws and their interpretation in the light of the evolving fields of international human rights law and the laws of war. Rather, the ISC also assumed far more activist roles: as a facilitator of dialogues between petitioners and the executive and as instigators of parliamentary legislation.

Subsequent chapters will expand on each of those processes, and thus follow the evolutionary development of Israel's national security framework in greater detail. What needs to be stressed at this stage, however, is that the story they describe does not focus exclusively on changes in the degree of influence wielded over time by each of the three branches of government. Within each chapter, equal emphasis is placed on a second level of analysis: the no less kaleidoscopic transformations that have taken place in the treatment that Israel's executive, legislature and judiciary (sometimes working in tandem, more often individually, and sometimes at cross purposes) have accorded to the various components of the conglomerate subsumed under the generic term 'national security'. It is to the identity of those components that attention must now be turned.

The quadruple dimensions of the national security legal framework

National security law, we suggest, is concerned with four principal clusters of themes, each of which designates a constituent dimension of the overall framework. Listed in order of their apparent constitutional importance, these four dimensions are here termed: the hierarchical; the functional; the spatial; and the temporal. Self-evidently, each of these dimensions encompasses a separate sphere of national security activity. What is perhaps less obvious is the precise identity of the separate legal issues to which each gives rise.

- Briefly summarized, the *hierarchical* dimension is concerned with the following questions:
    - What is the constitutionally ordained chain of national command with respect to national security issues?
    - Does there exist a decision-making hierarchy within the civilian government?
    - Which minister or official is designated as responsible for transmitting the government's instructions to the security agencies?
- *Functional* questions include:
    - Which agencies of government are responsible, individually or collectively, for national security activities other than the transmission of government instructions to the military (such as officially declaring the nation to be at war or in a situation that warrants the resort to emergency decrees and/or the imposition of martial law)?
    - Which mechanisms and measures are available to the legislature and judiciary for the purposes of monitoring executive decisions and the oversight of executive action in matters relevant to national security?
    - What provisions, if any, exist for resolving differences of opinion within and between branches of government over national security issues?
- *Spatial* questions ask:
    - To what extent has the content and tone of the national security legal framework been affected by territorial change, such as the geographical expansion or contraction of areas over which state agencies, and especially the military, exercise control?
    - Is the same legal framework applied to all regions under state control, or do there exist – concomitantly – separate legal 'regimes', one operative in the core area of the homeland and another in regions under military administration?
    - Do there exist legal constraints on the geographical deployment of the armed forces, either within the state's borders or beyond them?
- *Temporal* questions ask:
    - What provision (if any) does the legal framework make for state-sponsored violations of liberal democratic principles at moments of extreme threat to the survival of the constitutional order and/or the state?

- Are legal controls placed on the exercise of 'emergency powers' and their extension?
- Do provisions exist to ensure the speedy restoration of whatever civil liberties may have been suspended during the state of emergency?

Thus formulated, the quadruple framework of analysis presented here is not of course applicable solely to Israel's national security legal structure. On the contrary, basic to our argument is the contention that the issues covered by the four dimensions are common to most regimes, and certainly to all democracies. Where nations differ is in the form of answers that they supply to the questions raised.

Hierarchical issues have generated an especially wide span of possibilities. Although all democracies emphatically require the subordination of military affairs to civilian control, there exists no single and universally agreed legal formula for the attainment of that end. Presidential systems (such as exist in the United States of America, France, and Brazil) generally favor a unitary system of command. Control over the military is therefore vested in the president, who is identified as commander-in-chief of the armed forces. Where the legal framework also makes provisions for the functioning of a national security council (as is the case in the USA, Brazil, South Korea, and Turkey) the president also chairs that body. In constitutional monarchies, too, (the UK, Denmark, Spain, and Thailand) the head of state nominally exercises the function of commander-in-chief. Only in extreme circumstances, however, does the title carry anything other than ceremonial meaning.[1] Effective command over the military is invariably vested in the elected government, a fact made explicit in Holland where a constitutional amendment passed in 1983 formally transferred command of the country's armed forces from the monarch to the government of the Netherlands.

In some cases, the locus of control is even more precisely defined. Article 65a of the Basic Law (i.e., constitution) of the Federal Republic of Germany vests command over the armed forces in the person of the defense minister during peace time, but Article 115b transfers that responsibility to the federal chancellor in times of war. Article 117:3 of the Turkish constitution mandates that in times of war the duties of commander-in-chief be exercised on behalf of the president of the Republic by the chief of the general staff, who is commander of the armed forces. In Japan, where the post-World War II constitution prohibited the maintenance of any armed forces whatsoever, an amendment passed by the Diet in 2006 allowed that: 'In order to secure peace and the independence of our country as well as the security of the state and the people, military forces for self-defense shall be maintained with the Prime Minister of the cabinet as the Supreme Commander.'

Disparity likewise characterizes international treatment of the issues raised by the *temporal* dimension of national security. Certainly, most constitutions make some provision for alteration to the regular functioning of government during times of perceived threat to the nation's safety and stability. Under such circumstances, it is accepted that the executive branch can declare the existence of a state of emergency, a situation that has traditionally warranted the suspension of some civil liberties and even the imposition of martial law. Where countries differ, however, is in the overall mental framework that characterizes attitudes towards the circumstances thus created. Are they considered necessary – but undesirable – digressions from a set of legal norms that ought to be restored as soon as possible? Or is the emergency situation thought to justify the creation of a new and almost autonomous legal regime, the criteria of which are commensurate with the severity of the threat to the nation's well-being?[2]

In *Law in Times of Crisis* (Gross and Ni Aolain 2006) – a work to which we shall return at some length in our penultimate chapter – Professors Oren Gross and Fionnuala Ni Aolain identify three types of constitutional strategies that democracies can adopt when confronted with situations of national security emergency. One ('accommodation') is to make specific provisions in order to deal with individual situations; a second – and more drastic – is to altogether remove from the realm of constitutional law actions related to matters of national security taken during times of national emergency ('extra-legal action'); the third – and superficially most moderate – is to leave the existing constitutional and legal framework basically unchanged and hence to apply during national emergencies precisely the same norms and standards that are in effect during non-emergency times ('business as usual').

In modern democracies, by far the most popular of the three models is that of 'accommodation', in accordance with which specific constitutional arrangements are made in order to deal with periods of national crisis (Gross 2003a). Where that is the case, the special 'emergency' provisions that are enacted can affect some of the basics in the system of constitutional checks and balances that usually prevail. This is because they usually extend the range of powers to which the executive can resort, whilst curtailing those available to other branches. Articles 19 a–d of the Hungarian constitution, for instance, allow the president, in times of emergency, to issue decrees, to declare the country to be in 'a state of war', and to convene a 'national security council', It also invests the latter body with the power to recruit and order military actions without the need for parliamentary approval. Article 148:1 of the Turkish constitution bars any action being brought before the constitutional court 'alleging unconstitutionality as to the form or substance of decrees having the force of law issued during a state of emergency, martial law or in time of war.'

Most emergency regimes also permit some infringement of human rights – explicitly so in Article 103:2 of the constitution of the Netherlands and Article 37:4 in that of the Republic of South Africa. Because such provisions are considered potentially dangerous to civil liberties they are often limited to the duration of the period of emergency itself, a proviso specified in Article 37:2 of the South African constitution and in Article 230 of the Polish constitution. Under the US National Emergencies Act (1976) the president may declare a national emergency for a maximum period of one year, a term which can be renewed at the end of each year. The US Congress may terminate the national emergency in a joint resolution.

A limited number of democracies adopt the second of the Gross–Ni Aolain models, which they term 'business as usual'. Their constitutions either contain no emergency provisions at all, as is the case in Japan, or refer to emergency situations only obliquely. Thus the sole reference to emergencies in the constitution of Belgium is tucked away in Article 157, which specifies that martial courts may be maintained in a time of war. Until the passage of the National Emergencies Act of 1976, such was also the case in the USA. Indeed, the only emergency provision which appears in the US Constitution is to be found in section 9 of Article 1: 'The Privilege of the Writ of Habeus Corpus shall not be suspended, unless when in Cases of Rebellion or Invasion the public Safety may require it.'

Another expression of the 'business as usual' model can be found in the behavior of democracies that have enacted legislation enhancing the power of the executive to combat terrorism, but without specifically conditioning the use of these powers on the existence of a declared 'emergency' (Beckman 2007). During the first decade of the twenty-first century, the UK government twice adopted this policy. In the immediate wake of the 9/11 attacks in the USA, parliament passed the Anti-terrorism, Crime and Security Act (2001), part IV of which permitted the home secretary to order the indefinite detention of any non-British citizen suspected of being a terrorist. Following the 2005 bombings in London, parliament went on to pass the Terrorism Act (2006), section 23 of which allowed the police to detain suspected terrorists for 28 days without proffering charges (Walker 2007).

By definition, 'extra-legal action', the third Gross–Ni Aolain model, does not lend itself to legislative definition or precedent. With the exception of some rather oblique statements in a couple of judicial decisions, no evidence can be found for any formal judicial acceptance of this doctrine. Nevertheless, Gross and Ni Aolain (who do posit some historical and philosophical sources for the extra-legal model; see also Gross 2003b) suggest that in practice, this is precisely the way in which many states are approaching matters of national security. How far Israel too is doing so will constitute one of this book's foci of attention.

For many years, the *spatial* dimension was generally considered the least contested of all the components of national security law. Bluntly put, it was taken for granted that the armed forces exist in order to defend whatever the Government determines to be the state's interests, irrespective of geographical location. Article 97 of the constitution of the Netherlands reflects that state of mind, blandly stating that the armed forces exist in order 'to defend the interests of the Kingdom of the Netherlands and its interests in the world.' Since World War II, however, matters have sometimes tended to become more complicated. One reason is that, principally in reaction to the trauma of that conflagration, some countries have imposed geographical limitations on their deployment of force. The constitution of post-war Japan, for instance, explicitly forbids the overseas deployment of Japanese armed forces (which were themselves originally outlawed). Although the Basic Law of the German Federal Republic is considerably more opaque on this matter, a number of Constitutional Court cases in the 1990s established that German armed forces may not be deployed outside of NATO territory without a specific resolution of the Bundestag, which describes the details of the mission and limits its term. Hence, the participation of German units in the NATO forces in Kosovo in 1998–1999, and in the NATO-led International Security Assistance Force in Afghanistan since 2001 both required Bundestag approval, which was indeed forthcoming (Paulus 2002; Martinez 2006:2493).

Overseas deployments, however, frequently generate overseas military occupations, which in turn raise queries as to how much the legal regime applied in a defined geographical area under the control of a state's emissaries differs from that operative within the country's domestic borders. Traditionally, the legal regime of occupation was specifically intended to deal with areas which are temporarily controlled by one state, but are nominally still subject to the sovereignty of another. Under the international law of occupation (considered a customary part of international law, and applied with varying degrees of fidelity by states since the mid-nineteenth century) the legal regime prevailing in occupied territories is not the domestic law of the occupying state but the law of the sovereign state, as applied by the foreign military forces who can make some alterations for military needs (Benvenisti 2011). In recent years, however, new and more complex situations have arisen.

One notorious example is provided by the US detention base at Guantanamo Bay, in Cuba, to which, beginning in 2002, the US Administration transferred persons detained by US and Allied forces during the war in Afghanistan, denying them the right to judicial review of their detention on the grounds that Guantanamo lay outside the 'space' covered by the jurisdiction of the US constitution (Yoo 2006). (After a lengthy judicial process, which included four US Supreme Court decisions, this argument was finally rejected in *Boumediene* v. *Bush* 553 US 723 [2008]). Less well known, but equally relevant are those instances in which the European Court of Human Rights has tackled the issue of spatial differences in the context of the application of the European Convention of Human Rights (Hampson 2011). In *Bankovic* v. *Belgium* (2001), relatives of persons killed in the NATO campaign against Serbia brought a case against NATO states claiming that the bombing violated their right to life. Three years later, in *Issa* v. *Turkey*, the court was petitioned by Kurdish residents of an area in northern Iraq, some of the residents of which had been killed during the course of a Turkish anti-Kurdistan Workers' Party (PKK) operation in the region. Both cases were rejected, on the grounds that alleged violations of the European Convention of Human Rights can only be judged when the accused state exercises effective control over the area in question.

Domestic terrorist threats to 'homeland security' have given rise to an inverse formulation of the conventional deployment question. Instead of seeking to define the situations under which governments are entitled to deploy armed forces abroad, inquiry now focuses on asking whether they can be employed on counter-insurgency and law-enforcement missions within state borders. It is generally assumed that countries with common law traditions possess historical objections to the deployment of armed forces in order to deal with domestic matters, a principle that perhaps dates to Magna Carta and that accounts for many of the limitations on such deployments, at least in principle. A recent comparative study of this subject (Head and Mann 2009) shows that many democracies, including the UK, the USA, Australia, Italy, and Japan have all adopted measures which significantly reduce the limitation on the powers of the military to act within the state. In the UK, for example, several twentieth-century governments ordered the military to provide assistance to the police in domestic matters, including the prolonged struggle in Northern Ireland. In 2004, parliament passed the Civil Contingencies Act, Article 22:3 (1) of which allows the National Security Council (the body within the Ministry of Defence responsible for command of the armed forces) to order the deployment of armed forces within the UK to assist in any matter during an emergency. In the USA, especially since the declaration of the 'War on Terror' in 2001, protections against military involvement in domestic matters have also been eroded. Traditionally, the Posse Comitatus Act of 1878 prohibited the use of the army (and later also the air force) for the purposes of domestic law enforcement, other than in cases of explicit congressional authorization. Following 2001, however, the military became increasingly involved in the domestic 'war against terrorism' (Kohn 2003). In 2007, President George Bush asserted his power to use the military domestically in times of 'catastrophic emergency' without prior congressional authorization, and since 2008 a military brigade has been deployed within the USA. Contingency planning now envisages the widespread domestic use of service personnel to combat terrorism (Head and Mann 2009:53–6).

Even those constitutions that retain the strictest prohibitions on the deployment of the armed forces for domestic purposes recognize that exceptions will be made in times of natural disasters. This distinction is made explicit in Article 87a of the German Basic Law, which although imposing a total ban on the use of the military in an armed constabulary role does allow for unarmed troop deployment within Germany in order to provide disaster relief. In the chapters that follow, we shall adopt a similar distinction. Hence, the deployment of unarmed units of the IDF within Israel for non-violent purposes, which was a common phenomenon during the first decades of statehood, will be discussed within the context of the functional dimension of the national security framework, to which attention must now be turned.

Undoubtedly the most prominent of the issues covered by the *functional* dimension of the national security legal framework is the authority to declare war and proclaim the existence of a state of national emergency. Not surprisingly, therefore, most constitutions attempt to make explicit provisions for both procedures and mandate that some kind of legislative approval is required for a declaration of war. In France, indeed, that step can only be taken by the legislature (French constitution, Article 35). Even in the UK, where formal constitutional conventions do not necessitate parliamentary approval for a declaration of war, the government almost always does request such approval before embarking on any serious military action (Bowers 2003). Article 87a (4) of the German Basic Law empowers both the Bundestag and the parliaments of the *Lander* to order the armed forces to halt all domestic action, even during an emergency.

In practice, the delicate balance between executive and legislature has proved hard to sustain. Pressure to extend executive power has been particularly strong, as is clearly illustrated by the US example. The framers of the US Constitution famously adopted a mixed model when empowering Congress to declare war, raise and support the armed forces, and control war funding (Article I, section 8), and yet appointed the president as 'Commander-in-Chief' (Article II, section 2), a position that made him/her responsible for repelling attacks against the Republic. As the record of constitutional controversies since the early 1970s demonstrates, however, the arrangement thus constructed has become increasingly fragile. Presidents, it transpired, did not always feel required to receive congressional authorization before committing US troops to military action, sometimes (as in the case of the Korean and Vietnam wars) for extensive periods of intense fighting. By 1973, members of the Senate and Congress were convinced that the only way that they could rectify the imbalance thus created, and indeed ensure that the executive branch would in future observe both the spirit and the letter of the framers' original intent, was to pass a war powers resolution, which imposed strict limitations on the president's freedom to commit US forces to military action.[3] As constitutional lawyers often point out, however, these stipulations – even though passed by a two-thirds majority and thus overriding the president's veto – have consistently been ignored (Koh 1990; Ely 1993; Fisher 1995). Indeed, even the constitutional propriety of the War Powers Resolution remains a matter of some debate (compare Carter 1984, with Ramsey 2002, and Yoo 2002).

Other attempts to curb executive autonomy in national security affairs have usually assumed more conventional forms. By far the oldest is the ability to withhold budgetary allocations ('the power of the purse'), a constitutional constraint on executive freedom to resort to military action that was exercised by proto-parliaments in England as early as the fourteenth century. But although all democracies now follow that precedent, there remain considerable differences in the effectiveness of the manner in which they do. Only in the USA does the legislature scrutinize the defense budget in any detail, principally through the House Armed Services Committee. More often, military-related expenses retain the aura of a murky 'black box', the contents of which remain virtually impenetrable to parliamentary gaze. In Israel, for instance, not until the 1990s did the *knesset* challenge the convention whereby governments had presented the defense budget *en bloc* and, on grounds of 'state security', had refused to provide details of its various components.

Similar disparities occur with respect to two other traditional forms of parliamentary control over military conduct: legislation and investigation. Overall, however, the prevailing leaning in Western-style democracies is clearly towards an intensification of the resort to both mechanisms. In part, that trend reflects the degree to which Western armed forces have in recent decades reconstructed themselves, adopting modes of organizational transparency that invite intrusion by external bodies (King 2006). But in the main, the rise in the level of parliamentary scrutiny must be attributed to a widespread denial of the exceptionalism of military organizations, which are now expected to conform to standards, principles and norms considered de rigueur in society at large (Dandeker 1994; Moskos 1998). The effects have been felt across virtually the entire span of the societal-military interface. Throughout the Western world, legislation has transformed military recruitment policies, and in particular universal conscription, and has likewise revolutionized the status of women and homosexuals in the armed forces. Increasingly, it is also affecting the autonomy of the military justice system and the civil rights of servicemen and women. (Moskos *et al.* 2000; S. Cohen 2009).

Parliamentary reviews of military conduct, principally by means of subcommittees, have likewise become more intensive. True, in the USA, the Senate Committee on Armed Services, together with its various subcommittees, has always possessed an exceptionally broad remit, which extends to holding hearing before confirming the president's nominee for the position of 'Chairman of the Joint Chiefs of Staff'. Consequently, it has traditionally exerted a noticeably powerful influence over US national security policies. Increasingly, a similar pattern is emerging elsewhere too. The UK parliament, for instance, established a permanent Select Committee on Defense, consisting of 14 MPs, in 1997.[4] The following year, members of the Foreign Relations Committee and National Defense and Armed Forces Committee of France's national assembly conducted an enquiry into the role played by the French Government in the Rwanda genocides of 1994–1998, the very first occasion in the history of the Fifth Republic that the assembly had ever intruded into a presidential 'reserved domain'. Similar committees have been established, almost as a matter of course, in the new governments established in central and south-eastern Europe and Asia after the dissolution of the USSR and of Yugoslavia (*Report of the Conference on Parliamentary Oversight of the Security Sector* 2010).

Still more radical have been the changes in the balance of relationships between the executive and judicial branches in matters affecting national security. For many years it was considered virtually axiomatic that courts deliberately refrained from intervening in matters affecting national security, an area in which their deference to executive hegemony has traditionally been pronounced (Benvenisti 1993b). Hence, in many countries – and especially those influenced by the UK system of government – the primary instrument of civilian judicial oversight with respect to national security affairs, and in particular military action, for long remained the (Royal) Commission of Enquiry. But tribunals of that name, although independent and invariably chaired by a serving or former judge, nevertheless could only be established by an explicit government decision. Consequently, they did not convene unless public opinion was galvanized by an especially blatant instance of military incompetence and thus generated a degree of pressure for investigation that the government found impossible to resist. One of the earliest examples was the Royal Commission on the Health of the Army, established in 1856, in the wake of Florence Nightingale's revelations of the inadequacies of the medical care afforded to wounded British soldiers during the Crimean War. Equally famous, in its day, was the Investigatory Committee appointed in 1919 by the Legislative Council of the government of India into the 'Amritsar massacre' earlier that year. Chaired by Lord William Hunter, a Scottish politician and judge, this tribunal was created in response to public outrage at reports that 50 British soldiers in the Indian army had opened fire on an unarmed gathering of innocent men, women and children without any warning, causing 1,500 casualties.

Government-sponsored national commissions of enquiry continue to constitute valuable tools of national security oversight and review. They have been utilized in the UK to investigate both military conduct in Northern Ireland (the Saville Commission into the events of 'Bloody Sunday' in 1972) and the UK's involvement in Iraq from mid-2001 to July 2009 (the Chilcot Inquiry). Similar national committees have investigated the brutal murder of a local teenager by two members of the Canadian Airborne Regiment in Somalia in 1993 and the conduct of Dutch military personnel engaged in peacekeeping missions in Bosnia at the time of the Srebrenica massacre in 1995. Increasingly, however, the work done by *ad hoc* forums of this sort is being supplemented by developments in other forms of judicial review. Thus, recent years have witnessed the emergence of such international forums as the Inter-American Court of Human Rights and the European Court of Human Rights (which has passed judgment on, for instance, both Turkish control over northern Cyprus and the Russian–Chechnya war); the tribunals created by the United Nations in 1993 and

1994 with the purpose of prosecuting persons responsible for war crimes during the fighting in former Yugoslavia and Rwanda, respectively; and, in 2003, the International Criminal Court (Keller and Sweet 2008; Schiff 2008). A further development, which in many respects is even more remarkable, takes the form of hearings conducted before regular national courts, which have in several countries displayed an increasing readiness to abandon the attitude of restraint towards national security issues that was once the norm (Benvenisti 2008b).

Some scholars attribute this departure to the transformations that have taken place in the context within which judges now find themselves operating. Fifteen years of accelerating globalization, it has been argued, have altered the assessment of national courts about what the primary threats to the domestic order are and what strategies they will need to adopt in order to cope with them. National courts are increasingly discovering that the most effective way for them to maintain the space for domestic deliberation and to strengthen the ability of their governments to withstand the pressure brought to bear by foreign and local interest groups and powerful foreign governments is to ensure to the extent possible that their judgments complement rather than conflict with those of other national courts. Increasingly this requires them to monitor the opinions of other courts at both the national and international level and to engage in what amounts to tacit co-ordination' (Benvenisti and Downs 2009:71).

Nevertheless, it would be incorrect to exaggerate the universalism of this development. In this sphere of national security law, too, what remains striking is the diversity of responses. Different countries move at different speeds. Sensitivity to norms that reflect developments in international humanitarian law remains an essentially Western and Northern phenomenon. 'There still appears to be some time before the national courts of states such as China, Brazil and Russia are likely actively to engage themselves in inter-judicial co-operation.' (Benvenisti and Downs 2009) Even within the 'liberal' camp, moreover, considerable differentials are apparent. As will be demonstrated in Chapters 5 and 6, Israel's Supreme Court has begun to play a far more interventionist role in the determination of national security practice than is common in, for instance, the USA. The situation in the UK probably constitutes an intermediary case, and yet even there, it has been found, the military's complaints that it is becoming 'legally encircled' remain largely unfounded (Waters 2008).

Culture as a determinate

Broadly speaking, two approaches can be advanced to explain the variations thus apparent in domestic responses to challenges arising in each of the four dimensions of the national security framework. One emphasizes the role played by individual national experiences of an essentially practical nature, whose consequences are frequently expressed through the medium of idiosyncratic intra-state bureaucratic arrangements. This is particularly so with respect to questions related to *hierarchy* and *functions*, answers to which often hinge as much on ingrained national traditions of working relationships between senior military officers and their political masters as on the formal constitutional demarcations between executive, legislative and judicial spheres of activity. Most of the signposts relevant to this approach were laid down over half a century ago in Samuel Huntington's seminal work, *The Soldier and the State*, which still serves as a reference for even the most critical of more recent studies. James Burk (Burk 2002), for instance, has refined Huntington's thesis, *inter alia* by demonstrating the salience of differences between 'mature' and 'immature' democracies to an understanding of discrepancies in their modes of regulating the activities of their armed forces. In greater detail, Peter Feaver (Feaver 2003) has critiqued Huntington's 'objective control' template as a key to interpreting the recent US civil–military experience. Instead, he deploys agency theory in order to show how a protracted and inherently fluid process of trial and error has determined the interaction of civilian monitoring mechanisms (intrusive/non-intrusive) with military responses (working/shirking). The implication is that variations in modes of civilian control over their armed servants can best be explained by differences in the permutations produced by the same dynamic.

A second possible explanation for the discrepancies in individual national security frameworks adopts a broader perspective. In this view, responses to the challenges posed in the four dimensions of the national security legal framework, whilst certainly often assuming institutional form, are at root ideational. That is to say they are principally the outgrowth of highly subjective perceptions, which are manifest in the interpretations that members of a specific society place on certain events and the values that they attach to certain notions, places and actions. Hence, the decisive influence on the choice of response to specific questions in the national security sphere is neither bureaucratic convenience nor rational end-means assessments. Rather, the principal determinant is 'culture' – 'a social force that shapes cognition and perception of meanings and realities' (Hartman 1997:ix), which has itself been nurtured by the unique historical experiences of a specific group and the particular ways in which those experiences have been narrated and understood. Thus defined, culture becomes a deeply embedded intellectual prism, and as such acts as force that transforms policy orientations into concrete modes of action.

Analysts have long noted the role played by cultural associations and symbols in shaping the policy choices made by leaders of individual states and their responses to external stimuli, and especially to military threats (Klein 1991). Second-wave research in the field, however, has very much advanced on the rather primitive premises that at one time tended to associate 'strategic culture' with little more than the modes of war-fighting dictated by traits embedded in 'national character'. Scholars are now far more sensitive than was once the case to the argument that strategic culture – like all political culture – is manifest in cognitive, evaluative, and expressive dimensions, and hence to the need to identify the agents within any given society who carry such values (Johnston 1995a). Building on those premises, third-wave theory has developed further lines of enquiry – into the multiple sources of an individual country's strategic culture (myths and historical memories as well as geography and environment), into its numerous expressions (declaratory, organizational and symbolic), and above all, into its consequences, not only its influence on military conduct, but also on conscription policies, on battlefield restraint, and on styles of military leadership (Johnston 1995b; Rosen 1996; Legro 1996; Jandoral 1999; Kier 2002). Influenced by constructivism, scholars are now exploring the ways that strategic cultures evolve over time, delineating the processes whereby traditional components are handed down from generation to generation whilst new layers are added on (Lantis 2002).

This book is premised on the argument that the notion of strategic culture can likewise be used in order to explain differences in both the content and development of individual national security legal frameworks. They too are ideational phenomena that are shaped by 'recurring patterns of mental activity, or habits of thought, perception and feeling, that are common to members of a particular group' (Duffield 1999:769). That being the case, an understanding of their grainy individuality mandates an analysis of the specific cultural context from which each has emerged and within which each continues to operate. Our next chapter seeks to fulfill that need. Focusing on what is unique in Israel's national security heritage and experience, it is designed to trace why and how both translate into the modes of thought and behavior that have helped to make Israel's national security legal framework so distinctive.

2 Cultural contexts

Whilst numerous elements in the Jewish political experience have contributed to contemporary Israel's strategic culture, three strands exert an especially powerful effect on the content and form of the country's approaches to national security and on the national security legal framework. Listed in a sequence that accords with the length of time that they have been embedded in collective memory, they are:

- the legacy of Jewish political traditions developed against a backdrop of extreme and chronic vulnerability during the Exilic period;
- the heritage of civil–military relations bequeathed by the experiences of the Jewish community in mandatory Palestine; and
- the intense focus on national security issues and agencies, both principally defined in military terms, evinced by successive Israeli governments since 1948.

Although ultimately coalescing into one comprehensive prism, individually each of these elements affects the four dimensions of Israel's national security framework in distinct ways. Hence, each warrants independent depiction.

The lop-sided legacy of Jewish political traditions

For almost 2000 years, between Rome's demolition of the second Jewish commonwealth in the first century CE and the establishment of the State of Israel in 1948, the distinguishing characteristic of the Jews was their Exile. A major concomitant of that condition was a pervasive sense of vulnerability. Security – of residence, of livelihood, of religious freedom, and very often of life itself – could never be taken for granted. Lacking the most rudimentary attributes of political sovereignty, Jews everywhere engaged in an incessant struggle for both physical and cultural survival. Even seemingly 'non-Exilic' Diasporas, such as that of Sassanid Babylonia, Moorish Spain and nineteenth century *Mittleuropa*, all places in which Jewish communities enjoyed extended periods of civic tolerance and cultural freedom, accorded with this pattern. Since those episodes too ultimately ended in calamity and fresh dispersion, they became engraved in the collective Jewish memory as only temporary interruptions in what was otherwise an unrelenting cycle of rejection, humiliation, exploitation, persecution, expulsion and/or massacre – all experiences that reached previously unimaginable proportions in the Holocaust perpetrated by the Nazis and their accomplices during World War II.

Mainstream orthodox Jewish interpretations of that narrative harbored no doubts about either its causes or the way in which it would be terminated. From the very first, Exile and its consequences were interpreted in theological terms, as manifestations of the will and wrath of God. Israel had sinned, and Israel was therefore being punished. But therein, of course, lay a message of hope, because the same logic promised that once the Jews had served their Divinely-imposed sentence, they would be redeemed. In God's good time, and by means of a miraculous process in which the Messiah would play a crucial role, they would be restored to their ancient homeland and enabled to live in the state of sublime national security so gloriously foretold in the biblical book of Jeremiah (30:19): 'And Jacob shall return and be quiet and at ease; and none shall make him afraid.'

Comforting though such teachings undoubtedly were, their practical import was limited, since other than by praying and acting piously there was little that Jews, individually or collectively, could do in order to hasten their salvation. Meanwhile, how were they to cope with the here-and-now challenges presented by the need to ensure some modicum of security and survival in the present? Notwithstanding variations dictated by vast differences of location and situation, all Jewish communities developed and refined a remarkably similar set of broad strategies in order to answer that question. First amongst these was a resort to diplomatic negotiation. Given the paucity of conventional power resources available to its practitioners, Jewish diplomacy necessarily prioritized persuasion and conciliation rather than threat and confrontation. Hence, it came to be depicted in Jewish sources as *shtadtlanut* ('intercession', also 'petitioning'), a term that did not acquire pejorative overtones until the emergence of several 'activist' brands of Zionism in the twentieth century (Klieman 2008; Sandler 2007).

Other national security strategies adopted by Jewish diasporas tended to be more inward-looking, and were directed towards fostering the sense of unity and reciprocal responsibility of all Jews. During the nineteenth century, that enterprise attained formal institutional expression, with the foundation of several country-based Jewish organizations with multi-country agendas. (Their prototype was the Alliance Israelite Universelle, founded in Paris in 1860 with the purpose of safeguarding Jewish rights worldwide; its motto, *Tous les israélites sont solidaires les uns des autres*, was a French version of an old rabbinic teaching) However, the ties of association created by a shared fate and adhesion to a common set of religious beliefs had much earlier been cemented by the strict regulation of even the most mundane minutiae of personal and communal behavior. *Halakhah*, the multi-layered corpus of Jewish law that evolved through a process of constant interpretation and re-interpretation of the biblical and talmudic texts collectively designated '*torah*', played a crucial role in this enterprise. For whilst the foremost and most obvious function of *halakhah* was to elucidate how Jews could fulfill the Divine commands, it also provided a means of ensuring that all did so in basically the same fashion. By thus helping to preserve a sense of peoplehood and a singular identity, *halakhah* went far towards compensating Jews for their exile from their ancient homeland, providing a portable canon of almost uniform statutes and ordinances that, whenever circumstances demanded, could be – and was – transported across borders and even continents.

Thus described, *halakhah* served a purpose that was as much political as ritual. Transmitted from generation to generation by successive cohorts of scholar-decisors, all of whom adhered to the same prescribed rules of exegesis and jurisprudence and employed the same mixture of Hebrew and Aramaic that was the *lingua franca* of rabbinic discourse, *halakhah* established the world-embracing hierarchy of authorities and texts in accordance with whose teachings Jews conducted their private and public lives. As Daniel Elazar was the first to point out (Elazar 1981:21–58), it thus fostered the evolution and retention of a distinctly Jewish *political* tradition, with all that the term implies in the way of preferred modes of public behavior, favored institutions of self-government and accepted political norms. Because that tradition rested on biblically grounded teachings about the nature of man, the purposes of government and the role of covenants in shaping relationships, it constituted an essential part of the fabric of all Jewish civilization, traversing frontiers that otherwise set apart the customs of one community from another. Indeed, if Israel's loss of sovereignty did not mean the end of the Jewish community, surely one reason was rabbinic Judaism's success in developing a comprehensive alternative form of political life 'mediated by explicit and precise legal norms that sustained the collective thrust of Jewish spirituality' (Hartman 2000:xiii).

'Emergency measures', i.e., deviations from accepted practice promulgated in times of acute danger and justified by the need to ensure the survival of the polity and its way of life, constitute an integral feature of the Jewish political tradition. Rabbinic authorities have always claimed that, should short-term adherence to the strict dictates of the *halakhah* endanger its long-term preservation, they possess the power to suspend ordinary laws, to resort to sanctions not previously authorized and even to act in a manner that involves violating a portion of the *torah*. Folio 85b of tractate *Yoma* in the 'Babylonian Talmud', the massive record of protracted rabbinic discussions that was finally edited in the fifth century, summed up the prevailing attitude in a rule of thumb that has been echoed in all subsequent codes: 'Violate ... one Sabbath in order to enable the observance of many Sabbaths.'[1]

Clearly, such actions were not to be taken lightly (Elon 1994:513–36; Ben-Menahem 1991). No authority, no matter how renowned, could sanction a judicial deviation from regular law and practice unless convinced that the situation was indeed critical. Even then, protocol required the demonstration of right intent and displays of consideration for human dignity. Above all, emergency regulations were to be just that – interim steps taken in order to avert an immediately pending crisis or moderate its effects. Hence they were frequently designated *hora'ot sha'ah* ('temporary measures'), and justified in terms that similarly conveyed their transitory character. They were required because *ha-sha'ah tzerikhah le-kach* ('the hour requires it') or in order 'to safeguard the matter' (*le-migdar miltah*). Thus described, violations of the law could in fact be deemed commensurate with its observance. As one of the earliest recorded commentaries to Psalms 119:126 put matters, 'when "It is time to act for the Lord", Jews have "to violate Thy *torah*".'[2]

The regularity with which such phrases and teachings recur in the rabbinic texts of the medieval and early modern period belies any assumption that 'emergency measures' were a rarity. On the contrary, they seem to have been resorted to with considerable frequency. What is more, they were utilized in order to cover a wide range of circumstances that, in the Jewish context of the times, clearly carried national security connotations: the imposition of punishments not previously sanctioned on persons who informed against the community or otherwise slandered it; changing the accepted criteria for appointments to high judicial office so as to include suitably qualified converts; waiving the injunction against making payments to teachers of religious instruction (which, if upheld, would simply have acted as a disincentive to scholarship); and, not least, the commitment to writing of what was ordained to be an 'oral code of Law', the unity of which was in danger of being shattered by the circumstances of Jewish dispersion.[3]

So vast was this range that emergency regulations in fact became an almost routine feature of Jewish political life. A telling indication of that phenomenon is provided by changes in the provenance of synoptic analyses of their application in the great codes of law that served as constitutional references for the vast majority of medieval and early modern Jewry worldwide. In the *Mishneh Torah* (literally 'Supplementary Torah'), the magisterial and all-encompassing code compiled in Egypt by Moses ben Maimon (Maimonides; 1135–1204), universally recognized to be the greatest *halakhic* master of all times, the general discussion of emergency decrees is delayed until chapter 24 of his 'Laws Concerning the Sanhedrin' – a tail-end location roughly equivalent to that accorded to such matters in most modern constitutions. However, by the time of the composition of the next great compendiums of Jewish law, the *Araba'ah Turim* (literally 'Four Pillars') by Jacob ben Asher in the early fourteenth century, and the even more authoritative *Shulkhan Arukh* ('Laid Table') by Joseph Karo some 200 years later, matters had changed. In those texts, most emergency rights are enumerated in the clause that immediately follows the instruction to establish courts of law (the precise reference is section *Choshen Mishpat*, clause 2) – an up-front location that gives them a degree of prominence unmatched in any other constitution that we have been able to trace.[4]

The parallels with current Israeli constitutional practice are too stark to be overlooked. Almost as a matter of course, Israel's parliament, the *knesset*, now renews on an annual basis the emergency regulations that the government inherited from the British mandatory authorities in 1948 and that were written into Israeli law in the very first week of Independence. As will be seen, this practice, which in effect takes the traditional routinization of emergency rule to its logical extreme, has played a particularly large role in shaping the form of the *temporal* dimension of all national security legislation.

The impossible option: the resort to force

A close familiarity with emergency regulations constituted, however, just one of the Jewish political tradition's bequests to modern Jewish national security practice. Another, no less prominent, was a total renunciation of the use of force. Here, too, past collective experience played a decisive role. True, the Old Testament's historical portrait of the Children of Israel, beginning with the book of Exodus and ending with the last chapters of Chronicles, leaves no doubt that Judaism's earliest and most influential teachings were formulated and transmitted against a backdrop of almost incessant military activity. According to the narratives preserved in the Apocrypha, and especially in the books of Maccabees, Jubilees and Judith, warfare played a similarly crucial role in the formation of ancient Jewry's national identity during the period of the second commonwealth (516 BCE–CE 70). But the threads of continuity were violently severed with Rome's obliteration of the last vestiges of Judea's independence in CE 70 and her even more savage suppression of the rebellion that erupted in the province six decades later. Thereafter, the Jews transformed themselves into a non-bellicose people.

For one thing, they made every possible effort to expunge memories of warfare from the national consciousness. Even the Bible, otherwise a perennial fount of consolation and inspiration in times of Exile, was subjected to a process of rabbinic re-interpretation, whereby Scripture's takes of martial valor and heroism were deliberately divested of their plain meanings. King David, for instance, was transformed from a warrior into a scholar and his band of champions recast as irenic students. Likewise, military themes were airbrushed out of the traditions that celebrated the victorious rebellion against Seleucian rule led by Judah the *Maccabee* ('hammer') in the second temple period. *Chanukah*, the 'festival of lights', which commemorates the triumph, was instead invested with entirely other-worldly connotations and hence regarded as a quintessential application of the prophecy contained in Zechariah 4:6: 'Not by might nor by power, but by My spirit says the Lord of hosts.'

Simeon bar-Kochba, the fabled leader of the last-gasp Jewish revolt against Rome in the second century underwent an even more extreme form of literary metamorphosis – from an iconic national hero into a prototypical false Messiah. Concluding his exhaustive survey of this trajectory, Richard Marks writes: 'When most writers looked for the [Bar Kokhba] story's political meaning, they discovered a warning: it warned Jews not to seek national power by their own political, military efforts' (Marks 1994:204). Indeed, according to one tradition they had been expressly forbidden to do so. Burnishing a talmudic exegesis on the 'oath' thrice repeated in the biblical book known as the Song of Songs (2:7; 3:5; 8:4), generation after generation of spiritual authorities repeated the same warning: Divine decree expressly warned Jews not to undertake military activity in pursuit of national security by 'forcing an end' and conquering the Holy Land. Instead, as one fourteenth-century rabbi put it:

> We should follow in the footsteps of our forefathers, that is, prepare to approach the children of Esau with gifts, and with humble language, and with prayer to God, may He be blessed. It is impossible for us to meet them in war, as it is said [in the Song of Songs]: 'I have abjured you, O daughters of Jerusalem' not to provoke war with the nations.
> (Ravitzky 1996:227–8)

Given that background, it is hardly surprising to find a thundering silence with regards to military matters in almost all of the great classics of traditional Jewish philosophy and legal thought. The only author to deviate from that convention was Maimonides, who did include in his great code a summary of the biblical and talmudic rulings relevant to the initiation and conduct of armed conflict (*Mishneh Torah*; 'Laws of Kings and their Wars', Chapters 5–8). But this instance, although certainly Titanic, remained altogether exceptional, and did not set a precedent. None of the subsequent canonical authors and codifiers of either medieval or early modern Judaism ever examined in any depth what we have categorized as the *hierarchical* and *functional* issues associated with declarations of war and the management of military operations. Still less did they encourage their co-religionists to attain practical experience of such matters by pursuing military careers – even when that particular professional option was permitted by the local gentile suzerains. Rather, Jews developed what one scholar describes as an almost genetic aversion to bloodshed (Luz 1987), which persisted well into the modern period.

Eager to become fully accepted citizens of the Netherlands and the USA, handfuls of Jews did begin to enlist in the Dutch and American armies as early as the eighteenth century. In increasing numbers, the Jews of France, Germany, Britain and Italy soon began taking the same route to national identity. Nevertheless, even in the nineteenth-century heyday of Emancipation all such instances were exceptional. For the vast majority of both European and Oriental Jewries military service remained an anathema. Hence, the proportion of Jews who earned their livelihood by soldiering persistently lagged far behind that of the gentile average, and never comprised more than a fraction of the total Jewish population. Right up until World War I, when 'muscular Judaism' first came of age in central Europe (Presner 2007:187–217), military service in any shape or form remained for most Jews anathema. Far from being a right of citizenship to be exercised, or a career to be pursued, it was almost universally regarded as a burden best avoided.

From a cultural perspective, the most conspicuous effect of this situation was that, where attitudes towards national security policies were concerned, as a collective, Jewry entered the modern age with a decidedly lop-sided heritage. In contrast to the sophistication and competence that, as early as medieval times, characterized Jewish attitudes towards the enactment and enforcement of emergency judicial regulations as instruments of crisis management, approaches to the military dimensions of the national security repertoire remained stunted. A few idiosyncratic exceptions apart, Jews had no practical experience of the control of violence at the level of operational field command and, still less, of the exercise of supreme executive responsibility for national security.[5] Where it existed, Jewry's knowledge of warfare was generally limited to its supply side and restricted to so-called *hofjuden*, the 'court Jews' who purveyed military materiel to a disparate and not always distinguished list of central European rulers (Hodel and Rauscher 2004). Not one of that otherwise inventive circle, however, had exploited the experience thus acquired to theorize about the ways in which armies could be raised, equipped and deployed as instruments of policy, and yet at the same time prevented from upsetting the constitutional balance of civil–military relationships. In all such areas, even as late as the early twentieth century, Jewish thought clearly had much ground to make up.

The heritage of the Yishuv period

Initially, the founders and leaders of the political Zionist movement evinced no inclination to repair such deficiencies. Although in many other respects Zionism deserves depiction as a 'revolution' against past Jewish practices, where the exercise of force was concerned, the lines of continuity predominated (S. Cohen 2008:17–23). Partly, of course, this was because the vast majority of the movement's first leaders had no premonition that their ambition to secure the establishment of a Jewish homeland would require military action. Theodore Herzl, the Viennese journalist who founded the World Zionist Organization in 1897 and served as its president until his death in 1904, was convinced that what was needed to attain Zionism's purposes was an adroit admixture of financial inducements and diplomatic pressure. Hence, it was to the proper management of those two instruments that he devoted much of the discussion of government to be found in his programmatic manifesto *Der Judenstaat*, published in 1896. By contrast, military affairs are dismissed in a single line. The Jews' state, Herzl writes, will possess 'Just a professional army, equipped of course with every requisite of modern warfare, to preserve order internally and externally.' But as to the legal framework that would govern the raising, financing, training and, above all, the deployment, of that army, Herzl said not a word. Even as late as 1914, by which time Arab military assaults on early Jewish settlements in Palestine had already become serious enough to warrant the establishment of a local self-defense organization (*Ha-Shomer*, set up in 1909), most Zionists thought it unnecessary to adopt a new outlook. After all, and as one spokesman for the movement innocently proclaimed:

> The war for which we are being prepared is very simple, not dangerous in the least. What we desire is to engage in patient labor, work devoid of any bloodshed, work that is only civilized colonization. Diligent labor is our sword and bow. In the end, no one will oppose us in enmity.
> (Max Emmanuel Mandelstamm, cited in Shapira 1992:41)

The mood of confidence in the possibility of non-belligerency that thus permeated the early Zionist *Yishuv* (organized community in Palestine) did not last. Although its leaders soon developed their own brand of diplomacy (Sofer 1998), they could not rely solely on that instrument. Violence became increasingly pronounced in the two decades that separated the end of World War I from the beginning of World War II, a period that began with a series of fierce and bloody encounters between Jewish colonists and Arab villagers in Galilee and culminated with the wave of more ferocious and widespread attacks collectively known as the Arab 'rebellion' of 1936–1939. By the latter date, the *Haganah*, itself founded in 1920 as a nationwide successor to *Ha-Shomer*, had created the *Fosh* (*Pelugot Sadeh* ['field squads']), responsible for carrying out reprisal raids in response to Arab attacks on Jewish settlements. Even earlier, in 1931, the 'Revisionists', a right-of-center group who eventually broke away from the mainstream Zionist movement in 1935, had founded the more militant *Etzel* (*Irgun Tzeva'i Leumi*: 'National Military Organization') (Pail 1987).

With the outbreak of World War II, and especially once news of the Holocaust began to seep out, an increasingly proactive 'offensive' ethos came to dominate Zionist thinking. 'Henceforth force was to play a central role in realizing the political aims of the Zionist movement.' (Shapira 1992:288) This shift was expressed in two sequential stages. The first was organizational: the foundation in 1940 of the radical group that termed itself *Lehi* (*Lohamei Herut Yisrael*: 'Fighters for the Freedom of Israel', which the British authorities derogatorily referred to as 'the Stern gang') and in 1941 of the *Palmach* (*pelugot mahatz*: 'shock troops'), comprised of the elite of the *Haganah*. The second stage was operational. The cataclysmic years 1945–1947, especially, were marked by a spiral of increasing violence between Jews, Arabs and the British Mandate authorities, at sea as well as on land, creating a situation that virtually ensured that, during the following two years, the fate of the Jewish national enterprise would ultimately be determined on the battlefield.

Notwithstanding the progressively larger institutional arrangements by which it was accompanied, the development of Jewish military activism in the pre-state period was something of a haphazard phenomenon. Only in retrospect does the march of events from *Ha-Shomer* to the *Haganah*, and thence to the *Palmach* and – eventually – the IDF have the appearance of orderly and planned progression. At the time, there existed no blueprint for the military mobilization of the *Yishuv* and only a vague idea of how a fighting force, once established, ought to behave and be controlled (Eilam 1979; Van Creveld 1998:5–29). The only time when fundamental issues relating to the use – and abuse – of force seem to have debated in any depth was during the period 1936–1939, when the *Yishuv* felt the full force of what was known as 'the Palestinian revolt'. And even then, discussion generally eschewed topics related to civil–military relations and the questions associated with what we have termed the *hierarchical* dimension of the national security legal framework. Instead, attention was focused on either possible tactical responses to Arab terror or, at a more fundamental level, on the moral dilemmas generated by the resort to force (Shavit 1983; Don-Yehiya 1993). On its own terms, this was certainly a very fruitful exercise. It resulted in a thorough and public airing of the respective virtues of 'restraint' (*havlagah*) and 'response' (*teguvah*), and made popular the term *tohar ha-neshek* ('purity of arms'), which to this day remains one of the IDF's principal moral and legal compasses. But who might possess the authority to enforce the application of that particular gauge, and to judge post factum whether it had in fact been observed, were questions that were left very much up in the air and hardly discussed at all (Shapira 1984).

Historians have posited two broad explanations for that situation. The first, and most conventional, argues that no debate on the hierarchical dimension of the national security framework was required. In practice, after all, ultimate authority over the most powerful of the armed forces that the *Yishuv* was able to muster resided almost as a matter of course in its civilian organs of self-government. This was only to be expected in what were essentially militia groups, devoid of professional military cadres and intensely loyal to the civilian social networks out of which they grew. True, such loyalties were not altogether uniform. Differences between the rival political parties in the *Yishuv* that promoted different ideological agendas were almost always fierce and sometimes found expression in sporadic acts of violence, especially between factions on the Socialist left and 'Nationalist' right of the ideological spectrum. Nevertheless, the majorities in both camps agreed that, where matters affecting military activity against 'external' enemies were concerned (British as well as Arab), unity had to be maintained. In 1931, accordingly, control over the *Haganah* was vested in a 'national command' (*mifkadah artzit*), which comprised three civilian representatives of the majority labor movement and three representatives of 'civil' (non-Socialist) sectors of the *Yishuv*. As from 1937, this body was itself headed by a chairperson (*rosh ha-mifkadah ha-artzit* – abbreviated to *RAMAH*), acceptable to both sides. This system did not always function smoothly. Indeed, the history of the Command is punctuated with records of wrangles between, on the one hand, the incumbents of the post of *RAMAH* (especially, Moshe Sneh, 1941–1946 and Yisrael Galilee 1947–1948) and, on the other, David Ben-Gurion, since 1935 the chairman of the Jewish Agency Executive and the man who eventually dismissed Galilee (see Chapter 3). Whilst it lasted, nevertheless, the *mifkadah artzit* constituted a testimony to the supreme importance that the *Yishuv* attached to the attainment of a consensus on national security issues, an attitude that was likewise proclaimed to be equally important to the defense of the country after the attainment of Statehood (Horowitz and Lissak 1978:173–4; Shifris 2010:47–84).

The second historical explanation for the absence of any formal discussion of civil–military relations in the *Yishuv* during the Mandate period is considerably less benign. In this view, civil–military partnership in the 'organized *Yishuv*', as the dominant Labor alignment was known, was not at all an organic outgrowth of shared perceptions and outlooks. Rather, it resulted from a deliberate and carefully crafted bargain between persons representing the *Yishuv*'s civilian and military elites (Ben-Eliezer 1998). The two sides, it must be stressed, were not evenly matched representatives of different ideologies. On the contrary, the dialogue between them essentially took place in an intra-party context, albeit at an inter-generational level.

One side consisted of the *Yishuv*'s veteran leaders, principally drawn from the ranks of Labor Zionists, whose status reflected the fact that they had, over the years, fashioned the instrumental prerequisites for national regeneration, of which the most important were: a labor federation (the *Histadrut*); an educational and health system; a web of political parties; and – not least – rudimentary military frameworks. Even though they did not yet wield formal sovereignty over the *Yishuv*, a prerogative that still resided with the British mandate authorities, the veteran Zionist leadership certainly possessed enormous authority within it, a position that they were determined to hold on to until such time as independence was indeed attained.

On the other side was the younger generation of native-born *sabras* ('cacti'; the term of affection used by the *Yishuv* to designate its native-born offspring), a small but very influential cohort that had been deliberately brought up to believe that they were men and women of national destiny. As soon as they reached maturity, they assumed the designated role of their people's new elite with almost religious enthusiasm,[6] in the process imbibing and disseminating an entirely new canon of military-related myths. Theirs was the generation that first turned Masada, the desert crag that had been the site of the Jewish fighters' last stand against Rome in CE 70, into a place of pilgrimage during the 1930s. In the following decade its members flocked to the *Haganah* and the *Palmach.* In so doing, they gave practical expression to the firmness of their conviction that they possessed the means required for transforming a 'state-in-the making' into a reality. At the same time, however, they issued an implicit warning that, unless given their heads, they might act independently in order to do so.

As analyzed by what is known as the 'critical' school of Israeli sociology, the deal struck by these two parties was essentially a trade off: 'militarism' was exchanged for the threat of 'praetorianism'. Specifically, the *Palmach*'s young lions were promised societal regard, cultural predominance and priority of access to whatever resources the polity could muster. In return, they undertook not to use the means thus placed at their disposal to challenge the formal primacy of civilian primacy over the militias of which they formed a part. No written document spelled out the terms of this arrangement. Indeed, informality was essential to the entire framework that it established. Only thus could both sides be assured of the room for future maneuver that each thought it required. Nevertheless, once entered into, the arrangement exerted an influence that was profound. In immediate terms, the spirit of collusion thus established, runs the thesis, accounts for the overwhelming extent to which members of the three 'underground movements' acquiesced in Ben-Gurion's demand that, once the IDF was established, they divest themselves of their separate identities and merge into a single national army, upon which the Prime Minister was prepared to lavish enormous doses of esteem.

In the long term, the impact of the deal was even greater. Precisely because Israel's political and military leaders were unburdened by any constitutional commitment to the proper form that their relationship was supposed to take, they were able from the first to steer a flexible course that proved remarkably sensitive to changes of atmosphere and personality. This, it is held, explains why – notwithstanding the prevalence of military activity in Israel's early history – the country has never been even remotely threatened by the prospect of an army-led *coup d'etat*.[7] Simply put, the generals have never had need to resort to such extremes. Like their predecessors in the *Yishuv*, they have been able to obtain whatever they might have wished for simply by repeating their fidelity to the principle of military subordination to the elected government.

Quite apart from being far too cynical to be entirely plausible, that reading of the roots of modern Israel's civil–military partnership also suffers from several additional flaws. In particular, and as will be seen in the next chapter, it downplays the pivotal influence that Ben-Gurion exercised on the development of Israel's security culture, as on all other processes during the crucial years of the transition from the *Yishuv* to statehood. Nevertheless, the 'critical' reading of the genesis of Israel's arrangements for the management of the civil–military relationship does capture what seems to be one of that relationship's most prominent and enduring features. From their very inception, it shows, the arrangements were inherently informal, and in many important respects, by design opaque. Indeed, where the most important questions of hierarchical and functional principle were concerned – a category that includes such pivotal legal/constitutional issues as the authority to initiate hostilities or to desist from doing so, as well as the precise rules of engagement that were to apply should force be employed – those arrangements deliberately left much that was unsaid, or at best only vaguely expressed, and hence open to various interpretations. As we shall see, this was to be one of the Mandate period's most enduring contributions to the entire style of Israel's security law.

Writing in the mid-1980s, a period when Israeli public life suffered the shock induced by the disclosure of the 'General Security Services Cover-Up' (discussed in Chapter 5), a particularly unpleasant instance of the perversion of justice in the name of state security, Ehud Sprinzak advanced an additional gloss on the roots of Israel's informal style in the national security sphere, as in others. In general, he argued, the absence in a political system of clearly formulated rules for public behavior should be understood to reflect an underlying and essentially cultural unwillingness to accept the overriding supremacy of the rule of law across the board. Recent events, he argued, showed that Israel's political culture was overall characterized by 'an instrumental orientation to towards the law and the idea of the rule of law' (Sprinzak 1993).

'Illegalism', the term that Sprinzak used to define this trait, is hence not restricted solely to matters that concern (or, more accurately, are said to concern) national security. Rather, it pervades all areas of public life and stems from a get-up-and-go ethos that prioritizes ideological and state interests over subservience to the norms of behavior mandated by the rule of law. Moreover, it is very much an elite phenomenon. Its characteristic expression is not low-level corruption and/or a widespread disposition towards criminality on the part of the majority of the citizen body. Instead, illegalism's principal exponents – and defendants – are the political community's most highly respected politicians and ideologues, whose status and functions endow their actions and pronouncements with especial prestige.

Of the several reasons why 'illegalism', thus defined, should have been particularly pronounced in the *Yishuv*, two warrant particular attention.

- The first was Jewry's diaspora experience. The *Yishuv*'s leaders did not only lack any tradition of experience with military affairs (an aspect of their condition to which reference has already been made). Most of 'the founding fathers of Israeli Zionism', as Sprinzak calls them, also suffered the additional disability of coming from societies in Eastern Europe where notions of civil and individual legal rights were still unknown. 'For Jews who never even experienced the rudimentary elements of democracy, such as free elections, free press and majority rule, the niceties of the rule of law, impartial public administration, and civil service were completely irrelevant' (Sprinzak 1993:177).
- More specific, secondly, was the influence exerted by the experience of the regime governing the *Yishuv* itself during its formative period. Certainly, the British authorities whose administration of the Palestine mandate lasted from 1920 until 1948 did introduce a legal and governmental culture far superior in every respect to the corruption that had been endemic during the late Ottoman period. Nevertheless, the Zionists soon had reason to question the consonance between legality and legitimacy. Indeed, a series of British White Papers suggested that the two could be poles apart. The successive restrictions imposed by the mandate regime on Jewish land purchases and immigration were all 'legal', in the sense that they had been passed into law by due process. But in Zionist eyes, all were at root unjust, and a betrayal of Lord Arthur Balfour's famous declaration, issued in November 1917, that the British government was committed to seeing the establishment in Palestine of a 'Jewish National Home'.

Against that background, 'illegalism' attained the status of a crusade, and became an umbrella term for actions perpetrated in the name of a cause higher than the formal law. 'Illegal' settlement, 'illegal' immigration, 'illegal' military training – each constituted a path to national redemption. In retrospect, each too attained the respectability conferred by success. According to the official narrative of events, the State would never have come into existence had the *Yishuv* allowed its actions to be circumscribed by British regulations. On the contrary, the true lesson of the state-building enterprise was that nothing spoke louder than *bitzuizm* ('accomplishment', i.e., the art of getting things done). In comparison, constitutional pronouncements could carry little weight.

Understandable, and perhaps even justifiable in the mandatory period, such sentiments became entirely inappropriate once the State of Israel came into existence. At that point, the proper conduct of public affairs required that persons in authority adopt an emphatically negative attitude towards illegalism and instead foster, not least by setting a personal example, a respect on the part of citizens for the concept of the rule of law and a commitment to its upkeep. In Sprinzak's view, however, no such transformation occurred. True, Ben-Gurion certainly appreciated the enormity of the change wrought in the *Yishuv*'s condition by the attainment of independence. Indeed, he developed an entirely new doctrine of 'statism' (*mamlakhtiut*) in order to function as an agency for national re-construction (Kedar 2007, 2009). Nevertheless, the attitudes of mind and behavior ingrained by the older tradition of illegalism remained entrenched. 'Latent' according to Sprinzak, whilst Ben-Gurion was the height of his power, it once again became 'manifest' immediately after his retirement from the premiership in 1963, and enjoyed a new lease of life ('rediscovered illegalism'), with the formation of the second *Likud* government in 1981.

By that time, the impact on Israel's national security framework had long been apparent. Because it prioritized immediate and pragmatic considerations, the culture of illegalism had encouraged an attitude of mind that tolerated, and perhaps even encouraged, the postponement of the resolution of matters of principle likely to generate discord. At the same time, it fostered a hand-to-mouth approach to dealing with issues that acted as a disincentive to the establishment of formal procedures for the conduct of government business. Both traits influenced the content of Israel's national security legal framework as well as its style. Respectively, they help explain why it took so long for Israel's national security law to even begin to address two of the dimensions that we identify as integral to any national security legal framework: the *hierarchy* of national security decision-making (which authority is empowered to issue instructions to the military?) and the *functional* division of national security responsibilities (especially the ways in which the legislature and judiciary are to monitor executive actions).

The persistent shadow of warfare

Much though the character of Israel's national security legal framework thus owed to habits of Jewish thought and Jewish behavior deeply embedded in the Diaspora and *Yishuv* experiences, it cannot be described as simply a linear outgrowth of a single historical processes. Still less was there anything inevitable about its eventual form. As Aaron Klieman has pointed out (Klieman 1990:43–50), Jewry's past was rich enough to supply several alternative interpretations of Israel's relationships with the rest of the world and offered variant templates of the frameworks and procedures required in order to protect the nation's security. In his analysis, the relevant conceptions generally oscillate between three alternative worldviews, each of which can draw on biblical templates. One is the 'idealist' view, which assumes a condition of basic international amity that permits Israel to fulfill the function of a 'light unto the nations' assigned to all Jews by Isaiah 49:6. The second is the 'pessimist' view, based on the belief that Israel will always be an outcast state ('a people that dwells alone ... and not be reckoned amongst the nations' was how Balaam put it in Numbers 23:9) and as such, subject to the same hostile biases that typified anti-Semitic prejudices against Jews in previous ages. The third is the 'realist' view, which rejects the notion that Israel might, or ought to be in any way special. Instead, as a state like any other (the condition that the Israelites of old had on one famous occasion expressly asked to be granted; see I Samuel 8:5) she has to conduct her affairs in accordance with the same iron rules of realpolitik that governed all international behavior. Ultimately, once the State of Israel was established, the country's governing elite had to assess which (if any) of these three interpretations seemed best to reflect Israel's present condition and thereafter to determine how best to secure the country's future security.

From the very first, all such discussions have been conducted within earshot of gunfire. Essential to an understanding of the strategic culture that informs Israel's national security legal framework, therefore, is the fact that, at no time in the history of the State, has the country's leadership ever felt able to conduct a national security assessment in an atmosphere that even remotely resembles tranquility. Therein, indeed, lays Israel's uniqueness. She is not the first state to have been born into a situation of conflict. Neither is she the only small-sized country whose survival has been threatened by a hostile combination of far larger neighbors (Vital 1971). Her singularity, rather, lies in the longevity of the mutual hostility and enmity that has characterized Israel's relationships with her immediate geographical neighbors and in the protracted nature of the various conflicts which those sentiments have spawned. In the six decades of her existence, Israel has (by a conservative count, published in 2006) fought half a dozen inter-state wars, five – some say six – separate low-insurgency campaigns (LICs), and has engaged in some 150 major operations that the jargon of the security studies literature somewhat clumsily refers to as 'dyadic militarized interstate disputes' (MIDs), involving the threat, display, or use of military force against another state. In addition, she has conducted a much larger – probably innumerable – number of operations against targets that she classifies as 'terrorists'. Indeed,

> Israel is by far the most conflict-prone state in modern history. It has averaged nearly 4 MIDs every year. It has fought an interstate war every nine years. Israel appears on the top of the list of the most intense national rivalries in the last two-hundred-year period.
>
> (Maoz 2006:5)

Whether or not some, perhaps most, of those conflicts might have been avoidable is a question that now engenders considerable debate, not least within Israel. Avishai Ehrlich, then a professor of sociology at Tel-Aviv University, presented an initial version of a 'revisionist' approach as early as 1987, in an article that considered the Arab–Israeli conflict, not as an exogenous factor in Israel's development, but rather as a constitutive of Israeli society and state (Ehrlich 1987). Similar themes were later developed by several anthropologists, political economists and – especially – sociologists, of whom undoubtedly the most vocal was Baruch Kimmerling of the Hebrew University in Jerusalem. Particularly influential was Kimmerling's identification of Israel's leanings towards what he called 'cognitive militarism', defined as a *'latent state-of-mind'* (his emphasis), at whose core stands the conviction that 'military considerations, as well as matters that are defined as 'national security' issues, almost always receive higher priority than political, economic and ideological problems' (Kimmerling 1993:200). Thus described, 'cognitive militarism' encouraged Israel's elites, civilian as well as military, to seek primarily violent military resolutions to security problems that might be amenable to alternative treatment.

Partly because of the rambling style of his writing, and partly because some of his examples were patently inappropriate, Kimmerling's arguments often turned out to be less convincing than they at first seemed. Painting with a broad brush, he could only generalize about cognitive militarism's alleged impact on the 'social construction of the Arab–Jewish conflict' and on Israel's political, economic and administrative structures. Other observers, however, even when explicitly denying Kimmerling's premises and rejecting his terminology, presented analyses that in some respects moved along similar lines. The 'security subculture', they noted, had impacted on every facet of Israeli life, from literature and the cinema to women's rights, and from the economy to religious worldviews (Bar-Tal 1998). In an even more direct sense, the constant sense of being confronted by multiple existential threats has been shown to affect Israel's negotiating style, fostering a 'safety-first' posture that instinctively disfavors any diplomatic compromise even remotely likely to endanger what are considered to be core strategic assets (Klieman 2005).

Most intensive of all, however, has been the attention focused on the impact of Israel's security subculture on her civil–military relations. Early studies of the topic, published in the 1960s and 1970s, had generally tended to take a somewhat sanguine view of military influences over Israel's defense and security policies, suggesting that the military had been 'civilianized' just as much as the civilian sphere had been 'militarized' (Horowitz 1982; Lissak 1983). Even then, however, critical voices could be heard. One school of thought argued that the military already constituted an effective pressure group in those areas (Perlmutter 1969); another went as far as to claim that the military in effect constituted a full 'partner' in Israeli government, a situation facilitated by the existence of only nominal civilian control over the defense arena and weak instrumental control (Peri 1983:101–29).

More recent studies, although modifying those depictions in some important respects, nevertheless point in the same general direction. Some do so scathingly and in accusatory fashion, charging the civilian 'void' that allegedly lies at the heart of Israel's security and foreign policies with responsibility for a multitude of sins. Zeev Maoz, the author of an especially detailed and comprehensive overview of Israel's security behavior (Maoz 2006), is also by far the most critical of the pernicious consequences that he considers to have resulted from the faulty and often offhand manner in which strategic decisions have been arrived at. Thus, he finds 'absence of civilian oversight' responsible for the wanton arrogance with which Israel has so often, and so unnecessarily, wielded its military might ('most of Israel's wars were due to either its aggressive designs … miscalculations in conflict management strategies, or avoidable'); for the converse pattern of risk-shunning behavior in the management of peace diplomacy ('Israel has almost never initiated any significant peace effort. It was as responsible for the failure of peace-related efforts as were the Arab states or the Palestinians'); for several purportedly hare-brained schemes founded on the misguided assumption that Israel can employ violence to manipulate the domestic systems of other states and actors in the region; and for her 'ability to run a covert and unsupervised nuclear program that is driven by technocrats rather than by strategists and political leaders.'

Other analysts have sought to present a more balanced portrait. Thus, in his landmark study Ben-Meir drew on his vast knowledge of the subject to demonstrate that the situation was, as he put it, far more 'mixed' than is usually conceded. True, he acknowledged, in many spheres – notably strategic planning and defense organization – the protracted experience of imminent or actual warfare has held Israel's national security decision-making in thrall, so much so that 'civilian involvement is barely present.' (Ben-Meir 1995:179) In other areas and at some times, however, Ben-Meir found that civilian intrusion into military affairs, such as the conduct of military operations, in fact far exceeds the limits conventionally observed in Western countries. But that conclusion gives only small comfort. Even the most tolerant of contemporary analysts of Israel's national security decision-making take it virtually for granted that the military exercises an inordinate influence over that process, which hence continued to bear the marks of a long list of ingrained organizational efficiencies and almost inherent national pathologies (Ya'ari 2004; Freilich 2006; Michael 2008).

Legal studies of Israel's national security policies have followed an independent and somewhat different trajectory. Academic interest in the subject was a comparatively late development, which apart from a very few incidental exceptions did not make its appearance until the 1970s. Even then, much of what was written focused almost exclusively on the specifics of the legal problems generated by Israel's control over the territories conquered in the Six Days War and was authored by practitioners involved in its administration. An outstanding example was Meir Shamgar (Shamgar 1971), altogether one of the pillars of the Israeli legal establishment, who on his retirement from the IDF in 1968, after serving for seven years as Chief Military Advocate General (MAG), had been appointed Attorney General (and thereafter went on to serve as President of the ISC). However, evidence that the ISC was willing to hear petitions from Palestinian residents of the territories, and sometimes even to rule in their favor, prompted several independent legal scholars to analyze this Israeli version of the intersection of international law with judicial activism and national security. Yoram Dinstein, professor of law at Tel-Aviv University, soon became an especially influential voice, and in a series of articles written between the mid-1970s and late 1980s laid the foundations for future scholarship regarding the contents of the rules of international law regarding Israel's occupation of the territories (Dinstein 1974, 1978, 1979, 1981, 1983, 1984, 1988a, 1988b).

Subsequent scholarly interest shifted to the specifics of the decisions handed down by the ISC in cases that pitted human rights against state security interests. For the most part, their initial tone was self-congratulatory, a stance illustrated in 1981 when Moshe Negbi depicted the ISC as the protector of human rights in the Territories (Negbi 1981). Later writings, however, tended to be overwhelmingly critical. Amnon Rubinstein (1988) and Eyal Benvenisti (1989, 1992, 1993a) maintained that ISC judgments were effectively incorporating the territories into Israel, whilst Ronen Shamir (1990) and Gad Barzilai (1999b, 1999c) argued that, since they rarely overturned military policies, they also legitimized Israel's occupation of the region (see also Shelef 1993). In *The Occupation of Justice* (2002), a model of precision, elegance and erudition, Professor David Kretzmer of the Hebrew University supplied what was undoubtedly the most comprehensive analysis of the relationship between Israel's judicial system and the regions conquered by the IDF in 1967. Even so, what had by now become a cottage industry of 'Territories' studies', some of which was devoted to detailed discussions of ISC decisions handed down after Kretzmer's work had appeared, continued to flourish (e.g., Reichman 2001; Shany and Ben Naftali 2004; Cohen and Shany 2007; Am. Cohen 2007). A subsequent offshoot was scholarship devoted to examining the compatibility of IDF conduct vis-à-vis the Palestinians with the evolving demands of international law (Gross 2006, originally published in Hebrew in 2004, Ben Naftali and Michaeli 2004).

By comparison, the study of the broader framework of national security law and its application in Israel proper suffered from relative neglect. The first analysis of the scope of judicial review of national security considerations in free speech did not appear until 1988 (Shetreet 1988). Wider reviews took even longer to reach the bookshelves. Certainly, Menachem Hofnung's pioneering investigation of the tension in Israel between 'state security' and the 'rule of law' (Hofnung 1991, abbreviated English edition

1996) was worth waiting for. But although this landmark work filled several significant lacunae, it also exposed how many remained. Hofnung's masterful chronicle of the history of Israel's security legislation focused on emergency regulations and the attempts by the courts to introduce basic human rights into Israeli society at large, as well as the Territories. In the terms of the taxonomy that we presented in our previous chapter, he hence mainly concentrated on *temporal* and *spatial* issues. Topics that fall under the *hierarchical* or *functional* headings are barely touched on.

Subsequent studies have in large measure helped to fill several of the remaining gaps. Even when most successful and informative, however, they have tended to adopt a piecemeal approach. Within this category come, for instance, specialist studies of the relationship between the MAG and the attorney general (Shoham 2002) and, in greater number, of the role of the ISC with regards to issues related to foreign affairs and defense (Benvenisti 1992), its jurisprudence with regards to security claims (Bracha 1991), and its intervention in military matters, both operational (Arbel 2002; Finkelstein 2002; Ben-Naftali and Michaeli 2004; Tirosh 2004) and more generally societal (Barak-Erez 2002). Likewise, albeit without direct reference to national security matters, some attention has been paid to the roles played by different institutions in the processes whereby the government of Israel affirms its commitment to international treaties (e.g., Zilbershats 1995). Similarly sporadic in approach are analyses of various aspects of security-related legislation, a span that, under the influence of the birth of a 'constitutional' discourse in Israel's academia, encompasses Basic Laws (e.g., Bendor and Kremnitzer, 2000; Rubinstein 2000; Nun 1999 and 2004) as well as regular enactments relating to conscription (Siedman 1996). Many of these studies have appeared in *Mishpat ve-Tzava* ('Law and Army'), an academic-style journal that the MAG service in the IDF has published on a regular basis since 1983.

Individually, each of these works contributes substantively to our understanding of important elements in each of the four dimensions of the overall national security legal framework that we have identified. There remains, nevertheless, a need to pull the various individual strands together and show how in different periods they have created separate panoramas. The chapters that follow aim to fulfill that purpose. In addition to tracing the individual development of the temporal, hierarchical, functional and spatial dimensions that comprise Israel's national security framework, they also seek to explore the interplay of inputs, both civilian and military, that explain how and why that system as a whole has evolved over time. To that end, they follow a chronological sequence, the overall purpose of which is to explore the dynamics that have determined both the pace and the form of the changes which that framework has undergone.

Part II
Development

3 Centralization, 1948–1963

The primacy of Ben-Gurion and the priority of military security

In a confidential address delivered in February 1960 to the Foreign Affairs and Defense Committee of the *knesset*, Ben-Gurion frankly acknowledged that Israel's War of Independence, fought in 1948–1949, had not been as close-run a thing as popular mythology maintained (Gelber 2004:476). Modern historical research now tends to confirm Ben-Gurion's version (Kadish and Kedar 2006). True, Jewish forces entered the conflict under conditions of nominal numerical inferiority. Nevertheless, their ability to repel the invasions launched by multiple Arab armies, and indeed to revise in Israel's favor the boundaries of the Jewish state prescribed by United Nations (UN) Resolution 181 of 29 November 1947, owed far less to chance (or, in an alternative interpretation, to Divine intervention) than to the advantages bestowed by political and organizational factors. Israeli forces fought on interior lines and under a unified command structure. By contrast, their foes were widely dispersed and far too divided amongst themselves to coordinate their operations. Moreover, the longer the war lasted, the clearer it became that the IDF was the best led and best equipped of all the contestants, and could also draw upon a reservoir of supplementary financial and human resources provided by diaspora Jewry. So glaring were the disparities between the sides that by 1949 some IDF generals were pressing for yet more spectacular conquests: the entire region between the coastal plain and the Jordan River (the 'West Bank'); and the north Sinai salient centered on El Arish.

The self-assurance conveyed by such proposals soon gave way to a widely-shared and uneasy feeling that victory could prove transient. After all, the armistice agreements that Israel concluded with most of her neighbors at Rhodes in 1949 were intrinsically temporary arrangements, and for a variety of reasons never transmuted into the peace treaties that would have announced an end to hostilities (Caplan 1992; Rabinovich 1998). Hence, there remained the possibility (in some views, the probability) that sooner or later armed conflict would resume. Under those circumstances how Israel might retain its edge of military superiority became a critical question, which dictated the entire tone of the national security discourse.

The answer formulated by the architects of IDF operational planning was to develop a coherent set of strategic doctrines tailored to the rigidities of Israel's geo-strategic environment. Their general idea was elegantly simple: should the IDF ever have to conduct another full-scale war, it must seek to do so in an offensive manner, compensating for Israel's inherent demographic disadvantages and lack of geographical depth by mounting operations that would carry the battle to the enemy's territory and be characterized by a combination of surprise, speed and tactical maneuver (Handel 1994). By the mid-1950s, Moshe Dayan (the IDF's Chief of the General Staff, 1953–1957) had begun to elevate those doctrines into a more generalized strategy of pre-emptive warfare, which he suggested Israel trigger as early as 1954 (Golani 2001).

But bellicosity to that extreme was exceptional. For the most part, official efforts to maintain, and if possible enlarge, Israel's margins of security focused on two alternative policy options. One was to resort to diplomacy, a *modus operandi* that (as noted in Chapter 2) was deeply ingrained in Jewish public behavior, and that in the present context involved both cultivating the support of the great powers and pursuing openings to negotiation with Israel's Arab neighbors. The second option, rooted in *Haganah* practices, was to maintain an effective deterrent posture, principally by constantly improving the IDF's arsenal, but also by undertaking occasional military operations that clearly demonstrated Israel's resolve (Yaniv 1985).

As national security strategies, diplomacy and deterrence could of course complement each other and hence did not constitute severely polarized alternatives. The differences between them boiled down to questions of emphasis and timing. Those, certainly, were the principal points of contention running through the variant policy preferences advanced by the two men chiefly responsible for the formulation of national security policies in the initial period of Israeli statehood: Moshe Sharett (Foreign Minister, 1948–1956; and Prime Minister 1953–1955) and David Ben-Gurion (Defense Minister 1948–1953 and 1954–1963; and Prime Minister 1948–1953 and 1955–1963). Sharett, although not always opposed to the use of military force, as a rule – and often as a matter of principle – prioritized diplomacy and the observance of international law. Ben-Gurion, too, was certainly sensitive to Israel's dependence on a friendly international community, frankly admitting that 'We are dependent on the whole world like every country and more so than every other country' (cited in Bialer 1991:216–17). In contrast to Sharett, however, Ben-Gurion was by temperament far more inclined to think that, in the last analysis, military actions would speak louder than words (Caplan 2001). And, as later portions of this chapter will show, where national security matters were concerned, Ben-Gurion's opinion invariably prevailed.

Notwithstanding an entire library of biographical studies, it still remains difficult to pin-point the precise sources of Ben-Gurion's massive stature in the Israeli political arena throughout the first 15 years of statehood. Although undoubtedly a talented organizer and ruthless political infighter, he possessed few of the other attributes normally considered necessary criteria for hegemonic national leadership. His intellectual contributions to the ideology of Socialist-Zionism were, at best, marginal and decidedly inferior to those made by his closest political associate, Berl Katzenelson (Shapira 1984). He possessed no exceptional oratorical gifts, no physical presence to speak of and little of the charisma of Theodor Herzl or even of his own pre-War rival, Ze'ev Jabotinsky. His diplomatic skills, too, were limited and blunt, certainly when compared to the unique blend of faintly oriental finesse and deliberately acquired British charm deployed by Chaim Weizmann, the man who Ben-Gurion had effectively reduced to a figure-head in the Zionist movement by the mid-1940s.

Considering the extent to which he dominated Israel's national security policies, most remarkable of all was Ben-Gurion's very thin military record. His only first-hand experience of military service dated to 1918, when he briefly enlisted in the 38th battalion of the 'Jewish Legion' formed by the British government during World War I (Keren and Keren 2010). Once demobilized, he never held a senior post in the *Haganah*; neither did he ever command forces in action. Instead, he dedicated himself almost entirely to the *Yishuv*'s domestic affairs, and especially to strengthening the trinity responsible for organizing civil society: the *Mapai* party, the *Histadrut* (Labor Federation) and the Jewish Agency (of whose executive committee Ben-Gurion became chairman in 1935). Military matters remained very much a secondary area of interest until 1946, when he peremptorily demanded that the 22nd Zionist Congress, held in Basel, Switzerland, grant him the 'Security Portfolio'.

Thereafter, however, Ben-Gurion committed himself to studying the *Yishuv*'s military requirements and options with an intensity of almost obsessive proportions (E. Cohen 2002:142–54). Quite apart from making time to conduct a famous extended strategic 'seminar' in the spring of 1947, during the course of which he canvassed the views of *Haganah* and *Palmach* leaders, he also read widely and – even more importantly – began thinking originally. Of themselves, these typically auto-didactic attainments did not transform Ben-Gurion overnight into the *Yishuv*'s most authoritative military expert. But they did equip him with the tools required in order to confront those who placed themselves in that category. Combined with his political skills and psychological fiber, manifest in an absolute conviction that, once his mind was made up, he was unquestionably right, those were assets powerful enough to compensate for whatever failings he otherwise possessed.

Ben-Gurion's frenzy of security-related activity in 1947–1949 resulted in three consequences of especial importance. Chronologically, the first was his insistence, within weeks of concluding his 'seminar', that the troops

54 *Development*

available to the *Yishuv* be transformed from a collection of partisan units, principally structured in order to skirmish with local Palestinian irregulars and harass British military authorities, into a modern fighting force, capable of defeating the conventional Arab armies that Ben-Gurion predicted would soon invade (Gelber 2004:59–82). As will be seen below, with equal determination, Ben-Gurion set out to ensure that the new Jewish army, which he named *Tzevah Haganah Le-Yisrael* (the IDF), would, in the words of one formulation, be 'Ben-Gurion's army, fashioned by Ben-Gurion, loyal to Ben-Gurion, and an army that looked up solely to him as its source of authority and inspiration' (Shapira 1985:41).

Once victory was attained, Ben-Gurion emphatically ruled that there be no relaxation in the overall public mood of national security vigilance. As from 1949 he repeatedly warned that the Arabs were preparing for 'a second round' of fighting and hence insisted that Israel had no choice but to remain a 'nation in arms' (Ben-Gurion 1955:138–9). Failure to do so, he cautioned, would not only betray the memory of those members of the *Yishuv* who had fallen in the struggle for independence. It would endanger the far greater number of immigrants who thereafter flocked to make Israel their home. Over 100,000 newcomers arrived in each of the years 1948 and 1949, 240,000 more in 1950 and a further 175,000 in both 1951 and 1952. By 1953, just half a decade after Independence, the size of Israel's population had more than doubled. Enterprises directed at feeding, educating and housing citizens were considered to be just as relevant to national security as was their physical defense from hostile attack.

The temporal dimension

The temporal dimension of Israel's national security legislation was undoubtedly the first to feel the impact of the constant state of tension thus generated. As early as 19 May 1948, the Provisional Council of State (which functioned as Israel's legislature until February 1949, when elections were held to the first *knesset*) enacted the Law and Administration Ordinance, 5708–1948. Given retroactive power from the day of the declaration of independence, 15 May 1948 (Article 23), this measure immediately brought into being three legal avenues for the declaration of the existence of 'a state of emergency.'

One was specified in Article 11 of the Ordinance, which declared that:

> The law which existed in Palestine on the 5th Iyar 5708 (14 May 1948) shall remain in force, insofar as there is nothing therein repugnant to this Ordinance or to the other laws which may be enacted by or on behalf of the Provisional Council of State.

In practice, what this meant was the incorporation into Israeli law of, among other laws, the Defense (Emergency) Regulations (DERs) promulgated by the British mandatory authorities in 1945. Supplementing the Palestine (Defence) Order in Council of 1937 and the Emergency Powers (Defence of the Colonies) Order in Council of 1939, the DERs vested the executive branch with over 160 highly intrusive rights. Military commanders possessed an especially wide range of discretionary powers, including the authority to order house demolitions and deportations, to impose curfews, and to arrest, search and detain persons suspected of posing a threat to public order without judicial approval. The DERs also authorized a system of press censorship, which enabled the Military Censor to ban the publication of any information that 'in his opinion' might harm state defense, public order and/or public safety.

The second avenue established for the institution of an emergency regime was contained in Article 9 of the Law and Administration Ordinance, which conferred on the government, and even on individual ministers, the power to promulgate 'emergency regulations to such an extent as [ministers] consider desirable for the defense of the state, public security and the maintenance of supplies and essential services.' True, these powers were subject to limitations. No emergency regulations could be promulgated unless the Provisional Council (later the *knesset*) declared a state of emergency to exist (Article 9[a]). Even then, unless renewed, they would automatically expire after a maximum period of three months (Article 9[c]). Highlighting these provisions, Pinchas Rozenblutt, Israel's first Minister of Justice, argued that Article 9 had created nothing more than a restricted system of 'transitory enactments'. In fact, that was not the case. The emergency powers that it conferred on the executive became an integral part of the legal fabric of Israeli legislation. To this day, the 'state of emergency' declared by the Provisional Council on 19 May 1948 remains in effect, a situation that enables executive office holders to enact substantive provisions that could alter and suspend legislation emanating from the elected legislature (Hofnung 1996:52).

A circumstance facilitating that development can be identified in the third avenue that the Law and Administration Ordinance created for the institution of an emergency regime, which involved legislation. The simplest way of implementing that possibility was for the *knesset* to enact new laws, which were conditional on the existence of a state of emergency. In addition, however, Article 9c of the Law and Administration Ordinance also enabled the *knesset* to extend any emergency regulations originally enacted by the government.

These powers were liberally employed. New emergency regulations were announced every year until 1962, and by Hofnung's count 44 of them in 1948–1949 alone (Hofnung 1996:57). Equally significant is the span of subjects that they regulated, indicating how widely 'state security' was interpreted in this period. Thus, throughout the 1950s, emergency regulations regulated criminal law and the steps taken to control the Arab minority. In the 1970s and 1980s they became a method of dealing with strikes and of implementing the government's economic policies. Resort to DERs attained an equally lengthy pedigree. As early as 26 May 1948, Ben-Gurion exercised the powers granted by the DERs to disband the Jewish underground militias that had operated during the mandate period and to incorporate their forces into a single national army. On the same day, he also proclaimed the establishment of the IDF, to which he granted the status of the only legitimate armed force in the state.[1]

As Yifat Holzman-Gazit has documented, resort to the same tools revolutionized some aspects of property rights. Expressly noting that Israel was fighting for its life, the provisional government in the summer of 1948 issued emergency 'Requisition of Property' regulations, which permitted government officials to take immediate possession of private property, Jewish as well as Arab, in order to further, first and foremost, 'the defense of the State' (Holzman-Gazit 2007:88). Before the year was out, two additional sets of emergency decrees, both likewise justified on grounds of 'state security', had further legitimized large-scale land transfers. Thus, the 'Waste Lands Regulations' entitled the Minister of Agriculture to take possession of all agricultural plots which were not being cultivated, even if – as was commonly the case – this was because the Arab owners were being denied access to their land by Israeli security closures. The 'Absentees' Property Regulations' reinforced this warped logic by permitting the expropriation of lands considered to have been 'abandoned' during the course of the recent fighting by their previous Arab owners – even if they had meanwhile returned to their homes. Thus was created the ridiculous bureaucratic category of 'present absentees' (H. Cohen 2000).

In this particular area of national security concern, emergency decrees were eventually superseded by parliamentary legislation, a process in which the passage of the Absentees' Property Law in 1950 and the Land Acquisition Law in 1953 marked especially significant milestones. Nevertheless, the temporal dimension of overall national security thinking continued to reflect an attitude of mind that regarded the 'state of emergency' as the norm rather than the exception. Indeed, the only item of legislation passed in this period that explicitly recognized any temporal parameter in the national security sphere was the 1951 Civil Defense Law, which empowered the security forces to take actions during a 'time of attack', defined in the preamble to the law as the period between the sounding of an air-raid warning until the broadcast of an 'all clear' (Bichur 2003:142–5). But, crude though it was, even that rough attempt at temporal categorization, whose inadequacies were starkly revealed in 1991 (see below p. 110), proved to be exceptional. Neither the *knesset* nor any other agency devoted serious efforts to delineating the boundaries that might determine when the powers granted by emergency decrees could or could not be applied. Indeed, to judge by anecdotal evidence, in many quarters any such exercise was thought to be unrealistic. In his memoirs, Avner Bar-On (who acted as Chief Military Censor for 26 years) relates that when he took over the post in the early 1950s, he asked the then CGS, Yigael Yadin, how to define the 'harm to state security' that military censorship was supposed to prevent. Yadin, clearly irritated by the question, told Bar-On to ask the outgoing censor. But the latter was no more informative. 'It is impossible to define. After you have sat here for a while you simply know what is harmful to state security and what isn't' (Hofnung 1996:134).

The spatial dimension

Demarcations were somewhat more clearly defined with respect to the spatial dimension of Israel's national security legal framework during this period. Partly, this was because from the first there existed a distinct category of 'military' locations: army bases, aerodromes, port facilities, storage areas and the like. Oren calculates that by the 1950s some two thirds of these were of British mandate vintage, and had either been legally purchased by the Jewish Agency on the eve of the British departure or (as was the case in large parts of the Galilee) unilaterally seized by the IDF during the course of the fighting in 1948–1949. The remaining third had more recently been established by the Israeli Ministry of Defense, especially in the Negev, where the British infrastructure had been far less developed (Oren 2009:81–3). Whichever the case, all such properties constituted 'restricted zones', access to which was controlled exclusively by military personnel, who were also empowered to arrest persons whom they suspected of violating military rules of behavior (such as the ban on photography in and around those locations).

A second category of specifically military spaces consisted of the military cemeteries established in 1948 and 1949 in order to accommodate the remains of the comparatively high number of military personnel who had lost their lives during the course of the War of Independence.[2] Ben-Gurion originally wished to limit the number of such locations to just four main sites. But even when their number expanded (by 1951 there were over 150 military cemeteries, most adjacent to local civilian cemeteries), he insisted that they be clearly distinctive. As early as 1949, a national competition was organized amongst architects, who were invited to submit designs reflecting the wish that military cemeteries and gravestones would be distinguished from their 'civilian' counterparts by their landscape, décor and epitaphs. The Military Cemeteries Law, passed in 1950, took the further steps required to grant the cemeteries the status of 'national security shrines', places of private and public pilgrimage that were administered by a national agency (The Public Council for the Commemoration of Soldiers) all 11 members of which were appointed by the Minister of Defense (Katz 2007:79–91).

However, undoubtedly the largest and most blatant expressions of distinctive military 'zones' in Israel during this period were the areas declared to be under direct Military Administration (*mimshal tzeva'i*), and, as such, entirely separated from the legal regime in operation elsewhere in the country. Eventually, three such zones were established and allotted, respectively, to the IDF's regional commands. Thus, Northern Command was responsible for the 'Galilee area', a large region that encompassed much of the countryside between Nazareth (which housed the local military administration headquarters) and the Lebanese border. Central Command was responsible for the so-called 'little triangle', situated slightly north-east of the coastal plain between the Arab villages of Et Tira and Et Taiyiba, adjacent to the portion of Palestine ('the West Bank') that was annexed by Transjordan in March 1949. Finally, Southern Command ruled from Beersheba over the military administration that encompassed much of the Negev desert. Each of these regions housed heavy concentrations of non-Jewish citizens (mostly Muslim Arabs, but also Druze, Circassians, Bedouins and Christians of various denominations), who together comprised approximately 18 percent of the country's entire population.[3] The activities of the military commands were coordinated by the Commanding Officer (CO) of the Military Administration Department in the IDF, a professional officer who also served as the director of the Military Administration Department in the Ministry of Defense.

This system had evolved rather haphazardly. It owed its origins to the IDF's victories in the War of Independence, which spasmodically brought under Israeli military control several areas – and tens of thousands of non-Jews – that the 1947 UN partition plan had originally assigned to independent Arab rule. With the establishment of the State of Israel in 1948, the newly appointed Minister for Minority Affairs, Bekhor Shitrit, a Jewish lawyer from Tiberias who spoke fluent Arabic and was well acquainted with local Arab customs and society, expected to be granted the authority to incorporate the inhabitants of the newly conquered lands within his sphere of activity. Indeed, less than a week prior to the Declaration of Independence, he had distributed a memorandum to his future ministerial colleagues advising that political as well as moral considerations made it imperative that the Jewish state grant equality to all its Arab inhabitants, including residents of recently-conquered portions of the Galilee (Ozacky-Lazar 2006:18).

Since Shitrit also functioned as Minister of Police, his opinion could be expected to carry some weight. But in the climate of national emergency prevailing at the time, other voices prevailed. Local military commanders persistently warned Ben-Gurion that, even within the areas originally assigned to Israel under the 1947 UN resolution, Arab residents constituted a potential fifth column. Those who had fled – voluntarily or otherwise – hence had to be forcibly prevented from returning and their lands declared forfeit; those who remained had to be kept under strict surveillance. Where the newly-conquered territories were concerned, this opinion was further buttressed by the argument that, until such time as they were formally annexed to Israel, international law in any case mandated that they be governed solely by military commanders (Gelber 2004:412–13). Hence, in September 1948, the government formally decided on the establishment of a military administration – initially as a temporary measure.

Neither the termination of the fighting nor the conclusion of armistice agreements with Israel's neighbors settled the issue. As soon as the war was over, Ben-Gurion's initial instinct, which was shared by the CGS, was to disband the military administration other than in especially sensitive areas ('security zones') adjacent to the borders. But a cluster of committees, military as well as civilian, convinced him otherwise. Formally, the military administration was in 1949 dismantled only in the few remaining 'mixed' Arab-Jewish cities, such as Jaffa and Acre, or in those that no longer housed an Arab population of any significant size, such as Ramleh, Lod, Safed and Haifa. Elsewhere, it remained as prominent as ever. Additional proof of the mood now infecting attitudes towards the Arab population was provided in May 1949, when Shitrit was bluntly informed that, although he remained Minister of Police, the Ministry of Minorities would be shut down. Those of its responsibilities that were not transferred to the IDF were assumed by the newly established 'Minorities Department' in the Ministry of the Interior and by the Prime Minister's Advisor on Arab Affairs, another recently created office.[4] Belatedly, in January 1950 (almost a year and a half after it had begun functioning) the military administration was given legal basis, with the announcement that the regional military governors had assumed the authority of military commanders under the DERs of 1945 (Hofnung 1996:89).

During the course of the following decade, several informed observers queried not only the morality of the military administration but even its utility as a security measure (Ozacky-Lazar 2002:107,109). Nevertheless, under Ben-Gurion's aegis, it continued to enjoy the wholehearted support of officialdom – and was indeed between November 1956 and March 1957 extended to the Gaza Strip, which the IDF briefly occupied in the wake of the Sinai campaign. Mainstream government thinking was reflected in the recommendations submitted to the government in February 1956 by a committee that under the chairmanship of General (res.) Yochanan Ratner had been appointed to investigate the military administration. The perspective adopted by this body was publicly disclosed without any attempt at finesse by one of its members: 'Out of the 200,000 Arabs and members of other minority populations in Israel, we didn't come across even one who is loyal to the State.' Obviously, then, military rule over Arab citizens could in no way be relaxed. According to the official Ratner report, its maintenance was required in order:

1. To deter hostile activities, such as infiltration, sabotage, contact with the enemy and the transmission of information;

2. To supervise the Arab population and its traffic [partly in order to protect adjacent Jewish settlements and townships, especially those inhabited by new immigrants who were thought susceptible to intimidation] ...;
3. To prevent Arab refugees from returning to Israel and settling on abandoned lands and to preserve the existing property status quo.

(Ozacky-Lazar 2006:49–50)

All those tasks were carried out with almost ruthless efficiency. In the process, the areas under military administration were transformed into what amounted to a corpus separandum in which, thanks to the application of emergency regulations, the local commander's word constituted the only legal regime in existence – and one not subject to external judicial review. Freedom of movement was one early casualty. Article 125 of the DERs empowered military governors to declare any specified area 'off-limits' to those having no written authorization for entry or movement. This made it possible for any such area to be closed to Israeli Arabs, other than those who could obtain the necessary permission – a privilege usually granted only to those prepared to act as informers for the local representative of the General Security Services (*Shabak*) (H. Cohen 2010). Ninety-three out of the 104 Arab villages that remained in Israel after the mass exodus of 1948–1949 were at various times declared to be 'closed areas', a fiat that, in an irony of history, virtually ghettoized their inhabitants. Moreover, the limited and inequitable distribution of travel permits resulted in a situation whereby, on average, every year some 1,500 Arabs were branded as criminals in military courts for having moved surreptitiously from one village to another – usually simply in search of work, a bride, or a doctor (Koren 1999).

Even more substantial were the effects on property rights. Making full use of the powers granted by the cluster of emergency regulations affecting lands ('Requisition of Property'; Waste Lands; and 'Absentees' Lands'), members of the staff attached to the various military administrations carried out what amounted to a comprehensive land transfer. Indeed, according to one (admittedly rough) estimate, about 40 percent of privately owned Arab land was virtually nationalized, and either transferred to the Israel Lands Administration or leased to the Jewish National Fund (Kimmerling and Migdal 2003:147). Of the 370 new Jewish settlements built between 1948 and 1964, many of them *kibbutzim* whose members proclaimed their adherence to principles of social justice, almost 350 were established on what was termed 'abandoned' Arab property (Kimmerling 1983:122–3). Other studies report that early as 1954 more than one-third of Israel's Jewish population lived on land thus designated, and nearly one-third of the new immigrants (250,000 persons) were either directed to the 'new towns' built on former Arab land or settled in houses declared to have been 'abandoned' by Arab residents (Ozacky-Lazar

1998:356). As late as the eve of the Six Days War in 1967, 'abandoned' Arab villages were still being destroyed (Shai 2002).

As Amiram Oren (Oren 2009) has shown, the attitudes that legitimized those actions also affected land policies in Jewish areas of the country. There too, specifically military interests and concerns were granted an inordinate influence. For one thing, the IDF enjoyed virtual autonomy as far as its own property needs were concerned. During the War of Independence, individual IDF officers had felt free to requisition abandoned Arab property (sometimes for private use) without receiving proper authorization. And even though the more outrageous instances of misuse were subsequently corrected, and the IDF compelled to allow new immigrants to be housed in some of the bases that it clearly did not require, the primacy of narrowly defined 'security needs' remained unquestioned. Hence, the IDF was able to resort to liberal applications of section 125 of the DERs in order to obtain exclusive rights of access to large tracts of land (much of which, especially in the Galilee, had prior to 1948 been owned by Arab farmers) that it wished to use for training purposes. There existed no regulatory body charged with responsibility for verifying the IDF's claims of 'military necessity' where property issues were concerned, far less for assessing whether IDF land usages conformed to overall national projections for infrastructure development. As early as 1950 the IDF was excused from any formal obligation to attain permits from municipality or zoning committees before making substantial construction alterations to the facilities under its control. In practice, it restricted itself to informal consultations with the relevant authorities (Perez and Rosenblum 2007:399, n. 130–1).

Not only did the IDF demand – and receive – the authority to determine its own land requirements, even more remarkably, it was granted what amounted to a veto power over much civilian land usage. By convention, IDF approval came to be required for all major infrastructure development plans (roads, utilities and industry). Likewise, IDF input was solicited, as a matter of course, for all projections for population dispersal and new urban construction. These conventions and usages were incorporated almost without change in the Planning and Construction Law eventually enacted in 1965 (a draft bill had been prepared in 1954) thus ensuring that the IDF would continue to exercise a form of indirect control over extended areas, in which it declared a civilian presence to be undesirable (Perez and Rosenblum 2007).

The functional dimension

Throughout this embryonic period of Israel's national security law, the balance between the three branches of government was blatantly unequal. There was never any doubt that the executive wielded supreme influence. In part, that situation too reflected the uniqueness of the legacy inherited by the country's first generation of leaders. As has already been pointed

62 *Development*

out, where security matters were concerned they could not draw upon anything like a consolidated Jewish tradition of constitutional management. If anything, their own pre-State experiences with respect to the *Haganah*'s *mifkadaf artzit* (above p. 39) had taught them that in this area, especially, a large measure of executive autonomy was far preferable to any attempt to maintain a balance of power between the three branches of government. The persistent fear that Israel's physical survival still remained at risk further fuelled the public conviction that what the country most required was a powerful executive, a need that Ben-Gurion manifestly was fully prepared to supply and that in any case conveniently dovetailed with his personal preference for a domineering style of management in government affairs.

This attitude of mind necessarily impinged on the contributions that both the legislature and the judiciary could make to Israel's national security legal framework. The limited roles that each of those branches played can be illustrated by examining them in turn.

First, the legislature: Ben-Gurion certainly considered it appropriate for the *knesset* to perform a legislative function in the national security sphere, and on occasion encouraged it to do so. However, legislation was usually intended to promote the goals determined by the prime minister and to strengthen the executive, rather than to create any additional mechanisms of parliamentary review.

One example is the Prevention of Terrorism Ordinance enacted in September 1948. Nominally, the purpose of this measure was to enable the government to bring to trial members of right-wing Jewish underground movements (*Lehi* and *Hazit ha-Moledet*), members of which were allegedly responsible for the assassination in Jerusalem earlier that month of Count Bernadotte, the Swedish mediator. Ultimately, indeed, 335 persons were arrested, and although the assassins were never apprehended, three members of *Lehi* were tried in military courts on charges of conspiracy, and two were found guilty. As Barzilai points out, however (Barzilai 1999a), the apprehension of the persons guilty of this particular crime had never been Ben-Gurion's sole objective. The Prevention of Terrorism Ordinance was also a stage in his campaign to increase the powers available to the executive, in this instance by authorizing it to decide which group can be declared a 'terrorist organization' and hence a target of government action. As Article 8 of the Ordinance puts it:

> Should the Government declare, via a publication in the Gazette, that a particular group of persons constitutes a terrorist organization, that announcement will in any legal proceedings suffice to prove the criminality of the group, unless proven otherwise.

It is a tribute to the strength of Israeli democracy that these powers were only rarely invoked (in the 1950s against nationalistic and ultra-orthodox

Jewish fringe groups and in the 1980s against left-wing activists who met with Palestinians). Nevertheless, the very existence of this ordinance on the statute book demonstrates how unbalanced Israel's national security constitution always was.

Legislation was employed for different purposes when the government initiated the passage of the Defense Service Law (1949). This replaced the Ordnance passed on 21 May 1948 that had given retroactive force to the numerous, but thereto unenforceable, 'orders, proclamations, regulations and other directions concerning matters of national service' published by various arms of the Jewish Agency between 29 November 1947 and 14 May 1948 (Guvrin 1976). Henceforth, conscription was not to be derivative of emergency decrees. Rather it was to be – and, nominally, it has remained – an integral feature of normative Israeli behavior and as such subject to parliamentary debate and regulation. This impression seemed to be confirmed in 1953, when the *knesset* also passed the National Service Law, which imposed civic service obligations on unmarried religious young women who had been granted exemptions from military duty on the grounds that its performance would conflict with their traditional way of life. It was further reinforced when in 1959 the *knesset* passed a new and consolidated version of the Defense Service Law, which incorporated several amendments inserted to the original legislation over the course of the previous decade.

Parliamentary activity also extended to other spheres of national security relevance. During this period, the *knesset* enacted, at the government's initiative, a series of measures that acknowledged the centrality of military sacrifice in the national narrative, prominent amongst which was the law regarding Remembrance Day for IDF Fallen (1963), which enshrined that event in the annual national calendar. In recognition of the need to ease the financial burdens imposed on individuals and their families by extended stints of military duty, the *knesset* also passed a Demobilized Soldiers Law in 1949, the terms of which were later amended and updated in the 1952 Reserve Soldiers Law (Greenberg 2001:104–12). The extent to which parliament seemed to be assuming increasing responsibility for even some operational aspects of military affairs was meanwhile demonstrated by the passage of the Law on Shelters (1949) and the Civil Defense Law (1951), both of which were designed to limit the damage likely to be caused by another round of air attacks on Israel's population centers.[5] After considerable prodding on Ben-Gurion's part, the *knesset* in 1955 also passed a Military Justice Law, which replaced the 'IDF constitution' (*chukat tzahal*) that had been adopted under the terms of the Emergency Regulations in June 1948 (Z. Inbar 2005:69–134; Kedar 2008:202–17).

The impression of parliamentary activism conveyed by this legislative record is deceptive. Since the *knesset*'s intrusions were not the outgrowth of an articulate and coordinated conception of the role of the legislature in the national security legal framework, they tended to be diffuse rather than comprehensive. Instead of proceeding from first principles regarding the proper status and functions of the military in a democratic society, they constituted piecemeal, even random, responses to immediate problems and issues, each of which imposed its own individual logic and demands.

One result of this situation was that even where legislation was enacted, it was often incomplete. (The Defense Service Law, for instance, suffered from two glaring lacunae; focusing almost entirely on conscript service, it failed to specify the rights and duties of either professional soldiers or reservists). Another consequence, even more severe, was that entire areas of government activity in the national security sphere remained untouched by any legislation at all. As will be seen later in this chapter, the most glaring void was the absence of any legislation demarcating the division of responsibilities and functions between the most senior civilian and military echelons. Likewise absolved from any mention in the corpus of parliamentary statutes, however, were the two Israeli secret services: the General Security Service (GSS; *Shabak*) responsible for domestic security, whose agents worked hand-in-glove with the military administration, and the *Mosad*, which generally handled overseas operations, of which undoubtedly the most spectacular was the abduction of Adolf Eichmann to Israel in 1960. But although both agencies thus figured prominently in the annals of Israel security activity, the functions, duties and terms of employment of their personnel are nowhere defined and regulated in any legislation of the entire period. Indeed, the *knesset* did not enact a GSS Law until 2002; thus far, it has resisted public pressure to adopt similar measures with respect to the *Mosad*. Towards the very end of his tenure as Prime Minister and Minister of Defense, Ben-Gurion did charge an independent body, the Yadin–Sherf commission, with the task of investigating Israel's intelligence services. Characteristically, however, the resultant report, submitted in July 1963 (by which time Ben-Gurion was out of office), treated both agencies as though they were somehow beyond the realm of scrutiny. Indeed, it hardly refers to the *Mosad* and makes no mention at all of the GSS (Even 2007:26).

It is difficult to avoid the impression that so marked a degree of legislative abstinence was deliberate, and reflected the extent to which the parliamentary agenda was almost entirely controlled by the executive. This was often made explicit. Some laws expressly granted the government discretion with regards to their interpretation (for instance, the Defense Service Law of 1949 gave the minister of defense exclusive discretion to grant conscription deferments to individuals liable for military duty); others empowered the government to decide when – and whether – *knesset* legislation was to be implemented. This prerogative was explicitly stated in the final clause (no. 21) of the 1953 National Service Law ('The implementation of this law will not come into effect until the Government ordains' – a condition that to this day has not been met). It was latent, but no less forceful, with respect to the Law on Shelters and the Civil Defense Law, provisions in both of which were so persistently ignored by the ministries of the interior and finance that when Israel launched the Sinai campaign in 1956 over 60 percent of Israelis still lacked the protection that those laws were supposed to have assured (Bichur 2003:150–6 and 184–92).

The *knesset* played an equally subservient role when fulfilling its supervisory and monitoring functions with respect to national security affairs. True, parliamentary objections did compel Ben-Gurion to remove from the legislative agenda both an initial version of the Military Justice Law and a proposed 'Law on Defense and Security in Times of Emergency' (Kedar 2008:203). Otherwise, however, the record of the legislature's influence in the broader areas of national security was in this period very limited, and certainly considerably more so than in other spheres. Domestic affairs, and especially educational and economic issues, were debated with an intensity that befitted their ideological resonances, and on occasion proved contentious enough to cause riots (most famously, on 7 January 1952, when the *knesset* voted on the reparations agreement that Ben-Gurion had concluded with Chancellor Adenauer of West Germany) or even to bring about the fall of the government (as was the case in December 1952, when Ben-Gurion resigned over a dispute concerning religious education). But other than the 'Lavon affair' – a protracted series of enquiries into the shadowy details of the misguided and botched sabotage operation carried out by Israeli operatives in Egypt in 1954 during Pinchas Lavon's brief tenure as minister of defense (Teveth 1996) – security issues were generally treated with a degree of circumspection generous enough to grant the executive considerable discretion.

This background of the legislature's non-involvement in national security affairs explains why, in his massive survey of Israel's foreign policy decision-making process, Michael Brecher could find just two instances when, prior to 1960, the *knesset*, acting through its Foreign Affairs and Defense Committee, exercised what he judged to be 'effective restraint' on executive action in this sphere (Brecher 1972:132–3).[6] Indeed, although a committee under this name had begun to function as early as the first *knesset*, its precise statutory status remained unclear. Ben-Gurion found it easy enough to ignore the forum, and frequently did so, especially since its authority to fulfill certain supervisory functions with respect to 'the foreign policy of the State, her armed forces, and her security' was not specified in any official document until the publication of '*Knesset* Regulations' in 1963 (Bar-Or 2004). Meanwhile, for instance, the entire regime of military government over Arabs within Israel had been created and maintained without any parliamentary legislation or involvement during most of its existence. Occasional motions to place the subject on the *knesset*'s agenda, usually tabled just prior to parliamentary elections in an obvious ploy to gain Arab votes, were regularly voted down in the chamber, albeit by increasingly small majorities (Baumel 2002).

Knesset influence was even more restricted with respect to Israel's involvement in international agreements and treaties. Of all the international commitments undertaken by the Government of Israel, only those specified in the UN Convention on the Prevention and Punishment of the Crime of Genocide, which came into force on 12 January 1951, were formally submitted to the *knesset* for incorporation into Israeli law. In all other cases, members of the *knesset* were reduced to the role of spectators. The fact that they were only informed *post facto* of the government's actions denuded whatever comments they may have articulated of practical effectiveness. Documents as consequential as the armistice agreements concluded with Israel's neighbors at Rhodes in 1949 were treated as administrative rather than legislative matters. So too were initiatives as momentous as Israel's accession to the UN Organization and its adhesion to the Geneva Conventions in 1951. Official policy, which the executive dictated and in which the *knesset* acquiesced, was neatly summarized in a memorandum submitted to the UN Legislative Service in 1951: 'The legal power to negotiate, sign and ratify international treaties on behalf of Israel is vested exclusively in the government of Israel and is in the charge of the Ministry of Foreign Affairs' (Broude and Noam 2008:181–2).

Judicial influence was likewise restricted. As later chapters in this book will demonstrate, in subsequent decades the ISC was to redress much of the imbalance thus created in the functional dimension of the country's national security legal framework, to which it thus restored some sense of equilibrium. In the years covered by the present chapter, however, that development lay very much in the future. The judiciary was still too weak either to exert any substantive influence on the formulation of national security practices or to scrutinize them with any persistence. Partly, this was because the institutional independence of the ISC was far from assured. All justices were in these years essentially political appointments and although a draft Judges Law was tabled as early as 1951, not until two-and-half years later did legislation specifically regulate the appointment of justices and assure them of tenure. More to the point, the concept of the supremacy of law did not – as yet – possess anything like the prestige that it was later to attain. If anything, in some high places, where tolerance for 'illegalism' (above p. 41) tended to be pronounced, lawyers and the legal profession were objects of open disparagement. In this, as in so much else, Ben-Gurion (who had at one time himself thought of becoming a lawyer) set the tone. As he asked the Provisional State Council in September 1948, during the course of the debate on the Terror Ordinance:

> Have we been made for the legal principle, or has the legal principle been made for us?... As a law student, I know that no one can distort any text and invent far-fetched assumptions and confusing interpretations as can the jurist.
>
> (Kedar 2008:216 n.26)

That background encouraged an attitude of overriding deference on the part of the ISC towards government action in the national security sphere. By the international standards of the time, the restraint evinced by the Israeli judiciary might not have been considered exceptional, other perhaps than in the USA. What made it striking, nevertheless, was that it encompassed a remarkable forbearance towards the retention of the regime of emergency regulations. This was displayed as early as June 1948, when the Tel-Aviv district court (which then functioned as the supreme court) rejected a petition lodged by two leaders of the *Etzel* organization, Hillel Kook and Yaakov Meridor, who had been detained in connection with the recent attempt made by their organization to import their own ammunition on the 'Altalena' ship (*Kook* v. *Minister of Defense*, cited in Hofnung 1991:93).

In cases concerning Arab residents, the ISC displayed an even greater degree of pusillanimity. Prior to the mid-1950s (by which time even the most zealous of bureaucrats in the military administration was hard put to find any remaining Arabs who could be classified as 'illegal' residents), deportations were authorized almost as a matter of course. For the most part, justices limited themselves to a formal and technical review of the administrative procedures adopted when issuing the expulsion order. Certainly, when these were found to be faulty, the ISC did invalidate the executive action. Thus, in *Ahmed Showky Al-Karbutli* v. *Minister of Defense* (1949), it invalidated an administrative detention order against an Arab citizen because the government did not establish an appeal mechanism required by the DERs. But generally the purpose served by these decisions was to supply the IDF with guidelines as to how to avoid such mistakes in the future. Subsequent judicial scrutiny of administrative detentions and deportations too, was generally restricted to formal rather than substantive matters. Even when justices did voice some criticism of executive action in the name of civil liberties, they invariably sanctioned military orders, especially with respect to deportations. Indeed, to many observers it seemed that all the military governor had to do in order to win judicial approval for his actions was to cite 'security reasons', which was the only justification provided for ordering the deportation of the elders of Abu Gosh to Nazareth (Hofnung 1991:98–9).

In 1953, Justice Shimon Agranat (who had been born in Chicago, where he had also received his doctorate in law) did famously define free expression as a constitutional right that could only be overruled by executive action where there existed a 'near certainty' that its exercise would endanger the public good (*Kol ha-Am* v. *Minister of the Interior*). But this judgment, which has been described as 'Israel's *Marbury* v. *Madison*' (Lahav 1981:41), although undoubtedly a landmark with respect to judicial review in Israel and a striking example of the intrusion of the US tradition of liberal jurisprudence into Israeli practice, established no precedent as far as judicial attitudes towards more narrowly defined national security issues were concerned. It certainly did not influence judgments touching on the Arab minority, which was still considered a security risk. Hence, in 1965, 12 years after handing down his *Kol Ha'am* decision, Agranat himself refused to invalidate the procedures whereby a radical group of Palestinian nationalists was outlawed as a political party and hence denied the right to submit candidates for elections to the *knesset*. Instead, in *El-Ard Corp. v. Supervisor of the Northern District* he argued that the *Kol Ha'am* test was inapplicable to the use of emergency powers.

Two other judgments confirmed that trend of thinking. One was *Jaris v. Supervisor of the Haifa District* (1964), in which the ISC approved the decision of the authorities to refuse the registration of the *El Ard* group as a non-profit organization. The other was *Yardor v. Chairman of the Central Elections Commission* (1965), in which it approved the decision of the central elections committee to ban *El Ard* running for the *knesset*, on the grounds that Israel constituted a 'defensive democracy' (Saban 1996, 2008).

Judicial attitudes towards land expropriations followed a similar pattern of systematic deference to the executive branch. In effect, the ISC virtually rubber-stamped expropriation orders (usually against Arab landowners, but not exclusively so) issued by government agencies on grounds of national security, thereby contributing to the legitimization of the process whereby Israel gained control over what had thereto been Arab-owned land. Very few Arab petitioners managed to persuade the justices that they had been wrongly evicted and/or incorrectly classified as absentees, which was recognized to be the first step towards regaining their land. And even those who did so received no legal redress. In 1951, the ISC proved powerless to enforce its decision that the Christian Arab residents of the upper Galilean villages of Iqrit and Bir'im be allowed to return to their homes; having issued its evacuation orders, the IDF simply blew up the two villages. Two years later, it likewise took no action when the *knesset* enacted the Land Acquisition Law 1953, which retroactively granted legitimacy to the manner in which land belonging to the evicted inhabitants of Khirbat Jalama, in the eastern Sharon plain, had been illegally appropriated by members of a neighboring kibbutz, Lehavot Haviva (Holzman-Gazit 2007:116–17).

How extensively the judiciary could thus be side-lined in this period is further underscored by the evolution of the self-regulating agency known as the *va'adat ha-orchim* ('Editors' Council'). Dating back to an arrangement contrived during the Mandate period between the editors of the Hebrew press and the political leadership of the *Yishuv*, this forum had established a system of voluntary limitations based on a bargain struck between the parties: senior officials in the Jewish Agency had communicated confidential information to newspaper editors, on the understanding that it would not be published. Interestingly, the establishment of Israel as a democratic state, one of whose commitments was to the principle of free speech, did nothing to undermine this cozy – but essentially extra-legal – arrangement, which was now continued by ministers, generals and other senior state officials. On the contrary, in a supplement added to the original agreement in 1951 the editors expressly agreed to forego their right to petition the ISC with respect to freedom of the press, preferring to submit whatever complaints they might have about the military censor to a tribunal composed of editors and IDF representatives (Lavi 1987:11–34).

Military role expansion

Whilst the functions of both the legislature and the judiciary in Israel's national security framework were thus kept to a bare minimum, those of the executive branch, and especially of the military, enjoyed persistent growth. Indeed, the IDF experienced a development termed 'military role expansion', the process whereby the military, usually acting in a corporate capacity, 'penetrates into various institutional fields, such as economic enterprises, education and training of civilian manpower, fulfilling civilian administrative functions, and engaging in different forms of power politics' (Lissak 1976:13).

Although this phenomenon has been observed in several developing countries, in no other democracy did it flourish as much as in Israel, and certainly not in so benign a fashion (Lissak 1967). Without usurping the authority invested by law in civilian agencies of government, the IDF carried out a variety of functions far wider than the operational tasks conventionally associated with armed forces. Indeed, Ben-Gurion insisted that it do so. As he informed a cadre of newly commissioned officers early in 1949:

> While the first mission of the IDF ... is the security of the State, that is not its only task. The Army must also serve as a pioneering educational force for Israeli youth, both native born and immigrants. The IDF must educate a pioneering generation, healthy in body and spirit, brave and faithful, which will heal tribal and Diaspora divisions and implement the historic missions of the State of Israel through a process of self-fulfillment.
>
> (Ben-Gurion 1971:81)

Not only did Ben-Gurion thus formulate the credo responsible for supplying IDF role expansion with public respectability and justification. As minister of defense he also took a close personal interest in its several practical expressions. It was at his initiative, for instance, that in the 1950s the IDF Engineering Corps constructed and serviced the makeshift camps (*ma'abarot*) hastily erected to provide initial housing for the thousands of immigrants who otherwise had no roof over their heads. Likewise, it was

Ben-Gurion who, in his capacity as minister of defense, in the same period instructed the Education Corps to assume a similar range of public tasks: the dispatch of conscripts (principally women) to serve as supplementary teachers in under-privileged areas; the provision of means to help under-educated 18-year-olds to attain the literacy levels required to permit their enlistment; and the establishment of the paramilitary corps (*gadna*), a network that encompassed most of the youth attending high schools, who (as an Education Corps Order of the Day put it in 1950) were to be imbued with 'a sense of urgency in regard to building the State and to be on call at any moment to defend it' (Drori 2005:230).

Even closer to Ben-Gurion's heart was the use of the IDF as an agency for land settlement. Having reached political maturity in the 1920s and 1930s, when the importance of territorial possession to the success of the Zionist enterprise was considered axiomatic, Ben-Gurion forged what seemed to him a self-evident linkage between Israel's national security and the utilization of the lands now under State ownership. In that spirit, he encouraged the IDF high command to establish in 1950 an entire military framework, to which it gave the acronym *NAHAL* (*No'ar Halutzi Locheim;* 'Pioneering Fighting Youth'), designed to enable graduates of youth movements, men and women, to enlist in the IDF as consolidated cadres (*garinim*), and combine their conscript military duties with the maintenance of agricultural settlements in areas considered too harsh or too insecure for normal civilian habitation. After a somewhat shaky start, this enterprise enjoyed exceptional success. By 1956, *NAHAL* cadres had established 35 new *kibbutzim* and supplemented dozens of other settlements. In the process, they had heightened public awareness of the interface between military duty and agricultural labor and also added a new layer of meaning to the traditional Zionist-Socialist ethos of *kibbush ha-aretz* ('conquest of the land') as the very fulfillment of the Jewish national vision (Doar 1992).

In retrospect, there seems to have been only a slender legal basis for the IDF's assumption of so wide a range of non-combat roles on a regular basis. It might even be said that it contradicted the formal meaning of Article 18 of the Law and Administration Ordinance (1948), which authorized the creation of the military for 'the defense of the state'. Ostensibly, some authorization for military role expansion could be traced back to the clause in the Defense Service Law 1949 that required all conscripts (other than those drafted into the air force and navy) to devote one of their two years of mandatory duty to 'pioneer-agricultural training, accompanied by educational and cultural activity'. For Ben-Gurion, this remained a point of principle. When the IDF high command complained that it could not afford to dispense with so large a proportion of its manpower, he sanctioned an amendment to the Defense Service Law (adopted in February 1950), which gave the minister of defense discretion to grant conscripts deferrals from agricultural duties. Even so, he insisted that the new legislation retain the nominal commitment to agricultural work as an integral aspect of national defense service (Drori 2005:103–4).

Whether or not this basis was sufficiently sturdy to support the vast pyramid of the IDF's non-military activities was at the time never questioned by the press, the legislature or the military.[7] Thus unfettered by the prospect of either public scrutiny or administrative restraint, the executive branch of government was able to use the IDF in whatever capacity it thought fit. It also benefited from what amounted to a legal vacuum. Ben-Gurion exploited both situations. As long as he remained in power, his fiats remained the principal determinants of the true substance of the functional dimension of Israel's national security legal regime.

The hierarchical dimension

But it was with respect to the hierarchical dimension of Israel's national security framework that Ben-Gurion's dominance was most emphatic. Indeed, he had made clear his determination to ensure that he exercised sole authority over policy formulation and direction in this field even before the state formally came into existence. Protocols of the marathon discussions held in the last frantic weeks before independence by the 'Council of 13', the body that the Executive Council of the Zionist movement had early in April 1948 appointed as the provisional government-in-waiting, reveal that he would not budge from two specifications. First, he refused to accept the 'security portfolio' in the new government (the term 'Ministry of Defense' was not agreed upon until a later stage) unless his colleagues acknowledged the principle of unity of command. In practice, this meant that they would have to support his decision, originally announced on 3 May 1948 to abolish the position of *RAMAH* of the Haganah's *mifkadah artzit* held since mid-1947 by Yisrael Galilee, a member of a rival political party, *Mapam*.[8] Second, and no less important, neither would Ben-Gurion agree to proposals that he share the burden of war management with four other ministers, at least one of whom, he anticipated, would assuredly also be a member of *Mapam*. Rejecting all offers of compromise, Ben-Gurion adopted a take-it-or-leave-it attitude that infuriated his opponents, but ultimately wore them down. On 30 May 1948, fully two weeks after he had declared Israel's independence, his terms were unanimously accepted and the provisional government announced that it had made the following appointment: 'Minister of Defense, David Ben-Gurion' (Ostfeld 1994:94–101).

Whatever illusions Ben-Gurion may have harbored about the conclusiveness of that arrangement, and they cannot have been many, were soon shattered. Within weeks, the single-handed manner in which he insisted on managing Israel's national security affairs was again challenged, this time by members of the IDF General Staff. On 1 July 1948, less than a week before the first truce in the War of Independence was due to end, four generals submitted their resignations (Ostfeld 1994:619–22). Ostensibly, the reason for this barely disguised act of rebellion was dissatisfaction with the way in which Ben-Gurion was interfering in senior command appointments. As all sides appreciated, however, much more was at stake. The intrusion of partisan party political considerations continued to be one bone of contention – it was no coincidence that three of the four generals who had resigned were members of *Mapam*. Another, interconnected, was the notion of the unity of command. Ben-Gurion's conception, which he stuck to with unflagging obstinacy, was disarmingly simple: the minister of defense in effect constituted a supreme commander, in possession of the right, which he could exercise at discretion, to intrude upon all levels of command. The rebel generals and their political backers, although no less certainly committed to the principle of civilian control, rejected the implication that Ben-Gurion's prerogatives were monopolistic. Instead, they hoped to establish a more complex matrix, which involved setting up (or strengthening) several institutional filters of civil–military communication, such as a more independent General Staff, and a more diffuse system of civilian supervision and direction, such as had operated during the heyday of the *mifkadah artzit*.

Once again, Ben-Gurion had his way. Initially, he did bow to ministerial pressure when agreeing early in July 1948 that his conduct of the war be investigated by an inter-party commission composed of five other ministers and chaired by Yitzchak Greenbaum, Minister of the Interior. But this was no more than a gesture, the emptiness of which became apparent when he adamantly refused to allow the cabinet formally to discuss any of the commission's recommendations, all of which he bluntly rejected. Understandably offended, Greenbaum, now working against the ticking clock of the approaching resumption of hostilities, sought to argue his case on its merits. All he was proposing, he pleaded at the sixth and final meeting of the 'commission of five' held on 6 July 1948, was the rationalization and formalization of national security decision-making. Instead of running the war out of his own back pocket, Ben-Gurion should agree to the establishment of a more rational bureaucratic system, which would rest upon a written demarcation of civil–military responsibilities and the recognition of a 'War Cabinet' as the ultimate locus of authority, as had been the case in Britain during World War II (Shapira 1985:229–38). Those, however, were precisely the sort of arrangements that Ben-Gurion was determined to avoid. On 7 July 1948 he threatened to resign unless the Greenbaum commission's report was consigned to the archives. With only one day remaining before the end of the truce, the cabinet caved in.

The immediate consequence of this situation was that the War of Independence continued to be very much Ben-Gurion's war. Throughout, he remained almost the sole architect of strategy and the person responsible for almost every major operational choice, as well as for several tactical decisions (Tal 2003). Only where war-time diplomacy was concerned, did he consult with other ministers and allow Moshe Sharett any independence, especially with respect to the negotiations over additional truces. But no such procedures were permitted with respect to war management, an area in which the cabinet did not function as an advisory or consultative body, but merely as a forum to which the prime minister sporadically presented updates. Moreover, although there did formally exist a Ministerial Committee on Defense Matters, its meetings were infrequent, convened solely at Ben-Gurion's behest, and of no practical import. In terms of impact, Greenbaum's commission might just as well have never put pen to paper.

No less important were the long-term consequences of the situation thus created. Ben-Gurion's deliberately non-systematic style of national security decision-making established norms that remained in place throughout the next 15 years. Primary amongst these was opposition to the formulation and transcription of hard and fast rules. Ben-Gurion retained an abiding suspicion that, once committed to writing, decision-making conventions would be subject to legalistic scrutiny and conflicting interpretations. Executive license, i.e., Ben-Gurion's own freedom of action, would far better be preserved by combining *ad hoc* inventiveness with deliberate legislative abstinence. Thus freed of any constitutional straightjacket, the prime minister/minister of defense could entirely at his own personal discretion make senior appointments to military commands (a prerogative that, when exercised in 1949 effectively ended the army career of Yigal Allon, thereto the IDF's 'golden boy', but did wonders for that of Moshe Dayan).[9] He could also establish the convention whereby the CGS likewise was subject to the minister of defense's whims. Yigael Yadin, who was soon to be promoted to the highest post in the IDF, in 1949 asked Ben-Gurion to lay down explicit guidelines on relations between the minister of defense and the CGS regarding the initiation and pursuit of military operations. Ben-Gurion's response was as typical as it was blunt: 'No clear rules should be formulated until they had acquired more experience with the new system' (Kuperman 2005:674).

As several studies have shown, the history of Israel's 'reprisal raids' after 1952, and the processes whereby they culminated in the 1956 Sinai Campaign, provides numerous examples of the formalization of informality (Baron 1992; Morris 1993; Golani 1997; Tal 1998). Coherent though the purposes and priorities of Israeli actions may have been, from a procedural perspective their authorization reads like a chronicle of shambles. Although in some cases attributable to breakdowns in civil–military communications, for the most part the image of incoherence reflected the frequency of changes in the way in which the operations were authorized (or approved after the event) at the very highest levels of government (Kuperman 2001:10). Pinchas Lavon, who replaced Ben-Gurion as Minister of Defense when the latter temporarily took himself off to his desert bolt-hole at Kibbutz Sde Boker in December 1953, soon appreciated the need to change this situation. On his retirement from the post after just 13 stormy months, Lavon submitted a series of valedictory recommendations for a 'reorganization of the security system', principal amongst which were the establishment of a 'Defense Council' (akin to the US National Security Council), the appointment of a Deputy CGS, and the transfer of both the military administration and the office of military censor from the IDF to the ministry of defense (Kafkafi 1998:280–1). Once again, however, Ben-Gurion, who came out of retirement and succeeded Lavon as minister of defense, rejected the entire package outright. His relationships with both the CGS and his senior cabinet colleagues, he insisted, would continue to conform to the mould that he had previously cast: not a rational dialogue embedded in law but an outcome of a random and entirely unregulated sequence of verbal agreements and informal arrangements.

Under these circumstances, even the notion of cabinet responsibility – arguably one of the pillars of all democratic regimes – was neither articulated nor honored. Until as late as 1956, full cabinet discussions on security issues were so infrequent that, when they did take place, they generated a suspicion that Ben-Gurion had initiated them in order to ensure that his ministers would appear as responsible as himself for reaching decisions that he knew would meet with military and/or public disapproval.[10] The Ministerial Committee on Defense and Foreign Affairs, established that year, was initially considered to be a temporary expedient. The only forum that the prime minister consulted on a regular basis, usually every Thursday afternoon, consisted of a clique of hand-picked advisers: Shimon Peres (Director-General of the Defense Ministry), Nehemiah Argov (Ben-Gurion's military secretary until 1957) and – most influential of all – the Chief of Staff, Dayan, who Ben-Gurion also began to invite to cabinet meetings as from 1955 (Golani 2000:26, 30, 33). On one of the few occasions that Ben-Gurion permitted the establishment of a cabinet committee on a national security matter (the Rozen committee, which in 1959 by a vote of three to two recommended the dismantlement of the military administration over Arab citizens), he simply rejected the report without allowing anything other than perfunctory discussion (Ozacky-Lazar 2002:124–30).

To an extent larger than is often acknowledged, Moshe Sharett, who served as foreign minister from May 1948 until June 1956, and who also replaced Ben-Gurion as Prime Minister between December 1953 and November 1955, shared Ben-Gurion's inclination to limit the decision-making circle. However, he did persistently point out that national security policy-making had to take account of foreign policy considerations, and that there therefore existed no excuse for reprisal raids being launched without the foreign minister's acquiescence, or even knowledge (Morris 1993:245–55; Sheffer 1996:689–90, 721, and 852). But even these limited efforts to change existing practice suffered mixed fortunes. Ben-Gurion did occasionally agree to several consultative one-on-one 'arrangements' with Sharett. When he returned to the ministry of defense after Lavon's resignation in February 1955, he also maintained the custom earlier initiated by Sharett, whereby prospective reprisal raids were discussed by an informal caucus of *Mapai* ministers and functionaries (termed *havereinu*, 'our friends'). At no point, however, did he concede the need to grant these or any other decision-making forums statutory status. On the contrary, he sought to modify them whenever feasible. Most noticeably so was this so in December 1955 when he exploited the opportunity presented by Sharett's absence abroad to monopolize the authorization for one of the largest reprisal raids thereto. On 16 December 1955 Sharett vented his frustration in his diary. 'Ben-Gurion the Defense Minister consulted with Ben-Gurion the [acting] Foreign Minister and received the green light from Ben-Gurion the Prime Minister' (Sharett 1978:1309–10).

Once Ben-Gurion had maneuvered the resignation of Sharett from the post of foreign minister in June 1956, and assured his replacement by the less experienced Mrs. Meir, such stratagems became superfluous. National security decision-making was, if anything, more personalized during the last eight years of Ben-Gurion's premiership than had been the case prior to 1956. In critical areas, there no longer existed even the pretence of conformity with the norms of democratic government. Of the many examples of this phenomenon, two were particularly consequential.

The first relates to the initiation of the 1956 Sinai Campaign, an episode that surely ranks as one of the most thoroughly footnoted chapters in the history of the modern Middle East. It is now clear that Israel's response to the French offer of a military alliance was decided, not by the cabinet, but in the course of separate informal consultations that Ben-Gurion held with ministers from the *Mapai* and *Achdut Ha-Avodah* parties on 25 September 1956. When, the following month, the Prime Minister traveled to Paris, where he concluded the secret Sevres agreement that committed the IDF to war against Egypt in collusion with Britain and France, he was not accompanied by any member of his cabinet (none of whom, including Mrs. Meir, even knew of the journey) but by Dayan, Peres and Argov. At no point during the course of the negotiations did he make his signature dependent on ratification by his cabinet colleagues, whose subsequent discussion of the pact hence became almost a formality (Golani 1997:257, 276–9 and 397–9).[11]

A second example of Ben-Gurion's unilateral style is provided by his initiation of Israel's nuclear program. From the moment that he set this enterprise in motion in 1952, it remained the preserve of a very limited circle of bureaucrats and scientists. As such, and in this instance very much in keeping with the precedents set with regard to atomic development in both the USA and the UK, the subject was deliberately quarantined from both the legislature and other portions of the executive branch. As Avner Cohen points out: 'Ben Gurion [sic] did not obtain a cabinet decision on the secret project he had initiated, and he did not allow the issue to be

76 *Development*

debated in the military.' Even the *Mapai* caucus (*havereinu*) was kept in the dark (Am. Cohen 1998:71). Cohen also surmises that subsequently, too, it is doubtful whether Ben-Gurion told even his closest cronies about the underground reprocessing plant whose construction was being chaperoned by the French (Am. Cohen 2010:285 n.10). In order to avoid going hat in hand to the *knesset* in order to obtain funding for the nuclear facility, Ben-Gurion may also have established a secret 'war chest', composed of private donations from wealthy Jews abroad (Shifris 2010:158).

Finale

There are indications that, on the eve of his very last resignation from government in 1963, Ben-Gurion might have been coming around to the conclusion that his personalized form of control over national security policies would have to come to an end. One reason was his realization that the years were catching up on him (he celebrated his 75th birthday in the fall of 1962) and that he would soon have to relinquish his offices as both prime minister and defense minister, which would henceforth be held by two individuals. Another was evidence that his political base was becoming weaker. In the general elections held in February 1961, Ben-Gurion's *Mapai* party lost five of the 47 *knesset* seats that it had previously possessed in the 120-seat chamber, a situation that very much strengthened the bargaining potential of *Mapai*'s traditional coalition partners. Yisrael Galilee, the man who Ben-Gurion had ousted from the post of *RAMAH* in 1948 and who now headed the team of coalition negotiators representing *Achdut ha-Avodah* (which had split off from *Mapam* in 1954), was especially insistent on a broader distribution of responsibility for national security management. Included in the final version of the coalition agreement, therefore, were clauses that promised a strengthening of the *knesset*'s Foreign Affairs and Defense Committee (*inter alia* by the establishment of a sub-committee on nuclear affairs) and the creation of a permanent and active cabinet committee on security matters, to be known as *va'adat ha-sarim le-inyanei bitachon* (the 'Ministerial Committee on Security Affairs' [MCSA]; Shifris 2010:148).

In practice, the influence of these changes was marginal. Although certainly weaker than it had been, Ben-Gurion's hold on power was still strong enough to enable him to ignore the cabinet committee and to retain personal control over the nuclear project. Most important, he remained as firmly committed as ever to the notion that, where national security issues were concerned, matters would still have to remain under strict executive control, and that judicial intrusion and parliamentary supervision ought both to be kept to a minimum. Therein, it might be suggested, lays the significance of the process whereby in 1962 he established a commission in order to investigate the agencies responsible for the gathering and assessment of national security intelligence.[12] Not incidentally, this body was established by prime ministerial fiat, rather than – as is usually the case in such instances – as a result of a vote taken in the *knesset* on a government proposal. Equally significant was the composition of the commission, which consisted of just two persons: Yigael Yadin (who had served as the IDF's second CGS, 1949–1952) and Zeev Sherf, who had been secretary to the cabinet from 1948–1957. Absent from this body, therefore, and in stark contrast to the two subsequent commissions that dealt with the same subject (the Agranat Commission in 1973–1974 and the Steinitz Commission in 2003), were representatives of either the judiciary or the legislature. The intimation was clear. As far as Ben-Gurion was concerned, the role of law, as conventionally understood, was in national security matters to remain severely curtailed, certainly with regards to the most crucial elements of national security decision-making and implementation.

It remained to be seen whether or not this attitude would survive his own departure from government.

4 Diffusion, 1963–1977

If Ben-Gurion's departure from office in 1963 clearly terminated one era in Israel's political and constitutional history, the election of Menachem Begin as prime minister in 1977 equally assuredly ushered in another. The intervening period, however, constituted a national security drama in its own right, principally because it was bisected by the major Arab–Israeli wars of 1967 and 1973. Although fought in very different ways, those two confrontations shared several common characteristics. Each revolutionized the geo-strategic environment of the Middle East and each exerted a profound effect on the mood and mores of Israeli society. Equally influential was their impact, both individually and in combination, on the content and formulation of Israel's national security law, all four dimensions of which were, between 1963 and 1977, radically recast. For one thing, the ways in which supreme command was exercised during the wars mandated a fundamental reconsideration of the *hierarchy* of the national security apparatus. At the same time, its *division of functions* was revolutionized by the intrusion of new institutional actors into the decision-making process. Massive shifts in the contours of national security subject matter likewise entirely altered perceptions with respect to both the *spatial span* of the field and its *temporal* dimension.

Only in retrospect do those changes assume the appearance of some cohesion. At the time, they were haphazard responses to the immediate pressure of events, over which none of the individuals involved ever exercised more than minimal control. Nevertheless, with the benefit of hindsight it is possible to identify three principal features that bestow on the period a recognizable shape and form. One is the erosion of the hegemony of the prime minister over Israel's national security decision-making process. A second is the ambiguity that, especially at moments of crisis, pervaded civil–military relationships at the apex of the Israeli governmental pyramid. The third is the complexity of the dilemmas generated by Israel's control over the territories that the IDF conquered in 1967. This chapter will document manifestations of those trends and analyze their impact on both the substance of Israel's national security law and the role played by the various branches of government in its formulation.

Re-shuffling the pack: a new hierarchy of decision-makers

Differences of personality guaranteed alterations to Israel's national security decision-making framework as soon as Levi Eshkol succeeded Ben-Gurion on June 16 1963. Although Eshkol too combined the posts of both prime minister and minister of defense, he never claimed any particular expertise in security matters (his own specialty was economic management). Neither did he make any effort to imitate Ben-Gurion's authoritarian style. Eshkol's temperamental preference was for compromise over compulsion and for conciliation over confrontation. Hence, whereas Ben-Gurion had tended to ignore – or at best browbeat – cabinet members when formulating national security policies, Eshkol veered to the opposite extreme. Before taking any major defense decision he made it a rule to consult regularly with his colleagues, usually in the framework of the Ministerial Committee on Security Affairs (MCSA), and often in formal meetings of the entire cabinet (Brecher 1972:210–14; Naor 2006).

On 'technical' military matters, Eshkol was also far more inclined than Ben-Gurion to show deference to the professional expertise of senior IDF personnel. Indicative, in this context, was his working relationship with Yitzchak Rabin, who owed his appointment as CGS on January 1 1964 to his reputation (at the age of 41!) as the most experienced of Israel's serving soldiers. Far from fearing that so powerful a CGS might threaten prime ministerial authority, Eshkol looked upon Rabin as a partner, someone whose military talents were required in order to compensate for his own deficiencies in the national security field. Hence, he elevated Rabin to regular membership of the innermost consultative circle. Ben-Gurion had usually erected a strict firewall between ministers and generals, invariably insisting that the CGS present opinions to him in private. But Eshkol invited Rabin to submit national security assessments and propositions directly to both the cabinet and the MCSA, whilst also allowing him a degree of operational autonomy thereto unprecedented in Israeli history.

Diffusion, as thus practiced by Eshkol, proved to be an incremental process. Its earliest symptoms appeared during the Israeli–Syrian 'water war', which commenced in 1961 and dragged on intermittently until Israel's conquest of the Golan Heights in June 1967. Unlike Ben-Gurion, who had exercised strict personal control over the initiation of Israeli air strikes against Syrian artillery emplacements near the Sea of Galilee, Eshkol distanced himself from the quotidian details. Although no less sensitive than his predecessor to the escalatory dangers inherent in the resort to air power, Eshkol granted Rabin discretion to decide on the timing and scale of its use. As prime minister and minister of defense he limited his own input to supporting the CGS's decisions in cabinet, a posture that was particularly evident, and especially appreciated by Rabin, after the controversial Israeli air actions of November 1964 and April 1967 (the latter sometimes referred to as 'the first salvo of the Six Days War'; Elron 2005).

Eshkol could not possibly sustain so relaxed an attitude during the month-long crisis that preceded the outbreak of the Six Days War in June 1967. Even then, however, he adopted what was, by Israeli standards, a novel decision-making style. In 1956, when Israel had last gone to war, Ben-Gurion had kept his cards close to his chest, restricting consultation with respect to the impending hostilities to a small coterie of personal confidants (above p. 75). Most members of the cabinet were kept in the dark until the last possible moment. Eshkol's behavior was very different (Brecher 1974:402–9 and 423–31). Between 15 May and 5 June 1967, the Prime Minister met on six occasions with the ten ministers who comprised the MCSA, and another five times with all 18 members of the cabinet (one such session, on 27/28 May, lasted for 24 hours with only a short intermission). In addition, Eshkol addressed the *knesset*'s Foreign Affairs and Defense Committee once (17 May), the full *knesset* twice (22 and 23 May, when he also met privately with opposition leaders) and delivered one – almost disastrous – radio address to the nation (on 28 May). Less frequent, by comparison, were his 'off the record' consultations with smaller circles of advisers and ministers, only two of which (both on Saturday 3 June), were at all consequential.[1]

Although motivated by the best of intentions, Eshkol's attempts to broaden national security decision-making during the tense days of May 1967 backfired. Designed to avoid reaching hasty conclusions and to ensure that voice was given to every possible option, his consultative style generated an impression of indecision and – worse still – lack of confidence in the IDF's ability to defeat its foes. By the end of the month, Eshkol was under irresistible pressure, much of which originated in the IDF general staff (Gluska 2007:196–8), to relinquish the post of minister of defense. Virtually by acclaim, his designated successor was Moshe Dayan, the hero of the 1956 war and the one man now thought to enjoy the backing of both his fellow-*sabras* amongst Israel's generals and the leaders of the principal opposition parties in the *knesset*. On 1 June 1967, Eshkol finally succumbed.

With the benefit of hindsight, it is possible to identify Dayan's appointment as the point at which civil–military relationships in Israel embarked on a new course. For the very first time, senior members of the IDF general staff had formed themselves into a pressure group with the express purpose of affecting the composition of the Israeli cabinet. In so doing, they shifted the balance of civil–military power that Ben-Gurion had so carefully maintained. The unexpected magnitude and speed of victory during the Six Days War was bound to tip the scales even more. With public esteem for the IDF soaring to unprecedented heights, retired generals became electoral assets. Moreover, membership of the general staff became an accepted qualification for senior cabinet office.

Prior to 1967, Yigal Allon and Moshe Dayan had been the only former senior IDF officers to attain cabinet posts – and even they had been kept waiting by Ben-Gurion before being allowed to do so. Not until 1959, a full year after his retirement from active service, was Dayan appointed minister of agriculture. Allon, who had left the IDF in 1949, did not become minister of labor (as representative of the *Ahdut ha-Avodah* party) until 1961. After the watershed of the Six Days War, what had once been exceptional began to be a norm. Rabin, who retired as CGS in 1968, was immediately appointed Israel's ambassador in Washington, DC (a position which gave him enormous influence over security policy); his deputy, Ezer Weizman, who retired a year later, was the following day appointed minister of transport as representative of the *Gahal* (a precursor of the *Likud*) party in Mrs. Meir's coalition government. Rabin's successor as CGS, Chaim Bar-Lev, became minister of commerce just three months after his own retirement from active service in January 1972. Even though the IDF did sway dangerously on its pedestal of infallibility during the 1973 Yom Kippur War, thereafter too the process of 'lateral transfer' from senior military command to high government office continued apace, thereby contributing another layer to the diffusion of executive authority. Increasingly, civil–military relationships in Israel were to approximate more to what Peri termed a 'partnership' amongst parallel nodes of influence than to a hierarchical pyramid over which the politicians exercised unitary control (Peri 1983:101–29).

The immediate impact of Dayan's appointment in June 1967 on Israel's national security decision-making structure was, if anything, even more dramatic. From the moment that he assumed office, Dayan exploited his military record to don the mantel of the government's senior authority on security matters. With the outbreak of war on 5 June 1967, his position solidified. Outwardly, it is true, constitutional conventions were still respected. Eshkol convened the MCSA on each of the following five days, thereby conveying an impression of collective responsibility for the running of the war. But this was an illusion. The MCSA, which had been enlarged to 15 members in order to accommodate the expansion of the cabinet consequent upon the formation of a National Unity Government on the eve of war, was far too cumbersome a body to reach decisions with the speed required. Besides, where some of the most important issues were concerned, Dayan was not inclined to invite it to do so. Singlehandedly, and without cabinet authorization, the minister of defense permitted Israeli forces to remain in the positions that by the third day of fighting they had established, contrary to his own previous orders, on the banks of the Suez Canal. On what appears to be the basis of a personal mood change, and without so much as a prior telephone call to either Eshkol or Rabin, he likewise overcame his earlier objections to an attack on Syria, and at 7 am on 9 June gave a direct order to David Elazar, CO Northern Command, to unleash the IDF forces eagerly waiting to storm the Golan Heights (Golan 2007:251–2, 279–81, 301–9). Even when Dayan did design to consult with his cabinet colleagues, his attitude was hardly less imperious.

When my role [vote?] and Warhaftig's [the elderly Minister of Religious Affairs, who had no military experience whatsoever] carry the same weight, and a majority of two votes decides whether we go to war over two more kilometers – I don't believe this is the way to manage a complicated war.

(Segev 2007:389–90)

Victory increased Dayan's self-assurance. Although he had in fact made only a very marginal contribution to either the planning or conduct of the June 1967 campaigns, in political terms Dayan was without doubt their principal beneficiary. His reputation as a military genius soared to Olympian heights, ensuring that his views on security would be treated with a degree of reverence generally reserved for biblical prophecies. More concrete were the benefits that resulted from the massive physical expansion of the domain for which he was responsible. Other than eastern Jerusalem, each of the territories conquered during the war were placed under military control. To all intents and purposes they thus became Dayan's personal fiefdoms, areas in which no other minister possessed any official *locus standi*. Massive increases to the budget made available to the ministry of defense between 1967 and 1973 (Yaniv 1994:287–9) further widened the disparities between Dayan and his cabinet colleagues. As Abba Eban, the foreign minister of the period, ruefully recalled, after 1967 the minister of defense possessed powers of patronage with which no other minister could vie (Eban 1992:462–5).

Notwithstanding those advantages, Dayan never became prime minister. When Eshkol died in February 1969, he was succeeded by Golda Meir, who had firm opinions of her own as to how Israeli governments should go about their business. Like everyone else, Meir certainly admired Dayan. Her distinction, however, lay in that she refused to be overawed by him. Throughout her tenure of office she, like Eshkol, insisted that decision-making in the national security sphere be a collective affair and would include Dayan's detractors as well as his devotees ('One of the things of which I am most proud', she waspishly recalled, 'is that for over five years I kept together a government that included not only Dayan but also a number of men who disliked and resented him.' Meir 1975:379–80) The difference between Meir and Eshkol, and it was an important one, lay in the forum that she considered most suitable for decision-making. Eshkol, as we have seen, frequently had recourse to the MCSA. Meir, although recognizing the value of that institution, tended to use it as a rubber stamp, a place where ministers merely gave legal force to decisions that had been taken in what popularly became known as 'Golda's kitchen.'

As much a court as an engine of government, the 'kitchen' was very much Meir's personal creation (Medzini 2008:472–8). At its core it consisted of persons who fit into one or more of three categories: individuals with whom the prime minister felt comfortable; those who she considered experts in a specific field; and those whom she trusted. Probably the only person who fulfilled all three criteria was Yisrael Galilee, by now an *eminence grise* whose official title was 'Minister without Portfolio'. Hence, it was very rare indeed for 'kitchen' meetings to be held without him (Shifris 2010:259–60). Dayan, Allon (deputy prime minister since 1967) and Shapira, the minister of justice, were also almost always present, but otherwise membership was fluid and selective. Eban and finance minister Sapir were often invited, but not as a matter of course. Sometimes, ministers were outnumbered by members of the prime minister's private staff and senior unelected officials, a category that necessarily included the CGS. Most kitchen meetings were held at Meir's official residence in Jerusalem on Saturday evenings. Regular meetings of the full cabinet or, when necessary, of the MCSA, which by convention were held on Sunday mornings, hence often became formalities. The important decisions had already been taken the night before.

Probably the nearest Israel has come to possessing anything like the American National Security Council, Golda Meir's 'kitchen' exerted an enormous impact on policy formulation, especially during the War of Attrition that raged along the Suez Canal between the fall of 1968 and the summer of 1970. Every significant stage in that conflict was preceded by a kitchen discussion, often initiated by Dayan and attended also by the CGS, Bar-Lev. The spectrum of issues brought before the forum encompassed individual commando raids (such as that launched against Egyptian positions on Green Island in July 1969), air strikes against targets deep in the Egyptian rear in 1969–1970 (originally suggested by Rabin, soon after his posting to Washington) and, most dangerous of all, the confrontation with Russian-piloted Mig jets in the summer of 1970 and the mobilization of troops along the Syrian border later that year, during 'Black September' (Kober 2009:10–35).

With the outbreak of the Yom Kippur War in October 1973, decision-making became a more formal process. All ministers were immediately co-opted onto the MCSA, in which capacity they were convened by Meir over the course of the 20 days of fighting (6–25 October 1973) for 18 formal meetings, some of which were held twice on a single day and all of which were attended by the CGS or his representative. Even so, however, the 'kitchen' system continued to operate. Not surprisingly, Meir's confidence in Dayan had been seriously dented by the outbreak of war – and perhaps even more when he seemed to succumb to a mood of almost fatalistic pessimism during the early, dark days of fighting (Meir 1975:361). Hence, she on 17 separate occasions convened what were now termed 'political-security advisory meetings', to which she invited Galilee, Allon and the CGS (or his representative) as well as the minister of defense (Shifris 2010:261). The purposes of those gatherings varied. Sometimes, they were called in order to resolve differences of opinion between Dayan and the CGS, or to provide Dayan and the CGS with authorization for an operation about which they were agreed, but for which the minister of defense preferred to receive the prime minister's backing. But sometimes they were convened because Meir clearly had doubts about a specific proposal presented by Dayan. Whichever the case, the centralized form of control over operations that had been exercised by Ben-Gurion in 1956 and by Dayan in 1967, no longer appertained.[2]

Fumbling towards legislation: 'Basic Law: The Military' and its flaws

The first official agency to comment on the way in which the decision-making apparatus had operated immediately prior to the outbreak of the 1973 war and during its initial course was the commission of inquiry established by the government in November 1973 and which was chaired by the president of the ISC, Justice Shimon Agranat. This body, whose other members were one other justice of the Supreme Court, two former Chiefs of the IDF General Staff and the State Comptroller, was principally charged with investigating IDF conduct prior to the war and during its initial stages.[2] However, the commissioners also examined the civil–military interface, and in their *Final Unclassified Report* (Agranat Commission Report 1975:27–8) concluded that: 'Over time, faults have occurred in the fulfillment of the role that ought to be played in debates about national security and in decision-making in this sphere at the highest level by the *memshalah*' (literally, 'government', but in Israeli constitutional parlance referring to the body known in the UK as 'the cabinet'). Since Article 29 of the original version of Basic Law: The Government (enacted in August 1968) identifies the cabinet as a whole as Israel's executive branch, formally the war should have been managed by all ministers in concert. The frequency of 'political-security advisory meetings' demonstrated that such had not been the case. Hence, the Agranat Report recommended a reversion to Eshkol's system of consulting with a more compact MCSA.

> This will remove any pretext for shifting the focus of a debate on security or political-security matters from the Cabinet and its committees to forums constituted ad hoc and without cabinet authorization.
> (Agranat 1975)

The Agranat commissioners were certainly not the first observers to comment on the need to clarify Israel's national security decision-making hierarchy. They had most recently been pre-empted by prime ministers Eshkol and Meir. Within days of Dayan's appointment as minister of defense in June 1967, Eshkol had him sign a document that itemized the prime minister's prerogatives in the national security sphere. Soon after Meir assumed office in 1969, she and Dayan reportedly exchanged letters of commitment on the same subject, thus creating an epistolary corpus on which Israeli decision-making folklore bestowed the sobriquet 'the constitution' (Ben-Meir 1995:102).

Taking for granted that the nuclear issue must have dominated Israeli national security thinking throughout this period, Dr. Avner Cohen assumes that both sets of documents contained specific clauses relating to control over Israel's atomic arsenal. Thus, 'apparently' (as Cohen puts it), the first paragraph of the Eshkol–Dayan memorandum, which had been drafted at Eshkol's request by former CGS Yigael Yadin, 'asserted that the minister of defense could not initiate any use of nuclear weapons without the approval of the prime minister.' The Meir–Dayan exchange, which was drafted by their respective military secretaries and, as was usual, fine-tuned by Galilee, likewise 'apparently' dealt *inter alia* with 'the division of authorities and responsibilities between the two regarding the nuclear organization and its products' (Av. Cohen 2010:96, 290 n.60).

That case is impossible to verify. If it ever existed, the Meir–Dayan 'constitution' seems to have vanished into thin air (Ben-Meir 1995:102). By contrast, we do possess what purports to be the authentic version of the Eshkol–Dayan memorandum (Lempfrom 2002:555). But neither of the two short paragraphs in that document makes any reference at all to nuclear weapons. The first itemizes actions that the new minister of defense would not take without prior approval from the prime minister: initiation of general hostile action or war against any country whatsoever; military action in the course of war that oversteps bounds previously determined by the cabinet; military action against any country not thereto involved in hostilities; bombing of major cities in enemy territory unless the foe had already bombed Israeli cities; and retaliatory action in response to 'incidents'. Paragraph two designates the persons who the prime minister could 'summon in order to receive information', even without the knowledge of the minister of defense: the CGS, the CO of the IDF Intelligence Branch, the director-general of the ministry of defense, and the deputy minister of defense.

Even thus devoid of any reference to the nuclear issue, the text of the Eshkol–Dayan agreement is revealing, and speaks volumes for Eshkol's suspicions of Dayan's possible ambitions. Read in retrospect, however, it also provides an object-lesson in the limited value of the written word. For as long as Dayan continued to bask in an aura of infallibility and indispensability, which was the case until midday on 6 October 1973, no written formula was likely to limit his freedom of action. Neither, for that matter, was the absence of any direct reference to the minister of defense in Basic Law: The Government. As far as he and other ministers were concerned, control over the IDF was exercised jointly by the prime minister and the minister of defense.

Galilee articulated that position most explicitly just two days before the outbreak of the 1973 war, when a select group of ministers, hastily convened by Mrs. Meir in order to assess indeterminate intelligence information, weighed the pros and cons of ordering a massive mobilization of IDF reserves. Entirely ignoring the power arguably conferred on the cabinet by Article 33 of Basic Law: The Government to delegate its authority to individual ministers (Zamir 1996:523, compare Nun 1999), Galilee instead insisted that Meir and Dayan possessed an inherent right to act as they sought fit, without receiving cabinet authorization. The protocol of the meeting indicates that no objections were raised to his argument that:

> We have to tell ourselves, and the Prime Minister and Minister of Defense, that they can consider themselves entitled to issue mobilization orders, if they think necessary, prior to a meeting of the Cabinet.... I want there to be no delays in operational action.... We may be surprised.
>
> (Shifris 2010:253)

Notwithstanding the powers thus conferred on the prime minister and minister of defense, the Agranat commissioners, in what the public of the day undoubtedly considered to be their most controversial conclusion, refrained from assigning responsibility for Israel's failure to foresee the impending attack to Meir and Dayan, or indeed to any member of the civilian elite. Instead, they blamed the near-disaster on various named senior military officers, principal amongst whom was CGS Elazar. Even so, the commissioners did not restrict themselves to assessing personal failings. Something was very amiss with the existing system in accordance with which Israel's national security policies were formulated and implemented.

> From the evidence before us we have seen that there exist no clear definitions with respect to the division of authority, duties and responsibilities in security matters between the three relevant authorities in this area, i.e., the Cabinet and the Prime Minister, the Minister of Defense, and the Chief of the General Staff who heads the IDF.... The lack of definition of the powers existing in the present situation in the area of defense, which is an area of vital importance, makes effective action difficult, blurs the focus of legal responsibility, and even generates lack of clarity and confusion amongst the general public.
>
> (Agranat Commission, *Final Unclassified Report* 1975:25–6)

These faults were too fundamental to be amenable to bureaucratic remedies, of the sort that the commissioners recommended in order to improve the quality of intelligence analysis. Instead, they could only be corrected by the establishment of a new legal framework, which their report left to the *knesset* to devise.

It took the *knesset* almost two years of extensive discussion to fulfill that mandate and formulate Basic Law: The Military, which was enacted in March 1976 as an 'unentrenched' item of legislation (meaning that future changes would not require an extraordinary majority of members of the *knesset*). Given the time and effort invested in drafting the law, the end product seems rather disappointing. Because debates on its content were obviously – and perhaps inevitably – overshadowed by the sense of national trauma induced by the recent war, the statute was a decidedly lop-sided document. Legislators focused most of their attention on attempts to define relationships between the different actors most closely involved in the formulation of national security policy and its implementation, and hence on what we categorize as the *hierarchical* dimension of the national security legal framework. Far less comprehensive and sophisticated, however, was the treatment that Basic Law: The Military accorded to the three other dimensions. *Functional* questions, relevant to the demarcation of the roles supposed to be fulfilled by individual parts of the governmental mechanism, are simply glossed over. More seriously, the law provides no guidelines whatsoever with respect to either *temporal* distinctions with respect to national security affairs (do the same rules apply in times of war and of peace?) or to the *spatial* span of legislative application.

Each of those features of Basic Law: The Military will be discussed in turn.

The hierarchical dimension

The two most important sections of Basic Law: The Military are Articles 2 and 3. Article 2, which deals with the military's subordination to civil authority, states that '(a) The army is subject to the authority of the Cabinet' and (b) that 'the minister in charge of the army on behalf of the Cabinet is the Minister of Defense.' Article 3 focuses more specifically on the powers and status of the Chief of the General Staff. It begins (3a) by declaring the CGS to be 'the supreme command level in the army' and goes on (3b) to state that he 'is subject to the authority of the Cabinet and subordinate to the Minister of Defense.' Finally, Article 3c lays down that the CGS 'shall be appointed by the Cabinet upon the recommendation of the Minister of Defense.'

Clearly drafted with the memory of the October 1973 war in mind, Article 2a implies more than initially meets the eye. In addition to spelling out the primacy of civilian control over the armed forces (a proposition that no one in Israel seriously queried either before or after 1973) it also identifies 'the Cabinet' – a collectivity – as the source of that authority. This interpretation seems to be reinforced by subsequent clauses. Thus, the minister of defense supervises the army 'on behalf of the Cabinet' (Article 2b) and possesses no authority to formulate an independent policy. Likewise, since the CGS is 'subject to the authority of the Cabinet' (Article 3b), the minister of defense is merely the conduit through which the most senior officer in the armed forces receives government orders. No minister of defense can issue orders to a CGS independently of the cabinet.

Although thus articulating an apparently coherent constitutional statement of total and collective executive control over military affairs, Basic Law: The Military in fact contains several flaws. For one thing, its hypothesis flew in the face of Israeli experience. The law assumes that 'the Cabinet', a group of at least 15 persons (and sometimes up to 30), some of whom have no experience of military command whatsoever, could be capable of issuing orders to the military on a regular basis. That prospect was made especially unlikely by the fact that, as the Agranat Report emphasized, ministers possessed no independent means of assessing security situations, but had to rely upon the selective digests of intelligence material supplied by military sources. The notion of collective cabinet control over national security affairs was also contradicted by Israeli history. Only when Eshkol functioned as both prime minister and minister of defense (1963–1967) could the cabinet as a whole be said to have exercised any form of collective control over the IDF – and even then more thanks to Eshkol's managerial style than to any well thought-out constitutional arrangement. Otherwise, experience indicated that in Israel the real choice as far as supervision over the armed forces was concerned lay between the prime minister and the minister of defense. But the distribution of functions between these two persons is an issue that Basic Law: The Military nowhere addresses.

These deficiencies were compounded by legal inconsistencies, both within the Law itself and between Basic Law: The Military and other legislation. Article 3c offers a glaring example of an internal inconsistency, since it mandates that the CGS is to be appointed 'on the recommendation of the Minister of Defense.' This clause in effect grants the minister a veto over the highest appointment in the military hierarchy, thereby endowing him with a degree of power denied to any other single individual, including the prime minister (who in fact is not mentioned in Basic Law: The Military at all). Similarly, it is difficult to harmonize the doctrine of collective cabinet responsibility enunciated in this law with the stipulations of other items of legislation, which give the minister of defense sole license to act in certain national security spheres. One example is provided by the Military Justice Law, which was amended in 1975, in conjunction with the passage of Basic Law: The Military. In its older version, the Military Justice Law had defined 'Military Commands' as: 'Directives of the General Staff which the CGS has been authorized by the Minister of Defense to issue, orders of the General Staff...'. Article 2a of the updated version referred to an entirely new category: 'Directives of the Supreme Command' that 'would be issued by the CGS with the approval of the Minister of Defense.' If anything, this change bolsters the position of the Minister. It is quite clear that 'the Supreme Command' (a forum that is not mentioned in any other law, and whose composition and authority are therefore obscure) harnesses the CGS to the minister of defense, who is thus granted a far more active role in formulating commands than had previously been the case.

There existed at least two possible alternatives to the constitutional arrangement set down in Basic Law: The Military. One was to allow for the possibility that, especially in times of crisis, a single individual – who could be either the minister of defense or the prime minister – would be granted an exceptional degree of authority to issue orders to the military, thereby in effect functioning as 'commander-in-chief' (in all but name, that had been the status enjoyed both by Ben-Gurion prior to 1963 and by Dayan during the 1967 war). The alternative was to grant the minister of defense (or the prime minister) authority over the military as long as the cabinet had not decided otherwise. Under that arrangement the minister would be far more than a conduit between members of the cabinet and the armed forces, but not an independent agent. The Cabinet would retain the power to bring the arrangement to an end, but – as long as it lasted – would, if prudent, exercise self-restraint when reviewing the minister's conduct.

In *Dawikat* v. *Government of Israel* (1979, see below p. 136), the only occasion on which Israel's judiciary explicitly addressed Basic Law: The Military, the ISC provided an interpretation that came very close to the second of the above two alternatives. Thus, Justice Landau firmly rejected the argument, raised in the case, that in military matters the opinion of the minister of defense is superior to that of the cabinet.

> There is no substance to this claim.... True, according to Article 2b of Basic Law: The Military, the Minister of Defense is in charge of the army in the name of the Cabinet. But according to Article 2a of the same law the army is under the authority of the Cabinet. Also, according to Article 3b the CGS is under the authority of the Cabinet, even though he is directly subordinate to the Minister of Defense. The conclusion is that as long as the Cabinet has not made a decision on a specific issue, the CGS must obey the orders of the Minister of Defense. However, when an issue has been brought before the Cabinet, its decision obligates the CGS; the Minister of Defense is but one member of the Cabinet, and as long as he continues to be a member of this body, he continues to carry with his ministerial colleagues collective responsibility for its decisions, including those that were arrived at by majority vote against his own opposing opinion. The same applies to decisions by Cabinet-appointed committees.

Even in this view, however, Basic Law: The Military remains far from straightforward. Indeed, it leaves several questions unanswered.

90 *Development*

- Does the CGS possess a constitutional right to appeal a decision of the minister of defense to the prime minister or the entire cabinet? In practice, some have certainly done so, and in some views legitimately so (Bendor and Kremnitzer 2000:47). However, the wording and structure of Basic Law: The Military could be interpreted to suggest otherwise: the CGS is subordinate to the minister of defense, whose orders he cannot apparently query.
- Can the minister of defense, or the cabinet as a whole for that matter, issue orders directly to soldiers? Far from being far-fetched, this is in fact a highly practical question. True, Basic Law: The Military expressly identifies the CGS as the commander of the IDF – and thus implies that orders may not be issued directly by the minister of defense, but only through the military chain of command. Historically, however, this convention has often been breached, and soldiers have indeed obeyed orders received directly from a minister of defense. In some cases, sheer awe probably provided a sufficient incentive for them to do so (Ben-Meir 1995:62). But on other occasions they were motivated by sensitivity to Article 14 of Supreme Command Directive 3.0228, which specifies that the minister of defense approves all IDF promotions above the rank of colonel (*aluf mishneh*). Significantly, Basic Law: The Military makes no mention of this Directive, even though, as Nun points out, it clearly undermines the exclusively military hierarchy that the law attempted to preserve (Nun 1999:116 n.130).
- What procedure is to be adopted should an incumbent CGS unexpectedly become incapacitated, or should a designated CGS be prevented from assuming the post on the date that his predecessor resigns from service? In the summer of 1948, when the first CGS, Ya'akov Dori had become too ill to fulfill his duties, command over the IDF had been exercised by the CO Operations Branch, Yigael Yadin, even though Dori still retained his title, as did his official deputy, Zvi Ayalon, over whom Yadin leapfrogged when appointed the IDF's second CGS in November 1949. Still more glaring had been the hiatus created in April 1974, when Elazar resigned his office as CGS immediately upon reading the Agranat Report. At the time, no member of the General Staff held the title of deputy to the CGS, and it took Meir and Dayan a fortnight to agree upon Elazar's replacement (ultimately, they chose Mordechai Gur, the military attaché in Washington). Meanwhile, supreme command was exercised by the CO Operations Branch, Yitzchak Hofi, himself a contender for the top post, who resigned from service the moment it was awarded to Gur. Basic Law: The Military made no provisions to prevent the recurrence of such untidy precedents. Unlike Basic Law: The Government, which specifies a clear and automatic chain of succession should the prime minister be incapacitated (Article 16b: 'Should the Prime Minister be temporarily unable to discharge his duties, his place will be filled by the Acting

Prime Minister'), Basic Law: The Military makes no provision for the appointment of a deputy to the CGS or for the creation of any other such position.

Equally noticeable by their absence from Basic Law: The Military are any references to some of the other key actors in Israel's national security apparatus. One is the CO of the IDF Intelligence Branch who, given the lack of any independent agency capable of providing intelligence assessments, functions as the cabinet's main source in this area. Another, far more important, absentee is the prime minister, who is nowhere mentioned in Basic Law: The Military, and whose authority is somehow subsumed under the doctrine of collective cabinet responsibility. This omission ignores the fact that the prime minister does possess independent statutory authority over several non-military security agencies (the *Mosad*, the GSS and the Atomic Energy Commission) whose activities could certainly have military repercussions. It also seems to disregard historical experience. De-classified protocols of the discussions held on the very morning of the outbreak of the Yom Kippur War (6 October 1973) reveal that the prime minister certainly wielded a decisive influence over mobilization decisions. Indeed, it was Mrs. Meir who finally settled the last-minute debate between Dayan and Elazar as to how many reservists should be called up (S. Cohen 2000:84–6).

The functional dimension

Other than with respect to the relative hierarchies of the CGS, the minister of defense and the cabinet, Basic Law: The Military made very little reference to such functional issues as the division of spheres of responsibility in the sphere of national security law.

Particularly noticeable is the perfunctory manner in which it discusses the role of parliamentary legislation in this area. Altogether, there exist three references. Article 4 of Basic Law: The Military states that: 'The duty of serving in the Army and recruitment for the Army shall be as prescribed by or by virtue of law'; Article 5 declares that: 'The power to issue instructions and orders binding in the Army shall be prescribed by or by virtue of law'; and Article 6 stipulates that 'No armed force other than the Israel Defense Force shall be established or maintained except under law'.

Experience has shown that the authority granted to the *knesset* by these articles is open to various interpretations, and indeed has resulted in very different applications. On the one hand, the *knesset* has certainly assumed the powers granted it in Article 5, especially when enacting Article 2a of the amended Military Justice Law (see above p. 88), which mandates that military orders can only be given by the CGS – albeit sometimes with the approval of the minister of defense. But other articles have been followed less rigidly. Conscription, for instance, although certainly the subject of statute, has never been under exclusive parliamentary jurisdiction. Many powers in this area have in fact been delegated to the minister of defense, who now possesses, for instance, authority to issue blanket exemptions from military service to members of the Arab and the Jewish ultra-orthodox (*haredi*) communities, to whom the original Defense Service Law enacted in 1949 (new version 1986) nowhere refers. Finally, Article 6 has been almost entirely ignored. Until 2002 Israel's domestic security service, the GSS (*Shabak*) functioned without a legislative framework; the *Mosad*, which focuses on security activities overseas, still does so. Likewise, the *knesset* never once passed a law with reference to the South Lebanese Army, a military force that Israeli personnel armed and trained throughout much of the IDF's extended occupation of the 'security zone' established north of Israel's international border with Lebanon between 1982 and 2000. Parliamentary regulation of private security firms, which still rests upon legislation enacted in 1972 (the Private Investigators and Security Services Law) remains very rudimentary. Indeed, the only conditions that the latter specifies for the grant of a license to establish a private security firm are: proof of sufficient knowledge, a clean criminal sheet, and appropriate insurance coverage.

Likewise apparent are other deficiencies in Basic Law: The Military with respect to the *functional* dimension of national security legislation.

It does not provide, for instance, an answer to a possible Israeli version of the dispute that rages in the USA with respect to the War Powers Act. Are all issues other than those specified in Basic Law: The Military to be considered realms of exclusive executive responsibility, or is the *knesset* entitled to enact legislation in those areas too? Whereas such questions have been fully debated by the US Supreme Court, in Israel they remain very much *terra incognita*.

Are there limits on the functions of the minister of defense? The *Dawikat* formula seems to suggest that the only limits on his functions are explicit decisions taken by the entire cabinet. Absent such a decision on any specific matter, the minister possesses freedom of action. Would those rules of thumb also apply were members of the cabinet to be so evenly divided over a matter that a vote resulted in a tie, as has indeed happened in the past? Even then, would they also hold were the matter at stake to be a decision whether or not to go to war, as was the case on May 27 1967? As we shall see, even the new version of Basic Law: The Government (enacted in 1992, and reenacted in 2001) provides no more than a partial answer.

The temporal dimension

Basic Law: The Military entirely ignores the temporal dimension of the national security legal framework, most obviously by neglecting to include a clause stating that its provisions cannot be changed by emergency regulations, such as are to be found in such other legislative equivalents as Basic Law: The Knesset (1958, which is only partially 'entrenched') and Basic Law: The Government (1968, which was not 'entrenched' until revised in 2001). Two implications are immediately apparent. First: in times of war the cabinet possesses the authority to change the designated command structures, even though the Law nowhere gives any indication of the principles to be employed when doing so; second, and even harder to comprehend, the cabinet may resort to emergency regulations in order to bypass the need for parliamentary authorization when wishing to change enlistment practices or to create new armed forces.

The spatial dimension

Most glaring of all, however, is the absence of any reference in Basic Law: The Military to matters falling within the category of the spatial dimension. This Law makes no attempt to revise (indeed, does not even mention) the Planning and Construction Law of 1965, which created a procedure for the approval of military construction projects that was noticeably favorable to the IDF, and that did not begin to become subject to even the most cursory of judicial scrutiny until the 1990s (Perez and Rosenblum, 2007; Oren and Regev 2008:213–37). Even more noticeable is the absence in the law of any reference to the territories that the IDF had conquered in 1967.

The latter lacuna was especially extensive with respect to the West Bank, an area in which the situation created by the events of June 1967 presented problems that defied simple solution. One complicating factor was the unusually powerful emotions aroused by this region, whose associations with Jewry's biblical past were emphasized once Israeli official documents began referring to the West Bank as 'Judea and Samaria'. Then there were the demographics. Whereas both the Sinai Desert and the Golan Heights were – for different reasons – at the end of June 1967 devoid of any sizable civilian population,[4] that was certainly not the case on the West Bank. Although some 200,000 Palestinian inhabitants of the area had fled across the river Jordan during and immediately after the Six Days War, some 670,000 (including about 70,000 residents of east Jerusalem) remained and a further 19,000 were initially permitted to return soon after the fighting ended. Since another 350,000 Palestinians lived in the Gaza Strip, roughly half in refugee camps, the IDF suddenly found itself responsible for the welfare of about 1.1 million individuals, none of whom were citizens of the State of Israel (Morris 1999:336).

Decisions and non-decisions respecting the status of the Territories

Contrary to some post-war speculation, it is now clear that Israel's conquest of the West Bank was entirely unpremeditated (Shlaim 2000:244).

94 *Development*

Only reluctantly, and after several efforts at mediation, did the IDF enter into hostilities with Jordan on 6 June 1967. Prior to the Six Days War, no plans had been drafted in Israel to govern the West Bank, the future of which was, from the very beginning, a matter of speculation. Even before the fighting in the area came to its whirlwind close some government officials began tentatively to examine a possible power-sharing agreement with Jordanian officials and/or Palestinian notables. In the aftermath of victory, a far greater range of possibilities emerged. By and large, right-wing opinion, which was especially enthused by victory, favored an arrangement that would ensure a permanent Israeli presence on the West Bank. In the ruling *Mapai* party, however, opinions were considerably more cautious – and hesitant (Pedahtzur 1996).

Eshkol had hoped to bridge at least some of these differences at a cabinet meeting that he convened for precisely that purpose on 16 June 1967, less than a fortnight after the cease-fire. But the discussion, which stretched over four days, proved inconclusive. Ministers examined at length various options, including some form of deal with Jordan which would allow for a permanent Israeli military presence along the virtually unpopulated Jordan Valley (the 'Allon Plan') and the grant of a form of autonomy to the Palestinians (Dayan's proposal). Neither suggestion, however, garnered sufficient support to carry the day. Only with respect to the Golan Heights and the Sinai did the cabinet agree, by the narrowest of margins (10–9), to consider an exchange of territory in return for a peace agreement – and even then so secretly that neither the CGS nor any other member of the General Staff was informed of the decision. Moreover, when Yisrael Barzilai, a leader of the *Mapam* party who served as the minister of health, formally proposed applying the same land-for-peace formula to the West Bank, only two other members of the cabinet voted in favor of the motion (Pedahtzur 1996:55). On the other hand, the possibility that the area might be annexed to Israel was also ruled out. Any such action, it was widely appreciated, would require the granting of civil rights to the West Bank's Arab residents (who all Israeli ministers at this stage adamantly refused to term 'Palestinians'), a prospect that threatened to turn Israel into a bi-national state and thereby undermine its Jewish character. Moreover, annexation would also clearly infringe international law (Gordon 2008:5–6).

How sensitive ministers were to the latter consideration was proved by the manner in which Israel did annex eastern Jerusalem. Rather than risk the international opprobrium likely to be generated by specific legislation to that effect, ministers resorted to legal subterfuge. On June 27 1967 the cabinet rushed through the *knesset* all three readings of a bill that amended the 1948 Law and Administration Ordinance in such a way as to allow the government to re-delineate the borders of the State of Israel. Armed with that power, the grant of which only representatives of the Communist parties in the *knesset* opposed, the ministry of the interior on the same day publicized the precise geographical coordinates of the border amendments that it was making. Anybody with a map to hand could, of course, immediately discover that eastern Jerusalem had thus been incorporated into Israel. But nowhere in either parliamentary legislation or government decree was the city expressly named (Pedahtzur 1996:117–21; Gorenberg 2006:58–60).

The legal conundrum

Jerusalem, however, was clearly an exception. Elsewhere, the legal status of the West Bank remained opaque. So too, therefore, did the identification of the legal authority on which, in the absence of annexation, Israeli control over the IDF's conquests was based.

A straightforward solution to that dilemma was to declare 'the Territories' (henceforth capitalized) to be 'occupied' – a term that appears in the 1949 Fourth Geneva Convention, to which Israel had formally acceded in 1951, and which Israel had used during the IDF's brief period of control over the Sinai Peninsula and Gaza Strip between October 1956 and March 1957. Political factors, however, precluded a repetition of that course. 'Occupation', after all, was by definition, a temporary status; it implied that Israel would at some future date withdraw from the area. Dayan, who from the first had declared that Israel intended 'to stay' in the Territories, was certainly not prepared to undertake any such commitment (Gazit 2003:68); and even the most guarded references to the possibility (as were made ever so tentatively by Eshkol in an interview with *Newsweek* magazine in the spring of 1969) generated a storm of controversy that threatened to tear his parliamentary coalition apart (Pedahtzur 1996:122–3). Hence, Israeli jurists were required to exercise considerable more legal ingenuity. Some answered the call by denying the relevance of the term 'occupation' to the post-1967 situation on the West Bank (a denial supposedly substantiated by a critique of the pre-1967 claims of the Hashemite Kingdom of Jordan to sovereignty over the area).[5] Others, and especially Brigadier-General Meir Shamgar, who had been the IDF's chief military advocate general (MAG) since 1961, took a more inventive route and declared that Israel was not 'occupying' the Territories but 'administering' them. (Shamgar 1982:13) Although this formula was never formally submitted for cabinet approval, it was adopted by official Israeli spokesmen almost from the moment that it was mooted (Benvenisti and Zamir 1993:61). Its growing acceptability paralleled the increase in influence of its author (Rubinstein 1997b; Am. Cohen 2005). On his retirement from military service in 1968, Shamgar was appointed attorney general. In 1975 his career advanced yet further, and he became a justice of the ISC, over which he presided from 1983–1995.

Official enthusiasm for the 'administered' formula is easily understood. After all, it seemed to attain the best of all worlds. The term was sufficiently

96 *Development*

ambiguous to allow Israel to claim that the future disposition of the Territories was still undetermined. At the same time, it could be represented as at least roughly commensurate with international laws of occupation (Gordon 2008:26). Less frequently noted, but equally apparent, is the degree to which the 'administered' formula likewise informed academic legal analysis. Without explicitly saying so, it implied that the Territories were in some way detached from Israel proper. The distinctions between the two areas were not just geographical, but also those of regime, with each being governed by a different set of laws. Scholarly interpretations of this situation have tended, almost as a matter of course, to be segmented (Azoulay and Ophir 2008). One school of thought (Dinstein 1979, 1988a, 2000; Benvenisti 1993a; Kretzmer 2002; Gordon 2008) virtually restricts discussion to the law applicable in the Territories; another (Ben-Meir 1995; Hofnung 1996) focuses on analyzing the national security apparatus within Israel proper.

Our position is that compartmentalization of that sort does violence to the realities of the situation. Instead, we adopt an integrative approach, which seeks to make room for an examination of the interaction between processes at work in both 'spaces'. More specifically, we shall apply to the Territories precisely the same quadruple framework of analysis that we have employed when analyzing all developments relevant to Israel's national security law.

The multiple impact of military 'administration' over the Territories

In this reading, the impact of the 'administered' formula on the *spatial* dimension of Israel's national security law, although obviously obtrusive, was certainly not exclusive. The *temporal* dimension of national security legislation was similarly affected. Precisely because it sought to walk a tightrope between 'annexation', which conveys a sense of permanence, and 'occupation', which is a temporary circumstance, the 'administered' formula created a prolonged judicial twilight, during the course of which Israel's true intentions were left vague. This is an inherently unhealthy situation, almost as much for the rulers as for the ruled. Experience indicates that protracted occupations, quite apart from being likely to produce nationalist reactions that can stymie the chances of their success (Edelstein 2004), also endanger the fabric of the occupier's society. Democracies can survive and recover from periods of emergency rule, provided that the duration of the emergency is reasonably short. What they cannot abide are situations in which military government becomes the rule, rather than the exception. The 'administered' formula, however, very much contributed to that outcome in the Territories.

In addition, the 'administered' formula likewise fudged conventional *functional* boundaries in national security law. From the start, it was clear that the agencies of Israeli administration in the Territories would be military rather than civilian. For one thing, the establishment of a civilian bureaucracy in those regions would be more likely to create the impression that Israel was intent on their eventual annexation – an impression which, for reasons associated with domestic as well as international opinion, the government was keen to avoid. Just as relevant, however, were considerations rooted in bureaucratic convenience. It will be recalled that between May 1948 and December 1966 the State of Israel had subjected its substantial Arab minority to military government. During that extended period the IDF had amassed a vast store of institutional experience in enforcing a system of permits, curfews, land expropriations and restrictions on Arab access to all official services. What is more it had briefly refreshed its collective memory when all those measures were resuscitated immediately on the outbreak of the Six Days War on 5 June 1967 and kept in force in most of the Galilee throughout the following fortnight (Baumel 2002:154–5). It seemed almost a foregone conclusion that the skills thus acquired would also be applied by the IDF to the West Bank as soon as the fighting ended (Kimmerling 2004:377). After all, civilian bureaucrats would have needed to learn them *de novo*; military officials had merely to dust off recent manuals of administration and adjust them to the even larger numbers of Arabs whom they now governed.

Expedient though it thus appeared to be, the decision to entrust control over the Territories to the IDF in fact created an administrative maze – not least for the IDF itself. Even prior to 1967, Israel had been considered a prime example of country in which the boundaries between civilian and military spheres of activity had been eroded by two decades of 'military role expansion' (above p. 69 and Lissak 1983). 'Occupation', even when termed 'administration', exacerbated that characteristic. Only in part was this because the IDF – like numerous other armies of occupation in the modern age (including, most recently, US forces in post-2003 Iraq) – became responsible for running the daily lives of a large subject population, which it had to provide with essential civic services (Stirk 2009:96–121). More specifically deleterious was the crisis of identity with which the IDF was forced to live once Jewish settlers also began to move into the area. Initially, some of the newcomers were classified as military employees. Those who in 1975 established Ofrah, the first post-1967 Jewish settlement in Samaria and hence a landmark case, were described as construction laborers on IDF bases, to whom Shimon Peres, then minister of defense, granted ostensibly temporary permits for overnight stays (Gorenberg 2006:308–28). But that fiction could not long be sustained in the face of a far more complex reality. Local IDF commanders would eventually be enjoined – often at one and the same time – to protect Jewish settlers from Palestinian attacks, to punish them for acts of vigilantism, to co-operate with them on local security missions and to dismantle settlements whose established had not received prior authorization.

Finally, the decision thus to entrust control over the Territories to the IDF also affected the *hierarchy* of Israel's national security decision-making apparatus. When taken, in 1967, that decision at a stroke invested Moshe Dayan with what amounted to pro-Consular powers in the area. He was, in any case, then riding the crest of a wave of authoritarianism in the national security sphere. Specifically, he had already begun to assume a habit of acting as though he was the CGS's direct institutional superior, assuming a prerogative to intervene in military matters of an operational as well as strategic character. Where the Territories were concerned, he exploited those opportunities to the utmost. With the full and sometimes enthusiastic acquiescence of both of the prime ministers under whom he worked, Eshkol and Meir, Dayan assumed responsibility – often sole responsibility – not just for the formulation and supervision of military policies on the West Bank, but also their implementation (Shifris 2010:292). By any international standards, this was an extraordinary situation. True, recent history provides several examples of other senior agents of occupying powers who have likewise functioned in a dual capacity, as both supreme military commander and ultimate civil authority (Stirk 2009:72). None of the individuals concerned, however, has at the same time also been a powerful minister in the metropolitan cabinet, and thus capable of exerting an influence over the formulation of overall policy that was always massive, and occasionally pivotal.

Although there was nothing covert about the status that Dayan thus attained, its impact on democratic control over national security decision-making and implementation in Israel was nevertheless deleterious. One obvious casualty was the concept of cabinet responsibility. Admittedly, ministers did seek to influence policy in the area, especially with regard to the pace and scope of Jewish settlement activity. This was a subject that generated considerable public interest and was also hotly debated in the cabinet as early as September 1967, when Eshkol (in an unusually unilateral mood) sanctioned without any formal ministerial discussion the re-settlement of Kfar Etzion, a *kibbutz* located south of Jerusalem that had been overrun by Jordanian forces in May 1948 and left desolate until re-occupied by IDF forces in June 1967 (Pedahtzur 1996:191–2; Gorenberg 2006:107–19). But, even on settlements the minister of defense's views carried disproportionate weight (Gazit 2003:118). A Ministerial Committee on Settlements, chaired by Galilee, was not established until January 1970 (Shifris 2010:284). Thereafter, too, there seemed no need to question Dayan's policies. Any suggestion that some form of cabinet supervision might be required was easily forestalled by repeated IDF assurances that military rule in the Territories was benevolent as well as legitimate.

Equally substantial was the impact of this situation on the notion of parliamentary control. Certainly, the Territories and their future disposition were frequently debated in the *knesset*. Indeed, by a sheer statistical count, more hours in the plenum seem to have been devoted to those topics – even during the relatively quiescent first two decades of Israel's occupation – than to any other single item of public interest. But that impression is deceptive. By far the majority of debates on the Territories were concerned with general matters of policy; very few examined specific items of administrative military behavior. Not surprisingly therefore most such discussions ended without any decision having been made or even proposed, and it was very rare indeed for a matter affecting the Territories and their administration to be referred to a relevant parliamentary committee for more in-depth examination. As far as we have been able to ascertain, not until March 1985 (almost two decades after the Territories had come under IDF control) did a member of the *knesset* call attention to the anomaly inherent in the degree of autonomy enjoyed by military commanders in the region, 'who are responsible to no elected body other than the Minister of Defense' and go on to propose that the House debate the propriety of the fact that the area is administered in accordance with security regulations about which 'the *knesset* has nothing to say and is not even aware.' But this suggestion was apparently considered so outrageous that its author (MK Haim Ramon of the *Avodah* party) himself agreed to having it struck off the parliamentary agenda (*Knesset Protocol*, 18 March 1985, Available at: www.knesset.gov.il/Tql//mark01/h0000565.html#TQL).

The inadequacy of international law

Theoretically, the gap in national security oversight created by the absence of both cabinet and parliamentary supervision over IDF actions and policies in the Territories should have been filled by international law, and more specifically by The Hague Regulations of War annexed to The Hague Convention of 1907, and the Fourth Geneva Convention of 1949. Such, however, was not the case. Initial IDF policy documents, which specified the guidelines that Colonel Shlomo Gazit, the first Coordinator of the Military Administration, expected troops to pursue in the Territories – although emphatic in their insistence that IDF personnel rigorously respect the lives and property of local inhabitants – made no reference whatsoever to the requirements in this regard laid down in international law (Gazit 2003:56). Such lacunae cannot be attributed to ignorance. True, and as Hebron's first military governor, Colonel Tzvi Offer frankly admitted, officers appointed to govern segments of the Territories may have had only dim recollections of the courses in international law that they had audited several years earlier (Teveth 1970:55–65). But IDF lawyers, above all Meir Shamgar, were certainly familiar with the subject. Their overall attitude towards the requirements of international law, nevertheless, remained pragmatically selective. Those portions of the corpus that served the purposes of the military administration were accepted and implemented; others were pronounced inapplicable (Am. Cohen 2005).

100   *Development*

The Hague Regulations clearly came under the first category. For one thing, they grant an occupying army certain privileges: to make 'requisition in kind and services' for its needs (Article 52); to take possession of all moveable property which can be used for its needs (Article 53); and to levy 'contributions' for the needs of the army or the administration of the territory (Article 49). Even the limitations that the Hague Regulations set on military rule did not seem onerous. As itemized in Article 43, these amounted to imposing a duty on the occupying power to ensure public order and to respect ('unless absolutely prevented') the sovereignty of the prior sovereign, principally by enforcing whatever laws were previously in effect in the regions under its control (Schwarzenberger 1968:193; Dinstein 1983:218; Benvenisti 1993a:5–6). Those were requirements which the IDF welcomed with open arms. In fact, they coincided almost exactly with Dayan's policy guidelines, which were to promote stability on the West Bank by keeping military interference in the lives of the local inhabitants to a minimum and to resort to force only in order to suppress active resistance to Israeli rule. Quite independently of the Hague Regulations, he announced that the IDF would not replace existing Jordanian laws on the West Bank, provided they did not contradict Israel's security needs (Dayan 1968:138; Bavly 2002:45–8). If those laws denied Palestinians civil and political rights, as was indeed the case, then so much the better.

Adherence to the Fourth Geneva Convention, on the other hand, presented a far greater challenge. Unlike the Hague Regulations, the Geneva Convention focuses not on the residual privileges of the prior sovereign in occupied territories but on the rights of their civilian inhabitants to legal protection as individuals (Benvenisti 1993a:99–101) Hence, it can be interpreted as imposing far more curbs on military action, especially since it seems to outlaw – or at least make hard to justify – several of the actions that at a very early stage became hallmarks of IDF control, in the Gaza Strip as well as on the West Bank (Maimon 1993): deportations (Article 49); 'punitive' house demolitions (Articles 33 and 53; see Simon 1994); the arrest and transfer of terrorists into Israel proper for internment (Article 76); and administrative detentions (Article 78).

This lengthy list of possible restrictions on IDF discretion probably explains why military attitudes to the Geneva Convention underwent change. Initially, even before the war in 1967 officially ended, the Military Administration issued an order declaring that

> 'A military tribunal ... shall observe the provisions of the Geneva Convention of August 12, 1949 Relative to the Protection of Civilians in Times of War with respect to legal proceedings, and in the case of conflict between this order and the said Convention, the provisions of the Convention shall prevail'.
>
> (Kretzmer 2002:32)

This order was, however, soon revoked and not until 1982 was the Geneva Convention incorporated into Israeli military law, and even then only through a CGS command, and not through legislation (Sommer 1986). Thereto IDF lawyers instead argued that that since Judea, Samaria and the Gaza Strip were 'administered' rather than 'occupied' the Geneva Convention did not apply to those regions. Shamgar, the originator of the 'administered' formula, emerged as a particularly resourceful font of legal casuistry. It was he who reportedly suggested that the senior military official in the West Bank be entitled 'Commander' rather than 'Governor', a term that he felt would facilitate IDF claims to be acting under the conditions of 'military necessity' allowed for by the Hague Regulations (Teveth 1970:27). Shamgar also argued that the Fourth Geneva Convention is a conventional international agreement, hence inapplicable in domestic courts without domestic legislation (Shamgar 1982:13). Finally, and as a last resort, he posited interpretations of several specific articles of the Fourth Geneva Convention, which made them compatible with existing military policies. Bizarre, indeed according to Kretzmer barely comprehensible by conventional legal standards (Kretzmer 2002:187), those exercises can only be explained by their context. Shamgar was not creating a new legal regime; he was simply providing retrospective legal cover for the existing preferred policy.

The emergence of the Israel Supreme Court as a national security actor

Potentially, this was a dangerous path to tread. As has been seen, national security policies in Israel already suffered from a lack of adequate domestic oversight, which stemmed from the virtual absence of any substantive cabinet and parliamentary supervision over IDF actions in the Territories. The manner in which the military played fast and loose with the Geneva Conventions threatened to compound that situation by reducing to a bare minimum the intrusion of international law too. Under those circumstances, there existed a good chance that the IDF, acting under the auspices of the ministry of defense and its domineering minister, would come to constitute a law unto itself.

Credit for preventing that outcome rests primarily with the ISC, which during the course of the period covered by this chapter gradually assumed the role of national security overseer vacated by other civilian agencies of Government. As was so often the case with respect to the Territories, this process too was unplanned, and indeed unexpected.

In part, the intrusion of the ISC occasions surprise because it contradicted the prevailing reluctance of courts in the Western world to hand down decisions related to matters of national security and to interfere with military conduct (Benvenisti 1993b) – a tendency that, as noted in our previous chapter, had been especially pronounced in Israel prior to 1967.

But to this must be added, secondly, the ease with which the ISC could in this case have found several formal justifications for its non-intervention. One possibility, for instance, was to claim lack of jurisdiction over IDF activity in the Territories, on the grounds that, strictly speaking, those regions lay beyond the arc of Israeli sovereignty. Another option was to argue that the Territories were in any case governed not by Israeli laws specifically legislated for that purposed, but by international conventions – which Israel, as an 'administering' rather than 'occupying' power had voluntarily undertaken to implement. As Kretzmer has shown, this latter argument could have been supplemented by reference to earlier jurisprudence of the ISC, which had rejected the applicability of international conventions in domestic Israeli law, and allowed courts to refer only to customary international law (Kretzmer 2002:32).[6]

Instead of exploring any of these opportunities for adopting a self-denying posture, the ISC as from 1969 began to review petitions submitted against IDF actions by Arab residents of the Territories. What is more, and no less surprisingly, it did so without fully explaining either the basis for its authority to pass judgment on military actions taken in areas under IDF 'administration' or how its behavior dovetailed with the overall structure of Israel's national security law. Only in the 'Rafah Approach' case of 1973 (*Abu Chilu* v. *The Government of Israel*) did the ISC come anywhere near to reflecting on such issues – and even then briefly (the entire text takes up less than 14 pages) and in some respects implicitly.

This case originated in a petition submitted by Bedouin tribes against the IDF regional commander in the Sinai, who had ordered their eviction from an area known as the Rafah approach, on the grounds that their lands were required for security purposes. In the course of their judgment, members of the ISC analyzed four questions. First, wherein lays the source of the court's jurisdiction over actions undertaken by the IDF in the Territories. (Justice Landau's response was that because the soldiers are agents of the state of Israel they 'carry with them' the authority of the ISC to review their actions). Second, was the international law of occupation applicable to the Territories? (The State did not contest the argument that such was indeed the case). Third, what is the precise legal status of orders issued by the military commander? (Opinions on this question were divided. Justice Witkon argued that since in international law the military commander constitutes the legislative as well as the executive branch in occupied territories, his orders possess the force of statute. Precisely for that reason, however, they could not be reviewed by the ISC, which in those years did not have the authority to review legislation. But the majority opinion, articulated by Justice Landau, while agreeing that in the Territories the military commander's orders might indeed possess the force of statute, argued that as far as Israeli courts are concerned they are merely administrative acts and hence subject to ISC review). Finally, the court discussed the standard of review. On this point, too, Justice Witkon was in a minority when contending that the Hague Regulations, which permit the confiscation of private property for security reasons, constituted an international treaty and hence could not be applied by an Israeli court. The majority of judges invalidated Witkon's opinion, on the grounds that the State itself agreed to the petition being reviewed in accordance with the Hague Regulations. Eventually, Witkon withdrew his objections and the ISC unanimously rejected the appeal, declaring the confiscation order to have been based on bona fide military needs.

As thus handed down, the 'Rafah Approach' decision is disappointing and yet also indicative of future trends in ISC jurisprudence with respect to the Territories. It is disappointing because it provides only a cursory analysis of the pivotal issues raised by the occupation (Which international law applies in the Territories? What exactly is the legal status of the military commander? To how much deference is he entitled? Is it appropriate that the ISC review his actions?). At the same time, however, the decision is nevertheless informative, since it demonstrates how the ISC established a foothold in reviewing IDF actions in the Territories. In particular, it shows the collusion of the government in that process. Lawyers representing the State explicitly declined to table any of the arguments that might have been adduced in order to bar the court from adjudicating the 'Rafah Approach' petition. On the contrary, they declared their interest in judicial review of military decisions.

Scholarly opinion generally attributes the State's stand to a desire on the part of the executive to invest IDF control over the Territories with an aura of legitimacy (Shamir 1990; Kretzmer 2002:190). In this reading, the Government had much to gain by encouraging the ISC to hear Palestinian petitions (a process that showed how 'benign' IDF rule was) and very little to lose. After all, and as the 'Rafah Approach' case amply demonstrated, the ISC almost always approved the policies adopted by the IDF, even when they clearly flouted international law[7] – and was to continue to do so until the 1990s. Be that as it may, it is nevertheless possible, and necessary, to distinguish between the cynical nature of the Government's motives in encouraging the ISC to hear Palestinian petitions and the unplanned consequences of that process. Even the most hesitant of judicial interventions possessed the power to signal that the IDF could not completely ignore Israeli law and that its commanders had therefore to take care in order to avoid taking decisions that might be considered arbitrary and capricious. True, some scholars argued that by applying to the Territories the concepts of basic human rights applicable in Israel, the ISC was in fact abetting their incorporation into Israel and thereby violating international law (Rubinstein 1988). On the other hand, however, court action also possessed the potential to moderate at least some of the damage that that might otherwise have been caused to Israeli democracy by the maintenance of a two-standard judicial regime. Moreover, judicial review of military actions in the Territories could ultimately pave the way for ISC involvement in every other area of concern to national security too.

Which of these outcomes would materialize depended as much on developments in the executive branch of Israel's governmental system as on tides of judicial opinion. Formally, of course, Israel's national security constitution still vested control over policy formulation and implementation firmly in the Government's hands. If anything, indeed, that control had been buttressed in the post-Ben-Gurion period by the enactment of Basic Law: The Government and Basic Law: The Military, both of which proclaimed the same message: national security was a matter of collective cabinet responsibility. Reality, however, had long been somewhat different. Decision-making had begun to experience accelerating liquefaction almost from the day that Ben-Gurion relinquished office. By the mid-1970s, that process had reached chronic proportions. In this respect, the resignations in 1974 of both Meir and Dayan exerted an especially disruptive effect, since it removed from the political scene the two persons who over the previous five years had personified executive authority.

Notwithstanding his own record of achievement as both CGS and ambassador in Washington, DC, Yitzchak Rabin, who succeeded Meir as Prime Minister in June 1974, possessed nothing of her political stature. Indeed, by bowing to pressure to compete for the post with Shimon Peres, whom he narrowly defeated in a vote taken by the Labor Party executive, Rabin accepted a poisoned chalice. Had Rabin limited his ambitions, at least temporarily, to becoming Minister of Defense he might perhaps at least have been able both to enjoy the benefits conferred by the massive expansion of the IDF's budget after 1973 and, at the same time, to prevent the IDF from becoming a nexus of almost independent power. In the event, however, he forfeited both advantages and gained very little in return. His unhappy premiership, quite apart from being punctuated by a series of financial scandals, was from his first day in office also undermined by Peres, now minister of defense, who during three bitter years of rivalry made no secret at all of his intention to supplant Rabin. Significantly, the Territories constituted one of the principal battlefields over which they fought. In the public mind (the true picture was far more nuanced [Shifris, 2010:310–18]), Rabin sought to limit Jewish settlement activity in the Territories whilst Peres was prepared to countenance its expansion.

It is tempting to regard the Rabin–Peres rivalry as inconclusive. After all, although it long left a very bitter taste, neither side emerged victorious. Rabin, some months after declaring his intention to call for new elections, was forced to take extended leave from the premiership in April 1977, when his wife was discovered to have violated Israeli currency regulations. Peres, who as a result became leader of the Labor Party, lost the May election to Menachem Begin's *Likud* party. In fact, however, the damage was deeper. The episode undermined even further the principle of executive authority and unity, which had already been eroded. In the process, it also widened the opportunities for judicial intervention, as was evident when the attorney general, Aharon Barak, threatened to appeal to the ISC were the Government to decide that the Rabin family could put an end to the currency case by simply paying a fine.

Our next chapter will examine how much this experience affected relationships between the political and judicial forces in the Israeli national security establishment and the repercussions on the four dimensions of the national security framework as a whole.

5 Realignment, 1977–1995

Between 1977 and 1995 the national security framework established by Ben-Gurion, already weakened by the course and consequences of the 1967 and 1973 wars, fell almost entirely into disarray.

The first cause for that development, and in many ways the easiest to chart, is the destabilization of the political arena. Israel's era of single-party dominance terminated in 1977, when *Likud* replaced Labor as the largest party in the *knesset* and formed a coalition government led by Menachem Begin, the one-time commander of the right-wing *Etzel* underground militia, who for many years Ben-Gurion had deliberately ostracized. *Likud* went on to retain office, albeit with a reduced majority, after the next round of elections, held in July 1981. But its own supremacy was short-lived. It had to share power with Labor in a national unity government after the elections of 1984 and 1988, and was forced into opposition when Rabin, now a much more mature leader of the Labor party, was elected prime minister in 1992. Since each change of guard implied a change of policy, Israel's national security framework, in keeping with all other spheres of public life, had to accommodate itself to a far higher degree of turbulence than had previously been considered possible.

Behind the political see-saw lay a deeper socio-economic transformation. Successive general election results both reflected and stimulated shifts in power-relationships in Israeli society. Principally this was because they fueled a series of massive economic reforms. The first two *Likud* governments, especially, embarked on programs of liberalization that fatally and deliberately undermined both the *histadrut* (labor federation) and the *kibbutz* (collective settlement), traditionally revered as the twin totems of the Labor party's contribution to a just Socialist society. The new mantras of private enterprise and reduced government expenditures changed employment patterns and structures throughout Israel's economy, exerting a snakes and ladders influence on social standings that was exacerbated by parallel alterations in perceptions of collective identity. In effect, the 1977 elections heralded the demise of the hegemony of the old elites, principally comprised of male, bourgeois, secular Jews of Ashkenazi origin, members of which had dominated the country's politics, cultural life, industry and military ever since the era of the *Yishuv*. Increasingly, other ethnic, religious and (albeit more hesitantly) gender interests began to find voice, thereby bringing into the open a degree of heterogeneity that had thereto been either suppressed or latent.

Large-scale immigration added new elements to an already complex mosaic. Between 1987 and 1997 over a million newcomers arrived in Israel from the countries of the former Soviet Union (FSU). More dramatically, another 100,000 were airlifted by the Israel air force from the marchlands of Ethiopia and the Sudan. In many respects, the assets were enormous. At a stroke, Israel's non-Arab population increased by 20 percent. So too did its pool of military manpower (by 1997 one in every 12 new IDF recruits had been born and brought up abroad) and its work force, which in the case of FSU immigrants was often highly skilled. The other side of the coin was that massive immigration added new layers to what was already becoming a progressively atomized society, which was increasingly shedding its earlier conformity to centripetal norms. FSU immigrants, especially, resisted the 'melting pot' thesis that had been asserted by Ben-Gurion. Many refused to embark on the Jewish conversion course demanded by the Israeli rabbinate; several thousand proclaimed themselves to be Christians (As. Cohen 2007:157–72). All insisted on retaining their own cultural identity, principally by subscribing to Russian-language newspapers, theaters and clubs. No wonder that by the time the new millennium dawned, 'the image of a single, unified Israeli society' had evaporated and been replaced by 'a new system of competing cultures and countercultures' (Kimmerling 2001:15; Shafir and Peled 2002:213–59).

The new atmosphere made it difficult to sustain societal consensus in any area of public policy. Where national security issues were concerned matters were further complicated by developments taking place in the Territories. Here too, the 1977 elections marked a turning point, since they brought into office a government avowedly committed to amalgamating those regions into Israel as widely and as speedily as was politically possible. Post-1967 Labor governments had permitted Jewish settlements to be established in the central West Bank intermittently, and even then only after considerable cabinet in-fighting, especially in the period 1974–1977 (Gorenberg 2006:280–341). Hence, of the 90 settlements established over the Green Line between 1967 and 1977, only a handful were located in the central West Bank, always the most contentious of the newly-conquered lands. Most were sited either on the Golan, in the Jordan Valley or in the vicinity of Gaza. Once the *Likud* came to power in 1977, ratios changed. Settlement expansion, especially in the West Bank ('Judea and Samaria' in politically correct Israeli parlance), became official policy. Hence, over the next decade and a half, the government expropriated vast tracts of the countryside, much of which it declared to be 'state land', the use of which was subject to its discretion (Gordon 2008).

As had been the case within the Green Line immediately after the 1948 war, property transfer became the midwife to a demographic revolution. Whereas barely 2,000 Jews had inhabited the West Bank in 1977, their number rose to almost 23,000 in 1983, to over 69,000 in 1989 and to about 133,000 in 1995, by which time they were distributed on some 120 individual sites in an area that stretched from Hebron in the south to Jenin in the north (*Foundation for Middle East Peace* 2009). Moreover, although many of the Jewish settlements remained small, a few blossomed into major dormitory towns, which were linked to Israel by a network of newly constructed highways. The process of amalgamation was further accelerated by the adaptation of the tax regime operative in the Territories to the Israeli system and by the increasing integration of the economies of the two areas (Benvenisti 1989).

From an administrative and legal point of view, however, the situation remained anomalous. Since not even the most right-wing Israeli governments of the period ever annexed the West Bank, jurisdiction in the area remained under the aegis of the IDF and/or the ministry of defense, and not the *knesset*. Where most practical matters were concerned, even the degree of control exercised by the government was circumscribed. Studies of various topics – the administration of justice, zoning and planning regulations, the respect for human rights – consistently reveal the Territories to have constituted a state within a state, inhabited by two very distinct classes of residents.[1] One consisted of Jewish Israeli settlers, who enjoyed all the benefits afforded to citizens of a relatively liberal democracy obviously committed to the protection of basic freedoms. But the other, and much larger, population segment consisted of non-Jewish Palestinians who, although perhaps benefiting economically from the occupation, nevertheless were denied access to most human rights and resided in what became 'a legal no-man's land.' (Zertal and Eldar 2007:371–4) As we shall see, ultimately the ISC did address the discriminatory situation thus created. The process, however, proved to be protracted and awkward. Whilst under way, it was just as likely to aggravate the ambiguities inherent in Israel's national security framework as to solve them.

Intruding on all of the shifts in Israel's political and societal environments were multiple changes simultaneously taking place in the country's strategic landscape. The latter exerted an especially important influence on the national security framework, not least because they assumed such kaleidoscopic form. On the one hand, between 1977 and 1993 Israel made the most significant advances yet towards attaining regional acceptability, negotiating one peace treaty with Egypt in 1979, another with Lebanon (which was never ratified) in 1983, a third with Jordan in 1994, and signing agreements with the Palestine Authority in 1993, 1994 and 1996. At the same time, however, the IDF resorted to a widening spectrum of military operations. Quite apart from carrying out two ground invasions of Lebanon (operations 'Litani' in 1978 and the much more extensive 'Peace for the Galilee' in 1982, later renamed 'the first Lebanon war'), Israeli forces also launched two spectacularly successful air strikes, against the Iraq nuclear reactor under construction at Osiraq in 1981 and against Syrian air defenses in 1982. But as from the mid-1980s conventional missions of that sort were superseded by a more novel repertoire of force commitments. One prominent item on the IDF's new military agenda was the defense of the 'security zone' that, with the help of a local Christian proxy force, the South Lebanese Army, Israel carved out of southern Lebanon in 1985. Another was the containment of the Palestinian *intifada* (uprising) that erupted in December 1987 and took the form of 'low-intensity' riots, terrorist attacks and suicide bombings, which persisted even after the signing of the Israeli–Palestinian Oslo accords in 1993. Thirdly, there was the new military burden imposed by the need to develop and maintain a defensive capability against long-range rocket attacks on Israel's rear, such as were carried out by Iraqi 'Scud' missiles in 1991 and that Iran threatened to repeat, if possible with nuclear warheads, thereafter.

Quite apart from necessitating a new order of battle and force structure, Israel's changing operational landscape also mandated a re-assessment of strategic concepts that had thereto been considered axiomatic but that were now clearly losing their validity. Principal amongst these was the notion of battlefield 'decision' (Kover 2009:35–49). Future IDF campaigns could not be relied upon to follow the precedents set in 1967 and 1973. The latter had been short and sharp 'high-intensity' encounters, characterized by the rapid maneuver of large air and armored formations in the Sinai desert and Golan plateau, both regions largely devoid of civilians. 'Fourth-generation warfare', as it was soon dubbed, promised to be something entirely different. For one thing, it would probably take the form of protracted attritional struggles (as the Iran–Iraq 'war of the cities' in 1987 showed, this was also true of inter-state ballistic exchanges). No less important, civilians, far from being peripheral to the battlefield, were likely to be its main protagonists – not just as victims of attack but also as instruments of destruction. Under those circumstances, whether or not existing legal (and moral) tools and taxonomies could be adapted to the new conditions was bound to become a crucial question.

Consequences

Combined, the political, societal and strategic processes outlined above clearly necessitated fundamental revisions in Israel's national security legal framework. In each of its four dimensions, national security law confronted situations that mandated a re-clarification of both principles and their methods of application. With the agenda of national security issues containing so many items that were new, the old rules of analysis became increasingly difficult to sustain. Immobilism was not an option. Simply to extend the status quo was to run the risk of entrenching obscurity in a realm that cried out for clarity.

Most obviously was that so with respect to the *spatial* dimension. In the strict legal sense, it is worth repeating, the Territories conquered in 1967 remained distinct from Israel. In many political essentials, however, from 1977 onwards the boundaries between the two entities became increasingly permeable. One reason, already noted, was the boost given by *Likud* governments to the expansion of the settlement enterprise. A second was the incremental dependence of the economies of the West Bank and Gaza Strip on the Israeli market. Yet a third was the apparent irrelevance of the conventional geographical demarcations to new security concerns. Iraqi 'Scud' attacks in 1991 – one of the most traumatic events in Israel's military history during this period – were not directed exclusively at military installations. In fact, of the 39 Iraqi missiles known to have reached Israeli territory, the vast majority were aimed at urban centers. 'Low-intensity warfare' likewise fudged old borders. The *intifada*, although ostensibly directed against Israeli rule in the Territories, did not stop at the Green Line. Terrorist activities spilled over into Israel proper. Fifty of the 150 fatalities sustained by Israel's security forces between 1987 and 1993 were caused by attacks perpetrated within Israel proper, as were 177 of the 271 civilian deaths.

Equally apparent, secondly, was the ambiguity that infected the *temporal* dimension of the national security legal framework, making it difficult to determine when Israel was – and was not – in a 'state of war'. Officially, in all the years covered by this chapter the only time that Israel was declared to be in a state of 'extraordinary' emergency was during the week that commenced on the night of 16/17 January 1991, when US aircraft began the massive assault on Iraqi targets that presaged operation 'Desert Storm'. Immediately, Israel national radio broadcast an announcement instructing all citizens to break open the gas-mask kits with which they had been issued. But although fighting continued in Iraq until 28 February, with Scud missiles entering Israel air space until almost the last day, as from 22 January Israel had reverted to a 'routine emergency' regime (Ben-Meir 1992:333). Even the invasion of Lebanon in June 1982, the only occasion after 1973 when the IDF deployed large armored formations against the forces of a neighboring state (Syria), was originally termed an 'operation' rather than a 'war, albeit for political reasons rather than in response to any legal considerations. On the other hand, however, the threat of terrorist attacks loomed over Israeli society for much of the period – as much after the conclusion of the 1993 Oslo accords as prior to them. Moreover, hardly a day passed in this period when Israeli soldiers were not involved in violent action of some kind, both in southern Lebanon and the Territories, against at least one non-state actor, and often two or three simultaneously.

Definitions of the *functional* attributes of Israel's national security law were even more profoundly affected by the new ambience. Indeed, changes in the societal and cultural climate undermined the relevance of traditional classifications and subjected even the very term 'national security' to multiple processes of reinterpretation. Two conflicting conceptions became especially influential. One was expressed by what might broadly be defined as the religious right of the Jewish political spectrum, elements of which were in the years 1974–1975 caught up in a wave of almost apocalyptic fervor induced by the seemingly miraculous outcome of the Yom Kippur War. Only Divine intervention could possibly explain how the IDF, having entered into combat under the most unfavorable of conditions, had after just three weeks of fighting reached almost within gunshot of Damascus and Cairo. Against that background, spokesmen for the 'national religious' segment of Israeli society increasingly endowed land, the most tangible of national security assets, with transcendental meaning. In the process, they also dragooned religious faith into the service of territorial expansion, not least when presenting affidavits to the Supreme Court. Thus, during the course of *Dawikat* v. *The Government of Israel* (1979), the Court was informed (p. 11) that:

> The act of settling the land by the people of Israel is the real act of security, the most efficient and genuine. But the settlement itself does not stem from security considerations ... but out of a sense of vocation. This is why the [conventional] security argument, serious though it may be, has no meaning for us.

By contrast, citizens broadly identified with the secular left increasingly subscribed to liberal attitudes found in Western societies as a whole. Accordingly, they subordinated easily quantifiable military resources, the salience of which had once been considered axiomatic to any definition of national security, to what were later to be termed 'soft-power' attributes, prominent amongst which were a just society and the protection of human rights, freedom of speech and the grant of civic equality to Palestinians as well as Jewish Israelis.

Quite apart from being conducted with great intensity, the debate between these two camps and their various offshoots was also significant for taking place in a blaze of publicity. National security matters, once considered best enveloped in a thick cloak of secrecy, increasingly became topics of general discussion, leading to what Barzilai terms a 'partial democratization' of the national security decision-making process (Barzilai 1996:102–22). Only in part did the expansion of discourse take the form of formal and government-initiated *knesset* debates at moments of high drama, such as those which followed the announcement that Israeli and Egyptian negotiators had reached agreement at Camp David in 1979 or the declaration that the IDF had been ordered to embark on operation 'Peace for the Galilee' in 1982. More persistent, more indicative and certainly more critical was the volume of media coverage. By the 1980s, gone were the days when correspondents and reporters practiced 'deferential journalism', which involved their almost total subservience to dictates imposed by IDF spokesmen, the military censor and, perhaps most effective of all, their own sense of being drafted into the service of the national collective. In the competitive atmosphere fostered by the deregulation and increasing diversification of Israel's media,[2] media—military collusion gave way to confrontation. Critical newspaper coverage of the invasion of Lebanon in 1982 showed that even in wartime Israeli journalists could no longer all be relied upon to rally around the flag and to observe the rules of subservient discretion that had once been considered correct form. In more quiescent periods, norms had certainly changed. By 1995 it was taken for granted that 'The confrontation between the military and the media is as natural as the difference between day and night, between a thief and a policeman. It is inevitable ... it lies at the very foundations of a democratic state' (Emmanuel Rozen, a leading military correspondent, cited in Peri 2000:193).

It is characteristic of the climate of the period that the media did not restrict critical scrutiny of national security affairs to matters of high policy and grand strategy. Insider information about cabinet discussions concerning war and peace still remained good copy. So too did differences of opinion at senior levels of the IDF with respect to operational procedures Increasingly, however, the focus of media attention shifted to grayer areas, which had once been entirely off-limits but that were now generating increasing public interest: IDF fatalities as a result of training accidents; instances of petty and not so petty corruption in the military and the security services; maltreatment of conscripts; and sexual harassment of women soldiers. Advanced communications technologies made it almost impossible to monitor the flow of information on these and other matters and altogether cast doubts on the utility of the old censorship regime. They also ensured that public pressure would require Israel's framework of national security law to address a far wider span of essentially domestic topics than had once been considered necessary. Ultimately, the spectrum would range from inequalities in conscription policies to gender discrimination in service assignments and from conditions in boot camp to the epitaphs in military cemeteries (S. Cohen 2008:77–9).

The first institution to feel the effects of the new atmosphere was the *va'adat ha-orchim* (Editors' Council) – the self-regulating body that had ever since the Mandate period governed relations between the press barons and senior members of government (above pp. 68–9). The incipient irrelevance of the Council was demonstrated as early as 1983, when the *Hadashot* newspaper, whose editor was not a member of the body, violated the military censor's orders and published photographs which proved that two captive terrorists who were later pronounced dead had been alive when taken into custody by agents of the *shabak* (General Security Services). A second step was taken five years later when, contrary to the charter of the Editors' Council, Shemuel Schnitzer, the editor of the *Ha'ir* newspaper, petitioned the Supreme Court against the military's censor's disqualification of large sections of an article that revealed the identity of the director of the *Mosad*. The ISC's decision in Schnitzer's favor (*Schnitzer v. Chief Military Censor*, 1989), prompted successive ministers of defense to modify the Council's original charter, and in May 1996 the previous ban on appeals to the Supreme Court by member editors was finally lifted. But by then, the Council had in any case become virtually irrelevant. Many editors had discovered that they could easily avoid censorship by publishing information that had already appeared abroad (and which their own correspondents had sometimes planted). Others saw no reason to retain their membership. Once the *Haaretz* newspaper, one of Israel's most prestigious dailies, withdrew from the Council in 1995, its demise was virtually assured (Negbi 2005).

Media coverage, in addition to ensuring the wider dissemination of national security information, also provided a medium for the expression of differences of opinion. Given the demise of the security consensus consequent upon the end of single-party dominance, this was a particularly important development, whose effects became apparent every time a new policy program was set in motion (Arian 1995). Significantly, the environment thus created did not deter governments from taking national security initiatives. On the contrary and as already noted, this period witnessed more leaps in the dark – in the direction of both peace and war – than had ever before been attempted in a similar time span. Each innovation, however, was accompanied by a chorus of conflicting opinions, many of which were expressed by recently created non-government and non-party organizations. Operating against an overall background of increased public protest in Israeli society (Lehman-Wilzig 1992), these groups were distinguished by the fact that they were expressly established in order to influence national security policy one way or another.

The earliest prototypes were individual enterprises. An outstanding example is provided by the demonstrations staged immediately after the 1973 war by reservists demanding judicial enquiries into the deficiencies that had caused the IDF to fall victim to strategic surprise and calling for the resignation of the government. (As prime minister Meir later admitted, she was especially affected by the post-war protests mounted outside her office windows by Mottie Ashkenazi, who had commanded the only IDF outpost on the Suez Canal that was not overrun by the Egyptians in October 1973, Meir 1975:378). Soon thereafter, however, this new brand of actors on Israel's national security stage became more institutionalized, with three organizations being especially prominent.

In chronological order, the first was *Gush Emunim* ('Bloc of Faithful'), a movement formed in February 1974 by several dozen young graduates of national religious educational institutions. Their core comprised disciples of Rabbi Zvi Yehudah Kook, a religious authority who declared that any action on the part of a government that led to the relinquishment of Jewish control over any portion of the Land of Israel was sinful, and had to be resisted (Aran 1991:265–344). True to that directive, members of the *Gush* sought to derail the possibility of an Israeli withdrawal from all or part of the Golan and the West Bank (both of which options were aired during the period of Henry Kissinger's 'shuttle diplomacy' in 1974 and 1975), most blatantly by establishing settlements in those regions without awaiting prior sanction from any official authority. This tactic was employed to especial effect in November 1975, when a well-organized and highly publicized effort to establish a settlement at Sebastia, near Nablus, initially in the teeth of government opposition, ended in an almost total victory for *Gush Emunim*, moderated only slightly by prime minister Rabin's justifiably shame-faced announcement that he and the minister of defense, Shimon Peres, had reached a 'compromise' with the settlers (Gorenberg 2006:327–44).

Once the *Likud* came to power, no such contortions were required. With settlement expansion now official Israeli policy, *Gush Emunim* enjoyed a period of growth that was lubricated by generous government funding. Its settlement activities expanded, and it formed an administrative arm, 'The Council of Settlements in Judea, Samaria, and the Gaza Strip'. Success, however, came at a price. For one thing, *Gush Emunim* underwent a Weberian process of institutionalization, which took some of the shine off its pioneering fervor. More ominously, its millenarianism also spawned a Jewish vigilante organization, whose members committed several outrages against Palestinians on the West Bank in the early 1980s (Sprinzak 2000:96–128). With the movement thus tainted by association with criminality, *Gush Emunim* withered and eventually disintegrated.

Nevertheless, and as noted above, the settlement enterprise continued to thrive. Part of that success must be attributed to the continued enthusiasm for the expansion of the Jewish presence in Judea and Samaria evinced by the thousands of Israeli citizens who sought to live there (many of them religiously orthodox new immigrants from the United States; Klein 1991). Zertal and Eldar argue, however, that the settlement drive could never have flourished without the 'complicity' of the local Israeli military authorities as well as their political masters (Zertal and Eldar 2007:277–91). During the decade 1975–1985, they demonstrate, relationships between settlers, soldiers and senior politicians became steadily more collusive. The military provided essential help in establishing and protecting the infrastructure that the settlers required. Political backing was supplied by members of the right-wing *Tehiyah* political party, expressly founded in 1979 in order to further settlement interests, whose members formed part of the governing coalition from 1981–1984 and 1990–1992. True, this triangular honeymoon soon ended. Rabin's electoral victory in 1992 triggered a change in policy. Moreover, as from the mid-1990s, the rapport between local IDF commanders and the settlers came under increasing strain, with verbal clashes between them becoming frequent and physical confrontations not unusual (Zertal and Adler 2007:295–331). By then, however, the settlement enterprise was considered even by its critics (Jewish as well as non-Jewish) to have become, as *Gush Emunim* had always intended it to become, an entrenched feature of Israel's national security landscape.

Shalom Akhshav ('Peace Now') was in many respects the mirror-image of *Gush Emunim* (Peleg 2000; Feige 2003). Established in 1978, it too owed its origin to a determination on the part of a group of young activists to change the direction of Israel's security policy, initially by resort to extraparliamentary means. Their original target was what they considered to be Begin's foot-dragging approach to peace negotiations with Egypt in 1978. With time, however, *Shalom Akhshav* expanded its horizons. A landmark stage in that process occurred immediately after publication of the details of the massacre of Palestinians in the Sabra and Shatilla refugee camps situated in the southern suburbs of Beirut, perpetrated on 16 and 17 September 1982 by Christian Falange militiamen. Since Israeli forces had only days before entered the Lebanese capital (ostensibly in order to preserve law and order in the city) and had for weeks been coordinating their operations with Falange leaders, Ariel Sharon, the minister of defense, and his colleagues inevitably became targets of public outrage, both domestic and foreign. Protesting innocence, Sharon and Begin insisted that no Israeli, soldier or civilian, could be held responsible for an atrocity committed entirely by Lebanese citizens. *Shalom Akhshav*, however, spearheaded demands that the entire episode had to be investigated. Its efforts peaked with the organization of a massive demonstration in Tel-Aviv on 25 September 1982, after which pressure to establish an independent commission of inquiry became irresistible (Friedman 1989:159–68).

Although that success was never repeated, *Shalom Akhshav* went on to campaign for the IDF's withdrawal from Lebanon throughout the following two decades. Since the 1990s, it has focused on opposing Jewish settlement in the West Bank, monitoring and publicizing both the establishment of new settlements and the expansion of those already existing. Despite its avowed left-wing leanings, however, *Shalom Akhshav* persistently distanced itself from calls for conscientious objection to military service in either Lebanon or the West Bank voiced by some of its fellow-travelers, such as the *Yesh Gevul* organization (Dloomy 2005).

A third example of the emergence of a new form of attempted extraparliamentary public influence on national security affairs is *B'tselem* (literally 'In the image', derived from Genesis 1:27), which was established in 1989, two years after the outbreak of the first *intifada*. Initially, *B'tselem*'s activities transferred to the military realm the monitoring and reporting functions performed with respect to the settlements by *Shalom Akhshav*. Indeed, the organization's official English-language title is: 'The Israeli Information Center for Human Rights in the Occupied Territories.'

116 *Development*

Under that guise, it tracked and publicized alleged IDF violations of Palestinian human rights in the Territories, and subsequently those perpetrated by the Palestinian Authority too. By the 1990s, however, *B'tselem* had embarked on an entirely new course of advocacy. Taking advantage of the openness exhibited by the ISC, it began to present petitions that were based on its findings. This was an avenue never explored by either *Gush Emunim* or *Shalom Akhshav*, both of which had restricted their lobbying activities to the more conventional forms of public demonstrations and the fostering of contacts with specific sympathetic members of the *knesset* (MKs). In the long run, the route taken by *B'tselem* probably deserves to be considered the more effective. It was certainly more in harmony with the trend towards 'legalization', which became characteristic of Israel's national security discourse after the mid-1990s (see Chapter 6).

Dissent over foreign and military policies was not restricted to the public at large. It also became a feature of debates on these subjects within the more restricted circle of politicians and officials at the very apex of the decision-making pyramid. The result was a further weakening of the *hierarchical* structure that had previously underpinned the framework of Israel's national security law.

At root, that process reflected the relative instability that now characterized the political system. Since no single party managed to attain after 1977 the degree of dominance over the *knesset* that had previously been exercised by the Labor party in its various guises, coalition governments tended to be far weaker than was once the case, and hence less capable of implementing a unified political program. Even authoritarian prime ministers such as Begin and Rabin never managed to attain the same degree of control over policy-making and implementation as had been enjoyed by Ben-Gurion and Meir in their prime. Under Peres and Yitzchak Shamir, both of whom headed far shakier coalitions (between 1984 and 1990 they rotated the premiership of the National Unity Government, which Peres was instrumental in breaking up in 1990), dissent over national security affairs became even more pronounced. Two consequences followed from that situation. First, it allowed a greater degree of autonomy than had once been the case to individual ministers, especially if they had very definite ideas of their own about how to conduct national security affairs. Ariel Sharon exploited this opportunity to the utmost, both as minister of agriculture in Begin's first government (when he did much to assist the foundation of new settlements in the Territories) and as minister of defense in Begin's second government (when he was responsible for expanding the scope of the 1982 invasion of Lebanon). So too, over an even longer period, did Shimon Peres, who as minister of transport (1970–1974) and as minister of defense (1974–1977) played a critical role in providing government authorization, sometimes retrospectively, for some of the early settlements founded by *Gush Emunim* and who as foreign minister (1986–1988) entered into extensive negotiations over the future of the

West Bank with King Hussein of Jordan. Second, and especially during years of coalition stalemate (1984–1990), dissent within the cabinet also gave more scope for maneuver and action in this area to other groupings and institutions. Some were official branches of government, such as the IDF and the Supreme Court. Others, however, consisted of NGOs and (as was the case in the contacts that resulted in the 1993 Oslo agreement) even private individuals.

What also changed were the topics concerning which intra-executive dissent erupted. In previous eras differences of opinion within the ruling circle had usually concerned the initiation of military activities. Thus Sharett and Ben-Gurion had clashed over 'reprisal raids' during the 1950s and Eshkol experienced a tense relationship with senior echelons in the IDF during the 'waiting period' that preceded the Six Days War. After 1977, however, civil–military friction was just as likely to be generated by initiatives designed to establish peaceful relations between Israel and her neighbors. An early example of the latter phenomenon is provided by the reaction of Major-General Mordechai Gur (CGS 1974–1978) to the news, announced in November 1977, that President Sadat of Egypt had accepted Begin's invitation to come to Israel. Gur was totally ignorant of the fact that the conditions for Sadat's visit had been the subject of secret and intense negotiations conducted over several weeks between Hassan Tuhami (Egypt's deputy prime minister) and Moshe Dayan (who had accomplished a remarkable political comeback when appointed as Begin's foreign minister in 1977). Instead, and relying entirely on assessments provided by the IDF's Intelligence Branch, Gur feared that Sadat's announcement was just a smoke-screen, behind which the Egyptians were preparing another military attack. What is more, the CGS publicly voiced his suspicions during the course of a newspaper interview. According to Ben-Meir (Ben-Meir 1995:117), Ezer Weizman, who Begin had appointed minister of defense in 1977, wanted to punish Gur for his indiscretion by dismissing him on the spot. As matters turned out, Weizman's incarceration in hospital following a car accident prevented him from taking this unprecedented step. Tension, however, remained.

With the single exception of the 1994 negotiations with Jordan, every attempt to improve relations between Israel and her neighbors in this period generated similar discord, invariably within the cabinet. Dayan recalled that at Camp David, for instance, Begin was constantly aware of the misgivings that his territorial concessions to Sadat provoked amongst ministers back in Jerusalem, which he worked hard to allay (Dayan 1981:193–7). Further ministerial rifts broke out during the course of the negotiations subsequently conducted with the Egyptians over Palestinian autonomy. This time, however, the charge was that Yosef Burg, the minister of the interior whom Begin had appointed chair of the Israeli team, was being too intransigent – an attitude that provoked the resignation of Ezer Weizman from the ministry of defense in May 1980. More remarkable still were the domestic constraints that impinged on the Israeli–Jordanian negotiations of 1987. These, indeed, collapsed under the weight of Israel's top-heavy and inappropriately named 'Government of National Unity' when in April 1987 prime minister Shamir bluntly vetoed the agreement that Peres, his foreign minister – and arch political rival – had earlier that month reached with King Hussein in London (Zak 1996:270–1). The bitter taste left by that experience doubtless encouraged Peres to adopt an entirely different approach in the early 1990s, when informed of the negotiations that some Israeli academics had, at their own initiative, entered into with Palestinian contacts under Norwegian auspices (Gewurz 2000). Once Rabin too had been let into the secret, the two men agreed that the talks should continue on an entirely 'unofficial' and confidential track until as late a stage as possible. Even this ploy did not, however, defuse opposition. Once publicized, the Oslo agreements not only provoked cries of outrage from the *Likud*. Ehud Barak, who earlier in 1993 had been appointed CGS but who, together with all the IDF, had deliberately been kept entirely out of the loop, openly declared the agreements to be 'riddled with holes' (Savir 1998:81–2).

Decisions for hostile activities provoked intra-executive disagreements that were equally extensive. An interesting example is provided by the air attack on Iraq's nuclear facility at Osiraq, a mission that was carried out on 7 June 1981 but that Begin had given orders to plan for some 20 months earlier. In part, the postponement reflected external constraints, such as the need to avoid generating an international crisis during the final stages of the 1980 US presidential election campaign or, after November of that year, before Ronald Reagan had settled into office. Far more influential, however, were the delays caused by high-level domestic dissent, both military and civilian. Some senior IDF officers, including the CO Intelligence Branch, feared that an attack on Iraq might preclude offensive missions against Syrian installations in Lebanon, which they considered to constitute a far greater short-term threat. More bluntly, leading ministers castigated the mission as an exercise in adventurism that was sure to strike a fatal blow at the peace treaty with Egypt. Prominent spokesmen for that view included Yigael Yadin, now the deputy prime minister, as well as Ezer Weizman (prior to his resignation from office in May 1980), and the deputy minister of defense, Mordechai Zipori. Available accounts indicate that the Ministerial Committee on Defense discussed the Osiraq attack on six occasions between May 1980 and May 1981 without ever reaching a unanimous decision (Nakdimon 1993). Begin, however, remained determined to destroy what he considered to be the potential for another Holocaust, an outlook that was shared by Rafael Eitan, who had been appointed CGS in 1978. Two further developments enabled Begin to get his way. One was the opportunity afforded to him by Weizman's resignation to function as his own minister of defense. The other was the assurance Begin received (after much wooing on his part) from Yigael Yadin, to the effect that, although still opposed to the operation, the deputy prime minister would not make it a cause for resignation (Nakdimon 1993:197).

Intense and prolonged though it thus was, intra-executive dissent with respect to Osiraq was moderated by two extenuating circumstances. First, all parties to the debate respected the old rules of confidentiality, most obviously by not leaking to the press reports of differences of policy opinion amongst ministers. Second, in operational terms the mission was so spectacularly successful that even those who after the event still harbored qualms about its wisdom were reluctant to spoil the celebratory atmosphere by complaining that it might have revealed Israel Air Force (IAF) tradecraft (but others were not above whispering that the raid had been a 'gimmick', timed to give Begin an advantage in the upcoming general election [Nakdimon 1993:358–70]). Very different, on both counts, was operation 'Peace in the Galilee', the IDF invasion of Lebanon launched almost exactly a year later. In addition, and perhaps most important of all, whereas in the case of Osiraq Prime Minister Begin throughout remained firmly in control of the decision-making process, by June 1982 his exercise of supreme command had been undermined by Ariel Sharon, who Begin had appointed minister of defense in August 1981, soon after the aura of triumph induced by the Osiraq success had indeed helped him to win the general election of June 1981.

Intent on re-shaping the entire Middle East, Sharon had no sooner settled into the ministry of defense than he issued orders to the IDF to plan for a major offensive in Lebanon, designed to remove both PLO and Syrian influence from the country and to ensure that Israel's Christian Maronite ally, Bashir Gemayal, would become its president (Schiff and Yaari 1986:39–50). By December 1981, by which time the IDF had completed its staff work, Sharon was ready to present his plan (code-named *oranim* ['pines']) to Begin and then to the cabinet as a whole. But whereas Begin was soon persuaded to underwrite the entire scheme, other ministers evinced far more skepticism. At a cabinet meeting called in December 1981 to authorize the implementation of *oranim*, two senior ministers expressed stiff opposition, forcing Begin to withdraw the item from the agenda. Undeterred, Sharon offered Begin the option of 'small-*oranim*', i.e., a more limited IDF incursion into southern Lebanon that would not involve clashes with Syria. In June 1982, both the prime minister and his colleagues were under the impression that what they had authorized was indeed 'small-*oranim*'. Within days of the commencement of the operation, however, ministers were beginning to feel that they had been duped. Israel was at war with Syria, which was precisely the scenario to which they had objected (Naor 1986). Begin too found that Sharon was asking, often *post factum*, for approval of operations that contradicted the guidelines agreed to by the cabinet. Even after Sabra and Shatilla, he felt unable to criticize Sharon publicly. But other colleagues were less forgiving and one, Yitzchak Berman, the energy minister, resigned from the government.

Unlike previous wars, which had generally tended to assuage political controversy, the invasion of Lebanon was proving to be a cause of deep dissension (Barzilai 1996:123–55).

Responses

In theory, the existing framework of Israel's national security law should have been robust enough to accommodate the fundamental transformations thus taking place in the environment in which it operated. That being the case, no formal changes of structure were required. In fact, however, the situation proved to be considerably more ambiguous. In terms of the outer forms of institutional and administrative arrangements, matters did indeed largely remain much as they had always been. Hence, very few modifications were made to the organs responsible for determining national security law and oversight. Where substance was concerned, however, far more fluidity was in evidence. So much was this so that both the legislature and the judiciary responded to evolving circumstances in ways that were different – and sometimes contradictory.

The remainder of the present chapter analyzes those responses, branch by branch, in each case showing how they affected all four dimensions of the national security legal framework. Our discussion begins with a review of the actions taken by the legislature in this period, both with respect to the passage of new laws relevant to national security and in its capacity as an agency charged with oversight of executive conduct. At greater length, we then discuss the increasingly prominent responsibilities assumed in the national security field by the judiciary, both in the guise of national commissions of inquiry and, even more so, by Israel's Supreme Court.

The *knesset*

It will be recalled that prior to the 1970s the *knesset*'s role in national security affairs had been almost entirely marginal. Thereafter, too, the legislature presented no serious challenge to executive control over this realm. However, parliamentary involvement did certainly increase, finding expression in a wide range of activities.

Law-making – although traditionally considered to be the most important of all parliamentary functions – was in the area of national security the least influential. None of the several legislative acts passed by the *knesset* in the period 1977–1995 brought about significant changes in the way national security decisions were either arrived at, implemented, or monitored. Neither did they constitute building blocks in a coherent design aimed at attaining any such transformation. Legislation in this period remained piecemeal and ad hoc, and for the most part was designed to meet the short-term political needs of the government of the day.

Such was certainly the case with respect to those laws that affected the *spatial* dimension of national security. In this area, successive Begin coalitions adopted three items of legislation: Basic Law: Jerusalem (1980); the Golan Heights Law (1981); and The Law for the Compensation of the Sinai Evacuees (1982). In each case, however, the main purpose was declaratory.

- Basic Law: Jerusalem, which proclaimed united Jerusalem to be Israel's eternal capital, added nothing of substance to the far more subtle piece of legislation that had been enacted in June 1967 (see above pp. 94–5). Not until 2001 was an amendment passed which made any change in Jerusalem's status conditional upon the acquiescence of 61 members of the *knesset*.
- The Golan Heights Law, which pronounced the application to the region of 'Israeli law, jurisdiction and administration' likewise served no practical objective. During the course of the debate on the bill, Begin acknowledged that it would neither formally annex the Golan to Israel nor preclude any future government from negotiating the future of the area with Syria. Even at the level of individual citizens, the impact of the 1981 Golan Law was minimal. Jewish settlers in the region were in any case under Israeli jurisdiction – and hence did not require this item of legislation; Druze residents, who refused to accept Israeli identity cards, simply ignored it.
- The Law for the Compensation of Sinai Evacuees (1982) adhered to the same pattern. Its passage affected neither the implementation of the peace treaty with Egypt nor the evacuation of the Sinai settlers. The law was not passed until 31 March 1982, by which time the government had concluded compensation negotiations with the evacuees. The evacuation process, which was completed just three weeks later, was in any case an IDF operation carried out under the jurisdiction of the military governor of the Sinai, who neither requested nor required parliamentary sanction for whatever orders he issued.

Altogether, all three laws seem to have been motivated less by a desire to regulate the spatial dimension of Israel's national security legal framework than by narrow party political considerations. The real purpose of Basic Law: Jerusalem was to pacify Begin's right-wing opponents, who protested against the concessions to which he had agreed during the Camp David negotiations.[3] The Golan Law was also a domestic political maneuver. Although ostensibly a matter of urgent national necessity (the plea used to justify its rushed passage through the legislative process without the usual intermission of 14 days between the first and second readings), it in fact reflected a rather mischievous Begin's wish to sow dissension in the ranks of the Labor Party, whose views on the need to retain the region he knew to be divided. The Law for the Compensation of Sinai Evacuees (1982) was likewise a tactic, in this case a way of signaling that the Jewish settlers of the Yamit region were not being altogether discarded. In sum, in all three instances, legislation was employed as a means of bolstering the power of the executive, and not as a mechanism for effecting substantive change in national security practice.

Revelations of the failings that characterized decision-making process before and during the 1982 Lebanon invasion also prompted Israel's parliament to address the *hierarchical* dimension of the national security framework. It first did so in 1991, when a group of prominent MKs, none of whom was a former career officer, introduced a bi-partisan amendment (number 5) to Basic Law: The Government, which required all governments to set up a national security committee and create a national security staff. Since the proponents explicitly cited a Hebrew-language study recently published by Yehuda Ben-Meir as their source for this suggestion (Ben-Meir 1987), the swift passage of this amendment generated hopes that academe might at long last be influencing national security decision-making. That soon turned out to be an illusion. Without explanation, the requirement for a national security committee/staff was dropped from the consolidated revised version of Basic Law: The Government that was presented to the *knesset* in 1992. It re-surfaced in the 1996 revision, but again disappeared from the 2001 version, when it was sidelined to the Government Law. In practice, Ben-Meir's suggestion would not be acted upon before Israel had again experienced the twin traumas of yet another messy war in the Lebanon and, in its wake, yet another critical commission of inquiry (see Chapter 8).

Equally inconsequential was another revision of Basic Law: The Government, enacted by in 1992, entitled 'Article 51: Declaration of War'. The purpose of this article (re-numbered Article 40 in the 2001 version of the Law, but otherwise unchanged) was to clarify the mechanisms of civilian control over the armed forces. To that end, it laid down three specifications.

a   The State may only begin a war pursuant to a Cabinet decision.
b   Nothing in the provisions of this section will prevent the adoption of military actions necessary for the defense of the State and public security.
c   Notification of a Cabinet decision to begin a war under the provision of subsection (a) will be submitted to the Foreign Affairs and Defense Committee of the *knesset* as soon as possible; the prime minister also will give notice to the *knesset* plenum as soon as possible; notification regarding military actions as stated in subsection (b) will be given to the *knesset's* Foreign Affairs and Defense Committee as soon as possible.

This formulation, and especially subsection (a), leaves no doubt that the armed forces are by law subordinate to civilian control. As far as relations between the executive and the legislature are concerned, however, matters are less clear-cut. Subsection (c) only requires the Foreign Affairs and Defense Committee, and thereafter the full *knesset*, to be notified – at an unspecified date – of the cabinet's decision to go to war or take other military action. Cabinets are under no obligation to consult with the *knesset*, still less to obtain its sanction for the initiation of hostilities. In fact, they can bypass the full plenum entirely simply by recourse to the route made available by subsection (b). Granted, that clause would only appear to be operative when operations are undertaken in self-defense. But since Israel has consistently claimed that all IDF applications of military force fall into a 'self-defense' category, the supposed limitation is really meaningless. In point of fact, Basic Law: The Government in no way intruded upon the executive's supremacy in Israeli warmaking.

Peacemaking too remained an executive prerogative, with the *knesset* acting as little more than a rubber-stamp. True, Meir and Rabin had set a precedent when asking the *knesset* to approve the disengagement agreements that, under Kissinger's auspices, Israel reached with Egypt and Syria in 1974–1975. (The first Disengagement Agreement with Egypt passed in January 1974 by 76 votes to 35 and the second in September 1974 by 70–43; the agreement with Syria was approved in May 1974 by 76–36. Bar Siman Tov 2001). Begin likewise made a point of putting both the Camp David Accords and the Israeli–Egyptian Peace Treaty to *knesset* votes, for which he released *Likud* MKs from party discipline. Rabin adopted the same line with respect to the two Oslo accords (1993 and 1995) as well as the Jordan–Israel Declaration of August 1994 and the Treaty between the two countries in October 1994. The understanding reached by Arafat and Netanyahu in October 1998 at Wye Plantation in Maryland was the following month likewise placed on the *knesset* agenda.

Noting this record, in *Hillel Weiss* v. *Prime Minister Ehud Barak* (2001) the ISC was willing to acknowledge, for argument's sake and without extensive discussion, that parliamentary ratification of peace agreements constitutes a mandatory 'constitutional convention', even though it rejected the claim that *knesset* approval was required before an agreement was signed. But, contrary to the thesis advanced by Broude and Noam (Broude and Noam 2008), that reading cannot be construed as a true reflection of the executive's original intention. When invoking the need for parliamentary approval, Rabin and Begin probably had far more mundane and immediate purposes in mind. Both appreciated that the threat of parliamentary disapproval could provide an excuse for setting limits to the concessions that could be made to foreign representatives at the negotiating table. Conversely, a favorable *knesset* vote could be used as a means of legitimizing an agreement whose passage through the cabinet or the ruling party caucus was anticipated to be especially stormy. In the event, both ploys succeeded, and the executive's hegemony in the hierarchy of national security decision-making remained unimpaired. With the exception of

124 *Development*

Oslo II (which, amidst charges of bribery, squeaked through on 6 October 1995 by 61–59), all the international agreements submitted for *knesset* approval received comfortable majorities: the Camp David Accords by 84–19; the Israel–Egyptian treaty by 95–18; Oslo I (23 September 1993) by 61–50; the Jordan–Israel Declaration by 91–3; the Jordan–Israel Treaty by 105–3; and the Wye Memorandum by 75–19. Not surprisingly, therefore, the substantive impact of *knesset* debates on the content of the agreements submitted to its consideration was minimal. Not a single clause in the original texts was even modified, let alone rejected, as a result of comments made in the chamber.

Superficially, the 1992 revised version of Basic Law: The Government did seem to make a conspicuous effort to augment the legislature's role in clarifying the *temporal* dimension of the national security framework. Article 49 (which became Article 38 in 2001) specified that in contrast to the arrangements laid down in the 1948 Law and Administration Ordinance, declarations announcing the existence of a state of emergency would have to be submitted for parliamentary re-approval at least once a year. In practice, however, the *knesset* has never taken advantage of the opportunity thus given to it to distinguish between 'emergency' and 'non-emergency' units of time. Rather, its annual debates on Israel's security situation follow a standard ritual. At their conclusion, the *knesset* regularly declares Israel still to be in a state of emergency and that the existing emergency regulations are, therefore, still in effect.

The *knesset* played a more active role in this period with respect to the *functional* dimension of Israel's national security framework. Specifically, it exercised a greater influence than before on determining the areas in which actions taken by the executive would be subject to some degree of supervision by either the courts or the legislature. Here too, however, it would clearly be premature to speak of a fundamental parliamentary revision of the processes whereby Israel's national security policies were formulated and implemented. What the evidence supplies, rather, are additional signs of the extent to which legislators were becoming aware of the faults in the old order and beginning to outline a possible alternative.

It is indicative of the conservative characteristic of that approach that its principal expression was institutional rather than legislative. Indeed, as far as laws affecting the functional dimension of national security were concerned, the statute book of 1995 was almost identical to that of 1977. Once again, those differences that did exist could easily be attributed to attempts by the executive to manipulate the law for political goals, and not to any real change in the general balance of power in national security. As Gad Barzilai has demonstrated in considerable detail, one example is provided by the fate of the Ordinance for the Prevention of Terrorism, which forbade Israelis to conduct negotiations with known members of a terrorist organization without prior government authorization (Barzilai 1999c). When originally proposed in 1985, this Ordinance had a blatant political purpose – which is why its passage generated what was, even by Israeli standards, an especially acrimonious parliamentary debate. Only in part did this measure constitute an attempt on the part of the executive to retain absolute control over the conduct of foreign affairs, which is the way it was presented. More immediately, it reflected the intention of *Likud* representatives in the National Unity Government to muzzle those private citizens – principally those with left-wing leanings – who were seeking to enter into some form of dialogue with PLO representatives. Precisely the same motives, but this time in reverse, came into play when the Ordinance for the Prevention of Terrorism was repealed in 1993. Speaking for the motion, the minister of justice, David Liba'i, who represented the newly elected Labor government led by Rabin, blandly argued that the original law had been undemocratic, and hence had to be repealed. What he did not reveal was that, with Peres' connivance and Rabin's consent, private negotiations between Israelis and Palestinians had begun to move towards a critical stage at Oslo. In other words, the executive now clearly had an interest in manipulating its influence over the legislature in order to legalize actions that had hitherto been forbidden, and thereby avoiding possible appeals to the ISC. Hence, neither the introduction nor the dissolution of the Ordinance for the Prevention of Terrorism can be attributed to a new sense of independence on the part of the legislature. As had traditionally been the case, where national security issues were concerned, the executive remained the dominant branch.

Only with respect to the Emergency (Powers) Detention Law can legislation be said to have affected the hierarchical dimension of the national security framework. Passed in 1979, this law did away with some of the most draconian clauses in the DERs imposed during the last three years of the British mandate, and which were still in effect. Specifically, Articles 111–2 of the 1945 Defence Regulations had allowed regional military commanders to order the detention of any person they considered might pose a threat to 'the public safety, the defense of Palestine, the maintenance of public order, or the suppression of mutiny, rebellion or riot.' There existed no provision for judicial review over these detention orders, which were monitored only by an advisory committee which the military commander had to form. Moreover, although the ISC, sitting as the High Court of Justice, could review a detention order, it seldom did so, and even then only on technical grounds, never directly contradicting the decision of the military commander. The new law passed in 1979 created an entirely different situation. Besides limiting the right to issue a detention order to the minister of defense, it also narrowed the justification to reasons of state security or public security. Most important of all, the new law also subjected all detention orders to mandatory judicial review. Every extension of the original order (with the original order and the extensions limited to six months each) had to undergo judicial review too.

126 *Development*

Important though they were, these changes too must be placed in context. The case for these reforms had long been apparent (Bracha 1971; Dershowitz 1971) and the new legislation certainly struck a new balance between security concerns and human rights (Rudolph 1984). Nevertheless, it cannot be interpreted as a reflection of a more general desire on the part of MKs to exercise greater control over executive activity in the entire area of national security. Rather, the law owed its passage to the biography of the recently-appointed minister of justice, Shmuel Tamir, who had in 1946 himself been detained by the British mandate authorities under the terms of the Defence Regulations and thereafter incarcerated for two years in a detention camp in Kenya. From the first, Tamir had made no secret of his personal commitment to righting the wrongs under which he had suffered, and his success constituted 'a testament to what an individual committed to change can do.' (Rudman and Qupti 1990:475) It did not presage a mood of parliamentary initiative that might have stimulated a wave of similar legislation in other spheres of national security concern. As Hofnung points out, the prevailing climate of executive-legislature relationships clearly worked against any such prospect – even more so than had been the case in earlier periods (Hofnung 1991:123).

Whereas the *knesset*'s role in initiating and framing national security legislation was thus decidedly secondary, its activities as an agency that scrutinized executive actions in this sphere increased. Especially noteworthy, in this respect, was the expanding range of monitoring functions now performed by its Foreign Affairs and Defense Committee (FADC). Consisting of representatives of most coalition and opposition factions and (until March 2009) always chaired by a nominee of the largest party in the *knesset*, prior to 1977 the FADC had primarily served as a top-down channel of communications. Precisely because it was a compact body (usually comprising about 20 MKs) – and one, moreover, to which no Arab or Communist representatives were ever appointed – prime ministers had used the FADC as a means of keeping opposition leaders informed of national security developments that they preferred not to disclose to the *knesset* as a whole. In this respect, the precedent set by Ben-Gurion prior to the Sinai Campaign of 1956 (above p. 75) was followed by Eshkol in late May 1967 and by Rabin prior to the Entebbe rescue operation of 1976, albeit to a more limited extent.[4] Nevertheless, the FADC had gradually managed to extend its mandate. By the outbreak of the 1973 war, it had become routine for the committee to meet (sometimes on a monthly basis) with other senior members of Israel's security community: the ministers of defense and of foreign affairs, the CGS, the CO Intelligence Branch, and the heads of the GSS and the *Mosad*. A year after the fighting ceased, the FADC also established a special subcommittee to follow up on the Agranat Commission's recommendations regarding the IDF. Although ineffective, the exercise was nevertheless of symbolic importance, constituting 'probably the first occasion when the FADC actually attempted to supervise implementation by the IDF of specific actions and policies' (Ben-Meir 1995:49).

Changes in the composition of the *knesset*, and hence of the FADC, consequent upon the 1977 elections stimulated a burst of more effective action. Partly, this was because of the emergence of a more skeptical attitude towards all national security matters. More specifically, the change of gear reflected the personal disposition of the FADC's new chairman, MK Moshe Arens, a Massachusetts Institute of Technology (MIT) trained aeronautical engineer whose administrative skills had been honed during his long tenure as deputy director-general of Israel Aircraft Industries (1962–1971). As far as Arens was concerned, even the FADC was too large a body to conduct in-depth discussions of security matters, the most sensitive of which he therefore entrusted to a web of more intimate sub-committees with specific mandates: 'Intelligence and the Secret Services'; 'Research and Development'; 'Defense Industries'; 'Arms Procurement'; 'IDF Preparedness.' Since each of these groups followed the model of their counterparts in the US Capitol by employing professional staff of their own, they became repositories of national security knowledge in their own right. Indeed, with expertise thus married to constitutional authority, perceptible shifts began to take place in the relationship between FADC members and the senior ministers, officials and generals with whom they met on a regular basis. The FADC was no longer just a recipient of whatever security information the executive deigned to impart. Instead, it now became an initiator of some parts of the national security discourse. Its determination to fulfill that role became especially apparent in 1986 when Abba Eban, a former minister for foreign affairs who currently chaired the FADC, insisted on establishing a sub-committee to investigate how and why Israeli agents had, over the previous few years, come to pay Jonathan Pollard, an American Jew employed by the Naval Investigative Service in Washington, DC, for illicitly copying classified documents to which he had access. Only combined pressure by both *Likud* and Labor ministers in the National Unity Government ultimately put a stop to Eban's initiative (Ben-Meir 1995:50).

It would be wrong to conclude from this survey that such changes guaranteed parliamentary control over the implementation of Israeli national security policies, still less their formulation. Although zealous, the staff maintained by the FADC's various sub-committees could never be a substitute for a properly manned and fully authorized national security council, capable of providing civilian echelons with the degree of access to confidential security material that they required if they were to carry out informed assessments of alternative modes of action. In this period (and, for that matter, subsequently too) intelligence gathering and intelligence assessment continued to remain almost exclusively IDF preserves. What can be said, however, is that signs of change were becoming increasingly apparent, and that the upgraded status of the FADC provided an indication of the extent to which that was so. In this context, attention might again be drawn to Article 51 of Basic Law: The Government, passed in 1992, which specifies the steps to be taken in the event of Israel going to war. When listing the forums that the prime minister has to inform about the initiation of military activity, the article mentions the FADC first. Whether or not that order implies the precedence of the FADC over the *knesset* as a whole remains an open question. But whichever the case, the FADC had clearly earned its place in the very short roster of institutions recognized in Israel's national security law.

The judicial branch

Like the legislature, the judiciary too evinced sensitivity to changes in public perceptions of national security. Moreover, and again like members of the *knesset*, judges attempted to accommodate the new pressures on Israel's framework of national security law by upgrading existing institutional mechanisms and thereby investing them with new power. Two such mechanisms were especially prominent. The first was the national commission of enquiry, a tool originally created by the government for the almost explicit purpose of containing public pressure. The second was the Israel Supreme Court, which increasingly assumed the role of the voice of the conscience of the (non-existent) constitution.

National commissions of inquiry – the shift towards legalism

In Israel, legislation regulating the authority and composition of national commissions of enquiry was first enacted in the Commissions of Inquiry Law of 1968. Based on the UK Tribunal of Inquiry (Evidence) Act of 1921, this law sought to balance the functions attributed to the branches of government. Thus, it authorized the executive to appoint a commission of inquiry into any matter of 'public importance which requires clarification' and to define that forum's mandate. However, the law vested the authority to appoint the members of a commission with the president of the ISC and required that all commissions be chaired by a current or retired judge of either the ISC or a district court. The judicial character of a commission is also stressed in the provisions that entitle it to obligate witnesses to appear before it and to append operative recommendations to its report. True, and as one detailed study concludes, at the end of the day a commission of inquiry formally remains part of the executive, not of the judiciary (Klagsbald 2001:89–107). In practice, nevertheless, forums of that name have served as something quite close to a court, without many of the strings attached to 'pure' judicial institutions, and with an ability to view the large picture

The first tribunal of this sort to deal with a matter of national security concern was the Agranat Commission of Enquiry of 1973–1974 (see Chapter 4). But although mandated to investigate, *inter alia*, decisions taken by 'the responsible civil authorities' as well as their military counterparts prior to the outbreak of the Yom Kippur War, the commissioners had in fact focused mainly on military events and personalities. Their report refrained from passing any comment on the behavior of the politicians, whose conduct it claimed should be left to the judgment of the electorate. Hence, although the report did lay the groundwork for the passage of Basic Law: The Military, its only direct consequence was the resignation of the CGS and the dismissal of two other senior officers.

A different attitude was adopted by the two commissions of enquiry into national security affairs established during the period 1977–1995. The first was the Kahan Commission, comprised of two ISC judges and one retired general, which was set up late in September 1982 in order to investigate '[A]ll the facts and factors connected with the atrocity carried out by a unit of the Lebanese Forces against the civilian population in the Shatilla and Sabra camps' earlier that month. The second was the Landau Commission (one ISC judge, one district court judge and a former head of the *Mosad*), set up late in May 1987, ostensibly in order to investigate the methods of interrogation employed by the GSS, but in fact in order to ascertain just how deeply the organization had become infected by a culture of misrepresentation, doctoring of evidence and blatant lying under oath.[5]

When the Kahan and Landau commissions presented their reports (in February 1983 and October 1987, respectively), public discussion not unexpectedly focused on the strictures that they leveled against highly-placed individuals. In the case of the Kahan Commission, which was chaired by the then president of the ISC, but whose moving spirit was rumored to be his younger and healthier fellow commissioner, Justice Aharon Barak, these were certainly dramatic. Unlike the Agranat commissioners, Kahan and his colleagues clearly considered it their duty to evaluate the actions – and inaction – of all relevant persons, politicians as well as soldiers, whatever their office, rank or function, and to apportion responsibility wherever it lay.

> The absence of any hard and fast law regarding various matters does not exempt a man whose actions are subject to the scrutiny of a commission of inquiry from accountability, from a public standpoint, for his deeds or failures that indicate inefficiency on his part, lack of proper attention to his work, or actions executed hastily, negligently, unwisely, or shortsightedly.... No commission of inquiry would fulfill its role properly if it did not exercise such scrutiny, in the framework of its competence, vis-à-vis any man whose actions and failures were under scrutiny, regardless of his position and public standing.

>   In conclusion, regarding personal responsibility we will not draw a distinction between the political echelon and any other echelon.
>
>   (*Kahan Commission Report* 1983:65–6)

Acting in accordance with this gauge, the Kahan commissioners took the unprecedented step of criticizing not just the conduct of the CGS and the CO Intelligence Branch but also of the minister for foreign affairs, Yitzchak Shamir, and of the prime minister, both of whom they judged not to have taken sufficient personal interest in events in Beirut. More sensationally still, the commissioners declared Ariel Sharon unfit to hold the position of minister of defense.

Constitutional lawyers might reasonably have expected any such judgment to be grounded in references to specific items of legislation that laid down guidelines for the assessment of ministerial behavior. Especially is that so since, unlike the Agranat commissioners, who were unable to access any such text, members of the Kahan Commission had before them Basic Law: The Military, which had been on the statute book for the past seven years. Remarkably, nevertheless, the Kahan commissioners apparently decided to ignore that document, which is not mentioned even once in their entire report. Instead, they posited an entirely different system of national security government than was prescribed in the Law.

A clear example is provided by their depiction of the duties and functions of the minister of defense. Basic Law: The Military had identified the cabinet as the commander of the armed forces (Article 2a) and the minister of defense as merely the agent of his colleagues ('The Minister in charge of the Army on behalf of the Cabinet is the Minister of Defense', Article 2b). But in their summary critique of Sharon's action in 1982, the Kahan commissioners in effect likened the minister to a supreme commander of the IDF in his own right, someone whose functions were not limited to transmitting information from the cabinet to the armed forces (and vice versa) but who was capable of taking autonomous operational decisions, and could be charged with dereliction of duty when he did not do so. Specifically:

> It is our view that responsibility is to be imputed to the Minister of Defense for having disregarded the danger of acts of vengeance and bloodshed by the Phalangists against the population of the refugee camps, and having failed to take this danger into account when he decided to have the Phalangists enter the camps. In addition, responsibility is to be imputed to the Minister of Defense for not ordering [the IDF to take] appropriate measures for preventing or reducing the danger of massacre.
>
>   (*Kahan Commission Report* 1983:73)

In the case of the 1987 Landau Commission Report into the GSS, too, the systemic inferences were far more important than were any personal recommendations. (In fact, the report contained no personal recommendations. President Herzog, in an unprecedented move, had agreed to pardon all GSS officers allegedly involved in the 1984 killings before the investigation commenced). The Landau commissioners made the sanction for the resort to what they termed 'moderate physical pressure' during the interrogation of terrorist suspects – behavior for which they provided intrinsic legal and moral justifications – conditional on the fulfillment of defined procedural requirements. For one thing, they insisted that the courts be informed of all methods of investigation employed[6] and that judges have the discretion to reveal relevant information to either the prosecution or the defense. Secondly, the Landau Commission Report (pp. 80–1) recommended that all such methods be periodically reviewed by a ministerial committee, and presented for approval by a special subcommittee of the FADC. By thus strengthening the role allotted to both the legislature and the judiciary, the Landau Commission was seeking to effect a structural change that, if successful, would have weakened the influence over Israel's national security process traditionally wielded by the executive.

In the event, that did not happen. Resorts to commissions of inquiry did not re-design the framework of Israel's national security law. In some respects, those mechanisms merely helped to prop up certain features of the old system. In effect, commissions tend to serve as safety valves and as alternatives to criminal proceedings that might otherwise be justified. Moreover, even under the best of circumstances, their impact was almost certain to be limited. Commissions of inquiry are, after all, by their nature transitory mechanisms. No matter how dramatic the content of their reports, once they have been presented to the public their influence tends to fade. Even if governments do accept their recommendations, the commissioners have neither the authority nor the means to ensure that they are being properly carried out. Their ability to effect long-term change is therefore very circumscribed. The Agranat Commission gave birth to Basic Law: The Military, which was itself a weak document. The Kahan Commission's reinterpretation of that item of legislation never found statutory expression and even its best-remembered recommendation, the disqualification of Sharon to serve as minister of defense, was bypassed. Sharon continued to be a prominent force in Israeli politics. He served in a long line of ministerial posts (minister without portfolio 1983–1984; minister for trade and industry 1984–1990; minister of housing construction 1990–1992; minister of national infrastructure 1996–1998 and foreign minister 1998–1999) before becoming prime minister in February 2001. The Landau Commission's recommendations with respect to the dos and don'ts of interrogation methods were similarly overtaken by history. As succeeding chapters will show, in the new millennium the seismic experience of the first *intifada* made it clear to both the ISC and the State Comptroller that new norms were required.

In the final analysis, perhaps the most that can be said about the reports of both the Kahan and Landau commissions is that they interacted with simultaneous changes in Israeli public discourse on national security affairs. Together, the commissions contributed to a growing tendency to dress policy and political questions in legal terms. Amnon Rubinstein and Barak Medina have deduced that investigative commissions in Israel thus offer a legal alternative to the political process – a feature that they consider to be unique to Israeli democracy (Rubinstein and Medina 2006:1029). Be that as it may, their precise function and role remains imprecise and hence, as our concluding chapter will argue, needs to be redefined.

The Israel supreme court

Whilst the influence on the framework of Israel's national security law exerted by commissions of inquiry in this period was thus weak and intermittent, that of the ISC proved to be both persistent and more effective. In retrospect, this is hardly surprising, since the years between 1977 and 1995 witnessed a major change in that body's overall behavior as well as in its public profile (Shafir and Peled 2002:260–77). Joshua Segev attributes both developments to shifts in the ISC's perception of its own role in society. In his terms, instead of seeing itself as a 'conflict solver', the ISC, acting in its capacity as the country's High Court of Justice, progressively assumed the role of 'moral shepherd' (Segev 2008). Following precedents already set in other Western democracies such as France, Germany, Italy, and especially the USA, Israel accordingly began to experience a growing degree of judicial involvement in value-based political affairs (Barzilai 1999b). Portents of that trend were evident in the late 1970s, but became much clearer once Justice Meir Shamgar assumed the presidency of the ISC in 1983 (he was to hold the position until 1995) and, incidentally, the principle of judicial independence at long last attained formal recognition in Article 2 of Basic Law: The Judiciary, enacted in 1984. During Shamgar's presidency, the ISC dismantled all the old institutional and legal barriers impeding direct petitions, and became the most accessible of all supreme courts in the Western world. Any person, organization or legal entity that considered itself to have been wronged by any action taken by the government or any part of the executive could petition the ISC. The response was remarkable. According to one audit, in 1970 the ISC had been asked to consider only 381 appeals (barely 50 more than in 1960). By the end of the period covered in this chapter the numbers had grown dramatically: to 802 in 1980, to 1,308 in 1990, and to 2,209 in 1994 (Barzilai 1999b:19).

Barzilai attributes much of the growth in appeals to the ISC's ability to mobilize three sources of legitimacy: 'specific', 'diffuse' and, primarily, 'mythical'. But other influences may also have been at work. Potential petitioners soon appreciated that their chances of obtaining redress were measurably increased once the ISC matched its readiness to entertain claims against governmental agencies with a willingness to intervene in matters thereto considered political and hence outside the judiciary's jurisdiction. They increased still further the more Judge Aharon Barak gained authority. Widely considered to be a legal genius, the trajectory of Barak's career from wunderkind to grand old man was truly meteoric. Only 38 years old when he was appointed dean of the Hebrew University's Faculty of Law in 1974, Barak had the following year been awarded the Israel Prize for legal research. He also began a three-year term as Israel's attorney general in 1975, during which he participated as a member of the Israeli delegation to the Camp David negotiations with the Egyptians hosted by President Jimmy Carter. His appointment to the ISC in 1978 followed almost as a matter of course, as did his succession to Shamgar as president of that body in 1995 (Levitzky 2001).

From the first, Barak was determined to promote what became known as judicial activism. 'Everything is justiciable' was the phrase reported to have encapsulated his legal philosophy, and even though he probably never actually uttered that slogan it certainly captured the essence of his thinking. In part at Barak's instigation, the ISC made its presence felt in almost all spheres of public life, entertaining petitions on issues ranging from the way that the *knesset* functioned to the civil rights of the Arab Israeli minority. What is more, in their decisions, judges increasingly adopted positions that placed the ISC at the very forefront of the struggle for civil rights in Israel. Whilst liberal and left-wing opinion welcomed this situation, other sectors of society did not at all view it positively, claiming that the ISC had been 'captured' by liberals, whom it had in turn empowered (Mautner 1993).

It is important not to pre-date the impact of this surge of judicial activity on the structure of Israel's national security legal framework. As has already been pointed out, throughout the years covered by this chapter (and the next, for that matter), emergency regulations, some of them in existence since 1948 continued to remain in force. So too did the old, and always inadequate, arrangements governing civilian control over the military. Similarly, judicial control over IDF activities in the Territories remained circumscribed – even during the first *intifada*, when, as the MAG of the day acknowledged (Straschnov 1994:72, 86–7), IDF commanders in the Territories felt compelled to resort to numerous measures that infringed on the liberties of Palestinians, including administrative detentions, house demolitions, curfews and school closures. Moreover, although the number of petitions submitted to the ISC by Palestinians did rise sharply (by one count from an average of less than 30 per annum between 1968 and 1986 to about 200 per annum between 1987 and 1993), only some 60 percent resulted in partial or complete judicial decisions against the military authorities (Dotan 1999:328–35).

134 *Development*

Nevertheless, we shall argue, changes were occurring and a movement in the direction of future reform was gathering momentum. In each of the four dimensions of national security concern, the ISC was beginning to hand down decisions that, although at this stage still sporadic and disjointed, already had the potential to become the elements out of which a new doctrine of national security law could be constructed.

Inroads into the traditional functional divide – the Barzilai and Ressler cases

In Israel, as elsewhere in the Western world, national security issues have traditionally not been considered appropriate topics for judicial intervention. Hence, until the 1990s, courts generally advanced several justifications for refusing to consider national security cases on which they were asked to pass judgment (Benvenisti 1993b:159). In the USA, such 'avoidance doctrines' included the 'political question' argument; in the UK reference was made to the 'act of state' claim. In Israel, three more specific limitations were generally cited. One was that of standing – the ISC would accept petitions only from individuals personally affected by the decision of the government or its organs. The second was that of 'justiciability' – the ISC could not decide upon matters concerning which no judicial yardsticks existed. Finally, there was the argument of deference – the ISC recognized that security officials possess unique expertise in their field. Hence, their discretion should almost never be questioned on grounds of reasonability. Justice Agranat had formulated the *locus classicus* of this position as early as 1950:

> The jurisdiction of this court to review the competent authority's exercise of its power which emanates from the Defence (Emergency) Regulations, 1945, is of very limited character. When a given regulation confers upon the competent authority the discretion to action against an individual in any case in which 'it is of the opinion' or ' it seems to it' that conditions warranting this, then that same authority is the final arbiter in determining the existence of these conditions. In such situations the Court's function is limited to examining whether the authority exceeded its power under the law by virtue of which it was empowered to act, whether the said authority paid attention to the factors stated in the same law and whether the authority acted in good faith.
>
> (*Al Ayubi* v. *Minister of Defense* 1950:227–8)

Each of these barriers to judicial involvement in national security affairs had suffered some erosion prior to 1977, especially where issues relating to relations between the IDF and Palestinians in the Territories were concerned. Thereafter, however, the tempo of judicial intrusion noticeably increased – so much so that by 1988, the doctrines of standing and justiciablity had been all but abandoned. Two judgments deserve to be considered landmarks in that development. In the first, *Barzilai* v. *The Government of Israel* (1986) the ISC agreed to hear a petition submitted by an assorted group of MKs, academics, NGOs and private citizens – all of whom asked the court to disallow the presidential pardon granted, before trial, to GSS officials suspected of lying to the successive enquiries into the killing of two apprehended terrorists. (In what was patently a disingenuous remark, the ISC argued that it was prepared to discuss the petition, because it raised questions 'of constitutional importance'). The blow thus struck to the 'standing' doctrine was repeated in *Ressler* v. *Minister of Defense* (1988). In this case, the ISC agreed to hear a petition submitted by a private citizen against the manner in which the minister of defense was allowing increasing numbers of students in *yeshivot* (academies of advanced Jewish education) to defer their conscription into the IDF, almost always indefinitely. In years past, the court had rejected Ressler's petitions, on the grounds that since he could not prove that he had suffered personal damage as a result of the minister's actions he possessed no standing. Now, however, Justice Barak reversed that policy. Although paying formal tribute to the principle of standing, Barak hedged it about with so many provisos and exceptions that it in effect was abolished – and indeed was never again raised in court in the context of a national security issue.

During the course of his judgment on the *Ressler* case, Barak further broke with precedent when completely rejecting the argument that national security matters were not justiciable. Instead, in his opinion he ruled that there is no such thing as a topic for which there exists no legal standard. For example, every decision taken by a government official has to be 'reasonable' and may be annulled if it is not. Since the bottom line of Barak's judgment was that in the specific case of the deferments granted to *yeshiva* students the minister of defense's conduct did indeed conform to the standards of 'reasonableness', the inferences of his opinion were at the time generally overlooked. Indeed, several scholars developed a theory, according to which, the ISC, although evincing an apparent general willingness to intervene in national security matters, in effect was still not doing so (Hofnung 1991:275, Barzilai *et al.* 1994). However, by positing that there exists a 'normative' (albeit not necessarily institutional) solution to every issue, Barak had in fact set in motion a revolution that was to alter the balance of power between the judiciary and the other branches of government, in national security affairs as well as in other spheres.

Breaking the temporal and spatial borders: the true implications of Elon Moreh

In 1979, a Palestinian resident of northern Samaria petitioned the ISC, asking that it prevent the IDF from expropriating land that he owned near Nablus, on which there existed plans to construct the Jewish settlement of Elon Moreh. In response, the government claimed that the expropriation was motivated by security considerations, and thus permitted under Article 53 of the Hague Regulations. Two affidavits were also submitted. One, signed by the CGS of the day, Rafael Eitan, supported the government's position; the other, submitted by the minister of defense, Ezer Weizman, did not. On the contrary, Weizman claimed that the proposal to establish a settlement on the lands to be expropriated reflected political ambitions rather than security concerns. In *Dawikat* v. *The Government of Israel* (1979), the ISC accepted the latter position, and ruled that the planned expropriation violated the international law of occupation.

Even thus briefly summarized, the '*Elon Moreh* decision', as it became popularly known, clearly touches on several issues of constitutional importance. Indeed, it was for long considered to have marked a revolution in the way in which the ISC approached national security affairs (Shetreet 1986:320, Hofnung 1996:192). Recent scholarship has tended to be more skeptical, claiming that the *Elon Moreh* decision, whilst certainly commendable on its own terms, must not be misconstrued as a liberal manifesto, far less as an impediment to settlement expansion. If anything, the reverse was true. Precisely because the ISC limited its veto on expropriations to private property, *Elon Moreh* may in fact have facilitated settlement construction elsewhere. All governments now had to do was restrict expropriations to what were defined (accurately or otherwise) as 'public lands' – a category whose growth in size Zertal and Eldar claim to have been very much abetted by the loopholes in Palestinian land registration, zealously ferreted out by pro-settlement technocrats in Israel's legal service (Zertal and Eldar 2007:365–70). In other ways too, they argue, the *Elon Moreh* decision, rather than striking a blow at the occupation, helped to prop it up. Because military officers no longer had to justify the 'security value' of settlements, and would no longer be ordered to expropriate private lands, the IDF could pose as a 'benevolent ruler', under whose occupation the Palestinians had no cause to fear that their rights would be infringed (Zertal and Eldar 360–3). As a result, the *spatial* dimension of the Territories became even more ambiguous. The ISC did protect the private owner from confiscation, but allowed Israel to build settlements on all public lands, thus effectively annexing the latter into Israel proper, and permitting Israel to use them as it saw fit (Gordon 2008:128).

Be that as it may, there is another respect in which the *Elon Moreh* decision warrants consideration. Thereto, justices of the ISC – although long reluctant to provide precise definitions of the legal regime operative in the Territories (Kretzmer 2002:35–40)[7] – had clearly attempted to keep it distinct from the framework of regular Israeli government. *Elon Moreh* blurred much of that distinction. One way in which it did so was by clarifying relations between the minister of defense and the cabinet as a whole, implying that the situation of quasi-feudal autonomy once enjoyed in the Territories by Dayan was intolerable. Even though the ISC upheld the authority of the minister of defense to act as the government's representative, namely the military, it explicitly ruled that even with regards to the Territories all decisions taken by him were subordinate to those of the cabinet as a whole.[8] In terms of government, then, the *Elon Moreh* decision to all intents and purposes integrated the Territories into Israel. In both areas, the reigning policies were those determined by the cabinet as a collectivity, and not by either the military or spokesmen for security interests.

Subsequent ISC decisions made further contributions to the effective legal merger of Israel and the territories. *Abu Aita* v. *IDF Commander Judea and Samaria Region* (1983) imposed the Israeli tax system; *Kav la-Oved* v. *National Labor Court* (2007) supported the extension of the Israeli electric infrastructure, and eventually implemented Israeli labor law; *Gaza Beach Regional Council* v. *The Government of Israel* (2005) had already done the same for Israeli constitutional law. In many respects the tone had been set by *Jama'at Aschan Elmualamin* v. *IDF Commander Judea and Samaria Region* (1983), in which the Court permitted the expropriation of private Palestinian land in order to build a highway between Tel-Aviv and Jerusalem, which would be used by Israeli as well as Palestinian traffic. Arguing that the situation in the Territories was now one of 'prolonged military occupation', Barak ruled that the occupying power was entitled to more flexibility than was allowed by international law. Specifically, the government of Israel had a right, even duty, to develop infrastructure that would be of benefit to the local Palestinian population. In other words, its legal status had changed from a passive and limited custodian to an active manager – which is precisely its position within Israel itself. Eyal Benvenisti, for one, had no doubt about the implications. Indeed, as early as 1989 he had confidently asserted: 'The pre-June 1967 borders have faded for almost all legal purposes that reflect Israeli interests.' (Benvenisti 1989:1) Subsequent commentators have reached similar conclusions. By never delineating clear legal boundaries to executive action in the Territories, the Court has in effect been an accomplice to the legitimization of Israel's control over them, enabling successive governments to pose as 'benevolent occupants' (Kretzmer 2002; Gordon 2008).

Removing the hierarchical barrier – the Schnitzer case and its inferences

As far as relations between the ISC and the executive branch over security matters were concerned, there remained one further 'avoidance' hurdle to cross. After all, the judiciary's new-found willingness to review cases affecting national security did not necessarily imply that it had abandoned all traditional deference. It had still to show that it was ready to review the actions taken by security authorities and, if necessary, declare them illegal.

Between 1977 and 1995 the ISC began to embark on that path. In this period, it did so rather gingerly and without reference to any clearly defined doctrine or judicial program. Nevertheless, the cumulative effect of its actions, scattered and experimental though they undoubtedly were, remains unmistakable. Gradually, the Court positioned itself as a major component of Israel's national security framework, and thereby created the potential for judicial intrusion that was to be more fully realized in later years.

Enforcement was the first method employed by the ISC in order to lower the barrier of deference. It was also the most mundane. The Court simply compelled the executive to obey restrictions already embedded in law. To that end, it resorted to relatively traditional interpretative tools, and adopted much the same paradigm of supervision in the realm of national security that it applied to administrative agencies in other spheres. It assumed that the security agencies possessed substantive expertise and reviewed only their procedural conduct (Kretzmer 2002:188).

This attitude explains why, until the mid-1990s, most decisions of the ISC followed the same pattern. It would accept jurisdiction in almost all cases of appeals by Palestinian residents of the Territories, and would try to adjudicate them according to international law. However, justices did not address the propriety of the substance of whichever decisions they were asked to review. Rather, the ISC limited itself to reviewing the procedures that had been followed. Accordingly, substantive decisions taken by the IDF were almost never overturned, even when they seemed to contradict international law. The Court approved of the general policies of house demolitions,[9] deportations (*Afu* v. *IDF Commander in the West Bank*, 1988), and the internment of Palestinians in Israel (*Sajedia* v. *Minister of Defense*, 1988). At the same time, however, and further to its insistence on the observance of prescribed procedures, in both *Kawasme* v. *Minister of Defense* (1980) and *The Association for Civil Rights in Israel* v. *CO Central Command* (1989), the ISC demanded that the military authorities grant hearings before taking such actions.

From the ISC's perspective, the great advantage of the enforcement approach was that it avoided the charge that the judiciary was interfering unduly in national security decisions. Its disadvantage was that it restricted the ISC's room for maneuver. Provided executive agencies followed correct procedures, the Court in effect barred itself from reviewing their decisions, however problematic. Consequently, the ISC began to adopt a second method, which involved reviewing some decisions taken by the military and security services in accordance with standards applicable in other matters, of which the most conspicuous were reasonability and human rights.

Baruch Bracha dates the genesis of the process whereby the ISC thus departed from its traditional posture of deference to the beginning of the 1980s (Bracha 1991). As early as 1982 Justice Shamgar, when commenting on a military commander's exercise of authority in accordance with the Defence (Emergency) Regulation of 1945, announced that 'the Court will examine scrupulously the exercise of this power, and hence this Court no longer acts with the limitations and self-restraint characterizing the parallel English case law which examined the exercise of similar powers in England' (*Baransa* v. *CO Central Command*, 1982). In 1983, Justice Barak was still more specific about the criteria that were now being followed. 'the Court does not superimpose itself as a public official but rather examines whether a reasonable and air public official could have made a decision such as was actually made.' (*Jama'at Aschan Elmualamin* v. *IDF Commander Judea and Samaria Region*) Still more famously, in *Schnitzer* v. *Chief Military Censor* (1989), Barak wrote:

> Judges are not bureaucrats, but the principle of separation of powers obliges them to review the legality of the decisions of bureaucrats. In this matter there is no special status to security consideration. Those too must be applied according to the law, and those to must be subject to judicial review. As much as the judged are able and obliged to review the reasonableness of professional discretion in every area, so they must do in the area of security. This leads to the position that there are no special limits on the power of judicial review in matters of state security.

Military personnel could claim no exemption from that rule. Soon after the outbreak of the first *intifada* in 1987 the ISC began intervening in the discretion of the MAG to decide whether or not to indict soldiers suspected of misconduct through criminal proceedings. The first case it did so was *Zuffan* v. *MAG* (1989), when it instructed the MAG to review (in effect, to overturn) his previous decision not to indict Colonel Yehuda Meir, who had been found guilty of issuing orders to employ violence against detained Palestinians suspected of participating in an illegal demonstration. Disciplinary action and enforced early retirement, the punishments imposed by the MAG, were deemed inappropriate.

Soon thereafter, Barak began to supplement his by-now familiar arguments against discretion with another that was far more stringent. As the 1980s drew to a close he took the position that legislation authorizing actions by the security agencies had to be assessed in the light of its compatibility with fundamental human rights. Such rights were to be presumed to impose inherent limitations on the grant of discretion to an executive agency. Hence, every statute authorizing executive infringements of human rights was to be interpreted in way that gave them due consideration. Even though Israel did not yet possess a written constitution that explicitly guaranteed such basic human rights as freedom of

140 *Development*

speech, to which the ISC might refer when passing judgment, it was nevertheless to employ those rights as 'canons of judicial interpretation'.

In its fundamentals, this position too was laid out in Barak's *Schnitzer* judgment: Indeed, much of the significance of the *Schnitzer* decision lies in that it sent a signal, showing how the Court could invoke human rights as a means of revolutionizing accepted interpretations of statutes. Barak ruled that the military censor could now limit the freedom of speech only if there existed a 'near certainty' that the specific newspaper article would actually seriously injure state security. He then went on to explain:

> every statute – ... whether or not it involves state security – is interpreted according to the general principles of the system. State security cannot exclude those fundamental values; rather they are integrated with security considerations, whose form they influence ... [There is] a vast array of fundamental values that the Defence Regulations promote (state security, public peace and order) and harm (judicial purity, personal freedom, freedom of association, freedom of movement, freedom of speech, privacy, human dignity...) 12. In the interpretation of the Defence Regulations ... these fundamental values have to be taken into account ... as every statute in a democratic society is supposed to fulfill them.

In sum, 'Security is not an end in itself, but a means. The end is democratic government, i.e., a government of the people which guarantees individual freedoms.'

Precisely the same reasoning underpinned Barak's decision in *Morcos* v. *Minister of Defense* (1991), which concerned a petition, submitted on the eve of the 1991 Gulf War by a Palestinian resident of Bethlehem, who demanded that the IDF distribute gas masks to Palestinian as well as Jewish inhabitants of the Territories.

> The military commander [of the Bethlehem region] is duty-bound to operate on the basis of equality. He may not discriminate between different groups of inhabitants.... The ability of any society to stand up to its enemies is based on the recognition that it is fighting for values that deserve to be protected. The rule of law is one such value.

It is important to re-iterate that, until the mid-1990s, the *Schnitzer* and *Morcos* judgments remained exceptional. They did not immediately open the floodgates to judicial reversals of military decisions in the name of fundamental rights, and hence to a complete overhaul of the framework of Israel's national security law. At this stage, the ISC certainly preferred to proceed with caution. Hence, and as Bracha demonstrated at the time, much Court intervention in the field of human rights was in fact limited and hesitant (Bracha 1991:101 n.294). Likewise, Yoav Dotan's study of out-of-court settlements of Palestinian petitions during the first *intifada* showed that the 'informal' concessions thus promoted, whilst to some extent ameliorating the effects of the infringements of human rights in the Territories, also contributed to the process of concealing these infringements under the thick cover of 'legality'. Palestinians, he writes, 'did not win justice in the HCJ. Rather, they were, in some cases, allowed some mercies' by their rulers (Dotan 1993:356).

Even so, the importance of the new trend in judicial thinking should not be under-estimated. For one thing, and as Dotan goes on to argue, the ISC's declaratory posture, as articulated in its decisions, ensured that 'the shadow of the law' hovered far more intently over military and administrative behavior in the Territories than had previously been the case. Hence, 'The influence of judicial intervention on the actions of the Military Government goes much beyond what can be seen by reading the Court's formal decisions.' (Dotan 1993) Even more significant, secondly, was the potential inherent in the ISC's 'activist' position. The ISC was now signaling that, henceforth, it would not merely protect human rights by enforcing existing legislation and subjecting executive action to the test of 'reasonableness.' Administrative review could be supplemented by constitutional review, whose point of departure is whether or not an action upholds the principles of democracy.

It is within that context that the Hammas deportation case of 1992 (discussed in the preface, above) assumes watershed status. On the one hand, and much to the disappointment of some circles, the ISC did not halt the deportation, arguing that the deportees could exercise their right to a hearing even after they had been deposited on the Lebanese side of the Israeli–Lebanon border. At the same time, nevertheless, the ISC demonstrated its willingness to intervene and question the decisions of the government on a major national security issue and – no less significantly – to do so whilst the deportation operation was still in progress. It thus set two precedents. First, the deportation judgment marked the creation of a form of 'real-time' judicial decision-making in matters of national security. Second, and no less momentously, it demonstrated the ISC's willingness to set aside the tradition whereby its intervention in national security issues had generally been limited to matters of procedure. Henceforth, it was also increasingly to pass judgment on matters of substance.

Writing in 1996, Gad Barzilai deftly called attention to the importance of the institutional context within which members of the ISC, like all judges, have to operate. Much though the content of their decisions might be influenced by their judicial philosophies, they also have to take account of political realities, and particularly of the power of the legislature to overturn court decisions and of the executive to by-pass them (Barzilai 1996:192–3). By then, however, the latter possibilities had become even more remote than had been the case less than two decades earlier. During the period covered by this chapter, both the executive and the legislature had exhibited an apparently chronic inability to initiate the reforms in the national security framework made necessary by sweeping changes in Israel's social, economic, demographic and strategic environments. Hence, as Israel approached the new millennium, it was becoming increasingly unlikely that either branch would be able to respond coherently and in a coordinated fashion to whatever steps the ISC might initiate. Indeed, since the framework established by Ben-Gurion now continued to function only in name, there remained no institution other than the Supreme Court that might fill the vacuum.

How it attempted to meet that challenge must be the subject of our next chapter.

6 Legalization, 1995–2008

As from the mid-1990s an increasing proportion of national security issues in Israel were regulated by a steadily growing variety of legal mechanisms: statutes, ISC decisions and, albeit in a more attenuated sense, pronouncements issued by international legal tribunals. Even in the new environment thus created, nuclear affairs remained an enclave of traditionally unfettered executive decision and action. Where other aspects of national security policy-making and policy-implementation were concerned, however, the autonomy once enjoyed by the executive and its agencies became progressively circumscribed by a process of legalization.

Whilst several circumstances contributed to that shift, undoubtedly its primary cause was the willingness (and sometimes eagerness) of the ISC to intervene in most facets of national security conduct. The present chapter examines the reasons for the court's behavior, itemizes the various stages in the legalization process for which it was responsible, and analyzes the responses that it elicited from both the legislature and the executive.

1995 as a turning point

In Israel's political history, 1995 will always be remembered as the year of the assassination of Prime Minister Yitzchak Rabin, who had undergone a remarkable metamorphoses, from the emblematic symbol of Israeli militarism ('Mr. Security') to the recipient of the Nobel Peace Prize for his contribution to forging the 1993 and 1994 agreements with the PLO (Inbar 1999). Rabin's assassination certainly induced a sense of deep national shock. But although an event of profound symbolic significance, it did not – of itself – change the course of Israeli history. At most, it intensified, and thereby hastened, processes that were already under way. This was as true of the 'peace process' as of the fundamental sociological and political trends that, as noted in the previous chapter, had by the mid-1990s already become evident. Survey data show that public skepticism about the sincerity of Yassir Arafat's commitment to a lasting peace with Israel was clearly rising by November 1995. So too was public awareness of the threat posed to Israel's security by Iran's declared ambition to attain nuclear capabilities. In neither case did the assassination fundamentally alter the trajectory of national security perceptions (Arian 1999:93).

Especially was that the case in the more limited confines of the national security legal framework. In this sphere, 1995 certainly did inaugurate a new era, but for entirely different reasons. For one thing, it was in that year that the *knesset* on 10 February 1995 enacted the Law Implementing the Peace Agreement between Israel and the Hashemite Kingdom of Transjordan (originally signed on 26 October 1994), the first time that the legislature had ratified any such document in designated legislation – a precedent that was repeated on 17 January 1996 when the *knesset* likewise enacted the Law Implementing the Interim Agreement Regarding the West Bank and Gaza Strip (Jurisdiction and Other Provisions), otherwise known as the Oslo II accord, which it had narrowly ratified the previous October. A second turning-point occurred on 9 November 1995, when the ISC delivered its landmark verdict in *United Mizrachi Bank* v. *Migdal Cooperative Village*, in which it declared its power to strike down laws based on their violation of the two Basic Laws passed in 1992: Dignity and Liberty and Freedom of Occupation.

Each of these events clearly possessed its own immediate and formal justification. Thus, both the peace treaty with Jordan and the interim agreements with the PLO required legislation because they required some changes in existing Israeli laws, for instance with respect to jurisdiction and property. The *United Mizrachi Bank* decision could be seen as a consequence of a legal tradition developed over several decades, and besides seemingly had nothing directly to do with national security matters. That, however, is too narrow a view. As both Gavison and Kretzmer demonstrated, what was novel about the *United Mizrachi Bank* decision was that it was explicitly based on the theory of a 'constitutional revolution', which was bound to be extended (Gavison 1997; Kretzmer 1997). The ISC, having demonstrated its power to limit executive power in matters of social importance, could with increasing regularity adopt the same attitude towards national security affairs too. Indeed, that likelihood appeared even more feasible when, again in 1995, Aharon Barak succeeded Meir Shamgar as President of the ISC. Some of Barak's subsequent judgments were to show that, contrary to caricature, he was not an entirely unrestrained advocate of judicial intervention. In *MK Livnat* v. *Chairperson of the Constitution, Law and Justice Committee* (2001), for instance, Barak was deliberately to avoid intervening in the *knesset*'s internal procedures. However, as demonstrated in our previous chapter he had already adumbrated the thesis that security matters were at least as 'justiciable' as any other. As president of the ISC he could now assert that position even more forcefully.

It is now generally accepted that under Barak's presidency ISC jurisprudence, far from being restricted to matters that were essentially peripheral (as was once argued), moved to core interests (Mersel 2005). What also has to be noted, however, is that as far as national security matters were concerned, ISC activism in the years 1995–2008 evinced various forms, each of which developed at an independent pace and embraced all four of the dimensions of the national security framework. In the pages that follow, we shall chart the course of the ISC's behavior by noting its movement across a spectrum of six distinct modes of judicial operation. Listed in ascending order of intrusion these are here labeled:

1	2	3	4	5	6
Enforcement	Interpretation	Attribution	Facilitation	Transference	Constitutionalism

Figure 6.1

The differences between these various kinds of activity on the part of the ISC find expression in several parameters. They involve distinct roles for the judiciary, for the executive and for the legislature. They are based on alternative sources of law. Most importantly, they differ with respect to their underlying assumptions of the role of law in a democratic society.

1   As presented here, 'enforcement' constitutes the most basic stage of ISC behavior. In this situation, the court refrains from taking any initiative with respect to national security affairs. Instead, in its judgments, the ISC does no more than ensure that the executive is abiding by the rules and procedures that existing law already prescribes.
2   'Interpretation' represents a more advanced situation, in which ISC rulings – now referring to specified fundamental standards of Israeli law – provide a more expansive interpretation of existing statutory limitations on executive actions.
3   The ISC's role expands still further when its decisions adopt an avowedly narrow interpretation of executive authority. Not content with 'interpreting' the law – and still less with simply enforcing existing rules of decision-making procedure – the ISC now requires the legislature to exercise its law-making powers and explicitly state whether or not it is giving the executive a mandate to act in a particular manner. We term this stage 'attribution'.
4   'Facilitation' represents a fourth rung on the ladder of ISC behavior. This situation exists when the ISC does not restrict its role to adjudicating between parties, but acts as a go-between, most obviously by mediating between the executive and petitioners who claim to have a grievance about specific government actions taken in the name of national security.
5   In situations of 'transference' the ISC introduces a more extensive factor into the equation of considerations. This stage is reached when, in reviewing national security matters justices, rather than relying principally on Israeli domestic laws, begin consistently to adopt relevant corpuses of international law (such as the laws of war or international

human rights law), as criteria for the judgment of executive action in this sphere. 'Transference' does not necessarily imply that the ISC will automatically outlaw specific actions on the part of the government and its agencies. What is at issue, rather, is the basis upon which it will reach its decision. Sometimes, the act of 'transference' will articulate a preference on the part of the justices for international law. More often, it reflects their sensitivity to the absence of reference in Israeli domestic law to many of the issues that now arise in the national security realm.

6   Finally, there exists the possibility of what we here term 'constitutionalism'. Theoretically, this is the most radical option open to the ISC, since it defines a situation in which justices, basing their opinions on immutable principles embedded in either domestic or international law, decide to turn down executive actions, which they declare to be illegal.

The tradition of enforcement

As previous chapters have shown, for the vast majority of its history, the ISC had restricted its function in national security issues to one of 'enforcement' and had hence adopted an essentially passive posture when called upon to define Israel's national security law. Justice Agranat's decision in *Kol ha-Am* v. *Minister of the Interior* (1953; see Chapter 3), which had posited a doctrine of fundamental rights as limits on executive action, for over three decades thereafter remained an altogether isolated exception. The tone of ISC judgments had begun to change somewhat in the decade prior to 1995, which witnessed additional signs that justices might occasionally be prepared to shift their behavior to the category of 'interpretation'. Therein, indeed, lay the significance of both *Schnitzer* v. *Chief Military Censor* (1989) and *Morcos* v. *Minister of Defense* (1991). But not until the mid-1990s did that process gather enough momentum to make 'interpretation' standard ISC practice.

The regularization of 'interpretation'

It was in two major judgments handed down during the last half of the 1990s, both of which concerned the status of women in the Israeli military, that the ISC most clearly indicated its preparedness to advance beyond its tradition of 'enforcement' with respect to national security issues and instead adopt, almost as a matter of course, a policy of 'interpretation', as it was already doing in other areas of public life. The subject matter was well-chosen. Although the IDF had undoubtedly taken several significant steps during the previous two decades to upgrade the status of its female complement, progress towards gender equality had been much slower in the military than in civilian society. As a group, women soldiers were still considered very much inferior to their male counterparts. Most girl draftees were assigned to low-prestige clerical tasks, and even those who were integrated into combat units were employed solely as instructors (Sasson-Levy 2006). Moreover, and notwithstanding several attempts to discredit sexual harassment in service, a phenomenon that had in earlier decades reached almost epidemic proportions, the predominantly male culture still fostered an atmosphere which gave officers a virtual *droit de seigneur* over the young women under their command. As one of Israel's leading sociologists pointed out, the consequences of this situation of fundamental inequality were by no means restricted to the barracks. Thanks to the noticeably porous nature of Israel's military–societal boundaries, its deleterious reverberations were bound to be felt throughout society.

> A feedback loop dynamic leads from women's marginalization in the military to women's disadvantage in civilian life and back again.... The differential treatment of men and women in the military ... produces differential opportunities for mobility both within the military and in civilian life that privilege men.... The advantages men derive from military service are converted into advantages in civilian life. Military elites slip into roles in civilian elites where they contribute to the reproduction of gender equality and to the perpetuation of gendered processes within the military.
>
> (Izraeli 1997:162)

Alice Miller v. *Minister of Defense* (1995) addressed the first of these issues: gender equality in military assignments. It originated in a petition by Ms. Alice Miller, a South African-born flying enthusiast of draft age who was in every respect qualified for acceptance to the air force's fighter pilot training course, but who had been barred entry because of her gender. The court discussion indicates that the IDF considered several responses to Ms. Miller's petition that the ISC overrule the air force's decision (Seidman and Nun 2001). One was to base its defense on the formal General Staff orders that barred women from combat postings. Another was to argue that society was not yet prepared to tolerate an assignment policy that placed women in danger of being killed in action or – perhaps worse still – being captured by enemy forces. Interestingly, however, in their oral presentations, representatives for the State (i.e., the IDF) adopted neither position. Neither did they take issue with the justiciability of the petition, or claim to be in possession of classified security information that could not be submitted to the ISC. Instead, they addressed the issue of women pilots on professional grounds, citing the allegedly objective arithmetic of the cost of training a pilot vis-à-vis the possible returns. At the root of this calculation lay the observation that the value of pilots to the air force is measured by the amount of reserve service that they perform after completing their training. Because women are exempt from reserve duty once they give birth to children, and even if they voluntarily waive that exemption can always reclaim it at will, the overall length of time that they will spend in service is likely to be considerably less than that of men. It follows that, proportionately, women pilots will be more expensive to produce. Given the strains on the air force budget, cost-effectiveness – not gender discrimination – therefore dictates their exclusion from fighter pilot school.

In the absence of a developed field in Israel of jurimetrics – the study of where judges stand in terms of political and societal opinions – it is impossible to discern with any certainty the influence exerted on the opinions in this case by the prior leanings of individual justices. Nevertheless, a few observations can be made. Justice Kedmi, who wrote the minority opinion, was one of the two ISC justices on this case who were known to be relatively conservative. Although he did not question the ISC's authority to review IDF actions, in every other respect Kedmi's text adhered to the norms of judicial deference that had traditionally been invoked in order to grant the IDF what amounted to immunity from ISC scrutiny.

> My position is that principled decisions of those responsible for national security, as much as they refer to the needs of security, and to the proper ways to attain security, should be attributed a high degree of reasonableness; persons who contest those decisions carry a heavy burden, which is equal to the burden which is carried by a person who wishes to counter a presumption in statute. I would hesitate to intervene in such decisions unless convinced that they are extremely unreasonable, arbitrary or capricious … I do not feel that in this instance I have the tools, and especially the competence, required to examine the 'reasonableness' of the assumptions detailed above [that women will not serve as long as men.
>
> (*Alice Miller* v. *Minister of Defense*, p. 117)

Kedmi's argument was ultimately overruled by a coalition of three other justices – two of whom were women and the third (Justice Matza) a man who had in 1994 given voice to his liberal attitude in matters of gender when writing the basic decision on affirmative action for women in *Shdulat ha-Nashim* v. *The Government of Israel*, a case involving the election of women to the directorates of public firms. Matza, who wrote the decision for the majority in *Miller* too, began in somewhat muted tones. Much of his text reads like a conventional administrative opinion, dealing with the decision to prioritize state interest over a fundamental right. Matza analyses the decision of the IDF, and finds that factual basis is somewhat lacking; he refers to the arguments put forward by the army as 'hypotheses', and rejects them as unfounded. But the final paragraphs, which may have been added in response to Kedmi's opinion, were considerably more ambitious and emphatically articulated a strategy of 'interpretation.' Paragraph 22, for instance, reads:

This Court is not inclined to interfere in the professional decisions of the military. However, it was never doubted, and the attorney for the respondents admitted as much, that the decisions and orders of the military, representing the policy of the IDF, are subject to this Court's judicial review. Personally, I have no doubt that a policy which violates a fundamental right can provide an appropriate basis for intervention by the Court. A violation of equality, based on sexual discrimination, is a clear example of case which justifies intervention. This is the case before us.

It would be difficult to exaggerate the revolutionary nature of the claims thus presented. For one thing, they deliberately grant the ISC's new policy of intervention in military affairs a far longer pedigree than they in fact possessed. Citing no legal authority other than attorneys for the respondents, Matza claims – incorrectly – that there has never been any doubt about the ISC's right to assess the IDF's actions exactly as it would those of any other agency of government. He also turns on its head the qualification that judicial intervention of that degree would only be justified where fundamental rights are involved. Although equality is generally considered integral to Israel's fundamental rights,[1] the principal was rarely applied to gender equality (Halperin-Kadari 2004:27).

From an international perspective, too, *Alice Miller* v. *Minister of Defense* possesses a status that is distinctive. This is not because of the extent of gender integration that it presaged; after all, women have made equally substantial advances towards integration in other militaries too (Sandhoff *et al.* 2010). Rather, *Miller* deserves to be considered *sui generis* by virtue of its procedural characteristics. Even in the liberal West, national courts have rarely interfered with military decisions to draft or not draft to particular persons. (Conscientious objectors, such as Jehovah Witnesses in the USA during World War II, constitute a singular exception). And whilst international courts, especially European international courts, have occasionally declared gender discrimination in military organizations to be illegal,[2] Israel is the only country in which a national court has mandated gender integration in the armed forces and moreover compelled a branch of service to place an individual in a specific posting.[3] The fact that the ISC behaved in this way, without any specific constitutional leg on which to stand, speaks volumes for the radical and idiosyncratic nature of its activism.

Four years after thus undermining the IDF's exclusive control over its placement policies, the ISC took the same line with respect to an even more sensitive area of military administration: promotions to senior rank. In *Jane Doe* v. *Chief of General Staff* (1999), it upheld the appeal of a woman who petitioned against the promotion of Brigadier-General Nir Galili to the rank of major-general in command of a field corps, on the grounds that he had raped her several years earlier when he had been her immediate superior. A detailed analysis of that case shows just how far the ISC was prepared to go in bringing the IDF in line with legislation passed in 1998 that made sexual harassment in all walks of life a criminal offense (Shaked 2002). No longer would the military organization enjoy an extraordinary degree of tolerance. True, Galili was not removed from his present command, still less cashiered, as many feminists insisted should have been the case. Otherwise, however, the three judges, who in this instance were all women, came down firmly on the side of the appellant, showing even less consideration for the opinions expressed by senior officers than had Justice Matza in the *Miller* case. They explicitly took no account of the fact that Galili had already been tried by an IDF disciplinary tribunal, which had in 1996 punished him by delaying his promotion for two years. Still more demonstratively, the justices also refused to be swayed by testimony given on Galili's behalf by the CGS, Shaul Mofaz, who declared that failure to promote Galili would endanger the IDF's operational capabilities. 'The considerations that have to be weighed', wrote Justice Strassberg-Cohen (who had sat on the bench during *Miller* case too), were entirely different. Specifically:

> ...the supreme importance of the IDF's moral probity; the need to uproot the phenomenon of sexual exploitation in situations of the subordination of soldiers to their officers; the need to strengthen public confidence in the IDF, not just as a professionally efficient body, but also as one that possesses credibility, probity, and a high moral standard, especially in the context of relationships between commanders and their soldiers.
>
> (Shaked 2002:459)

Subsequent to the Galilee case, the ISC's resort to a strategy of 'interpretation' in national security matters became almost routine. Moreover, the process itself followed an almost identical pattern. Deploying a human rights reading of the relevant statute, the ISC consistently subjected the IDF to the standards of human rights imposed on other administrative agencies. On that basis, in *Wichselbaum* v. *Minister of Defense* (1995) it granted parents the right to personalize the epitaphs on military gravestones. It also permitted bereaved parents access to the reports of the military committees that investigated the cause of death (Doron and Lebel 2001).

Most strikingly of all, in 2000, the ISC reversed its previous opinion on the legality of the IDF's protracted incarceration of Lebanese citizens, whose detention in Israeli prisons was intended to exert pressure on the Hizbollah organization to release Captain (res.) Ron Arad, the air force navigator who had fallen into captivity on 16 October 1986, when his Phantom F-4 exploded in mid-air. For over a decade after the incarceration practice was first initiated in 1988, the ISC had consistently (albeit not unanimously) rejected appeals for release submitted by the detainees. Instead, it had repeatedly resorted to an expansive interpretation of the Emergency Powers Law (Detentions) of 1979. This interpretation authorized the minister of defense to detain, for renewable terms of six months, any individuals whose imprisonment he considered necessary for reasons of national security, even though the detainees were not themselves involved in threatening activity. But in *John Does* v. *Ministry of Defense* (2000), a majority of a special panel of five justices, chaired by Aharon Barak changed that opinion and adopted a new and more restrictive interpretation of the Emergency Powers Law. It was now understood to mean that the minister could only order a detention when in possession of clear and substantive evidence showing that the specific individual constituted a threat. Barak, who wrote the opinion, stressed that the new interpretation far better reflects the fundamental rights doctrine that the ISC was committed to uphold. Most of the detainees were immediately released.

The singularity of this case lies in its context. The ISC, after all, was certainly not alone in opposing detention without trial. As Benvenisti points out, in reaction to the policies adopted by several governments after 11 September 2001, especially, precisely the same stand was taken by other national courts and international tribunals, including the US Supreme Court, the German Constitutional Court and the UK House of Lords (Benvenisti 2008a). But in none of those instances were the justices required to weigh the individual rights of detainees against the impact that their release might exert on the life of a soldier known to be in enemy hands. That, however, was precisely the dilemma faced by the ISC.

Attribution – sending the case back to the knesset

In addition to thus intensifying its amplification and application of fundamental rights principles to national security concerns, in the years spanning the turn of the new millennium the ISC also began to employ what is here termed a strategy of 'attribution.' This involved handing down decisions that required the legislature to exercise its law-making powers and explicitly state whether or not it is giving the executive a mandate to act in a particular area of national security concern.

The application of this strategy was first demonstrated in the way in which, late in the 1990s, the ISC addressed the exemptions from military service granted to students in ultra-orthodox theological seminaries (*yeshivot*). In accordance with an arrangement that Ben-Gurion had reached with representatives of the ultra-orthodox (*haredi*) community as long ago as 1947 (Friedman 1995), successive ministers of defense had over the years regularly granted draft deferments to *haredi* males who claimed to be engaged full-time in the study of traditional Judaism's sacred texts. But what had once been a limited occurrence, which in 1948 affected less than 400 individuals, had mushroomed into a widespread phenomenon.

152   *Development*

Total *haredi* draft deferments jumped to 8,257 in 1977, the year that *haredi* political parties first joined a government coalition, and thereafter grew exponentially. By 1985, they had already reached 16,000 and – given the relatively high *haredi* birth rate – were projected to double themselves yet again over the next decade.

Although a handful of members of the *knesset* had occasionally sought a parliamentary debate on this topic in the 1980s, their efforts had been time and again thwarted by political pressure. As all the major parties were aware, even to hint that the existing arrangement might have to be altered was to run the risk of irrevocably antagonizing the *haredim*, without whose support no coalition government could possibly survive. As has been seen (Chapter 5), Yehudah Ressler, a Tel-Aviv advocate, had by the late 1980s finally got the ISC to agree to consider his petition to the effect that *haredi* draft deferments violated the principle of equality. But although Ressler thus managed to overcome the original 'standing' hurdle, his petitions had no substantive effect. In *Ressler* v. *Minister of Defense* (1988), for instance, the ISC concluded that the existing arrangement of draft deferments was 'reasonable', and hence refused to intervene.

In the late 1990s, however, that argument was becoming increasingly difficult to sustain. For once, the statisticians were correct. At the end of that decade, some 35,000 *haredim* declared themselves to be full-time *torah* students. By then, indeed, some 4,000 deferments were being granted to *haredi* males of conscript age every year, thereby depriving the IDF of almost 10 percent of its annual Jewish conscript potential. Publication of these figures induced Ressler, who on this occasion was joined by MK Professor Amnon Rubenstein, to petition the ISC once again. The sequence was surprising. In *Rubinstein* v. *Minister of Defense* (1998), the ISC did not discuss whether or not the government might be violating a fundamental principle when granting so many draft deferments. Instead Justice Aharon Barak, who authored the opinion, used the scope of the phenomenon as grounds for declaring that the decision was too principled to be left to the sole discretion of the minister of defense. On divisive issues such as this, where a balance had to be struck between conflicting interests and rights, the ISC's view was that decisions should be taken by the *knesset*, and not the executive.

Even thus baldly summarized, the *Rubinstein* decision clearly marked an advance on the position adopted by the ISC in the *Miller* and *Galili* cases. In the latter instances, the court had used its interpretative authority in order to redefine the boundaries of a particular principle in law. Where *haredi* draft deferments were concerned, however, it was extending its responsibilities to encompass the preservation of the separation of powers – a system of checks and balances basic to the democratic structure as a whole. Hence, the ISC was using its authority in order to compel the legislature to legislate. What form the new legislation should take remained, of course, open to debate (although Barak made it clear that the justices reserved the right to intervene once again should they consider that the *knesset* was indeed violating a fundamental principle). But at the present stage, procedure took precedence over substance. In effect, the ISC enunciated what amounted to an Israeli version of the 'non-delegation' doctrine notoriously articulated by its US counterpart in the 1930s. That it did so with respect to a topic affecting national security was not incidental. This particular sphere was selected for the declaration of a new doctrine, not despite it being the least regulated of all areas in Israeli public life, but precisely for that reason. The time had come to end the system of executive hegemony that had prevailed for so long and to encourage legislative involvement in this area.

The ISC reiterated its commitment to this approach in *The Public Committee Against Torture* v. *The Government of Israel* (1999), in which it reviewed the authority of the General Security Service (GSS) to apply moderate physical pressure to suspected terrorists. Here too, the justices knowingly departed from their own previous practice. In the past, they had persistently resorted to 'avoidance doctrines' when petitioned to review the position of the Landau Commission, which had concluded that 'necessity' (i.e., national security) might warrant a resort to some degree of force on the part of GSS operatives when interrogating suspects. In this case, however, the justices took a different tack. Once again writing for the majority, Justice Aharon Barak ruled that the only way that force could be used in investigations could be by express legislative authorization. Although Justice Cheshin, in a concurring opinion, acknowledged that a plea of 'necessity' could perhaps justify resort to physical torture in an extreme ('ticking bomb') situation,[4] coming on the heels of the precedent that it had recently set with respect to *haredi* draft deferments, the direction that the ISC was now taking was unmistakable. First, it was denying 'national security' even a shadow of the deference that it had once enjoyed as a matter of course (Justice Kedmi, who was prepared to grant the government a lengthy period of grace in order to prepare the necessary legislation, was overwhelmingly outvoted by his colleagues). Second, the ISC was now insisting that the legislature assume responsibility for subjects that had moved to the forefront of Israel's national security concerns: the equitable distribution of the burden of military service and the preservation of basic human rights even under circumstances of national danger.

Early in the new millennium, Benvenisti suggested that these two decisions represent an attempt on the part of the court to create checks and balances in the area of national security (Benvenisti 2001). If so, they deserve notice as an unusual – and important – effort by the ISC to employ judicial decisions as a means of dividing the responsibility between the different branches of government. However, it must be noted that the ISC made no further attempt to employ this form of judicial 'traffic control', a maneuver that our concluding chapter will argue possesses several merits.

Intermission: the impact of the 2nd intifada, 2000–2006

Predominantly, the decisions relative to national security taken by the ISC between 1995 and 2000 concerned 'domestic' military matters: individual service placements, sexual mores in the ranks, and enlistment policies. Topics bearing on the IDF's operational conduct and rules of engagement were noticeably absent from the agenda. In large part, that bias can be attributed to a prevailing atmosphere of relative security tranquility, which allowed attention to focus on less bellicose subjects. Of course, the reality of the overall security situation remained sober. During those years the IDF was still very much a fighting force, heavily involved in defending its 'security zone' in southern Lebanon against Hizbollah attacks. Likewise, Israeli citizens, on both sides of the Green Line, were still subject to suicide bombings and drive-by shootings perpetrated by other Palestinian groups. Nevertheless, a corner seemed to have been turned. Surveys conducted throughout the period revealed a slow but steady decline in public threat perceptions, a trend both boosted and justified by the fact that 1999 was the first year in Israel's entire history that not a single civilian died as a result of a terrorist attack (Ben-Meir and Bagno-Moldavsky 2010:56–60). On the political front, too, tensions seemed to be abating. The framework of Palestinian–Israeli security cooperation, established in the years 1993–1995 when Rabin was still alive, had been buttressed by the agreements signed by Yassir Arafat and Binyamin Netanyahu at the Wye plantation summit in October 1998. And although progress towards a comprehensive agreement stalled thereafter, hopes that the process might be resuscitated revived after the general elections in 2000. Netanyahu's successor as prime minister, Ehud Barak, not only immediately carried out his campaign promise to withdraw all IDF forces from southern Lebanon. With equal alacrity he also pushed for the convention of an American–Israeli–Palestinian summit at Camp David, intended to settle Israeli–Palestinian differences once and for all (Ben-Ami 2006:250–3).

That outcome was not attained. Instead, in the aftermath of the Camp David failure relationships between Israelis and Palestinians rapidly deteriorated. On 29 September 2000 they entered a new violent phase with the outbreak of another *intifada*, which was much bloodier than its predecessor. Whereas 421 Israelis had been killed during the first *intifada* (1987–1993) and some 1,000 injured, for the second *intifada* (which petered out in 2005) the figures were, respectively, 1,070 and 8,000. On the Palestinian side, the cost was yet higher: some 5,000 fatalities and 25,000 injured during the second *intifada* as opposed to less than 2,000 killed and 2,000 injured during the first (S. Cohen 2008:179 n.3). Clearly, that background was not conducive to sustaining a judicial focus on 'domestic' aspects of military affairs. The real question was whether it would altogether permit the ISC to maintain the momentum of its growing intervention in national security issues.

In large part, the answer was influenced by the IDF's claim that the second *intifada* had created an entirely new national security situation. Outbreaks of violence on the scale witnessed during and after September 2000, ran the military's argument, rendered obsolescent all former definitions of the Israeli–Palestinian conflict. Given the number of troops now committed to suppressing the uprising, and the firepower that they had to employ, it no longer made sense to speak of IDF missions in the territories in terms of constabulary operations, designed merely to restore law and order (Sa. Cohen 2009:129–213). Rather, the present campaign warranted categorization as a military confrontation or, in the formulation contained in a legal deposition submitted in December 2000 to the CGS by Colonel Daniel Reizner, the MAG's advisor on matters of international law, 'an armed conflict short of war' (cited in Harel and Isacharoff 2004:195).[5] Similarly inventive skills were also employed in order to revise definitions of the enemy. If the IDF was to be able to justify its own resort to force, many of the old terms ('law-breakers', 'disturbers of public order') clearly had to be abandoned. On the other hand, Palestinians could not be accorded the status of 'combatants', a definition that might entitle them to the rights due to prisoners of war. Instead, in response to *The Public Committee against Torture in Israel* v. *The Government of Israel* (2006) the IDF was to maintain that all Palestinians fighting against Israel fell into a category that the Americans fighting in Afghanistan had already termed 'illegal combatants' (Roberts 2003). From the military point of view, this was the best of all possible designations. As 'illegals', Palestinians were denied the protections due to both soldiers and civilians; but as 'combatants', they remained legitimate targets of Israeli military activity.

Peri contends that the second *intifada* witnessed a resuscitation, and indeed exacerbation, of many of the problems that had plagued the formulation and execution of Israel's national security decision-making ever since the State's foundations (Peri 2006:91–108, 123–36). Since no statutory steps had been taken since 1974 to demarcate spheres of civil–military responsibility (spheres whose borders in any case tend to become fuzzy during 'low intensity conflicts' the world over; S. Cohen 2003), that situation is hardly surprising. As will be seen (below pp. 214–15), not even the establishment of a National Security Council in 2000 had done anything to repair the well-known deficiencies in relations between the IDF and the cabinet.

Relations between the military and the ISC were more complex – and for that reason more interesting. On the one hand, the ISC accepted that Israel's conflict with the Palestinians had indeed entered a new phase ('armed conflict little short of war'). Hence, it recognized that military personnel might be required to resort to more force than was acceptable in constabulary operations. Nevertheless, it did not revert to the attitude of deference to IDF discretion characteristic of its behavior during the first three decades of Israel's existence. Even during the second *intifada*, the

156 *Development*

ISC maintained the tempo of its increasing intrusion into military affairs. All that changed was the form and direction of its activity. Instead of restricting its attention largely to domestic military matters and pursuing strategies that we have termed 'interpretation' and 'attribution', the ISC increasingly focused on relations between the IDF and external, non-Israeli bodies. In so doing, it also adopted several new methodologies, of which the most pronounced and influential were 'facilitation' and 'transference'.

Facilitation

Palestinians and Israelis have never been the only parties to play a role in their conflict. At various times, events have also been influenced by a wide variety of other 'actors'. During the first decades of Israeli occupation, the latter category consisted primarily of either neighboring Arab countries or more distant states with an interest in Middle Eastern affairs, including, of course, the great powers. Non-state actors, even the UN, usually acted in little more than an observatory capacity. That balance altered, however, after the late-1980s, when increasing numbers of NGOs, some based in Israel, began to evince an interest in the conflict and its impact on Palestinian society. According to one count, whereas only one Israeli human rights NGO was active in Israel prior to December 1987, by 2002 the number had risen to 26 (Berkovitz and Gordon 2008:881).

In addition to undertaking conventional humanitarian work, these groups also turned to legal means as a primary vehicle for the attainment of their goals. Organizations such as '*Adalah* – The Legal Centre for Arab Minority Rights in Israel', 'The Center for the Protection of the Individual', 'The Public Committee against Torture', '*Gishah*', 'Physicians for Human Rights', 'Rabbis for Human Rights', and especially the most renowned human rights NGO – 'The Israeli Civil Rights Association' – all invested much of their energies in petitioning the ISC. As has been seen (Chapter 5) the court did not resist this tendency. On the contrary, it encouraged it, not least by lifting the 'standing' requirement. The removal of that barrier exerted a further multiplying effect, so much so that by the late 1990s, for many of the NGOs, petitions to the ISC often constituted their major activity. In essence, the political discussion over the territories had by then become a legal dialogue.

Throughout this development, the ISC had limited its function to providing a forum in which the two sides – usually the IDF and one or more NGOs representing Palestinian rights – might mediate their differences and search for some middle ground. During the second *intifada*, however, the ISC began to play a more active role, functioning as a go-between and mediating in its own right, even during exchanges of fire, between Palestinians and their NGO representatives on the one hand and the IDF on the other.

Early indications of the ISC's readiness to assume that role appeared in the spring of 2002, a period of especially heightened violence. During March 2002, 26 IDF soldiers and 105 Israeli civilians were killed in a spate of especially viscous suicide bombings, the most horrendous of which, responsible for 30 deaths, took place on March 27, the first night of the Jewish festival of Passover (which is traditionally marked by a communal gathering and meal) at the Park Hotel in Netanya. In retaliation, the cabinet instructed the IDF to undertake a large-scale infantry and armored assault on the terrorist infrastructures located in Palestinian-controlled cities (operation 'Defensive Shield'). Between 29 March and 6 May 2002, Ramallah, Nablus, Jenin, Bethlehem, Tul Karem, and Kalkiliyah all became scenes of heavy exchanges of fire, which ultimately claimed the lives of 29 IDF soldiers and almost 500 Palestinians (Harel and Isacharoff 2004:251–60).

Initial ISC interest focused on the city of Jenin, where the fighting was especially and unexpectedly intense and where the scale of property destruction was reported to be exceptionally high. During the very first days of the operation, one NGO (Physicians for Human Rights) claimed that the IDF was firing on vehicles transporting medical supplies to Palestinians, and petitioned the ISC to halt the practice. Although the court did not bluntly reject the claim, on the justiciability of which it passed no comment whatsoever, the overall tone of its response was muted. For one thing, it argued, the facts were still unknown; besides, the IDF had announced its intention of respecting international law (*Physicians for Human Rights* v. *IDF Commander in the West Bank* [8 April 2002]). The following day, the ISC was again petitioned, this time on the grounds that the IDF was violating the rule that gave house owners the right of hearing before their property was destroyed. Again, the ISC said nothing about the justicability of the case. But it did accept the State's argument that appeals against impending house destructions could not be granted during battle (*Adalah* v. *IDF Commander in Judea and Samaria* [9 April 2002]). Before another 24 hours had elapsed, the ISC was petitioned for a third time, *inter alia* by The Association for Human Rights in Israel, which asked that the IDF be ordered not to target civilian populations and in general to follow IHL with regards to the protection of civilians. On this occasion, the State did respond with a 'non-justiciable' claim, which the ISC accepted. 'Substantively and institutionally', reads the decision in *Canon (Law) and others* v. *IDF Commander of the West Bank* (10 April 2002), 'it is impossible to give the relief that the petitioners ask for.'

At that point, the lines seemed clearly drawn: there was to be no judicial review of military actions whilst fighting still raged. Within four days, however, the 'protected' area of autonomy thus granted to the IDF was narrowed by the ISC's response to a fourth petition regarding the Jenin operation. Formally, the issue in this case concerned a secondary matter: would Palestinians killed in the fighting be buried by their own side or by

158   *Development*

the IDF? Behind this question, however, lurked the highly combustible accusation (voiced by the petitioner, MK Barake) that the IDF had committed a massacre in Jenin and wished to bury the dead in order to conceal its extent.[6] Intervening for the first time in the Jenin series of petitions, Justice Aharon Barak decided to break new ground. Instead of attempting to reach a decision as to the respective merits of the two sides, in *MK Barake* v. *Minister of Defense* (14 April 2002) he sought to broker an agreement between them. Eventually, it was agreed that in order to dispel any suspicion that the IDF was trying to hide something, Red Cross staff would participate in the identification and burial of the dead. In effect, Justice Barak thus assumed a new role. In addition to being the senior member of the highest court in the land, he now also appointed himself to be a kind of national mediator.

Barak followed his own precedent on two further occasions: during the IDF's siege of the Church of the Nativity in Bethlehem (April–May 2002) and its incursion into Rafah in the Gaza Strip (May 2004). Both operations raised humanitarian issues that, in Barak's opinion, no democratic state could ignore, even in times of war. In Bethlehem, attention focused on the extent of the IDF's duty to deliver food, water and additional necessities to the 180 clerics and other civilian personnel who were being held hostage in the Church of the Nativity by some 40 armed Palestinians, especially when all such deliveries weakened Israel's bargaining power regarding the hostage-takers (*Al-Madani* v. *Minister of Defense* [2 May 2002]). In Rafah, the matter at issue was the supply of medical supplies and food to the thousands of Palestinian residents in an area to which the IDF was laying siege. In both cases, Barak's stated premises were absolutely clear. Israeli jurisprudence would have no truck with Cicero's notorious pronouncement '*silent enim leges inter arma*', a proposition that he considered contradictory not only to international humanitarian law but also to the ethos upon which Israel was founded. As he wrote in his *Al-Madani* judgment (pp. 34–5):

> The values of the State of Israel are Jewish and democratic. We have established here a law-abiding state, which fulfills its national aims and age-old vision whilst also acknowledging and implementing human rights in general and human dignity in particular. Those two objectives exist in harmony and suitability not opposition and estrangement.

Non-justiciability (which was the response entered by the State), therefore, was out of the question. But so too was the non-interventionist position that had been articulated by Justice Strasberg-Cohen with respect to an earlier petition to the ISC concerning the situation in the Church of the Nativity (*Custodia Internazionale Di Terra Santa* v. *The Government of Israel* [24 April 2002]). Refusing to sit on the sidelines, Barak on both occasions again donned the mantle of go-between. In the Church of the Nativity case he brokered an agreement between the IDF and NGOs regarding the way in which food would be delivered to the captive civilians and monks. Two years later, when passing judgment in *Physicians for Human Rights* v. *IDF Commander in Gaza* (2004), he likewise ruled that – even whilst military operations were in progress – the IDF must allow the passage of vital supplies in quantities that were acceptable both to the military authorities and the petitioners.

Transference

Barak's decisions in the Jenin, Church of Nativity and Rafah cases did not just signify an expansion in the scope of the ISC's impact on Israel's national security behavior. The manner in which those decisions referred to international law also indicated that an equally fundamental shift was taking place in the locus of the authority to which the court was now appealing. True, several previous ISC decisions had also made mention of a corpus generally identified as either the international law of armed conflict or international humanitarian law. But other than in the *Dawikat* judgment of 1979 with respect to the settlement of Elon Moreh (above p. 136), appeals to universal principles embodied in international law had been relatively limited. Only after the outbreak of the second *intifada* did International Law (now capitalized) come to constitute a primary source of jurisprudence, rather than simply an adjunct to domestic legislation. Likewise, only then did the ISC begin to find in International Law a reason for challenging executive actions in the national security realm.

Part of that change can be attributed to developments in the international legal arena, of which the most important were the establishment of several international tribunals specifically mandated to adjudicate situations of military occupation and to provide institutional interpretations of international humanitarian law (IHL) and/or the international laws of armed conflict. Thus, as from the mid-1990s, war crimes' tribunals were created by the UNs Security Council (UNSC) and by special agreements with states. In 2003 a permanent International Criminal Court with wide jurisdiction began to operate. More importantly, the re-emergence of the UNSC as a dominant force in international politics indicated that it would become increasingly difficult to ignore decisions taken by international tribunals, even if they lacked enforcement mechanisms. On another level, several states began to apply, sometimes vigorously, the doctrine of universal jurisdiction, which allows national courts to adjudicate international crimes (Bassiouni 2008; Schabas 2010).

These developments clearly influenced both the content and the style of the ISC discourse. For one thing, its decisions of this period reference the international law of armed conflict far more frequently than had previously been the case. More significantly, they also exhibit a noticeable tendency to make IHL an indispensable ingredient of the assessment of the legality of IDF action in the Territories. This was a shift of especially significant proportions, since it implied that the justices had abandoned whatever hopes they might at one time have harbored that the politicians might be relied upon to change or curtail IDF policies. Confronted with evidence that, in fact, ministers were usually giving *ex ante* approval to IDF actions in the Territories, the ISC seems to have felt that it constituted the only civilian institution now capable of influencing the shape and direction of national security policy. International law was enlisted for that purpose – not least by being referenced as a boundary marker that the justices would employ in order define the acceptable limits of IDF actions.

Barak first gave notice of the new direction in *Ajuri* v. *IDF Commander of West Bank* (2002). Ostensibly, the issue in this case was hardly novel: an appeal against an IDF decision to relocate the family of a deceased suicide bomber from the West Bank to the Gaza Strip. The decision, too, accorded with precedent, in that the ISC allowed this instance of 'assigned residence' for one of the three people to whom the government sought to apply the policy. Where Barak broke new ground, however, was in the principles that he enunciated in his decision, with which all of his colleagues on the bench concurred. First, he declared the Fourth Geneva Convention (Article 78 of which relates to 'assigned residence') to be applicable and enforceable by the courts – a position that had thereto been considered at best debatable, but was henceforth never questioned. Second, he interpreted Article 78 of the Fourth Geneva Convention far more strictly than had previously been conventional, limiting future cases of assigned residence to persons who could be proved to have been directly involved in a crime. As a political maneuver, this was a characteristically masterful stroke. Without explicitly announcing that such was his intent, Barak thus ensured that assigned residence would simply disappear from the IDF's repertoire of punishments. Indeed, since *Ajuri*, it has never again been used. More to the point, Barak had also given notice of his determination to ensure that the ISC, in its position as Israel's senior interpreter of international law, would henceforth be regarded as a major component in the national security decision-making process.

The latter position was stated even more explicitly in Barak's judgment in *Beit Sourik Village Council* v. *The Government of Israel* (2004). This was one of a series of cases revolving around the 'security/separation fence' that Israel began to construct in 2002 in an effort to impede the movement of terrorists intent on attacking Israeli civilian targets.[7] Israeli military officials were persistently to credit this obstacle barrier with responsibility for reducing the level of Palestinian incursions and attacks (e.g., Almog 2004). Its opponents highlighted, by contrast, the economic, social and psychological hardships that what they termed 'the separation barrier' or 'apartheid wall' was causing to numerous Palestinians living in the vicinity of its alignment, as well as the injustices inherent in the fact that in many instances it was built on Palestinian-owned land (Arieli and Sfard 2008). In *Beit Sourik*, Justice Barak sought to balance the conflicting aspects of the case. Accepting the State's argument that the barrier was designed to serve security purposes, and not to promote a political program, Barak was prepared to sanction some infractions of human rights, such as the confiscation of private lands situated on the route of its construction. Where he drew a line, however, was on granting the military sole discretion in the determination of what actions could and could not be taken. As he wrote in paragraph 48 of his judgment:

> The military commander is the expert regarding the military quality of the separation fence route. We are experts regarding its humanitarian aspects. The military commander determines where, on hill and plain, the separation fence will be erected. That is his expertise. We examine whether this route's harm to the local residents is proportional. That is our expertise.

Idiosyncratic though Barak's interpretation of the proportionality principle might have been from a strictly legal perspective (Cohen-Eliya 2005), as a declaration of institutional judicial empowerment it deserves to be considered a milestone. In this presentation, 'proportionality' is a standard rather than a rule, a term that has constantly to be interpreted by the courts and remains open-ended even subsequent to its application in a specific case (Am. Cohen 2008). In that meaning, moreover, the terms 'proportionality' and 'reasonableness' (its corollary) allowed the ISC enormous flexibility, not least with respect to the extent of its own intervention in a particular issue. Hence, it did not have to be an external observer of national security decision-making. On the contrary, its deliberations and assessments could constitute an essential part of the process. With respect to the separation barrier that was certainly the case. Since *Beit Sourik*, almost every kilometer of its alignment has been subjected to judicial review and almost every issue raised by its construction has reached judicial decision. Moreover, whenever the tension between security needs and human rights did not seem otherwise amenable to harmonization the ISC has played an active role in seeking and designing alternatives, such as secondary roads around the barrier and the placement of 'gates' at various points along its route in order to allow the passage of Palestinian agricultural traffic.

Ten days after the ISC issued its *Beit Sourik* decision, the International Court of Justice (ICJ) published its *Advisory Opinion – Legal Consequences of the Construction of a Wall in the Occupied Palestinian Territories*. The two documents, both available at www.asil.org/ilib/ilib0712.htm#j2, disputed several essentials. Contradicting the ISC, the ICJ argued that the real goal behind the barrier (which is pointedly termed a 'wall') is political; it is designed to facilitate the annexation of some of the territories, an action forbidden by international law. Likewise, the ICJ declared the construction of the barrier to be in violation of international human rights laws and international humanitarian laws, a situation that it called upon all states to end. But not even this condemnation (incidentally, the first and thus far the only occasion on which the ISC has come into direct conflict with an international tribunal) caused the ISC to retract from its basic position with respect to the need to apply international law to matters related to Israel's national security. On the contrary, in his judgment in *Mara'be* v. *The Government of Israel* (2005), Barak invested considerable energy in arguing – contrary to much of the evidence – that disputes between the ISC and the ICJ revolved around facts rather than the law *per se*.[8] On the basic principle, the content of international law and its status, the two sides were, so he maintained, in complete agreement.

Given that background, it is hardly surprising to find that the ISC enunciated similar principles when petitioned with respect to the legality of the IDF policy of what were termed 'targeted killings', attempts to take the life of a previously specified individual alleged to be involved in terrorist activities or planning to perpetrate a terrorist attack. Acknowledging the need for both operational speed and surprise, the ISC could not insist that it review each proposed targeted killing mission operation prior to action being taken, which is basically what it declared itself competent to do with respect to the construction of the separation barrier. But in all other essentials the positions adopted with respect to the two sets of cases were the same. Although some IDF preventative strikes might indeed meet the demands of international legality, especially if it could be shown that the target had taken a 'direct part in the hostilities', this form of military activity would always be subject to legal restrictions. Once again, Barak summed up his position with the utmost clarity. Giving judgment on *The Public Committee Against Torture in Israel* v. *The Government of Israel* on 14 December 2006 (his very last day in office as president of the ISC), he wrote (paragraph 60):

> [W]e cannot determine that a preventative strike is always legal, just as we cannot determine that it is always illegal. All depends upon the question whether the standards of customary international law regarding international armed conflict allow that preventative strike or not.

And the only institution that could make that assessment was, of course, the ISC itself.

The road rarely taken – constitutional review and complete ban based on international law.

Substantial though they undoubtedly were, the steps thus taken by the ISC to influence national security decision-making were not altogether unrestrained. In fact, other than in one peripheral instance,[9] justices seemed deliberately to stop short of the radical tactic of striking down actions taken by the executive or the legislature on the grounds that they conflict with a constitutional or otherwise immutable principle of Israeli and/or international law. Rather, the ISC was careful to leave the other branches a means of amending their own policy – primarily, it seems, out of respect for the government and the *knesset*.

Even when the ISC did deviate from that path, either by totally banning a particular national security policy or by declaring it to be unconstitutional, its behavior must be attributed more to the extenuating circumstances of each individual case than to the influence of a general policy. Three instances are in this respect illustrative.

- One is *Adalah – The Legal Center for Arab Minority Rights in Israel* v. *OC Central Command* (2005), colloquially known as the 'early warning' decision, in which the ISC, then still under Barak's presidency, declared unlawful the 'neighbor practice' – a procedure whereby the IDF used civilians as intermediaries, tasked with persuading terrorists holed up in their neighborhood to give themselves up peacefully to the soldiers surrounding them. Ostensibly, this decision rested on the ISC's judgment that the practice violated the principle that civilians must never be involved in battlefield operations. But it may also have been influenced by the wish of the justices not to be excluded from the operational arena. After all, the conditions under which the 'neighbor practice' was employed, a hostile area in the midst of an operation, invariably left the commander with no opportunity to consult with any non-military agency of assessment, or even with the internal legal advisors of the military, and especially not with the ISC. Hence, no matter how many legal limitations might be put on the 'neighbor practice', it would in the last analysis still remain beyond the span of judicial control. Under those circumstances, Barak may well have thought it best to wipe the slate entirely clean, and outlaw the practice altogether.
- *Abu Zafya* v. *Minister of Defense* (2009) provides another instance of an ISC decision against the government that warrants consideration as an exceptional judgment rather than a link in a chain of premeditated constitutional review. At issue was the right of Palestinian access to a major highway (Route 443, linking the coastal plain and the Jerusalem hills) which had been built, in part, on private land in the Territories that the ISC had in 1983 been permitted to be requisitioned from its Palestinian owners (*Jama'at Aschan Elmualamin* v. *IDF Commander Judea and Samaria Region* [1983]). In response to persistent Palestinian attacks on Jewish traffic along the route during the years 2000–2002, the IDF had barred access from the adjacent Palestinian towns of Ramallah and Bituniya, thereby effectively making it altogether off-limits for Palestinians. In its judgment, the ISC unanimously declared the IDF's action to be illegal.

Once again, the decision lends itself to two levels of interpretation. Formally, it rested on the argument that the punishment (the closure of the road to all Palestinian traffic) was disproportional to the threat of violence, especially since the latter could be reduced by such alternative means as checkpoints and an increased military presence. Clearly, however, other considerations also intruded. When originally sanctioning the requisition of the land on which the road was built, the ISC had assumed that its construction would also benefit the Palestinians. From that perspective, the closure of Route 443 – in addition to all its other faults – also made a mockery of the ISC, and that was something that could not be tolerated.

Broadly similar considerations also influenced the ISC's attitude to Article 5 of the Criminal Procedure Law, which a majority of judges declared in February 2010 to be unconstitutional (*John Doe* v. *The State of Israel*). Originally enacted for a period of 18 months in 2005, and renewed for a further three years in 2007, Article 5 made it possible, in very specific cases, to hold a hearing regarding detention of a person suspected of terrorist activities without his/her presence, provided that the detention period thus imposed would not exceed 20 days.

Ostensibly, this decision seemed to set a precedent, since it was the first occasion on which legislation directly supporting national security was declared unconstitutional (in this case, on the grounds that it violated the right of the suspect in security offenses to liberty and a fair trial). Once again, however, closer inspection reveals several other sides to the picture. For one thing, the justices took pains to point out that since the article was applied very rarely, their decision would have little practical impact. Especially was this so since their judgment did not prevent the executive from resorting, in cases of extreme emergency, to other measures, including the ban on meetings between suspects and their lawyers, which would in any case render judicial review entirely ineffective. Last, and certainly not least, the judges obviously found unpalatable the fact that Article 5 had originally been justified by an assumption that judicial review could 'impede' investigations. Clearly, so direct an attack on the judicial process could not possibly be tolerated.

Far more indicative of ISC policy during this period, we argue, are those cases in which it refrained from banning a national security policy, or from declaring a particular item of legislation to be unconstitutional, even when presented with an opportunity to do so.

One such occasion arose in July 2002 when, after tense debate, the *knesset* finally complied with the ISC directive to regulate the contentious issue of the non-enlistment of *haredi* males (handed down in the *Rubinstein* decision of 1998), and passed the Service Deferral Law. In most essentials this item of legislation adopted the recommendations submitted the previous year by a government-sponsored commission, chaired by former Supreme Court Justice Zvi Tal (hence it is popularly known as the 'Tal

Law'). At its root lay a complex scheme designed to provide *haredim* with the opportunity to enter the workforce by offering them exemption from military service at the age of 24, provided they first undertook the largely symbolic step of enlisting for an abbreviated spell of military or civil service. No sooner had the Tal Law been enacted, however, than petitions were submitted to the ISC, claiming that this arrangement violated the constitutional principle of equality, and demanding that it be struck down. The text of the ISC's decision in *The Movement for the Quality of Government and others* v. *the Knesset and others* (2005) leaves no doubt that the justices shared many of the petitioners' misgivings. Even so, they refrained from acceding to their wishes. Rather than declare the Tal Law unconstitutional, the ISC announced that it would grant the experiment a period of grace. Not until 2011 would the case be reopened and the legality of the legislation be re-assessed.

ISC attitudes towards the 2005 disengagement from the Gaza Strip followed a similar trajectory. Although showing some sympathy for the settlers who were slated to lose their homes and livelihoods, the justices rejected a petition to declare that implementation of the government's policy would violate their property rights and human dignity. Instead, the majority decision in *Gaza Beach Regional Council* v. *The Knesset* (2005), from which Justice Edmond Levy dissented, deemed the evacuation itself to be legal, because the violation of the rights of the settlers was proportional compared to the national interest. The ISC would do no more than make slight improvements to the compensation package that the evictees were due to receive.

Finally, note must be taken of the ISC's attitude towards the Citizenship and Entrance to Israel (Temporary Measures) Act passed by the *knesset* in 2003, which instructed the minister of the interior not to grant any resident of the Territories either a permit to reside permanently in Israel or Israeli citizenship. This law did not apply to Jewish settlers, who are in any case Israeli citizens. In effect, therefore, it targeted Palestinian spouses of Arab-Israelis. It was said to be justified on the grounds that it closed a loophole that had in the past been exploited by terrorists. However, in *Adalah* v. *Minister of Interior* (2006), petitioners to the ISC claimed that it violated the fundamental right to human dignity, equality and family life.

Once again, opinions amongst the justices were divided. Barak, who wrote the minority opinion in May 2006, invoked his now familiar doctrine denying national security matters a privileged status.

> We must treat human rights seriously both in times of war and in times of calm. We must free ourselves from the naïve belief that when terror ends we will be able to put the clock back. Indeed, if we fail in our task in times of war and terror, we will not be able to carry out our task properly in times of peace and calm. From this viewpoint, a

mistake by the judiciary in a time of emergency is more serious than a mistake of the legislature and the executive in a time of emergency. The reason for this is that the mistake of the judiciary will accompany democracy even when the threat of terror has passed, and it will remain in the case law of the Court as a magnet for the development of new and problematic rulings.

(*Adalah* v. *Minister of Interior*, Article 20)

However, on this occasion, the majority of the ISC was prepared to meet Barak's arguments head-on. Justice Grunis, who wrote a concurring opinion for the majority, explicitly rejected Barak's 'ratchet' hypothesis, and instead emphasized the here-and-now nature of the risks likely to be incurred by not according priority to interests of state security over human rights.

Granted, if the petitions before us are denied and it is held that the law remains valid, there will be a violation of the right to family life of an unknown number of Israeli citizens. On the other hand, if the petitions are granted and it is held that the law is not valid, there will be a violation of the right to life and physical and emotional integrity of an unknown number of persons. Since we are dealing with unknowns on both sides of the equation, there is no alternative to taking into account the possibility of error. In my opinion, greater weight should be attributed to a fear of error on the side of the equation containing the right to life.

(*Adalah* v. *Minister of Interior*, Article 8)

And there followed a telling peroration, in which Grunis went on to query whether Israeli national security policies had to differ from those of any other nation state under threat.

The opinion of my colleague, the President [of the Court], abounds as usual with citations from all parts of the world and is replete with references to many thinkers and scholars. Notwithstanding, [he] does not provide even a single example of a country that has allowed the entry of thousands of enemy nationals into its territory for any purpose during a time of war or of armed struggle. Certainly, there is no example of a Court that has ordered a State to allow the entry of thousands of enemy nationals into its territory.

Responses

Although the ISC thus invariably stopped short of striking down actions taken by the executive or the legislature, the cumulative impact of its various forms of intervention in national security concerns was bound to generate responses on the part of the other two branches of the governmental triad. Interestingly, however, in each case the reactions were in this period likewise diffuse.

The legislature

Legislative responses to ISC activism in the broad field of national security were especially inconsistent. Over time, they in fact moved back and forth along a noticeably kaleidoscopic spectrum comprised of four very different types of *knesset* activity: adherence, pre-emption, rejection and delegation.

- *Adherence* is the most passive of all legislative responses to the new environment, since it involves little more than parliamentary acquiescence in whatever interpretation the court imparted to a particular statute. This was the response adopted with respect to issues such as the adherence of the military justice system to fundamental rights, the right of bereaved parents to personalize the epitaphs on military gravestones, the disclosure of conclusions reached by military enquiries into accidental deaths and with respect to the equality of women soldiers in the IDF. In each case, since most MKs supported the ISC's decision (alternatively, since opponents could not muster a majority), no legislative initiatives were required. The new situation was simply incorporated into the existing law.
- *Pre-emption* lies at the opposite end of the passivity–activity scale. It constitutes a response, not to any specific decision on the part of the ISC, but to the overall ambience created by its record of judicial intervention. In this category, the *knesset* legislates on an issue affecting national security in the anticipation that, were it not to do so, the justices, following their own precedents, could instruct it to do so. As thus illustrated, 'pre-emption' seems to constitute the best of all possible worlds, principally because it satisfies the institutional interests of both sides to the on-going dialogue between the judiciary and the legislature. One the one hand it allows the *knesset* to retain the legislative initiative. At the same time, however, 'pre-emption' represents a success for the ISC too. It indicates the extent to which the *knesset* has internalized the judiciary's persistent calls to repair the legislative lacunae in national security affairs that date back to the era of Ben-Gurion.

Examples of 'pre-emption' are still comparatively rare. Nevertheless, two instances indicate the sort of outcomes to which it can lead. The first is the amendment (number 31) that in January 2001 the *knesset* passed to the Law of Families of Soldiers who Fell in Battle (Compensation and Rehabilitation), which had originally been enacted in 1950. The result of a long campaign by war widows and bereaved parents to modify the 'means tests' that determined the amount of monetary compensation that they would receive, the amendment signified not only the ability of a pressure group to re-frame public discourse (Laron 2002) but also the sensitivity of the *knesset* to the need to pre-empt what was likely to be a successful appeal to the ISC. The second example is the Reserve Duty Law, which was enacted in 2008 after a similarly protracted and high-profile campaign conducted by individuals and groups claiming to speak on behalf of the most numerous component of Israel's military complement. A landmark in several respects, this entirely novel enactment not only itemized – for the first time in Israel's history – the precise duties of reservists and the nature of the compensation to which they are entitled. Equally significantly, it also created a legislative review mechanism, which endowed the *knesset* with a supervisory role over this area of IDF concern.

- *Rejection.* Notwithstanding the rough and tumble atmosphere that invariably pervades public discourse in Israel, there have been remarkably few direct confrontations between the *knesset* and the ISC over national security issues. Both sides can claim some credit for that state of affairs. As noted above, the ISC has been reluctant to declare an item of parliamentary legislation to be illegal. But the *knesset* has likewise generally refrained from adopting what is here termed a policy of 'rejection', which would require it to enact legislation that deliberately overturns a judicial decision. Probably, this is because most MKs recognize the enormity of the damage that any such action might cause, especially when the ISC bases its decisions on its understanding of the requirements of international law. Under those circumstances, to enact laws contrary to a judicial decision is in effect to run the risk of being branded in violation of human rights by the world at large – a political price that, for national as well as personal reasons, few MKs are prepared to pay. This consideration explains why the only security issue concerning which rejection seems to have been thought a viable option concerned the non-enlistment of *haredi* males. Since this is a matter of domestic concern that is unlikely to generate much international interest, let alone opprobrium, most MKs clearly considered judicial displeasure with the Tal Law (which fell far short of the ISC's expectations) to be far less threatening than the alternative: a coalition crisis that would threaten the stability of the government. With respect to both the Lebanese detainees and the security services' use of physical pressure in investigations (see above, p. 153), however, the prospect of international displeasure seems to have tipped the scales. Hence, despite much initial patriotic posturing, in both cases, the *knesset* ultimately backed down from its declared intention to take the route of 'rejection'. Instead, as will be seen, it tuned to the alternative of 'delegation'.

- *Delegation.* As here defined, 'delegation' constitutes an attempt on the part of the legislature to find a way to circumvent a court decision with which most MKs disagree, but to do so without causing a direct confrontation with the judiciary. Reduced to its essentials, the solution to that problem consists of deliberately involving the executive branch in the arena of discourse. This is accomplished when the *knesset* uses its legislative authority to restore to government agencies some of the authority and discretion over national security issues denied to them by the ISC or, when necessary, to enact laws brining such powers into being.

The General Security Services Law of 2002 offers a striking example of this procedure, not least because its origins can be traced directly to the 1999 ISC decision in *The Public Committee Against Torture* v. *The Government of Israel.* That judgment, it will be recalled, had not declared that resort to physical pressure during interrogations would always be unlawful. What it had required, rather, was the establishment of a statutory mechanism that would determine the circumstances required for the use of physical pressure to be legally authorized. In essence, the GSS law was designed to fulfill that requirement.

As with similar laws in other democratic countries, the GSS Law (which is said to be modeled on its British counterpart) attempts to balance the needs of national security and the fundamental principles of a democratic country, with varying degrees of success (Zimerman 1997). But that is not its only function. More specifically, this measure also attempts to harmonize the push of constitutional oversight (by the legislature and the judiciary) with the pull of institutional leeway. The *knesset* attained that end by in fact delegating to the GSS decisions as to how to use its powers, thereby effectively immunizing it from external controls.[10] In sum, the enactment of the Law reduced rather than enhanced the likelihood of judicial intervention in GSS activities which now enjoyed the protection of the various firewalls that the *knesset* thereby erected.

Executive responses

As reflected in the corporate behavior of the IDF, executive responses to the growing legalization of national security were likewise diverse. In some areas, submission to judicial decisions and parliamentary legislation – on the part of the military institution as a whole, and not just individual soldiers – was self-evidently reluctant. The clear, albeit unspoken, message was one of grudging submission. In other spheres, however, IDF responses were far more positive. They conveyed an impression that the IDF had adapted its own ways of thought and action to those of the ISC and the *knesset,* and was hence acting in accordance with the spirit as well as the letter of their decisions.

A useful guide to understanding that spectrum of responses is provided by Harold Koh's studies of the ways in which international law are incorporated into domestic settings (Koh 1996, 1997, 1998). Koh concludes that the transition of any item of legislation from a matter of external pressure to a part of domestic law necessitates its passage through various political, social and legal filters. Each stage represents and facilitates an advance in a progression that Koh terms 'internalization.' This process may commence with the imposition of a norm in response to external pressure but can culminate with an internal appreciation of its intrinsic value. Guided by that insight, we suggest that in the present instance too, the spectrum of the responses shown by the IDF (and to some extent by the GSS too) to the twin 'external' pressures of ISC decisions and *knesset* legislation can usefully be divided into two principal categories: non-internalization and internalization.

- *Non-internalization.* Non-internalization can take several forms, common to which is the fact that the target institution has not assimilated the new norm into its own corporate culture. At the most extreme, this will result in a policy of open rejection. In a milder form, non-internalization will result in the new norm simply being disregarded. A third possibility is submission, a situation of grudging acquiescence, in which compliance results from submission to external pressure, which can be exerted by the judiciary, NGOs and/or the legislature.
- *Rejection.* At a corporate level, outright rejection, which in the national security realm translates into explicit refusal on the part of the IDF or the GSS to implement an ISC decision or *knesset* law, is absent from the Israeli experience. Some individual soldiers, usually of very low rank, have certainly on occasion pronounced their intention to disobey the norms thus prescribed, but as far as is known no senior officer (or person of comparable rank in the GSS) has ever done so. This is not surprising. Adherence to ISC rulings and *knesset* laws constitutes an essential facet of Israel's self-perception as a liberal democracy. Open defiance of judicial decisions would jeopardize the legitimacy of the entire Israeli system of government.
- *Disregard.* If reports by NGOs and the media are to be believed, situations in which institutional behavior simply does not follow the law or its interpretation by the courts have been far more common. However, the evidence as to the extent of this phenomenon is not always conclusive. Undoubtedly, disregard seems to have been widespread, even systematic, in the GSS prior to the 1987 Landau Commission Report, when investigators regularly applied physical pressure during interrogation of Palestinian suspects, and with equal consistency denied doing so in testimony in court. But accusations advanced in *The Public Committee Against Torture* v. *The Government of Israel* (1999) that the practice per-

sists are not at all easy to quantify. Likewise, it is difficult to evaluate reports that some IDF units continued to use 'early warning' or 'neighbor policy' practices even after the ISC declared them to be illegal, and that neither the IDF nor the police had implemented court orders to dismantle illegal settlements. Are these isolated instances, and comparatively rare occurrences? Or do they reflect an institutional attitude that is more widespread? As the next chapter will argue, one of the unintended consequences of the entire process of legislation as outlined here is that the ISC has become the institution principally responsible for the imposition of law in national security affairs, and yet clearly is incapable of monitoring that entire realm by itself. In the absence of any other verifying body, whatever evades the attention of the ISC remains open to doubt.

- *Submission.* Situations of 'submission' arise when institutions acting in the name of the executive branch conform to court orders and parliamentary laws, but do so grudgingly and without being convinced that this is the correct route to follow. Consequently, the institutions cannot be relied upon to apply the norm fully and/or effectively of their own volition. In order to get them to do so, the judiciary has constantly to monitor executive behavior and apply pressure when it needs to be changed. This can be an effective course of action, especially when exerted vis-à-vis military organizations, which are more accustomed than most to obeying orders. However, it can also be expensive. The application of external pressure requires a large investment of time and energy on the part of agencies, such as the courts, that are prepared to monitor the behavior of the executive branch and compel them to comply with the law.

The 'separation barrier' cases supply an example of the tensions between the judiciary and the executive to which submission can thus give rise. It will be recalled that the ISC declared the barrier to be legal, provided that its alignment accorded with security considerations, not political designs. It also instructed the ministry of defense, the body responsible for the barrier's construction, to minimize the damage it caused to Palestinian rights and property. However, as Arieli and Sfard show (Arieli and Sfard 2008), the ISC considered the ministry's compliance with this ruling to be far from satisfactory. Petitions were presented with respect to almost every kilometer of the barrier's alignment, and in numerous instances the justices rejected the route offered by the State, on the grounds that the bureaucrats concerned were either ignoring its directive to be considerate of Palestinian rights or presenting justifications for its chosen alignment that were no more than half-truths. On one notorious occasion (*Azun Chairperson of Municipal Council* v. *IDF Commander in the West Bank* [2006]), the justices discovered that they had been lied to by the head of the department responsible for the barrier's construction. No action was taken against the person concerned, but the previous approval granted to the alignment was retracted (Arieli and Sfard 2008:142–4).

- *Internalization.* Following Koh, we define internalization as a reflection of a shift in the institution's own corporate culture. Its operatives comply with the law not because they are compelled to do so, but in response to an inner conviction that it is correct to do so. This shift in attitude, he shows, is most likely to occur when there exists (or is created) within the institution itself a component that has a clear and corporate interest in promoting compliance with the new norm throughout the entire organization. That circumstances changes the character of debates about the norm. Instead of reflecting a tussle between the institution and external forces, those debates become dialogues amongst domestic constituencies, all of whom share a common organizational culture and interest.

An excellent example of precisely such a process is provided by the mandate given to the IDF's International Law Branch (known by its Hebrew acronym as *DABLA*) soon after the outbreak of the second *intifada* in the year 2000 (Am. Cohen 2011). Convinced that developments in both the laws of armed conflict and IHL were becoming increasingly relevant to Israel's military operations against Palestinian terrorism, the MAG of the day made *DABLA* personnel responsible for making IDF officers conversant with legal requirements in both areas. Two features have characterized their *modus operandi* in carrying out those orders. First, they restrict their activities solely to this area of jurisdiction, an attribute that distinguishes *DABLA* personnel from their counterparts in the US military, who do not focus exclusively on IHL (Dickinson 2010). Second, although *DABLA*'s role is defined as entirely advisory, it is also designed to be very action-oriented. Hence, ever since the year 2000 *DABLA* has supplemented its original presence in training exercises by providing what is termed 'operational' legal advice. Under this framework, *DABLA* representatives are attached to commanders in the field, with the purpose of supplying them with information and direction before and during on-going operations.

DABLA's impact must not be exaggerated. Not even the most rose-tinted of views could justifiably claim that, thanks to this unit, all Israeli military personnel have internalized IHL, to the extent that compliance with its requirements has now become second nature. The continuing incidence of IHL violations, rare though they are when IDF conduct is compared to that of other armed forces in similar situations, proves that such is not the case. What can be said, nevertheless, is that *DABLA* personnel, in their capacity as legal advisors to IDF commanders in the field, already exert a far greater influence over Israel's national security behavior than might perhaps be expected and have the potential to exert an even greater impact in the future. Simply by virtue of its existence, the unit ensures that at the very heart of the Israeli national security apparatus there functions an institution that considers IHL to be intrinsic to its organizational culture and mission.

The compound implications of 'legislation'

As described in this chapter, then, the process of 'legislation' experienced by Israel's national security framework since the mid-1990s has been a far more broadly based phenomenon than is often acknowledged. Certainly, the ISC was the prime mover behind this development, adopting an increasingly 'activist' jurisprudence that advanced purposefully, even if sometimes erratically, from its traditional and conventional stance of enforcing existing legislation through the successively more radical stages that we have designated 'interpretation', 'attribution', 'facilitation', and 'transference.' What remains significant nevertheless is the extent to which other branches of government also participated in that process. Legislation – the growing use of legal tools in order to regulate Israeli national security conduct – even if perhaps it initially gave the impression of being forced upon the legislature and executive, gradually elicited various forms of acquiescence and even cooperation. Since the advent of the new millennium, especially, it has won increasing acceptance amongst law-makers and some parts of the executive too. As the example of *DABLA* illustrates, it can even be said to have undergone a process of internalization on the part of the military.

That said, a broader perspective indicates that the record is not altogether straightforward. At the end of the period covered by this chapter, Israel's national security framework was no more cohesive than at its beginning. If anything, the opposite was the case. Certainly, ISC activism had contributed to the emergence of new emphases in Israel's national security discourse, and in particular to the degree of attention now paid by all sectors of government to issues related to human rights and to the standards of IHL. But once attention has shifted from the agenda of the framework to its functioning as a unified system, a more compound picture begins to emerge. Legislation, it transpires, quite apart from necessarily being a non-linear development, was also unbalanced in terms of its systemic consequences. Instead of facilitating the synchronization of mutually coherent policies in all four of the dimensions of the national security framework, it had done much to impede such efforts. Principally this was because the ISC's experiments with various methods of judicial control over individual facets of that framework had created a capricious situation, in which some issues in the realm of national security are subject to one form of regulation, others come under another system and yet a third category continue to be free of any judicial oversight altogether.

The concluding chapters of this book will examine in greater depth the reasons for the emergence this state of quasi-chaos and suggest some ways in which the problems to which it gives rise might be solved.

Part III
Perspectives and prescriptions

7 Diagnosis
Israel's hybrid national security legal framework

Whereas previous chapters have traced the evolution of Israel's national security law in chronological form, the perspective adopted in the present chapter is analytical. Taking a synoptic view of the historical record, it has two principal purposes. One is to identify the underlying attitudes towards national security needs that found expression in the successive periods of development. The other is to portray how the confluence of those attitudes has prevented Israel's national security framework from assuming a cohesive form and has instead retained its character as a disjointed and even hybrid construct.

As a framework for conceptualizing underlying attitudes towards national security needs, in this chapter we adopt the three models of legal behavior during times of national security emergencies posited by professors Oren Gross and Fionnuala Ni Aolain: 'business as usual', 'accommodation', and 'extra legal action' (Gross and Ni Aolain 2006). In their depiction, these three forms of legal behavior constitute separate points on a spectrum of responses to the circumstance created by acute threats to national security – a situation that is broadly considered to exist when the safety of the regime and/or state is endangered by imminent or actual violence, whether man-made or as a result of the forces of nature.

The 'business as usual' model occupies one end of that response spectrum. Its proponents deliberately refrain from according national security emergencies a unique status in law. On the contrary, basic to this model is the assumption that moments of crisis, however acute, need not affect the fundamental provisions of the existing constitution, and indeed should not do so. As Gross and Ni Aolain point out, that view was most famously articulated in 1866 by Justice Davis of the US Supreme Court, in *ex parte Milligan*:

> The Constitution of the United States is a law for rulers and people, equally in war and in peace, and covers with the shield of its protection all classes of men, at all times, and under all circumstances. No doctrine, involving more pernicious consequences, was ever invented by the wit of man than that any of its provisions can be suspended

during any of the great exigencies of government. Such a doctrine leads directly to anarchy or despotism, but the theory of necessity on which it is based is false; for the government, within the Constitution, has all the powers granted to it, which are necessary to preserve its existence; as has been happily proved by the result of the great effort to throw off its just authority.

By contrast, proponents of 'accommodation' (the second of the Gross–Ni Aolain models) argue that Justice Davis' opinion in large part reflected the exceptional nature of the historical period during which it was framed. In this reading, *ex parte Milligan* articulated a reaction to the way in which the Union Government under President Lincoln had taken several constitutionally dubious actions during the American civil war. Hence, it must be considered atypical. Contrary to Justice Davis' contentions, the vast majority of state constitutions do in fact acknowledge the extraordinary nature of the circumstances created by threats to national security, whether they are the result of domestic violence or of foreign attack. Indeed, precisely because it recognizes the uniqueness of national security requirements at times of crisis, the 'accommodation' model allows governments to suspend normal legal procedures in order that they might act more freely for the public good.

Temporal provisions supply one practical expression of this attitude, providing for the implementation of 'emergency measures' for the duration of the crisis. But it is also evident in the *hierarchical* dimension (allowing for national security matters to be controlled during the emergency through a specially created chain of command) and in the *functional* dimension (the creation of special institutions with responsibility for a specific area of national security). As noted in Chapter 1, even the Constitution of the USA, perhaps the best known example of a constitution which contains no specific emergency clauses, shows traces of the 'accommodation' perspective. Under section 9 of Article I it allows limits to be placed on *habeas corpus* in times of invasion. According to some interpretations, it also grants presidents, in their capacity as commanders-in-chief, extraordinary powers in times of war.

The 'extra-legal' model (the third part of the Gross–Ni Aolain trinity) takes 'accommodation' to its logical conclusion. At times of severe threat to national security, it argues, conventional legal frameworks have to be dispensed with altogether. Hence, the constitutional provisions concerning extraordinary government license (as envisaged in the 'accommodation' model) are superfluous. The 'extra-legal' model prefers that in emergency situations, governments and their agencies do not seek the cover for their actions provided by the constitution. Instead, they ought to assume responsibility for their actions, leaving decisions about whether those actions were or were not justified to subsequent discussion by other branches of government. That, argue Gross and Ni Aolain, is precisely the stand taken by Justice Cheshin in *The Public Committee Against Torture* v. *The Government of Israel* (1999, above p. 153). As a rule, Cheshin acknowledged, agents of the General Security Services who resorted to physical force during the interrogation of suspects were violating the law. However, moral responsibility clearly renders the conventional legal framework inapplicable in a 'ticking bomb' situation, where the agent has reason to believe that the suspect is withholding information vital to defusing an imminent threat to national security. Under those circumstances, the law has to bow to reality and accept the validity of extra-legal action. Indeed, it will be recalled, Justice Cheshin expressly assured potential GSS investigators that the State would never prosecute them for employing reasonable physical force in 'ticking bomb' circumstances.

Because the studies conducted by Gross and Ni Aolain focus principally on emergency situations in the context of violent conflicts, they concentrate on what we have termed the *temporal* and *spatial* dimensions of national security decision-making: for which length of time are emergency measures employed and in which locations? In this chapter, we suggest that the Gross–Ni Aolain taxonomy can be extended, and hence applied to the national security framework as a whole and in all four of its dimensions. Especially is that so when account is taken of the differences in the institutional agencies to which each of the three models gives prominence, a facet of the analysis that we consider Gross and Ni Aolain to understate. For instance, the 'extra-legal' model, precisely because it altogether dispenses with the need to apply an existing legal framework, grants an extraordinary degree of independence and power to the executive, the only branch of government that can benefit from an environment devoid of any application of law. By contrast, the legislature is the principal beneficiary of the 'accommodation' model. By applying provisions that were inserted into the constitution in advance of the present emergency, this model transfers the locus of decision-making to the body that created the constitution and in so doing specified when, where and by whose actions its emergency clauses would take the place of the provisions normally applicable. Finally, the application of the 'business as usual' model prioritizes the courts. This is because its real meaning is not that national security requires no special treatment, but that whatever treatment may be required should be determined on a case-by-case basis, rather than by constitutional provisions formulated in advance. Since only courts can decide specific cases, it is they who ultimately are responsible for determining the correct balance, at any particular moment, between the needs of national security and the preservation, in both the short- and long-terms, of other important rights and interests that could be affected by government action.

Thus modified, the tripartite classification posited by Gross and Ni Aolain provides a useful organizing device for understanding the dynamics of the evolution of Israel's national security legal framework. It also

180 *Perspectives and prescriptions*

helps to illuminate the changes in emphasis that have taken place over time in its basic format.

Briefly summarized, three distinct phases of development can be identified. During the first, which stretched from the foundation of the state in 1948 until Ben-Gurion's retirement from office in 1963 (a period covered in Chapter 3, above), Israel's national security legal framework most closely approximated the 'extra-legal' model. The extensive use made of the emergency powers inherited from the British Mandate gave especially articulate form to this paradigm, the dominance of which was buttressed by the personal hegemony over national security affairs exercised by David Ben-Gurion, in his dual role as both prime minister and minister of defense. In this sphere, neither the legislature nor the judiciary wielded any significant influence.

As Michael Walzer has observed, extra-legal measures possess clear advantages. They offer the prospect of flexibility and of the assumption of responsibility on the part of specific individuals (Walzer 1974). Nevertheless, extra-legal measures are only beneficial when applied over the short term. Once a state of emergency becomes prolonged, extra-legal exceptions become the rule. This situation is likely to corrode any system. It is especially deleterious to the governments of states which, in conditions of protracted emergencies, find themselves habitually conducting their business outside the law. Maturing democracies, especially, are hence likely to wish to replace the situation of 'extra-legality' as soon as is reasonably possible.

Such was the case in Israel by the early 1960s when Ben-Gurion's retirement from office further facilitated efforts to shift the focus of Israel's national security legal framework in the direction of the 'accommodation' model. As shown in Chapters 4 and 5, between 1963 and the early 1990s, a large number of people participated in this enterprise, including several of Israel's prime ministers, other cabinet ministers, members of the *knesset* and justices of the ISC. Thanks to their efforts, several areas of national security concern that had previously been left in legislative limbo (one of the most important being constitutional control over the armed forces) during the 1970s and 1980s became subjects of parliamentary statutes and/or national enquiry.

The scope covered by those legislative achievements cannot mask the piecemeal manner in which they were attained. By and large, attempts to shift Israel's national security regime from an 'extra-legal' to 'accommodation' format were stimulated more by the pressures of unpremeditated events than by a carefully considered and synchronized program of reform. For instance, it was the 1973 Yom Kippur War and its aftermath that set in train the process that eventually resulted in the passage of Basic Law: The Military in 1976; likewise, it was the exponential growth in the number of service deferments granted to *haredi* males that triggered the enactment of the Service Deferral ('Tal') Law in 2002. That *modus operandi* helps to explain why the shift from 'extra-legality' to 'accommodation' was not linear and coordinated. At best, change could only stumble forward in fits and starts. Indeed, in some areas the executive branch found it convenient to reverse the process altogether, and to revert to an older mode of 'extra-legal' behavior. This was an especially marked characteristic of official Israeli conduct in the Territories. But it was also evident within Israel proper, where the 'state of emergency' declared in 1948 was unfailingly renewed every year.

By the mid-1990s, at the latest, it was clear that the legislative program initiated in the late 1960s had not brought into being a robust successor to the 'extra-legal' model. Rather, all it had produced was a weak, and somewhat chaotic, version of 'accommodation' that, in its existing form, was incapable of rising to the challenges to Israel's national security law mandated by drastic changes in the country's societal, international and military environments. It was at that stage that Israel entered a third phase of constitutional development where national security matters were concerned. Justices of the ISC discarded the attitude of deference and restraint that, only a handful of exceptions apart, they had traditionally adopted towards national security issues. Instead, and especially under the energetic presidency of Aharon Barak, they began to play an increasingly prominent role in this field, not just as arbiters of the sort of military conduct that is forbidden and permissible under Israeli law, but also as communicators of the international standards with which the IDF is expected to conform. This involved a shift in judicial perspectives. Members of the ISC did not implement the pre-existing 'accommodation' model, which focused on the division and separation of power between different branches of government in matters of national security. Instead, almost their entire jurisprudence focused on the balance between rights and security interest. Ultimately, this shift prodded the national security framework in the direction of a 'business as usual' model.

Whilst the general dynamics of the movement from one model to another is thus clear, the consequences of the process must not be oversimplified. At no point during the 1970s and 1980s did 'accommodation' entirely replace 'extra-legality'. Neither, more recently, has Israeli practice conformed exclusively to the 'business-as-usual' mode. Rather, the present condition of Israel's national security legal framework in effect resembles a palimpsest comprised of successive layers, none of which entirely conceals residual traces left by their predecessors. Hence, when examining the development of Israel's national security legal framework, it would be mistaken to focus attention solely on the accelerators, the forces of innovation and the conditions that stimulated the transition from one of the models identified by Gross and Ni Aolain to another. If the dynamics of the process of change are not to be over-simplified to the point of distortion, equal emphasis must be placed on the brakes, the circumstances that tended to retard the pace of movement, and sometimes to bring it to a complete halt.

182 *Perspectives and prescriptions*

The remainder of the present chapter seeks to demonstrate the interplay of those competing pressures, principally by illustrating their effects on the substance of the national security framework in each of its four component dimensions. Employing that methodology, the analysis will first assess the attainments and limitations of the efforts undertaken to shift the emphasis of discourse and action in this field from an 'extra-legal' mode to one of 'accommodation'. Thereafter, a similar audit will be made of the consequences that have resulted from the increasing tendency of the ISC to move Israel's national security legal framework in a 'business as usual' direction.

From 'extra-legality' to 'accommodation': a balance sheet

The temporal dimension

Israel first adopted an 'accommodation' mode with respect to the temporal dimension of national security in 1992, when the *knesset* revised Basic Law: The Government, another revised version of which was passed in 2001. True, even then emergency regulations very much remained integral to the constitutional fabric. Article 39a of the 2001 law expressly underscores the prerogative of the executive to resort to emergency regulations when required, whilst Article 39c empowers emergency regulations to alter or suspend any other legislation. Nevertheless, the legal sanction thus accorded to extraordinary government action very much differs from Article 9 of the 1948 Law and Administration Ordinance, which had for many years been used to regulate not just military-related affairs but also matters as diverse as labor laws, regulation of foreign currency, and the import of diamonds. Moreover, during the pre-1990 'extra-legality' phase, the declaration of a state of emergency, once it received *knesset* approval (a requirement that had to be fulfilled within three months) had retained its validity until expressly revoked by a vote in the legislature. The 2001 law, however, requires *knesset* ratification on an annual basis.

Other laws, too, similarly provided evidence of the determination to subject the temporal dimension of Israel's national security legal framework to regulation via legislation, in accordance with the requirements of the 'accommodation' model. Thus, Basic Law: Human Dignity and Liberty of the Person (1992), which is generally recognized to have been a cornerstone of Israel's 'constitutional revolution' (Sapir 2010), specifically added two riders to the clause (Article 12) acknowledging that 'when a state of emergency exists ... emergency regulations may be enacted ... to deny or restrict rights under this Basic Law.' One was that 'the denial or restriction shall be for a proper purpose'; the other was that it could only remain in force 'for a period and extent no greater than is required.'

This tone was likewise reflected in an amendment to the Civil Defense Law that was passed in 1997. It will be recalled that the original law, passed in 1951, had recognized only a 'time of attack' as a situation that warranted the granting of special powers to the executive. However, in the light of the experience of both the 1991 Gulf War, when Israel was targeted by almost forty Iraqi 'Scud' missiles, and of intensive rocket attacks on Israel's northern settlements in the mid-1990s, that provision was revised. Thereafter, government agencies – and particularly the military – would also be allowed to exercise extraordinary powers whenever a 'special situation in the rear' was officially declared to exist. In this case, too, however, time restraints apply. According to Article 9:3a of the revised Civil Defense Law, 'special situations' terminate automatically after 48 hours (if unilaterally proclaimed by the minister of defense) or after five days (if proclaimed by the entire cabinet). Extensions can only be sanctioned by the FADC of the *knesset*, which has to be informed 'immediately' of a cabinet decision to implement the 'special situation' clause. These procedures were followed several times in subsequent years, most noticeably in July 2006, in response to Hizbollah rocket attacks on northern Israel and in December 2007 and December 2008, when Hamas fire was directed at Israeli settlements in the vicinity of the Gaza Strip.

For all their occasional prominence, the efforts thus made to shift the temporal dimension of Israel's national security framework from an extra-legal model to one of accommodation were never likely to be more than partially successful. Primarily, this is because of the extent to which the continued existence of the state of emergency has come to serve as the legal basis for official activity in numerous areas of life. As early as the 1960s, the ISC ruled that powers given to the executive under emergency regulations can also be used in other areas as long as the emergency situation continues to exist (*Attorney General* v. *Ostreicher*, 1963). How liberally this sanction has been interpreted became evident in 1999, when the ISC was petitioned to annul the state of emergency (*The Association for Civil Rights in Israel* v. *The Knesset* [pending]). It then transpired that thereto, no less than 21 laws had been enacted under powers granted to the government in emergency situations, several of which are only tangentially related to 'real' threats to national security and deal with matters such as labor relations, detention and price regulation. Under those circumstances, to revoke the state of emergency is in effect to unravel part of the very fabric of Israel's entire legal structure – a prospect so daunting that it perhaps explains why, 11 years after first being presented, that particular petition is still pending.

The spatial dimension

Attempts to shift the emphasis from an 'extra-legal' basis to a model based on legislative 'accommodation' were equally inadequate when applied to the spatial dimension of Israel's national security framework. True, once again, a definite change in tone could be discerned with respect to the role of the legislature in defining the physical contours of Israel's borders. Ben-Gurion had never felt required to submit to the *knesset* any of the borders agreed upon at Rhodes in 1949 during the course of armistice negotiations between representatives of Israel and her neighbors. For various reasons, most of which were related to consideration of domestic politics, that precedent was entirely overturned after the Six Days War. In 1967 the *knesset* ratified changes to the Law and Administration Ordinance whereby Israeli jurisdiction was extended to east Jerusalem. In 1980 it formalized the annexation of east Jerusalem (Basic Law: Jerusalem) and in 1981 passed the Golan Heights Law, which incorporated within Israel's borders territory conquered from Syria in the Six Days War.

Withdrawals from individual portions of the Territories were likewise submitted for the approval of the legislature. Unlike Ben-Gurion, who had not thought it necessary to ask the *knesset* to vote on the decision to pull back IDF forces from the Sinai in 1957, Begin insisted on delaying the dismantling of the Yamit settlements in 1982 until the *knesset* had both ratified the peace treaty with Egypt and passed the Law for the Compensation of Sinai Evacuees. Likewise, practical preparations for the implementation of Ariel Sharon's disengagement program, in accordance with which, in August 2005 Israeli forces withdrew all military installations and civilian settlements from the Gaza Strip, did not move into high gear until the previous February, when the program was ratified by the *knesset* by a margin of 59–40, with five abstentions. Even though the borders thus established gained scant international recognition, from a domestic point of view they did at least seem to be geographically clear.

This appearance of legislative activity is, however, deceptive. If anything, *knesset* contributions to determining the spatial dimension of Israel's national security framework continued to be limited – so much so that they provide a particularly striking illustration of the various weaknesses that altogether undermined efforts to substitute a model of legislative 'accommodation' for the previous format of 'extra-legal' decree. Closer examination reveals that, for the most part, such legislation as was enacted related by and large to peripheral spatial issues. Moreover, since in most such instances *knesset* approval was a foregone conclusion (as was the case with respect to the Jerusalem and Golan laws as well as the Yamit and Gaza withdrawals), the chamber really constituted a venue for decisions that were ceremonial rather than substantive. With respect to the most pressing spatial item on Israel's national security agenda, the future form and alignment of Israel's border with her Palestinian neighbors, the *knesset* had absolutely nothing to say. Instead, it left this thorny topic entirely to the discretion of the executive, which – after much humming and hawing – eventually resorted to the older mode of 'extra-legal' action. In this instance, the method employed was the decision, taken by the cabinet in April 2002, to construct the 'separation barrier.' But although the route taken by this enterprise (ostensibly determined by security considerations) generated considerable debate and legal controversy, abroad as well as in Israel itself, not once did the *knesset* venture to express an opinion on the matter, still less claim a right to exercise any supervisory role. Instead, as has been seen, disputes over the barrier's alignment were adjudicated on a case by case basis by the ISC.

Another glaring omission from legislative treatment in the spatial sphere is the multi-faceted nature of the legal regime that has developed over time in the West Bank. The unitary system initially created by the establishment of an IDF military administration that applied the international laws of occupation in those regions has long disappeared into history. It has been replaced by what Nir Gazit has described as a situation of 'fragmented sovereignty', a patchwork of legal regimes that cuts across all identifiable administrative boundaries and geographical borders (Gazit 2009).

One major divide derives from the presence in the West Bank of over a quarter of a million Jewish settlers, who possess Israeli citizenship and who are subject to Israel's penal code, civil code, and many administrative regulations (Gordon 2008:28). But boundaries are further blurred by the multiplicity of regimes that now apply to different Palestinian groups in the areas conquered by Israel in 1967 that have not been formally annexed (Gordon 2008:169–224). Ever since the 1993 Oslo Accords, full Israeli martial law is supposed to apply only to Palestinian residents of regions designated 'area C'. Residents of areas 'A' and 'B' are formally subject to laws of the Palestinian Authority (established in 1994), which shares with Israeli forces control over 'area B' and is autonomous within 'area A', although it must respect Israeli supremacy in some specific issue like water and customs there too. However, even parts of 'area A' have on occasion been the targets of Israeli military incursions and control, as was the case during operation 'Defensive Shield' in the early summer of 2002. Moreover, although IDF forces were withdrawn from the entire Gaza Strip in 2005, the rise to power in that region of Hamas, an organization which both tolerates rocket attacks on neighboring Israeli settlements and towns and refuses to allow any humanitarian contact with the Israeli soldier that it holds in captivity, has resulted in an Israeli ground and naval blockade so extensive that much international legal opinion considers the entire region to still be under Israeli 'control' (Mari 2005; Martin and Warner 2005. Compare, however, Shany 2005 and Zemach 2009).

Unless and until these anomalies are regulated by international agreements that are written into Israeli law, the spatial dimension of Israel's national security legal framework will, to all and intents and purposes, remain anchored in the 'extra-legal' mode dictated by its reliance on the virtually exclusive prerogatives wielded by the executive branch and its security agencies.

The functional dimension

During the Ben-Gurion era, when executive dominance was virtually taken for granted, questions related to the functional dimension of Israel's national security legal framework had been all but irrelevant. Quite simply, the government and its agencies had assumed – and by default were granted – authority to handle national security issues in whatever way the executive considered appropriate. Ostensibly, that is no longer the case. Various items of legislation enacted since the late 1960s have set down what appear to be clear guidelines that apportion responsibility in this area. Thus, Basic Law: The Military identifies several topics that the *knesset* has to regulate by way of statute: the formation of armed services other than the IDF; conscription; and the authority to issue military instructions. Likewise, Basic Law: The Government allots to the *knesset*, and particularly to its FADC, specified functions with respect to the legalization of initiation of hostilities. In addition, legislation has regulated, or defined with greater precision than was once the case, the allocation of functions amongst government agencies within a specified area of national security relevance. One example is the GSS Law of 2002. Another is the Reserve Duty Law of 2008, which declares (Article 8) that emergency orders for mobilization of reserve forces must be approved by the cabinet and reported to the FADC.

Thus, to list the areas relating to the functional dimension of Israel's national security framework that have been regulated by legislation is, of course, to highlight the enormity of those that are still untouched. One glaring omission from the statute book is a specification of the precise responsibilities and sphere of activity of the *Mosad*. Another is an indication of the criteria that are to determine the assignment of IDF units and resources to non combat-related missions. Nun (Nun 1999; Elyasuf 1988) rejects the opinion that the topic might be covered by references to 'recognized (non-military) service' in the amended Defense Service Law of 1995. So too, apparently, do lawyers in the ministry of defense who have therefore recently begun drafting for *knesset* consideration a 'Law Concerning IDF Responsibilities in the Rear', which, amongst other things, would also formally legitimize the utilization of military personnel at moments of national civilian emergencies, such as may be occasioned by a flood, earthquake or other form of natural disaster (Elran 2011).[1]

But in addition to thus laboring under the burden of inadequacy, which, as has been seen, was the case with respect to the spatial dimension, efforts to move the functional dimension of Israel's national security legal framework in the direction of an 'accommodation' model were also, and more seriously, impeded by the obscurity of much of the legislation that has been enacted. Relations between senior office-holders in the military and civilian echelons constitute a prominent example, and one that by virtue of its self-evidently crucial importance has generated considerable discussion. On this subject, the wording of Basic Law: The Military is especially fuzzy, providing scant guidance as to how to implement the general rule laid down in high-sounding declaration contained in Article 2a: 'The army is subject to the authority of the Cabinet.' As has long been asked (Hadar 1977): does the law therefore expect, or permit, the cabinet as a whole to supervise every action taken by every soldier? Can even ministers of defense do so? If so, then what precisely are the duties and responsibilities of the CGS?

Bendor and Kremnitzer suggest that such queries can be solved by positing a functional distinction between strategic and tactical decision-making (Bendor and Kremnitzer 2000:50–1, 59–60). Authority at each level, they argue, is a correlate of responsibility for what transpires within its boundaries. Hence, they interpret Basic Law: The Military to mean that, whereas the strategic level of activity is subject to direct control by the cabinet, and perhaps more specifically by the minister of defense, issues of a tactical or technical nature are the preserve of the CGS. This distinction was implicit in the Agranat Commission's comment that the minister of defense does not constitute a 'super-CGS' but the military's political controller (*Agranat Unclassified Report* 1975:25). It also seems to have been accepted by the Winograd Commission, which investigated decision-making before and during the 2006 Second Lebanon War. Stressing the linkage between authority and responsibility, it too considered the civilian echelon to be responsible solely for strategic decisions, but not for issues related to the specific technical and logistical aspects of the IDF's preparedness for battle (*Winograd Commission Partial Report* 2007:132, paragraph 115). In his testimony to the Turkel Commission, established in order to investigate the circumstances preceding and during the boarding of the Turkish vessel 'Mavi Marmora' by IDF naval forces on 31 May 2010, Defense Minister Ehud Barak sought to make the same point. 'The political echelon determines what has to be done, and it bears responsibility for this. The military echelon determines how to do this, and it bears responsibility for this' (*Turkel Commission Testimony*, 10 August 2010:12).

Matters are never quite that straightforward. Historical studies indicate that distinctions between the strategic and tactical layers of military operations have always been notoriously hard to define. They are even more difficult to discern in the current operational environment, which is characterized by the amplifying effect that technology and communications exerts on even the most limited of military missions – a circumstance that has given rise to the phenomenon of the 'strategic corporal' (Betts 2000). Those circumstances explain why the boundaries that, in theory, are thought to separate strategic from tactical levels of decision-making have in practice regularly been breached: political leaders have frequently been tempted to exploit the opportunities that now exist for micro-managing local operations; even in the most democratic of countries, generals have likewise been accused of attempting to influence strategy (E. Cohen 2000; Roman and Tarr 2002).

Both tendencies have been particularly pronounced in Israel. As is well known, senior IDF personnel have consistently participated in strategic decision-making in a wide variety of areas. In addition to virtually adjudicating debates regarding specific military operations (Peri 2005; Michael 2007), they have also been known to vet appointments in public service and to determine land uses and rights of access to the coastline (Ben-Meir 1995; Oren and Regev 2008). More often overlooked by students of the field, but nonetheless occasionally blatant, have been the cases in which ministers of defense have exercised functions at the tactical and operational levels of command. At the time, no constitutional eyebrows were raised when Dayan took personal control over the operations mounted to release hostages on the hijacked Sabena aircraft in 1972, nor even when he participated in operational discussions (during the course of which he occasionally tendered 'ministerial advice') during the 1973 Yom Kippur War. If anything, and in the absence of any clear legal directive to the contrary, that is precisely how convention seems to have required ministers of defense to act. Only the Agranat commissioners implicitly denied that interpretation of Israel's national security hierarchy, when limiting the assignment of responsibility for IDF failures in October 1973 entirely to the military echelons. Subsequent tribunals adopted a very different line. In 1983, the Kahan commissioners specifically faulted Defense Minister Sharon for not exercising sufficient operational authority (above p. 129). The Winograd commissioners likewise insisted on naming political names.

> A leader who initiates a large-scale military action has duties towards the State, towards the IDF personnel who risk their lives and to the citizens – of Israel and of Lebanon alike. Amongst these duties is the need to consider whether the military operation is at all necessary, whether its timing and nature are appropriate, and whether – given regional data – it is likely to succeed. In our view, the hasty decisions taken by the Olmert Cabinet with respect to the initiation of the war did not meet these criteria. Therein lay the failure of the Prime Minister as a leader who, in cases of an initiated military operation, is duty-bound to lead his country sagely and responsibly.
> (*Winograd Commission Partial Report* 2007:131, paragraph 106)

Unless and until the *knesset* addresses the duties of each of the actors at the apex of the national security decision-making chain complex once again, and in consequence re-drafts Basic Law: The Military in a way that clarifies much that is still obscure with respect to the management of Israel's security policies, the 'accommodation' model can no more be said to apply to the functional dimension of Israel's national security legal framework than to any of its other components. Located in a hazy borderland, this dimension – especially – is burdened with residual traces of the 'extra-legal' tradition, which only judicial intervention seems to be powerful enough to restrain.

The hierarchical dimension

But it is with respect to the hierarchical dimension of Israel's national security legal framework that the limitations of the results attained by efforts to shift matters in the direction of an 'accommodation' model are most apparent, and that the discrepancy between appearances and reality is most conspicuous. Formally, several steps were taken to remedy the most pernicious of the faults inherent in the 'extra-legal' method of national-security decision-making inherited from the Ben-Gurion era. In this respect, Basic Law: The Government and Basic Law: The Military, originally enacted by the *knesset* in 1968 and 1976 respectively, constitute obvious milestones. Article 40 of Basic Law: The Government identified the cabinet as the authority responsible for initiating a war. Article 2a of Basic Law: The Military declared the same forum to be in command of the military ('The army is subject to the authority of the Cabinet'). Together, these items of legislation thus appear to establish a clear chain of command with respect to national security matters, an impression seemingly confirmed in the year 2000 by the passage of the GSS Law, Article 4a of which likewise specifies that the cabinet constitutes the supreme authority in national security affairs.

Once again, however, matters were never quite that clear-cut. For one thing, as noted in Chapter 5, the legal framework thus established by the *knesset* suffered from too many internal inconsistencies to allow for the emergence of a coherent and consolidated process of decision-making in the national security sphere. Many of the difficulties stemmed from the fact that none of the above-mentioned laws restricted themselves to establishing cabinet control. In one way or another, all also referred to specific ministers, and did so in ways that obscured the very framework that they were supposed to clarify. Article 2b of Basic Law: The Military, for instance, states that the minister of defense is 'in charge of the army on behalf of the Cabinet', but does not elaborate on what that job description might entail or on the extent of the authority that it grants to the incumbent of the post vis-à-vis either the CGS or the cabinet as a whole. Likewise, Article 4b of the GSS Law identifies the prime minister, who is not mentioned at all in Basic Law: The Military, as the person 'in charge' of the GSS. Another institution not once referred to in Basic Law: The Military is the *knesset.* However, Article 40 of the 2001 version of Basic Law: The Government stipulates that this forum (and, more specifically, the FADC) has to be notified of the commencement of war, whilst Article 6 of the GSS Law also grants it a supervisory role over the GSS.

More scrupulous drafting might have bypassed some of the difficulties thus raised. But the obstacles impeding the transition from an 'extra-legal' format to one of 'accommodation' ran much deeper. At root, they reflected the enormous discrepancy that existed between the prescription for national security decision-making mandated by *knesset* legislation and the methods of action dictated by political realities. Control by 'the Cabinet' over military conduct, for instance, is rendered virtually impossible by the sheer size of that body, which is itself a by-product of the fact that all Israeli governments have been coalition governments – and are likely to remain so in the foreseeable future. A forum that for many years has invariably consisted of over two dozen persons,[2] each of whom – no matter how inexperienced in military matters – usually feels required to express an opinion, cannot be expected to conduct operations in an efficient manner. Neither can it be relied upon not to leak classified information to unauthorized sources. For both reasons, principals in the realm of national security decision-making, a group that embraces senior military personnel as well as the prime minister and minister of defense, have tended to empty the notion of 'cabinet control' of its intended meaning. As was demonstrated by the sequence of events during both the first (1982) and second (2006) Lebanon wars, norms in this area were barely affected by the passage of Basic Law: The Military in 1976. Instead, practice continued to conform to the patterns established during the Six Days War (1967), the War of Attrition (1968–1970) and the 1973 Yom Kippur War. At most (albeit not always) the cabinet as a whole was informed about the general outline of proposed operations, to which ministers were asked to give their consent. Just how unsatisfactory a way this is of going about the business of supreme command is illustrated by the Winograd Report's depiction of what happened in the cabinet room on July 12 2006, when prime minister Olmert proposed that the IDF launch a full-scale attack on Lebanon.

> The Cabinet did indeed take the decision, but it did so in the guise of a political forum that expressed support for the Prime Minister, Minister of Defense and the IDF, to all of whom it also gave backing. The most amazing and critical conclusion is that the only significant decision taken by the Government of Israel – the body that has the authority to decide (and to refrain from taking a decision) – in the period covering the initiation of the campaign was to support the decision to embark on a military operation. [It took this decision] knowing that there was a probability that it would result in rocket attacks on the rear, but without knowing how the campaign would end, and without knowing the scale of the proposed action, its goals or its real purpose. [The decision was taken] after two and half hours of talks, without a serious debate, and without satisfactory answers being given to the relevant questions posed by ministers in possession of considerable experience in relation to security affairs.
> (*Winograd Commission Partial Report* 2007:24, paragraph 61)

As has been noted in several previous chapters, almost all prime ministers have sought to solve the problems presented by the cumbersome size of the cabinet by consulting with smaller groups. Indeed, ever since 1962, a MCSA has been a permanent feature of all governments. Significantly, however, the status of that forum has always been indeterminate. Only Eshkol felt required to consult with the MCSA on a regular basis during wartime (above pp. 79–80) Otherwise, the preference has been for more informal groups. Ben-Gurion set a precedent when limiting discussion of sensitive national security affairs to a small entourage of trusted aides. Mrs. Meir likewise invited to her 'kitchen' gatherings a limited number of close advisors and cronies. Whilst both traditions have continued, they have recently been supplemented by the establishment of an 'inner circle' of selected ministers, which is even more exclusive than the MCSA. Thus, the coalition government put together by Binyamin Netanyahu in 2009 contains both a MCSA, of which 15 ministers are full members and another five listed as 'observers', and a much more powerful forum known as 'the seven', which consists of the principal ministerial representatives of the parties that comprise the coalition and trusted ministers with national security experience.

Analysts conventionally focus attention on the ways in which this multi-layered system might have adversely affected the quality of Israel's national security decision-making (Freilich 2006:641; Maoz 2006). Also worthy of notice, however, is its dubious constitutional status. Of all the inner caucuses thus formed, only the MCSA has managed to get its name written into the statute book, albeit very belatedly and laconically so, in the guise of the National Security Committee of the Cabinet (NSCC), a forum first referred to in the earlier versions of Basic Law: The Government and now mentioned in The Government Law of 2001 (not to be confused with Basic Law: The Government of 2001, the implementation of which it was designed to assist). This, too, however, is less helpful a document than might have been expected. Its principal contribution to the national security framework is to give formal expression to the dominant role that the prime minister usually plays in the decision-making process. Unlike Basic Law: The Military, for instance, which makes no mention of this office, The Government Law specifies that the prime minister is to chair meetings of the NSCC, the other members of which are the ministers of defense, foreign affairs, finance, justice and the deputy prime minister. Other matters, however, remain obscure. Specifically, The Government Law does little to clarify the legal status of the NSCC or to define its precise functions.

A compendium known as the *takanon avodat ha-memshalah* ('regulation respecting the work of the Cabinet') attempts to repair those lacunae.[3] It ordains (Article 43) that when setting the agenda for meetings of the NSCC, the prime minister is to act on the advice and recommendation of the head of another body, the *mateh le-bitachon leumi* (which translates, rather confusingly, as the 'National Security Staff' [NSS]). However, since the holder of the latter office is appointed by the cabinet on the recommendation of the prime minister (Article 3 of the NSS Law enacted in 2008, see below) the *takanon* in effect buttresses prime ministerial influence over national security decision-making. In other respects, the *takanon* is even less helpful. Article 44, for instance, states that decisions taken by the NSCC are final and cannot be appealed to the cabinet as a whole. Quite apart from virtually emptying the notion of 'cabinet responsibility' of all meaning, this regulation could also place Israel's most senior military officer, the CGS, in an impossible situation. Should a difference of opinion arise between most ministers on the NSCC and the minister of defense, the person who Article 2(b) of Basic Law: The Military appoints to be 'in charge of the military on behalf of the Cabinet', who should the CGS obey?

In part, this question was anticipated in *Dawikat* v. *The Government of Israel* (1979), where the ISC addressed relations between ministers of defense and their cabinet colleagues, as well as the chain of command from the minister of defense to the CGS. The ISC noted that only with respect to decisions affecting the initiation of a war does the law (in this case Basic Law: The Government) require a declaration by the entire cabinet. Otherwise, where military decisions are concerned, the minister of defense is by default free to take his own decisions, unless overridden by the cabinet or by a committee appointed by the cabinet. This conclusion is actually not very helpful. Barring any cabinet intervention, shall the IDF always act in accordance with directives issued by the minister? Can the prime minister interfere?

Experience suggests that answers to such questions are far more likely to be determined by the extent of political clout available to the minister of defense of the day than by any hard-and-fast legal interpretations. Powerful ministers, such as Dayan, especially when they also function as prime minister, as did Ben-Gurion, and also possess a record of senior military command (Rabin, Sharon, Ehud Barak) obviously stand a far better chance of getting their way than do those who do not command such assets, as was the case with Lavon in the 1950s and Peretz in 2006.

The ISC and the rise of the 'business as usual' model

By the mid-1990s, at the latest, it had become clear that justices of the ISC were willing – and in some cases even eager – to play a much more prominent role in national security affairs than had thereto been common. An early indication of that change was provided in *Ressler* v. *The Minister of Defense* (1988), when they practically eliminated the standing doctrine. This departure from previous practice had several repercussions. For one thing, it solved the technical problems often presented by the sheer physical difficulties that otherwise denied access to the ISC to specific victims of alleged executive wrongdoing (such as the Palestinian militants and their hostages holed up in the Church of the Nativity in Bethlehem in 2002). Furthermore, by doing away with the need to identify such persons, the removal of standing also allowed the ISC to deal with almost all issues, hypothetical or not, that could arise.

Similarly consequential were the steps taken by the ISC to limit, sometimes drastically, its adherence to the doctrines of political questions and operational issues, which had thereto restricted its scope for intervention in national security affairs. Only with reference to the thorny question of the legality of the Jewish settlements established since 1967 on the West Bank has the ISC accepted a plea of 'non-justiciability', and hence persistently refused to pass judgment, principally on the grounds that the questions involved are political rather than legal in the strict sense.[4] Otherwise, however, it generally showed itself willing to deal with national security issues, almost irrespective of their precise subject matter.

No less significant than the increased tempo and scope of ISC activity as from the 1990s is the substance of its jurisprudence. In the terms of the concepts employed in this chapter, the justices did not deploy their influence in a way that might have buttressed a climate of 'accommodation' in Israel's national security framework. For instance, in none of the judgments handed down in this period did the ISC evince any inclination to lay down any fundamental constitutional principles that might demarcate spheres of authority amongst the other branches in the realm of national security – something that it had shown signs of being willing to do (albeit hesitantly) in *Dawikat* v. *The Government of Israel* (1979). Instead, ISC decisions after the 1990s focused almost to the exclusion of all else on balancing specific human rights and national security interests, an enterprise that Aharon Barak subsequently declared to be the hallmark of Israeli jurisprudence with respect to constitutional law (Barak 2010) and that is also characteristic of the 'business as usual' model of behavior depicted by Gross and Ni Aolain. In other words, what it reviewed was not the constitutional propriety of the executive's use of its national security powers but whether or not they were employed 'reasonably'. One consequence of that policy was that, unless blatant violations of human rights had occurred, the ISC invariably acquiesced in positions adopted by the executive. Another, however, was that judicial application of the 'business as usual' model embraced all four dimensions of the national security framework and hence can usefully be analyzed on a dimension by dimension basis.

The temporal dimension

Significantly, the ISC has never upheld a distinction between different temporal 'zones' where national security is concerned. Individual justices have, on occasion, made remarks indicating that they recognize such distinctions, and have expressed general uneasiness with the broad powers that emergency regulations give to the executive. However, the ISC has never annulled the declaration of emergency situation, and has almost never put actual limits on the broad use of emergency powers.

The ISC's persistent postponement of a decision in *The Association for Civil Rights in Israel* v. *The Knesset*, which explicitly questions the legality of emergency regulations, is entirely commensurate with that attitude. After all, and in clear conformity to the perspectives adumbrated in the 'business as usual' model, as far as the ISC is concerned, *knesset* declarations that renew the state of emergency are a given, which do not usually necessitate judicial review. Similarly, in *Levy* v. *The Government of Israel* (2005) the justices refused to accept a petition that they prevent the executive from resorting to DERs in order to close off an area of Israel adjacent to the Gaza Strip, an action designed to prevent opponents of the disengagement program from reaching the area. Once again, the only test that the ISC was prepared to apply was that of 'reasonable behavior', with which it declared the government's action to be in compliance.

More interesting is the way in which the ISC adhered to a 'business as usual' mode of judicial behavior with respect to the situation prevalent in the Territories during the second *intifada*. Ever since the year 2000, the State has advanced the claim that the term 'occupation' no longer adequately describes the situation prevailing in the Territories. Instead, it has posited the existence in those regions of 'armed conflict short of war' (above p. 155), a situation that warrants the adoption of a more flexible and lenient attitude with respect to IDF operations in the area. Here, too, the ISC has accepted the State's position, and has accordingly adjusted its own temporal depiction of the prevailing situation, allowing that an 'armed conflict' exists even when the intensity of violence has abated. What it has not altered, however, is its insistence on its continued duty to review military actions in accordance with the gauge of the protection of human rights. As much is demonstrated by its decisions in *Ajuri* v. *IDF Commander in the West Bank* (2002), *Physicians for Human Rights* v. *CO Southern Command* (2003), and *The Public Committee Against Torture* v. *The Government of Israel* (2006).

The spatial dimension

ISC applications of the 'business as usual' model with respect to the spatial dimension of Israel's national security framework have followed a similar pattern. Once again, at the level of principle the justices have tended to adopt whatever positions were advanced by the State. Thus, in *Abu Aita* v. *IDF Commander in Judea and Samaria Region* (1983) and in *Jama'at Aschan Elmualamin* v. *IDF Commander in Judea and Samaria Region* (1983) the ISC provided the legal framework that facilitated the incorporation of the Territories into Israel. Subsequently, however, it supported the form of re-organization that Gordon has termed 'outsourcing' (Gordon

2008:169–77), supporting the government's position with respect to the construction of the separation fence after 2002, the disengagement program in 2005, and the end of the Gaza occupation. At each turn of the spatial wheel, the ISC related to petitions only when they seemed to concern the alleged violation of a human right. Provided its basic requirements in this area were met, however, it maintained a non-interventionist stance. At a micro-level, how much this mindset could prove beneficial to the Israeli authorities was shown by the ways in which the ISC's attitudes towards the supply of electricity to the Territories conformed to changing governmental needs. In *Electricity Company for Jerusalem District* v. *Minister of Defense* (1972), the ISC had agreed that the concession to supply electricity to the occupied city of Hebron would be awarded to an Israeli company, rather than a Palestinian concern, thus enabling the IDF to use this commodity as a form of 'benevolent' control (Kretzmer 2002:64). In *Jaber Al Bassiouni Ahmed* v. *The Prime Minister* (2008) the ISC went one stage further. Provided that minimal humanitarian requirements were met, it now permitted the government of Israel to use the supply of electricity as a form of punishment; Palestinian consumption could be limited.

When no infringement of human rights could be proven to have taken place, judicial acquiescence in executive policies with respect to the spatial dimension of national security was even more blatant. ISC judgments with respect to military construction projects provide a case in point. The Planning and Construction Law of 1965, which had virtually excluded the public from exercising any influence over military construction projects, remained in force and virtually impervious to ISC criticism. Much though individual justices might decry 'the anachronistic premise of the taboo of security considerations' (as did Justice Rubinstein in *Hoshaya* v. *The State of Israel – Ministry of Defense*, 2007), they could offer little in the way of concrete relief to petitioners who complained about the arbitrary manner in which the IDF had begun building one large military base adjacent to their houses and was planning another entire complex of installations without considering the project's possible environmental consequences. Only with respect to the second case (*Adam Teva va-Din* v. *Ministry of Defense*, 2010) did the ISC make some headway, and eventually browbeat the ministry of defense into conducting an environmental study, albeit not a hearing. In the first instance, it did not get even that far, and sufficed itself with some general comments about the need for consultation in the future.

Judicial acquiescence in the broad framework of executive policies is also evident in the extent to which the ISC allowed the government to employ the IDF on missions not directly connected to the protection of Israel from external enemies. Thus, in *Federman* v. *Minister of Police* (1995), the ISC rejected a petition based on the claim that the minister had acted illegally when dispatching a contingent of Israeli policemen to Haiti, where they participated in an international aid force organized by the

USA. In a unanimous opinion, written by President Shamgar on the eve of his retirement, the ISC ruled that the right of the government of Israel to command the country's security forces was not limited by law to any specific geographical locality, and that it derived from the executive's unilateral authority to conduct foreign relations. (Whether or not this conclusion merely reflected an absence of appropriate legislation, which the *knesset* could repair by intervention, remained an open question). Likewise, in *The Legal Forum for the Land of Israel* v. *the Government of Israel* (2005), the ISC rejected an appeal against the assignment of IDF soldiers to law and order duties within Israel proper. Instead, it ruled that the authorities had been acting within reason, and hence legally, when ordering the troops to prevent demonstrations against the disengagement program from getting out of hand. In this instance, the ISC cited the last ten words added in 1991 to Article 18 of the Law and Administration Ordinance (1948):

> The Cabinet shall form military forces, on land, at sea and in the air, which shall be authorized to take all necessary and legal actions for the protection of the State, *and for the attainment of its security and national goals.*

The functional and hierarchical dimensions

With respect to both the functional and hierarchical dimensions of national security, the ISC's attitude of restraint found expression in its reluctance to declare which institution of government is authorized to make decisions affecting Israel's national security and to specify a precise constitutional correlation in this field between the executive branch, its various agencies, the legislature, and the various *knesset* committees. This had always been contentious ground. Where the initiation of military operations was concerned, opportunities for misunderstandings and conflicting interpretations had, if anything, multiplied since 1992 when the *knesset* had passed Article 51 of the new version of Basic Law: The Government (re-numbered Article 40 in the 2001 version, but otherwise unchanged). Even the title given to this article ('Declaration of War') was misleading. 'Declaration' was problematic because it did not reflect what the article actually talks about, which is in fact conflict 'initiation' ('40a: The State may only begin a war pursuant to a Cabinet decision'). Without further clarification, 'war' too is an unhelpful term, since it seems to relate to one type of military activity to the exclusion of others. In this respect, Article 29 of the older version of Basic Law: The Government had been much more straightforward since it authorized the cabinet 'to undertake in the name of the State, subject to any law, any act the doing of which is not enjoined by law upon another authority'. Read in a military context, the old version had thus intimated that every major use of force would require cabinet approval. Did the new version imply that such was no longer the case?

In 2006 the ISC was explicitly asked to address that question. Noting that the military campaign initiated that year in response to the Hizbollah ambush of 12 July had been declared an 'operation', MK Yossi Beilin petitioned that the cabinet should have declared its decision to embark on a 'war', and notified the FADC, in accordance with the procedure set out in Article 40c of Basic Law: The Government (*Yossi Beilin* v. *Prime Minister*, 2006). In response, the ISC trod warily. Its judgment began by identifying the areas in which Basic Law: The Government was obscure. 'Begin a war', the phrase used in Article 40a, was obviously very imprecise; after all, it could encompass a 'declaration' of hostilities – a procedure that, as the justices noted, is now considered irrelevant, certainly as far as the application of international humanitarian law is concerned (Dinstein 2005:30–4). But they confessed to being unable to ascertain whether the legislators had intended the procedures prescribed in Article 40c (cabinet decision and notification of the FADC) to be applicable to the onset of all forms of hostilities or to restrict them solely to cases in which the executive determined that it had embarked on a 'war'. As matters turned out, the ISC was saved from the need to determine the issue. Before it could issue judgment, the cabinet had indeed approved of IDF operations in southern Lebanon and Prime Minister Olmert had addressed both the FADC and the full *knesset*. Nevertheless, in an abstract sense, the issue raised by MK Beilin still awaits clarification.

Precisely the same attitude of judicial reticence is reflected in the absence of any direct reference on the part of the ISC to questions related to civil–military relationships at the very apex of the decision-making pyramid, the level conventionally referred to as 'supreme command'. Indeed, the court's silence in this area is even more noteworthy when it is remembered that this especially sensitive aspect of both the functional and hierarchical dimensions of Israel's national security has been a subject of persistent concern. Who made decisions respecting the conduct of military operations, and how they did so had constituted foci of attention during the wars of 1973, 1982, and 2006 and had indeed been discussed at length by each of the commissions of inquiry established in their wake. The ISC, however, took no part in the debate that ensued. Its non-intervention in this issue, which is all the more remarkable for contrasting with its activism in other spheres, can only be explained by the fact that, since no human rights issues were involved, judges considered intrusion on their part to be unwarranted.

Precisely the same considerations came into play where ISC review of the conduct of Israel's foreign relations is concerned. In this instance, however, they caused the pendulum to swing from a position of judicial non-involvement to one marked by a high level of activism. The reasons for that shift are easily explained. For many years, the ISC (following

British practice in this field) declared the conduct of foreign relations, a brief that includes granting approval to international agreements entered into by the state, to be one of the prerogatives of the executive. Accordingly, it argued, initially implicitly and as from the 1960s in an explicit fashion, that decisions taken by the executive branch in this sphere did not require parliamentary approval. At the same time, however, the ISC also ruled that international agreements entered into by the executive do not affect domestic Israeli law. They remain international obligations which cannot be enforced by Israeli courts.[5]

With Israel's administration of the Territories, that position became increasingly difficult to sustain. Because Israeli law did not apply in the areas conquered in 1967, the ISC had to base its jurisprudence on the international law of occupation, especially where human rights were concerned. Its attitude towards Israel's external obligations changed accordingly. Even so, however, the direction of movement was *sui generis*. The ISC did not now insist on the legislature's right to participate in international treaty adoption. In fact, in *Hillel Weiss* v. *Prime Minister Ehud Barak* (2001), for instance, it explicitly rejected that option. Instead, it considerably enlarged its own authority to do so (Hirsch 2009). In so doing, it explicitly subordinated the 'accommodation' model of conduct, which prioritizes legislative activity, by adopting a 'business as usual' mode of conduct, which augments judicial authority.

For one thing, justices of the ISC have very much enlarged the span of treaties that they recognize as falling within the scope of customary international law, a designation that automatically makes them part of Israeli law and hence subject to their adjudication. Especially relevant, in this respect, is the ISC's declaration that much of the international law of belligerent occupation falls within that category (for instance, in *Yesh Din* v. *IDF Commander in the West Bank*, March 2010), a position that in effect incorporates these international norms into Israeli law. Second, following American precedents, the ISC has vigorously applied the interpretative doctrine, which requires it to interpret Israeli legislation in a way that is consonant with international norms (e.g., *John Doe* v. *The State of Israel*, 2008). Since, as has been noted on several occasions, the ISC adheres to a very expansive doctrine of interpretation, which allows it to aggressively interpret every statute, this change further strengthens its claim that international agreements are applicable in Israeli law.

Why the business as usual model?

Conveniently, students of Israeli jurisprudence do not have to go far to discover the considerations underlying the ISC's choice of a high level of 'business as usual' activism with respect to human rights. They have explicitly been laid out by Justice Aharon Barak, who published an extensive review of his judicial philosophy, entitled 'A Judge on Judging', in the

Harvard Law Review in 2002 (Barak 2002).Written by the person who did more than any other individual to bring Israel's military response to armed conflict within the orbit of judicial review, this article deserves to be read as much as an exculpatory manifesto as a work of scholarship. Self-confessedly intended to justify the degree of activism for which the Barak court had become famous, 'A Judge on Judging' set forth a series of explanations for its contention that no alternative course of action could possibly have ensured that Israel, even in a time of war, continued to function as a democracy that respected the rule of law and protected individual freedoms.

Basic to the position advanced by Barak is his explicit rejection of the contention that national security constitutes an exceptional sphere of judicial activity. Against that premise, which lies at the root of the 'accommodation' model as well as 'extra-legal' practice, Barak advances three claims. The first, in order of both appearance and importance, is normative.

> We, the judges in modern democracies, are responsible for protecting democracy both from terrorism and from the means the state wants to use to fight terrorism.... The protection of every individual's human rights is a much more formidable duty in times of war and terrorism than in times of peace and security. If we fail in our role in times of war and terrorism, we will be unable to fulfill our role in times of peace and security. It is a myth to think that we can maintain a sharp distinction between the status of human rights during a period of war and the status of human rights during a period of peace.
>
> (Barak 2002:149)

Barak's second argument appeals to positivism. In point of fact, he points out, there exists no yardstick for differentiating between times that are and are not considered national emergencies. 'The line between war and peace is thin – what one person calls peace, another calls war. In any case, it is impossible to maintain this distinction over the long term' (Barak 2002).

Finally, Barak advances what has come to be called the 'ratchet' claim – concessions conceded to emergency considerations during a period of conflict are likely to remain in force even when peace is restored.

> I must take human rights seriously during times of both peace and conflict. I must not make do with the mistaken belief that, at the end of the conflict, I can turn back the clock…
>
> Indeed, we judges must act coherently and consistently. A wrong decision in a time of war and terrorism plots a point that will cause the judicial graph to deviate after the crisis passes. This is not the case with the other branches of state, whose actions during a time of war and

terrorism may amount to an episode that does not affect decisions made during times of peace and security.

(Barak 2002:149–50)

The distinction that Barak draws between the judiciary and other branches of state is not restricted to the context of the 'ratchet' claim. It is also central to his analysis of the unique character of the roles that judges have to perform in democratic society and of the manner in which they should carry out their functions. On both subjects, Barak is prepared to take unequivocal positions. Thus, he argues that the role of judges as guardians of individual rights becomes especially important in times of national emergency, precisely because it is then that public pressure to infringe on those rights is most likely to be pronounced.

> …democracy ensures us, as judges, independence and impartiality. Because of our unaccountability, it strengthens us against the fluctuations of public opinion. The real test of this independence and impartiality comes in situations of war and terrorism. The significance of our unaccountability becomes clear in these situations, when public opinion is more likely to be unanimous. Precisely in these times, we judges must hold fast to fundamental principles and values; we must embrace our supreme responsibility to protect democracy and the constitution…
>
> (Barak 2002:150)

It follows that, since they are thus uniquely placed to defend democracy, judges must also perform their functions in ways that reflect and buttress their distinctiveness, and at the same time clarify their relationship with other branches of government.

> To my mind, a judge is not an agent who receives orders, and the legislature is not a principal that gives orders to its agent. The two are branches of the state with different roles: one is legislator and the other is interpreter. Indeed, legislatures create statutes that are supposed to bridge the gap between law and society. In bridging this gap, the legislature is the senior partner, for it created the statute. But the statute itself cannot be implemented without being interpreted. The task of interpreting belongs to the judge. Through his or her interpretation, a judge must give effect to the purpose of the law and ensure that the law in fact bridges the gap between law and society. The judge is a partner in the legislature's creation and implementation of statutes, even if this partnership is a limited one.
>
> (Barak 2002:35).

Richard Posner may perhaps have exaggerated when citing the latter passage as an instance of the hubristic judicial philosophy advocated by

Barak, who he altogether characterized as a 'legal buccaneer' (Posner 2007). Even so, it does provide a key to an understanding of the considerations that might explain Barak's preference for what we here refer to as a 'business as usual' model for the handling of Israel's national security affairs. Institutional factors would certainly have distanced him from the alternative of an 'accommodation' model. The latter, after all, mandates a form of judicial restraint. It requires that judges restrict their opinions to matters of process rather than substance, to drawing the lines instead of filling in the picture. All they have to monitor is whether, in the case to hand, agents of the executive have indeed followed procedures ordained by the legislature. Thus envisaged, 'accommodation' enjoins the judiciary to avoid, as far as possible, overturning decisions taken by qualified bodies and to limit itself to ensuring that parliamentary statutes are obeyed.

The 'business as usual' model, by contrast, begins from entirely different premises. Specifically, it denies that legislatures (or, where relevant, the framers of constitutions) can possibly foresee every contingency that may arise with relation to the needs of national security. Hence, neither can they supply, in advance, solutions to each of the problems to which those contingencies may give rise. Given those conditions, it simply makes no sense to expect judges merely to enforce whichever directives may be laid down in statute. Rather, and precisely as Barak demanded, they must act as 'interpreters', whose function is to assess the balance between individual rights and national security requirements on a case by case basis, and whenever a situation requiring court intervention might arise. Against that background, Barak's choice of the 'business as usual' model was virtually pre-ordained. From his viewpoint, its advantage lay in the extent to which it allows courts to relate to legislative statutes as expressions of general standards of required conduct (such as proportionality, reasonableness, and the like) rather than as determinants of specific rules of behavior that have to be followed to the letter.[6] Only by adopting this model could judges be given the scope for the exercise of the discretion that he considers to be vital for the defense of democracy.

A balance sheet

Although Barak is perhaps the most vocal of judges who support the ISC's adoption of a 'business as usual' mode of behavior, he is not the only scholar to have done so (Cole and Lobel 2007). Neither have his views respecting the role of courts in national security been left entirely unchallenged or without comment. Eric Posner and others have written extensively on the same subject (Posner 2006; Posner and Vermuele 2007). With more limited reference to Barak's jurisprudence, so too has Gideon Sapir (Sapir 2010).

The following summary will not retrace that ground. Rather, its purpose is to distinguish between the different consequences that have resulted from what we have described as the bifurcate behavior that has characterized ISC conduct since the mid-1990s: on the one hand, a high level of judicial activism, which has found expression in the adoption of a 'business as usual' model where human rights are concerned; and on the other a reticence to intervene in matters concerning the division of constitutional powers. Precisely because they have been so different, we shall argue, these policies have tended to produce compound results in the three areas of concern principally affected by their implementation.

- As far as the defense of Palestinian human rights is concerned, judicial activism – although certainly not without blemishes – generally deserves to be considered at least partially effective.
- As a means of shielding Israel from international criticism, the strategy has been even more successful.
- By contrast, its impact on the coherence of the national security framework as a whole has been almost entirely deleterious. Precisely because it has adopted an ad hoc and 'business as usual' mode of behavior towards human rights issues, the ISC has probably prevented the formulation of constitutional principles most likely to have contributed towards their long-term protection.

The human rights record

Judicial activism, as practiced by the ISC, has met with a mixed reception. Critics focus attention on its allegedly limited results in terms of the protection of Palestinian human rights. Some of the failings in this area can be attributed to procedural defects. Judicial intervention, by definition, cannot be anything but arbitrary. Courts do not take the initiative in deciding which cases to investigate; they can only react to petitions presented by individual or corporate applicants. True, the ISC has done much to enlarge the size of the potential plaintiff cohort, principally by abandoning the standing requirement and divesting itself of such other avoidance techniques as the 'political question' doctrine. Nevertheless, its agenda remains subject to the vagaries of public demand for its services.

Once judicial procedures do get under way, other biases intrude. The ISC is a common law court and, as such, restricted to reviewing the facts of the specific case at hand. Accordingly, its ability to view the wider picture is limited. Especially is this so since evidentiary proceedings in administrative petitions to the ISC are notoriously incomplete. The justices conduct no investigations and base their decisions on information provided by the parties, supplemented only by general knowledge. That background perhaps helps to explain the apparently very low proportion of cases in which the ISC can be said to have accepted the validity of Palestinian complaints against Israeli actions. Sommer (Sommer 2010), for instance, found that between 1997 and 2004 only about 15 percent (50 out of more than 350) of petitions presented to the ISC in this area were successful.

A more sophisticated analysis, however, reveals a more complex picture. For one thing, it has been argued, the readiness of the ISC to accept petitions from and on behalf of Palestinians constitutes a contribution of its own to the protection of human rights, and certainly is without international precedent. As Kretzmer points out (Kretzmer 2002:197), British courts, and especially the Privy Council, did act in a like manner when reviewing petitions emanating from British colonies and former colonies. Nevertheless, the two cases are far from identical. The British courts acted on the assumption that the colonies were legitimate components of the British empire; they would never have designated them as being 'administered' by the home country, still less 'occupied'.

Then there is the statistical evidence. As early as 1999 it was clear to Dotan that the ISC was employing a variety of methods in order to assist petitioners without declaring action taken by the executive and its agencies to be illegal (Dotan 1999). Hofnung and Weinshall-Margel have further refined the picture. After examining more than 200 cases concerning actions taken against Palestinians by the IDF and GSS in the name of 'anti-terrorism' and 'national security' during the period 2000–2008, they concluded that in some areas the statistical likelihood of a successful petition was in fact rather high (Hofnung and Weinshall-Margel 2010). Overall, certainly, some 60 percent of petitions related to national security failed. But those that concerned the separation wall and military operations recorded a 60 percent rate of success, which was much higher than in any other sphere of ISC judgments.

The national interest

Whilst the impact of ISC activism on the defense of Palestinian human rights is thus mixed, its contributions to Israeli national interests seem to be far more straightforward. Especially is that so if analysis focuses on the period since the year 2000, which has witnessed an intensification of efforts in various parts of the world both to apply to Israeli politicians and military personnel the process of universal jurisdiction – in accordance with which national courts can bring to trial and convict foreign nationals for international crimes committed elsewhere – and to cause the International Criminal Court (ICC) to indict Israelis for crimes against humanity allegedly committed in the context of the Arab–Israeli conflict (Cassese 2008; Hurwitz 2009; Ronen 2010; Benoliel and Perry 2010; Shany 2010). Few sectors of Israeli political society can afford to ignore such moves or to adopt an attitude of disdain that might deny their importance. Government officials, civil as well as military, retired as well as serving, have already been affected; some have had to cancel – on occasion at the very last moment – their plans to travel to countries where they have reason to fear that they will be arraigned under the rule of universal jurisdiction.[7] Members of the ISC possess additional incentives for attempting to thwart efforts to apply universal jurisdiction and/or instigate proceedings under the auspices of the ICC. Quite apart from genuinely wishing to avoid embarrassment to the State of Israel, they also have personal and professional reasons for ensuring that they will continue to be considered fully accepted members of the international legal community, a transnational network in which, on an individual basis, several ISC justices have indeed long played prominent parts.

Judicial activism helps serve those purposes. Partly, this is because it buttresses the professional credentials of the members of the ISC, demonstrating the extent to which they are cognizant of the concerns expressed by their international colleagues, even when disagreeing with the specifics of some of their opinions. This characteristic is nicely illustrated by the ISC's response to the famous advisory opinion, which the International Court of Justice (ICJ) published in 2004, declaring the separation wall to be a violation of international law. Even though Barak, who wrote the judgement (*Mara'be* v. *The Government of Israel*, 2005), disagreed with the ICJ's conclusions, he was careful not to take issue with the positions expressed in the advisory opinion any more than was absolutely necessary. For national as well as professional reasons, he clearly felt it important to emphasize that, where the principles of international law are concerned, the ISC and the ICJ are in complete accord.

Intervention on the part of the ISC in specific cases has also served another purpose. It has activated the internationally-recognized principle of 'complimentarity', according to which neither international tribunals nor national courts may take action in cases of international criminal law if the relevant domestic court has demonstrated its ability and willingness to execute its jurisdiction (Delmas-Marty 2006). In other words, judicial activism has become a means of undercutting whatever pretext may otherwise exist for international intrusion into Israeli domestic affairs. This tactic appears to have been successfully applied when the ISC managed to convince the government of Israel to initiate an independent investigation into the targeted killing of Salech Shechade in 2002, an operation in which 14 innocent civilians were also killed (*Hass* v. *MAG* [2008]). Accepting that this investigation constituted an instance of 'complimantarity', the Spanish court immediately dismissed the private criminal claim on the incident that it had previously agreed to adjudicate under the universal jurisdiction process.

Notwithstanding that achievement, there of course exists no guarantee that the ISC will continue to provide protection from attempts to apply universal jurisdiction. Principally, this is because in most cases concerning IDF conduct in the territories, it has tended to confine itself to behaving as a court of administrative review. Provided that the military justice system has taken action, the ISC has usually refrained from intervening in criminal prosecutions of Israeli soldiers accused of violating the military code, preferring to defer to the decisions of the MAG (Ben-Naftali and Zamir

2009). This may lead to accusations that the ISC is attempting to side-step its duty to show that Israel is making a bona fide attempt to prosecute war crimes or is in possession of a criminal justice system sufficiently independent and effective to do so.

The national security framework

It is with respect to its impact on the national security framework as a whole that the record of judicial activism is most open to criticism. At this systemic level, two faults appear to be especially pronounced.

First, extended and protracted judicial intervention has intruded to what seems to be an excessive degree on the autonomy that, as Samuel Huntington pointed out, military organizations are entitled to expect, not least in democratic societies (Huntington 1957). More recently, other observers have also cautioned that armed forces which are subjected to micro-management do not necessarily thereby become more law-abiding, and certainly not more proficient. On the contrary, they tend to seek ways of shirking their professional responsibilities and/or resort to subterfuges in order to avoid any scrutiny at all (Sarkesian and Connor 1999; Feaver 2003). Such, it has been argued, are precisely the dangers that presently confront Israel. Particularly is that so since extensive and protracted judicial intervention is not an isolated phenomenon. It has fed, and been complemented by similar attempts to dictate IDF norms of conduct on the part of a motley collection of (often competing) civilian groups, prominent amongst which are parents, off-duty reservists, gender activists and rabbis (S. Cohen 2006).

Whilst most fears of military shirking in the realm of judicial investigation have not thus far been realized, the same cannot be said of senior political behavior. On the contrary, excessive and protracted judicial activism as practiced by the ISC in accordance with the 'business as usual' model appears to have provided politicians with a pretext for not taking the necessary legislative steps to create a viable and normative legal framework in the field of national security. After all, they have argued, petitions respecting alleged crimes committed by both military and civilian agencies of government can always be submitted to the ISC. As a corollary, they have also intimated, even if only *sotto voce*, that conduct which has not been expressly outlawed by the ISC must, by definition, be legal.

The obverse side of that coin has been occasional executive disregard for even the semblance of due procedures with respect to national security decision-making. 'Disengagement', the sanitized name given to what was in truth a unilateral withdrawal on Israel's part of IDF forces from the Gaza Strip and the dismantling of all Jewish settlements both there and in a small portion of northern Samaria, supplies a particularly blatant example. Disengagement was almost entirely the brainchild of prime minister Ariel Sharon and the small circle of personal advisers and family members with whom he consulted on a regular basis at his private ranch (hence known as the 'ranch forum', an updated version of Mrs. Meir's 'kitchen'). At no stage subsequent in its development did the program follow accepted procedures. Plans to carry out previous pull-backs of Israeli forces (from the Sinai in 1956, from portions of the Golan Heights and the Suez Canal in 1975, from the Sinai in 1982, and from successive layers of southern Lebanon after 1985) had all been preceded by at least a modicum of staff work and cabinet debate, and invariably communicated at an early stage to the *knesset*.

Sharon broke with all those precedents. He initially floated disengagement in a speech that he gave in December 2003 to a quasi-academic gathering (the fourth 'Herzliya Conference') held in one of Israel's swankier resort hotels. His announcement had not been preceded by a cabinet discussion, still less by an inter-departmental examination of disengagement's possible implications. Neither did the announcement trigger a return to the regular constitutional process. Instead, and to a degree that might have made even Ben-Gurion blush, Sharon took unilateralism to an extreme. Thus, he brushed aside the misgivings voiced inside both his own *Likud* party, a majority of whose registered members voted against disengagement in a special ballot, and in the IDF, whose CGS made no secret of his distaste for the program. Only thereafter, in February 2004, did he officially present disengagement to the *knesset*. Since at no stage did the ISC call the executive to order (as it was eventually petitioned to do in *Gaza Beach Regional Council* v. *The Knesset*, 2005), to all intents and purposes Sharon became a law unto himself.

Thus seen, the policy of judicial 'activism' pursued by the ISC assumes an appearance that deviates from the popular image. Far from articulating a view of the place of the Supreme Court in all aspects of public life, it has in fact encompassed a remarkably narrow area of interests. Therein, we suggest lies the second – and most important – systemic defect consequent upon the ISC's adoption of a 'business as usual' mode of behavior. It has encouraged the tendency of its members to define their functions in restricted terms. They have been far more concerned with protecting individual human rights than with laying down clear constitutional principles with respect to the exercise of governmental authority and the separation of political powers (Rubinstein and Medina 2006:173–264). This tendency, we argue, has been especially pronounced in the realm of national security affairs, where it has produced an especially lop-sided situation. Focusing almost exclusively on human rights issues, the ISC has almost entirely ignored the vast range of other issues with which a coherent national security legal framework must necessarily be concerned. Its reputation for judicial activism notwithstanding, the ISC has persistently – and deliberately – remained entirely silent with respect to many of the large and fundamental issues that could reasonably be expected to figure prominently in a constitutional discourse on national security: the proper division of authority between the branches of government with respect to war initiation; the precise nature of the relationship between the cabinet, the minister of defense and the CGS; and – perhaps most contentious of all – the legal status of the Territories.[8]

Our view is that this policy has been mistaken. Indeed, it can be said to have undermined the very efforts to protect human rights in which the ISC invested so much of its energies. After all, a clear definition of spheres of control in national security is not only advisable in the abstract constitutional sense, it is also a necessary condition for the long-standing protection of human rights. That, indeed, is one of the lessons drawn form the experience of other democracies, in which the establishment of clear boundaries of executive action has been recognized as the essential foundation upon which all attempts to control the misuse of governmental power must ultimately rest (Koh 1990:208–28; Issacharoff and Pildes 2005). From that perspective, the ISC's adoption of a 'business as usual' mode of conduct must be judged a disservice to Israeli democracy. Primarily, this was because it nurtured a tendency to avoid formulating and stipulating clear rules of national security conduct, based on first principles of good government. Instead, 'business as usual' encouraged treatment of all national security issues, including those affecting human rights, on an ad hoc and even arbitrary basis, and without consideration for the uniqueness of the general characteristics that distinguish affairs of state in this area from any other. Hence, even if a strategy of 'business as usual' has enabled the ISC to prevent and/or repair the most egregious of human rights violations, it has not provided any guidelines for the prevention of a recurrence of similar incidents in the future. Potential violators of human rights norms, such as the military or the GSS, can still never be entirely certain where justices might draw the line between appropriate and inappropriate behavior. Bystanders, a category that includes the Israeli public as well as international legal observers, are also left in a state of uncertainty – as are, even more so, potential victims.

In the absence of a sufficient degree of certainty, instability is almost bound to ensue. In this sense, the ISC's adoption of a business as usual model must be deemed largely responsible for the state of semi-chaos that now characterizes Israel's national security legal framework. Rather than imposing coherence on the framework, actions taken by the ISC have in fact contributed to the persistence of its hybrid form. Instead of prodding the other branches of government to function in accordance with a clearly defined set of standards across the entire board of national security activity, the judiciary has left vast areas of that subject entirely open to legislative and executive discretion. No wonder, then, that Israel's national security framework now resembles a tripartite three-legged race in which the participants, although proclaiming their wish to head in the same general direction, invariably find themselves tripping each other up.

Our final chapter will offer some suggestions as to how that situation might be repaired.

8 Prognosis
Modes of reform

Israel's current national security legal framework clearly stands in need of reform. As previous chapters have demonstrated, in all of its four dimensions far too many issues remain unregulated. The division of responsibility between the various branches of government for both the formulation and implementation of national security policies has never been clearly defined. Worse still, neither has the need for agency oversight ever been fully acknowledged. Consequently, although Israel is undoubtedly committed to the principle of civilian supremacy over military conduct, the country still lacks a statutory body, or cluster of statutory bodies, specifically tasked to ensure that the security agencies and military services adhere to norms, both national and international, relevant to the use of force. As has always been the case, fulfillment of that assignment continues to depend on a ramshackle and uncoordinated apparatus, the components of which range from a self-regulating system of military justice to ISC judgments, and from ad hoc commissions of enquiry to sporadic parliamentary probes. Although this melange has certainly managed to correct the most blatant faults in Israeli national security practice, the time has clearly come to search for a more synchronized arrangement capable of coping more efficiently with the challenges of the future.

That quest is hindered by two frequently cited obstacles. The first, and most comprehensive, is the absence from the Israeli legislative landscape of a written constitution. Notwithstanding the existence of 11 'Basic Laws', which are designed to serve as the building blocks of a future constitution, and notwithstanding too the obstinacy with which proposals for the drafting of a constitution are aired from time to time (e.g., *Israel Democracy Institute* 2005), there seems little prospect that any such document will garner sufficient support to ensure *knesset* approval in the foreseeable future. Hence, Israel will continue to lack a text of the sort that in other countries lays down the functions, privileges and duties of the branches of government and prescribes the manners in which each may (and may not) exercise its powers. That being the case, all such arrangements will be subject to the sort of improvisation that has become so pronounced a characteristic of Israel's national security style.

In many senses, the second impediment to reform is an outgrowth of the first. As Gad Barzilai has pointed out, Israel's national security laws, precisely because they are not grounded in a durable constitutional template, are especially prone to manipulation by whichever branch of government happens to be most willing and able to exploit that circumstance. In other words, as periodically formulated and implemented, Israel's national security legal framework is a manifestation of political influence; its format at any moment in time reflects the ability of one elite or another to control national policies and block domestic opposition to such efforts (Barzilai 1999a). Ben-Gurion, for instance, sought to entrench his hegemony over national security by dragooning law into political service. Subsequent legislative alterations, such as were articulated in Basic Law: The Government and Basic Law: The Military, reflected the extent to which authority in this area had become more diffuse. When the overall balance of power again changed, and the Supreme Court began to play a more active role in every aspect of Israeli life, the national security framework experienced yet another shift, placing greater emphasis on sensitivity to norms expounded in international humanitarian law.

Taken to its logical conclusion, that historical interpretation can be presented as an excuse for immobility. After all, its implication is that the necessary pre-condition for any reform or fundamental change in national security law is a complete overhaul of both the style and structure of all Israeli politics. Otherwise, dominant elites would simply block the enactment of whatever legal change they assessed as inimical to their interests or, worse still, manipulate the proposed reform in a way that would benefit those interests. We submit, however, that an alternative argument can be made. Hopes for reform are not forlorn; neither are all changes doomed to abuse by interested parties. Provided they are appropriately enacted, laws – including national security laws – can and do exert an influence over the way in which institutions interact and carry out their functions. But they will best be able to fulfill that function when the expectations and ambitions of their framers are not set too high. Hence, we suggest that instead of submitting a program for the comprehensive and across-the-board reform of Israel's entire national security framework, it would be more realistic to formulate a piecemeal program, which recognizes the requirements of each of its component dimensions: the spatial, the hierarchical, the functional and the temporal.

Before itemizing the specifics of our suggestions, we consider it important to clarify the principles upon which they are based.

The first, and perhaps most obvious, is that all proposed reforms in Israel's national security legal framework, as in any other context, must take account of political realities. Otherwise, they will be ignored, at best, or – in the worst scenarios – used manipulatively to enhance the powers of whichever institution is able to deploy its political power.

As noted in our preface, the approach that we consider most usefully considers such restraints is 'legal process theory', as developed by scholars principally associated with the public choice school under the heading of 'due process of lawmaking'. Hence, our conclusions are based on two of the principles conventionally associated with this school of thought. One is that the separation of powers is essential to the proper working of the democratic political system. Clear borders between the functions of different branches are required in order to promote the proper operation of government. Second, within the overall framework of the system, the role of supreme courts (whatever their precise nomenclature) is important but limited. Their task is to preserve the separation of powers arrangement, but not to interfere in its substantive content (Farber and Frickey 1991:118–31). Provided those boundaries are respected, we consider that in Israel the attainment of the correct equilibrium will require only minor adjustment to the institutional scaffolding of the present legal system.

Admittedly, this approach grants a large degree of credit to the willingness of all component parts of that system to support the continued functioning of current institutions. For that reason it is unlikely to appeal to either Marxist or rational choice theorists, who assume that the conduct of institutions and individuals is largely determined by group or personal interests, rather than those of the collectivity as a whole. However, as our historical chapters have demonstrated, the development of Israel's national security legal framework provides no evidence that might support those approaches. Accordingly, our conclusions will also bypass them. Instead, we limit our proposals to reforms that recognize the current division of governmental powers, and attempt to operate within the confines of this system. That approach also accounts for the methodology employed in this concluding chapter. We deliberately avoid adopting a one-size-fits-all approach that seeks to repair the weaknesses of the current national security legal framework in its entirety. Rather, we address each of its four dimensions in turn, seeking to identify the type of reform necessitated by the uniqueness of its specific needs.

Briefly summarized, we propose the following:

- Present faults in the *spatial* dimension of the Israeli national security framework, when they touch upon matters located within the pre-1967 borders ('the Green Line'), can be corrected by no more than incremental improvements in present arrangements. Rectification of the spatial faults relating to the Territories, however, mandate what we term 'transformational' reform, a major re-structuring that can only result from a dramatic external stimulus, such as a negotiated or imposed settlement of the Israel–Palestinian conflict.
- Where matters relevant to the *hierarchical* dimension are concerned, the required remedial measures appear to be far less drastic. We refer

- to them as 'corroborative' reforms since they amount to reinforcing an existing trend to introduce new legislation affecting this sphere.
- Most deficiencies in the *functional* dimension, by contrast, present a challenge that requires structural improvements. We conclude that both the legislature (the *knesset*) and the judiciary (the ISC) must change the thrust of their intervention in the national security legal framework and that, more importantly, major efforts be invested in cultivating agencies that can fulfill the role of 'sentinels' of national security practice.
- Most substantial of all, however, are the reforms required in the *temporal* dimension, especially with regard to the continuation of a 'state of emergency'. Our analysis suggests that the existing deficiencies in this area cannot be repaired by anything less than a fundamental re-alignment of the way in which the ISC conducts itself. That end can only be attained by discarding traditional common law attitudes towards the functions of courts and the adoption of new patterns of thought. Hence, in this case we advocate a program of 'cultural' reform.

The purpose of the pages that follow is to discuss each of those proposals in greater detail.

The spatial dimension

Even in the twenty-first century, military control over land resources within the internationally recognized borders of the State of Israel remains excessive. Indeed, it has been calculated that within the Green Line alone Israel's defense establishment still exercises direct and indirect control over half the country's land surface. In addition, it possesses exclusive rights of access to over one-third of the coastline and massive swathes of air space (Oren 2007). Moreover, the amalgam of interests and agencies generically known as the 'security sector' continues to enjoy extraordinary legal status where property is concerned. In contrast to civilian individuals and corporations, for instance, the IDF possesses exceptional status in the Planning and Construction Law, which permits it to erect military-related installations almost without any prior approval from the relevant civilian agencies. It is all but exempt from legislation requiring environmental preservation. And the cloak of secrecy under which it often operates is exploited to avoid paying property taxes to the scores of local authorities within whose jurisdictional territory lie hundreds of military camps and facilities.

Nevertheless, the differences with the situation that prevailed during the first decades of statehood (see Chapter 3) are marked and warrant notice. In recent decades, especially, IDF land privileges have been affected by the same sort of insistence on transparency and accountability that has revolutionized military–societal relations in other areas of Israeli life and has resulted in a growing public inclination to subject the claim of 'national security interest' to critical scrutiny (Oren and Newman 2006). Economic considerations have provided further incentives. Civilian demand for real estate, for both housing and commercial development, spiked dramatically with the arrival of over one million new immigrants from the former Soviet Union and Ethiopia during the 1990s, and has since been sustained by demographic increases and a constant rise in the standard of living. Under those circumstances, the continued existence of large military installations in the metropolitan center of the country has come to seem increasingly anomalous. Indeed, as early as August 1993, the government published a formal decision to the effect that the IDF would re-locate bases situated in the center of the country to peripheral areas (notably the Negev) and transfer control over the vacated properties to the Israel Lands Administration (Oren and Regev 2008:177).

Thereafter, additional attempts to exercise some form of public control over the spatial dimension of the national security framework followed almost as a matter of course. The State Comptroller periodically scrutinized the way in which the IDF was violating existing regulations with respect to such matters as the payment of licenses and land taxes, not giving due consideration to environmental and safety factors when undertaking construction, and delaying the relocation of its bases away from the metropolitan area (Oren 2007:158). Academic and media interest in IDF compliance also increased. And, when petitioned, the ISC also played a role, for instance, when adjudicating the objections raised to the location of the massive complex that the IDF planned to construct in the Negev as replacements for those it was vacating in the area of Tel-Aviv (e.g., *Adam Teva va-Din* v. *Ministry of Defense* [2010]). Critics continue to protest both the belatedness and sluggishness of these corrective measures (Perez and Rosenblum 2007; Oren and Regev 2008). But the fact that they are taking place at all indicates that within the Green Line the spatial dimension of national security requires no new agencies or procedures. We consider it safe to assume that the autonomy exercised by the military establishment with respect to land resources will continue to be eroded, slowly but nevertheless surely. Provided they are properly utilized, existing mechanisms are adequate to ensure the required degree of incremental improvement.

That is emphatically not the case where the Territories are concerned. Partly, this is because of the patchwork nature of the legal regimes operating there. Formally, the ISC treats the entire area of the West Bank as one unit in which the legal regime is the law of occupation, whilst the Gaza Strip is defined as 'not occupied' and outside Israel's control. Reality, however, undermines the validity of both those classifications. Israeli and Palestinian residents of the West Bank are subject to a variety of legal regimes. Palestinian inhabitants of the Gaza Strip are very much influenced by the IDF's supervision of their ability to travel to and from the area. Altogether, in fact, the Territories retain the characteristics of 'a legal frontier' (Gazit 2009), areas in which the executive can, if it so wishes, easily undermine any national security constitution that we can think of. The longer this situation persists, the more it perpetuates the existence of a legal no-man's-land in which the balance between the branches of government degenerates into disequilibrium. The roles of the legislature and the judiciary are especially affected. The *knesset* fulfills virtually no legislative function where the Territories are concerned. Conversely, and partly in consequence, the ISC has adopted an activist posture with respect to those regions, especially whenever actions taken by the executive there seem to violate human rights.

Imbalances of that magnitude cannot be repaired merely by incremental reforms. What they require, rather, is a 'transformational' process, which will subject the entire spatial dimension of the national security framework, where it affects the Territories, to drastic change. Lawyers do not possess sufficient political clout to instigate so drastic a shift. As matters stand, neither do legislators. The initiative must come from the executive, and will in all likelihood only do so as a result of a powerful external stimulus, such as the negotiation (or imposition) of an arrangement that will proclaim the resolution of all Israeli–Palestinian territorial differences. Until such time, in all matters affecting the Territories, the spatial dimension of Israel's national security framework will continue to be seriously flawed.

The hierarchical dimension

From an overall historical perspective, the management of the hierarchical dimension of Israel's national security framework can be said to have come full circle. The series of experiments undertaken ever since the mid-1970s with the purpose of dismantling the system of unitary control over national security affairs established by Ben-Gurion are now widely recognized to have ended in failure. Far from making possible the emergence of a more orderly and structured hierarchy of decision-making and implementation, the various attempts at de-centralization invariably resulted in confusion and chaos. Yitzchak Rabin, whose own experience of Israeli national security decision-making at the very highest level went back to Ben-Gurion's day (he received his first General Staff posting in 1954), appears instinctively to have appreciated that the remedy to this situation was to be found, not in further diffusion, but in a return to the highly centralized practices of the 1950s and 1960s. Hence, as soon as he had led the Labor Party to victory in the 1992 elections, he reverted to Ben-Gurion's precedent and combined the posts of prime minister and minister of defense, a practice that (with the exception of very brief spells during the premierships of Begin and Shamir) had fallen into abeyance after Dayan's appointment as minister of defense in June 1967. Rabin's example was followed by Shimon Peres, who succeeded to both positions after Rabin's assassination in November 1995, and more extensively (July 1999–March 2001) by Ehud Barak.

Since both Rabin and Barak were also the first retired Chiefs of the IDF General Staff to attain the very highest elected office in the land, there exists a temptation to attribute their combination of the two offices to essentially personal considerations, principal amongst which was their conviction that their past military attainments best qualified them for the defense portfolio. Although both men presided over cabinets that contained other former generals, including former holders of the office of CGS,[1] in neither case could other ministers parade anything like the prime minister's wealth of security experience and achievement. Rabin, quite apart from leading the IDF to victory in 1967, had also been minister of defense for almost six consecutive years, 1984–1990. When Barak retired from the IDF in January 1995, after almost 36 years in service, he had the distinction of being the most highly decorated soldier in the Force's history.

In addition, however, structural factors played a role. Notwithstanding the deficiencies pointed out by the Agranat Commission in 1974 and the Kahan Commission eight years later, little had been done to reform Israel's system of national security decision-making. Even at the end of the century, observers such as Ben-Meir (Ben-Meir 1995) were still noting the apparently congenital tendency of Israeli governments – invariably ad hoc coalitions of politicians, harnessed together by a temporary mixture of electoral chance and personal advantage – to trivialize strategy by making policy decisions on the hoof and almost entirely on the basis of narrow military advice. Despite some initially energetic huffing and puffing, the 'Center for Political Research' (*merkaz le-heker medini*), set up at the ministry of foreign affairs in 1974 in the wake of the Agranat Report, never attained the resources required to enable it to fulfill its intended function of counterweight to the IDF Intelligence Branch. An enquiry conducted by the State Comptroller two decades after the Center's foundation discovered that the unit had degenerated into almost complete atrophy (State Comptroller Report 1995:319–24).

Still more glaring was the failure to impinge upon the IDF Planning Branch's monopoly over national security operational preparations. Fierce opposition on the part of successive ministers of defense (who in this case acted as faithful spokesmen for the IDF brass) until 1999 stifled all attempts to bring together senior ministers, soldiers and government officials in a body that possessed a mandate to conduct broad-based analyses of national security affairs in all their manifestations. Even thereafter, the bureau established by Prime Minister Netanyahu under the high-sounding title of the *mo'atzah le-bitachon le'umi* ('National Security Council', [NSC]) turned out to be a rump agency, denuded of any clearly-defined tasks, let alone statutory status. Analysts apportion blame for this circumstance fairly widely. Included amongst the culprits are: the IDF, which fought a fierce rearguard action in defense of its traditional privileged status; the clique of prime ministerial advisers who were instinctively suspicious of 'professional' strategic counsels that might prove politically unpalatable; and individual prime ministers, who preferred to pursue their own visions without having to deal with the 'ifs' and 'buts' of pedantic bureaucrats (Maoz 2006; Ya'ari 2006). Whichever the case, the NSC was starved of both manpower and financial resources and – more importantly – of access to the very persons it was supposed to serve. The fact that its offices were located in an isolated installation situated in farmland on the outskirts of a Tel-Aviv suburb, rather than adjacent to the government compound in Jerusalem, symbolized and exacerbated its marginality.

So too did the frequent turnover in its directorship. In the nine years that separated the establishment of the NSC from the passage of a new National Security Staff Law in 2008 (see below), six individuals were appointed successive heads of the body. None completed their full intended term of four years, and one (Efraim Halevy, the distinguished former head of the *Mosad* [1998–2002], who was appointed the NSC's second director in October 2002) resigned in obvious frustration after just eight months in the job. His successors, too, were almost totally excluded from the innermost decision-making circle with respect to such major national security initiatives as the construction of the separation barrier or the decision to disengage from the Gaza Strip (Although General [res.] Giora Eiland, who headed the NSC 2003–2006, did play a significant role in implementing the disengagement program, he had not been party to its original formulation). Notwithstanding the existence of the NSC, therefore, the hierarchical dimension of Israel's national security framework continued to suffer from basic structural faults. As had almost always been the case, the decision-making chain of command remained highly personalized, chronically unstructured and almost continuously prone to breakdowns in communication between its various components.

All these anomalies became especially evident during the second Lebanon War of 2006. Formally, throughout that conflict the constitutional requirements were fully observed. As required by Basic Law: The Military, it was the cabinet as a whole that on 12 July took the decision to resort to large-scale military action in retaliation for the Hizbollah ambush of that morning, which had resulted in the death of eight IDF soldiers and the abduction of two others. On the following day (and hence again as required by Basic Law: The Military), prime minister Ehud Olmert informed a specially convened session of the *knesset* of the decision. He also maintained a regular schedule of both cabinet consultations and parliamentary briefs throughout the ensuing 34 days of fighting, during which the IDF also allowed the media unprecedented access to military information and personnel. Hence, on the face of things, this seems to have been the most 'democratic' and appropriately managed war in Israel's entire history.

Appearances, however, are often deceptive. The Winograd Commission, which was established in the autumn of 2006 in order to investigate both the civil and the military management of the war, came to very different conclusions. Especially was this so in its first 'partial' Report, published in April 2007, which dealt specifically with matters of constitutional interest. (The final 'full' Report, published in January 2008, focused far more on the military aspects of the campaign). As portrayed by the Winograd Commission, cabinet decision-making in 2006 had been virtual rather than real. Ministers, including both the prime minister and the minister of defense, possessed no direct and independent access to intelligence capable of helping them formulate an informed opinion with regard to available policy alternatives. All were entirely dependent on whatever the military agencies chose to tell them.

The faults in this situation might have been ameliorated had either the prime minister or the minister of defense possessed experience of senior military command. But for once in Israel's history, that was not the case. Both were self-confessedly 'civilians': prime minister Olmert had served much of his political apprenticeship as mayor of Jerusalem; defense minister Peretz had made his name as a trade union leader. Those records of public service did not equip them to question the prudential value of recommendations tabled by the IDF, or to demand that the military present them with clear cause and effect scenarios or a menu of alternative courses of action. Therein, in fact, lay the primary flaw in the hierarchical system of national security decision-making that Rabin and Ehud Barak had revived. It was too dependent on the personal qualifications of whoever happened at any given moment to be in charge of the apparatus as a whole. Absent individuals with the experience and status of Rabin or Barak, military input, although nominally submitted only in an 'advisory' capacity, would be left unchallenged.[2] Hence, according to Winograd, in July 2006 ministers voted to approve the recommendation that Israel go to war without really understanding what exactly it was that they were endorsing (*Winograd Partial Report* 2007:123–5).

Although thus critical of the cabinet as a whole, the Winograd commissioners singled out minister of defense Peretz and Prime Minister Olmert for particular censure. The former did not scrutinize the military's operational plans, he did not verify that the armed forces were prepared for battle, and did not adopt a general perspective in order to examine the harmony between the courses of action that were proposed and approved and the goals that were specified. In addition, Peretz failed to take sufficient steps to compensate for the deficiencies in his own knowledge of military affairs by soliciting outside advice and did not question forcefully enough the prime minister's decisions by presenting his own opinion with respect to the wider questions raised by the campaign (*Winograd Partial Report* 2007:116, 139–41).

This criticism is open to several objections. One is legal: as was made clear in *Dawikat* v. *The State of Israel* (1979), once the cabinet as a whole has reached a decision, ministers of defense are not at liberty to make independent judgments. They too are bound by the rule of collective responsibility. Then there are the practical administrative considerations. The IDF is necessarily the most powerful bureaucratic component within the ministry of defense. Hence, it is bound to exert a dominant influence on the views and opinions expressed by whoever happens to be minister of defense, especially if he or she possesses little personal military experience. Under those circumstances, any attempt on the part of ministers of defense to persistently second-guess their senior military advisers would undermine the principle of the unity of command. For them to establish independent 'think tanks' of their own would also adversely affect their relationships with the IDF, and would in any case duplicate work that (as will be shown shortly) the Winograd commissioners expected a 'National Security Staff' to carry out.

The Winograd commissioners were also severely critical of Ehud Olmert's conduct prior to and during the fighting. Specifically:

> We find the Prime Minister responsible, in both a ministerial and personal sense, for the flaws in the decisions taken, and for flaws in the decision-making process. The Prime Minister formulated his opinions without having been shown detailed plans and without demanding that they be presented to him. Hence he could neither analyze their specifics nor authorize them. Moreover, he never demanded real alternatives for consideration, and did not exhibit appropriate skepticism with respect to the military's opinions. In this he failed.
> (*Winograd Partial Report* 2007:115)

More succinctly:

> We could find no evidence that the Prime Minister consulted in a systematic manner with security experts outside the system, that he insisted on hearing other opinions in the IDF, and that he challenged in any depth the heads of the national security system with regard to alternative courses of action and their implications.
> (*Winograd Partial Report* 2007:13)

This was a somewhat strange line to take since, as we noted in Chapter 4, the constitutional status of the prime minister in the national security hierarchy is not self-evident. Basic Law: The Military makes no mention at all of this office, which is also only referred to en passant in those passages of Basic Law: The Government that deal with military operations. Nevertheless, reflecting custom rather than the law, the Winograd commissioners took an entirely different approach. Although careful to mention that the prime minister was legally (as opposed to politically) only responsible for conduct under his control, the commissioners nevertheless used bold type to emphasize their assertion that:

[The Prime Minister] is the leader who is personally responsible for the fact that the state and its army are embarking on a war. It is the responsibility of the Prime Minister to define the principal tasks [of the military], including the manner in which they are to be carried out and an extensive review of the probability of their attainment.

(*Winograd Partial Report* 2007:135)

In fairness to Olmert, the Winograd commissioners can perhaps be accused of protesting too much. After all, they did not restrict their criticisms just to the substance of the prime minister's decisions, the most critical of which was to embark on a war whose strategic goals were not at all clear. More seriously, they also castigated the manner in which those decisions had been reached, and especially his failure to canvass alternative opinions. Was this an altogether reasonable charge? After all, Olmert – who had barely been in office two months when the crisis erupted – cannot reasonably be held responsible for the absence from Israel's national security structure of an agency equipped to supply decision-makers with a sufficiently wide spectrum of alternative courses of action. Neither can he be blamed for the fact that no military plans were in place in order to deal with the scenario that he confronted on 12 July 2006. Given those constraints, his options that morning were in fact very limited. Prime ministers can hardly be expected to go around creating, from scratch, makeshift consultative forums in the midst of a national emergency, still less to veto operational proposals tabled by the IDF branches responsible for planning and intelligence on the basis of nothing more substantial than their personal instincts. Either improvisation would have involved going outside the only decision-making apparatus that was in place, and hence would have been just as likely to invite criticisms from a commission of enquiry as did the course that he in fact took.

A sense that much of their criticism of Olmert's activity (and inactivity) may have been unwarranted perhaps explains why the Winograd commissioners, in their 'Partial Report', focused considerable attention on examining how such situations could be avoided in the future. Their main recommendation followed almost inevitably from their view of the prime minister's centrality in the national security decision-making hierarchy. In order that incumbents of that office might be equipped to fulfill their functions in a professional manner, they had to be given direct access to an apparatus that was far more substantial than the existing NSC (which had played no role at all during the Second Lebanon War) and also far more permanent than an ad hoc coterie of personal advisors, selected on almost a catch-as-catch-can basis. Hence, included in a lengthy list of recommendations designed to transform the NSC into a truly effective tool of policy planning was the demand that its staff be 'radically strengthened, in both quantitative and qualitative terms, *inter alia* by employing persons with varied experience and from varied backgrounds, who would also be able to refer to available advisers and research papers' (*Winograd Partial Report* 2007:148, recommendation 4).

This recommendation came as no surprise. After all, one of the five Winograd commissioners was Professor Yehezkel Dror, recipient in 2005 of the prestigious Israel Prize for his academic attainments in political science, who had for almost two decades been advocating that:

> in order to facilitate high-grade grand-strategic thinking ... it is essential that there exist a professional policy planning staff alongside the government and the Prime Minister, who should also have available a bureaucratic framework for crisis management.
>
> (Dror 1989:334)

What was remarkable, however, was the context within which this proposal was presented. As formulated by the Commission, it reads almost entirely like a bureaucratic correction to a structural fault. In fact, however, it also had fundamental constitutional implications. A powerful NSC would not merely provide prime ministers with the assistance that that they require in order to assess national security options. More substantially, and more dramatically, it would place incumbents of that office in virtual sole control of policy-making in the national security sphere. Thanks to the NSC's support staff, the prime minister would possess access to information and assessments unavailable to any other minister, including the minister of defense. As a result, the principle of collective cabinet responsibility for national security decisions, a principle that rests on the concept that all elected officials share responsibility for government and that is embedded in Basic Law: The Government, and even more so in Basic Law: The Military, would be superseded by the individual responsibility of the prime minister. Constitutional convention might possibly grant holders of that office extraordinary status in the national security hierarchy (the issue is debated in Nun 1999); existing laws certainly do not do so. Indeed, it is worth repeating, as matters stand in this realm prime ministers possess no explicit statutory status whatsoever.

It is important to point out that the Winograd commissioners were certainly sensitive to the dangers inherent in conferring too many powers on the prime minister, and hence sought a golden mean. Their quest led them to balance their proposal for the establishment of a strengthened NSC with the recommendation that, in times of national security emergency, executive authority would be delegated to a 'War Cabinet'. Consisting of a small number of ministers who would be responsible for the overall management of national security affairs, this body, the commissioners recommended, would be a temporary device and hence would dissolve itself as soon as matters returned to normal. For as long as the emergency persisted, however, it 'should meet on a regular basis, and discuss the overall format of developments as well as major specific issues. Members of this forum should include, amongst others, ministers who possess experience in political and security affairs, without regard to coalition requirements'.

(*Winograd Final Report* 2008:580, recommendation 2)

Members of the Winograd Commission (a retired judge, a professor of law, a professor of political science, and two retired generals) might arguably be forgiven for failing to mention that this recommendation was in essence not novel at all. Precisely the same forum (a 'War Cabinet') had been mooted as early as July 1948 by the Greenbaum Committee and, it will be remembered, forthwith rejected out of hand by Ben-Gurion (see Chapter 3). Less easy to pardon are two other lapses. One is the truly astounding naivety of the Winograd commissioners' supposition that it would be possible to put together a forum in possession of so much prestige and power 'without regard to coalition requirements' – a supposition contradicted by even the most cursory acquaintance with the Mad Hatter's tea parties that frequently masquerade as consultations in multi-party Israeli governments. The second flaw is more formal. At no point in their Report did the Winograd commissioners formulate with any specificity the legislative changes that the implementation of their recommendation would require. Indeed, with the exception of one mention of the need 'to anchor' a beefed-up advisory body on national security 'in law' (*Winograd Partial Report* 2007:148, recommendation 7), they hardly referred to the need for new legislation at all. They seem to have assumed that the existing framework of laws needed little amendment.

Our own position is that such is not the case. In their present state, neither Basic Law: The Military nor Basic Law: The Government guarantees the principle of collective responsibility that the Winograd commissioners intended to uphold through the device of a 'War Cabinet'. If anything, the need for legislative reform to that end has been intensified by the passage of the National Security Staff (NSS) Law in 2008.[3] Although Article 1a of that measure intimates that the new administrative framework is designed to serve the entire executive ('The Cabinet shall have a National Security Staff'), subsequent passages create an unmistakable imbalance. Article 1b explicitly identifies the prime minister as the primary beneficiary of its work ('The NSS shall serve as the advisory body for the Prime Minister and the Cabinet in foreign and security affairs of the State of Israel'); Article 1c designates the incumbent of that office as the person who is the agency's prime mover ('The Prime Minister shall operated the NSS and shall lead it'). Admittedly, the practical effects of this reform have yet to become fully evident. Other than a substantial increase in the NSS's budget, which doubled between 2008 and 2010, and the relocation of its offices to the government compound in Jerusalem, the only tangible change in recent years has been the intimacy of the working relationship between Prime Minister Binyamin Netanyahu and Dr. Uzi Arad, whom he appointed to head the new NSS in 2009 and who frequently functioned as his personal envoy and adviser. Even so, and as the Turkish flotilla incident of May 2010 is reported to have illustrated, the IDF's influence on operational intelligence, planning and decision-making remains paramount.[4] Moreover, it retains its enormous intelligence and planning staff and, no less critically, its own lines of direct communication to the prime minister by means of the latter's military secretary – a position that has over the years grown in importance and influence without being referred to in any existing law whatsoever.[5]

Under those circumstances, there clearly exists a need for further legislative measures designed to attain an appropriate hierarchical equilibrium between prime ministers and their colleagues, as well as between the military and civilian echelons. However, what form those measures should take still remains an open question. A study published in April 2008 by a team of researchers at the Institute for National Security Studies (INSS), an independent think tank informally associated with Tel-Aviv University, advocates the adoption of a new IDF Law (Even and Gross 2008). This measure, the proposal argues, would preserve and even extend collective government responsibility over national security affairs by itemizing the areas of military activity deemed to require the prior sanction of the cabinet as a whole. Existing legislation specifies only two such instances: the initiation of war and the appointment (on the recommendation of the minister of defense) of a new CGS. Were the INSS recommendations to be accepted, the new IDF Law would also mandate cabinet sanction for the determination of the objectives of a military operation and the specific goals of a war. Moreover, the IDF would be required to obtain cabinet approval for its annual 'work plan', a document that spells out in some detail its proposed schedule of training exercises, weapons' tests and human resource allocations.

A system of that type offers obvious advantages when applied to routine matters, such as the examination of routine military agendas. But at moments of crisis, where time is usually at a premium, a forum consisting of the entire cabinet is likely to be more of an impediment than an asset. Our own position, therefore, is that even were all the components of the Institute's proposal to be fully adopted, supplementary reforms to the existing basic laws (the government and the military) would still be required. These do not mandate fundamental changes, of the sort likely to radically revise the present structure (and, for that reason, to generate opposition). Rather, we categorize the measures required with respect to the hierarchical dimension of Israel's national security framework as 'corroborative' reforms, designed to adjust and revise the existing framework rather than to construct an entirely new legislative structure.

Hence, with respect to the hierarchical dimension, we suggest three specific measures.

- The granting of statutory status to the sort of 'inner mini-cabinet' that the Winograd commissioners had in mind. Formally, such a forum has existed in rudimentary form ever since 1962, in the guise of the 'Ministerial Committee on Defense'. What it has never attained, however, is legal recognition or the benefit of a detailed specification of its powers and composition. Instead, prime ministers, beginning with Ben-Gurion, have tended to resort to convening 'kitchens', non-statutory gatherings of personal confidantes. In some readings, such forums are legitimated by under Article 33 of Basic Law: The Government, which authorizes the cabinet to delegate powers to individual ministers (see, however, Nun 1999, 2004). But even if such is indeed the case, 'kitchens' of the traditional type run the risk of undermining the entire notion of collective responsibility for national security, which legislative amendments can best preserve.
- A second requirement is for a clarification of the constitutional relationship between the prime minister, the cabinet and the minister of defense where matters affecting national security and military operations are concerned. It will be recalled that, to a certain extent, that need was fulfilled in 1967, when prime minister Eshkol and his new minister of defense, Moshe Dayan, signed a document delineating their respective freedom of action. However, and as the ISC pointed out in its *Dawikat* decision, by 1979 all such arrangements had clearly been allowed to lapse, and have never since been renewed. The most convenient and most appropriate way to correct that situation is by inserting relevant amendments into Basic Law: The Government.
- Finally, existing legislation must also be amended to address the degree of autonomy allowed to the CGS. Attention with respect to this topic conventionally focuses on whether the law in its present state provides sufficient guarantees for the subordination of the military high command to political control (Ben-Meir 1995; Bendor and Kremnitzer 2000:44–66; Kasher 2005; Rubinstein and Medina 2006:981–7). As Nun points out (Nun 2002), it is also important to preserve the status of the CGS, who in Article 3a of Basic Law: The Military is designated 'the supreme command level in the army'. Nun suggests that one way of attaining that aim is to specify that the minister of defense cannot intrude on the CGS's conduct of 'tactical' operations without full cabinet approval (surely a recipe for interminable squabbles. Since who is to determine, *ex ante*, what is and what is not 'tactical'?). In 2007, the *knesset* took another route, when passing legislation that forbade senior office-holders in the IDF, the police force and the security agencies from becoming either MKs or cabinet ministers within three years of their retirement from service (The Law Relating

to the 'Cooling off' Period for Personnel in the Security Forces). This requirement ensured that there would be no repetition of the delicate situation created in November 2003, when Shaul Mofaz somersaulted into the office of minister of defense barely four months after retiring as CGS, a circumstance that necessarily undermined the autonomy and authority of his successor and one-time deputy, General Moshe Ya'alon, over whom Mofaz had so recently exercised command. The next step, surely, is to draft legislation that might specify the independence of the CGS more explicitly.

The functional dimension

The reforms necessitated by the current state of the functional dimension of Israel's national security framework can be divided into two distinct categories. One comprises areas of functional relevance which require little or no reform. The other encompasses a larger range of issues, deficiencies in which have become so glaring that they require an innovative program of far-reaching change.

The employment of military personnel on non-military tasks falls within the first category. Even if, as is sometimes claimed (Nun 1999; Bendor and Kremnitzer 2000:38), the IDF's traditional posture of 'military role expansion' possesses insufficient authorization in law, at this point in time there seems little point in tackling the issue. Primarily, this is because the entire process has long lost the momentum that it once enjoyed, so much so that the IDF is now clearly engaged in a reverse process: 'military role contraction' (S. Cohen 2008:93–6). Budgetary pressures, together with drastic changes in both societal and professional military views on the proper functions of the armed forces, have combined to drastically reduce IDF involvement in the national building programs that were once considered flagship symbols of the military's commitment to society: land settlement; the provision of supplementary education for underprivileged communities; immigrant absorption. Increasingly, civic services once performed by conscripts are now being carried out by volunteers, many of whom have received discharges from military duty.

As is the case the world over, the IDF continues to play a prominent role in providing relief during cases of natural disasters (floods, forest fires, etc). Through its 'Rear Command' (*pikud oref*), established in 1992, it also assumes a large proportion of responsibility for civil defense. Neither activity, however, in any sense represents the sort of threat to democratic government that might require legislative correctives. If anything, it is the incremental process of de-militarization that might require statutory acknowledgement. During his term of office (2007–2011), the 19th CGS, General Gaby Ashkenazy, on several occasion publicly mused that Israel might soon have to adopt an entirely new method of conscription. The discharges from military service now granted to Arab citizens, *haredim* and large numbers of Jewish women who claim to follow a religious lifestyle, he pointed out, will soon result in a situation in which only 50 percent of all Israeli 18 year olds will be drafted. One way of repairing that inequality, Ashkenazy has suggested, would be to require all youngsters excused from military service to register for civic duty.[7] In that atmosphere, changes in the law that might sanction the employment of military personnel on non-military tasks seem entirely irrelevant.

Other areas of activity related the functional dimension of the national security framework, however, do require an innovative program of fundamental reform. Especially is that so where the crucial issue of agency oversight is concerned. Notwithstanding more than six decades of almost uninterrupted military activity in the name of national defense, *quis custodiet ipsos custodes?* ('who will guard the guardians?') remains an open question in Israel. Although there certainly do exist several competing contenders for the role of national supervisor of military conduct, not one of the candidates is equipped to ensure that the task is carried out either efficiently or adequately.

One obvious source of potential watchdogs is the security services themselves. Indeed, national security agencies everywhere have traditionally claimed to be the most suitable investigators of their own activities. No other organization in the country, runs the argument, disposes of the manpower and skills required to supervise national security affairs; no other can do so without revealing state secrets and/or jeopardizing the health of the services responsible for national defense. Those arguments underlay the creation of such internal supervisory mechanisms as the IDF 'Ombudsman' (*netziv kevilot ha-hayalim*) first established in 1972, and the 'Comptroller of the Security Establishment' (*mevaker ma'arechet ha-bitachon*), first formed in 1976. Although both positions are nominally occupied by civilians, the individuals concerned have always been retired senior officers who present their annual reports directly to the CGS. By and large, IDF ombudsmen have focused on providing service personnel and their families with a channel of communication for the voicing of personal grievances about alleged misconduct by junior and senior officers (a subject that appears in almost three-quarters of the 6,000 cases dealt with on average every year). Comptrollers of the security establishment, by contrast, generally concern themselves with financial (mis)management and planning procedures. In neither case, do the reports presented by these offices relate to proper norms of behavior vis-à-vis enemies, nor attempt to set standards in such areas.

The latter issues do certainly fall within the purview of the MAG, who commands the entire IDF military justice system. Although the relationship between holders of this office and attorney generals is complex (Shoham 2002), the Military Justice Law of 1955 clearly grants the former wide powers of investigation and adjudication as far as military conduct is concerned. Successive occupants of the post have certainly exercised those mandates, especially since the outbreak of the first Palestinian *intifada* in 1987, when the incidence of IDF violence against Palestinian civilians began to jump to unprecedented proportions. Reportedly, Brigadier-General Amnon Strashnov, who served as MAG between 1986 and 1991, immediately attempted to take the disciplinary and judicial measures required to curb the worst excesses (Strashnov 1994:157–97).[8] Prospects that allegations of misconduct could be pursued to the very highest levels of the IDF hierarchy were very much enhanced during the second *intifada* when one of Strashnov's successors, *tat-aluf* (Brigadier-General) Menachem Finkelstein, became in 2002 the first MAG to be elevated to the rank of *aluf* (Major-General), a promotion that was intended to allay fears, earlier expressed by Finkelstein himself, that persons of lower rank 'might favor military commanders and refrain from initiating court-martial proceedings against senior military personnel – even when such action might otherwise appear to be justified' (Finkelstein 2000:178).[9]

Not even the best of military justice systems, however, can be left entirely to its own devices. As Strashnov admitted, justices who are part of the military organization will always be prone to pressure exerted by their colleagues in the field forces, who typically warn that too rigid an adherence to judicial rules will both undermine troop motivation and invite operational failure (Strashnov 1994:371–403). Mindful of that situation, and especially when matters of principle are at stake, all democracies insist on some form of external supervision, designed to ensure that the armed forces (and other national security agencies) adhere to appropriate legal norms. Where they differ, however, is in the determination of which institutions might be deemed most suitable for the assumption of that responsibility and, no less important, how they ought to carry out their tasks. Those are precisely the questions which are now re-surfacing in Israel, where the array of possible answers is also especially wide.

As has been demonstrated in earlier chapters, one especially prominent candidate for the role of civilian overseer of national security conduct is now the ISC, which has in recent decades increasingly thrust itself to the very forefront of the struggle for civilian supremacy over all aspects of military behavior. The ISC does not merely perform its traditional function as the defender of individual civil liberties against military encroachment. Filling a vacuum left by the inactivity of other potential public bodies, it has also, and sometimes even more prominently, become the address of first resort with respect to wider questions of national security interest, a situation which has in fact transformed it into the arbiter of policy issues and even operational decisions. For reasons already itemized (see Chapter 7) we believe that the latter process might now be advancing to a stage at which it could cross the boundary that divides appropriate from inappropriate judicial conduct. Unless arrested, it threatens to impinge on the autonomy required by the agencies charged with the defense of the national interest and, in the long run, to damage the status of the ISC too.

We suggest that the first requirement that needs to be fulfilled if such dangers are to be averted is for the ISC to initiate a change in its own practices. Necessarily, it must retain its primacy as the country's principal defender of individual human rights. But where matters of more general national security policy are concerned, we suggest that it readjust its patterns of behavior. Rather than itself continuing to play a direct role in determining policies through the adoption of a 'business as usual' pattern of behavior, it should act as a 'traffic cop', restricting its intervention to adjudicating the constitutional propriety of national security legislation and to indicating which government authorities it considers best equipped to act in specific situations.

Significantly, such has long been the tradition prevalent on the European continent, where national courts are often expected to approve laws before they are implemented and thereby ascertain whether the new legislation complies with the constitution. That requirement is mandated by Article 16:3 of the French Constitution, which requires that the French Constitutional Council be consulted before the enactment of emergency measures. It has also been adopted in Germany, where in 1994 the Federal Court ruled that Bundestag approval was required prior to the dispatch of German troops to participate in UN peacekeeping operations in Somalia and former Yugoslavia, a decision that led to similar procedures being adopted in 1998 and 1999 prior to German military deployment in Kosovo.

A review of ISC decisions reveals that only in two instances has it adopted a similar approach: *Rubinstein* v. *Minister of Defense* (1998) and *The Public Committee Against Torture* v. *Government of Israel* (1999). But both instances, quite apart from focusing on the margins of national security issues (the conduct of interrogations of detainees and the draft deferments granted to *haredi* males, respectively), were also isolated. Overwhelmingly, the ISC has evinced marked reluctance to hand down opinions on national security affairs that might be construed as judgments on the constitutional propriety of an action and/or as interpretations of the institutional separation of powers. It will be recalled that the ISC fought shy of doing so in the *Dawikat* judgment of 1979, which left open the issue of the relationship between the cabinet and the minister of defense. Likewise, in *Beilin* v. *The Prime Minister* (2006) the ISC refused to pass an opinion on the definition of 'war', and of the constitutional powers of the cabinet to initiate an operation of that name in accordance with the provisions laid down in Article 40a of Basic Law: The Government. In the latter case, especially, it let pass an opportunity to clarify several questions of crucial relevance to the hierarchical dimension of the national security legal framework: do the military actions mentioned in Article 40a ('The State may only initiate a war pursuant to a Cabinet decision') include those that are not *prima facie* wars of self-defense, and perhaps therefore illegal under international law? Wherein lies the difference between a 'war', as specified in Article 40a and a 'military action', as specified in Article 40b ('Nothing in the provisions of this section will prevent the adoption of military actions necessary for the defense of the state and public security'). And perhaps most important of all, especially in the light of the experience of 2006, what procedures ought to be followed when 'military actions' are contemplated. Who, within the government, is authorized to initiate them, and who is responsible for their conduct?

It is generally agreed that the contribution made by the *knesset* to the hierarchical dimension of Israel's national security framework has, by and large, likewise fallen far short of expectations. The working group set up by the Israel Democracy Institute under the chairmanship of former President of the Supreme Court Meir Shamgar advocated rectifying those deficiencies by reinforcing the *knesset*'s supervisory functions. Thus, several of the constitutional proposals tabled by the group in 2005 specify ways to reform the existing balance of relationships between the executive and the legislature, in the latter's favor. One suggestion is to supplement the existing Article 40 of Basic Law: The Government, which grants the executive exclusive right to initiate a war, with a new clause granting the *knesset* the authority to '... order the Cabinet to halt any war and any military activity' (IDI 2005, Article 104). A second suggestion (Article 137) proposes transferring to the *knesset* the power to ratify treaties, except when national security consideration requires otherwise (Article 139). Yet another (Article 188) advocates that the powers to legislate emergency decrees, which under the present system are transferred to the cabinet as soon as the *knesset* declares the existence of an emergency situation, remain the prerogative of a special parliamentary committee.

Whether or not each of these proposals possesses intrinsic merit is itself open to question. For instance, do the advantages of encouraging the legislature's micro-management of a military operation, as implied by proposed Article 104, outweigh its disadvantages? Why not just leave the *knesset* with the power to terminate a war by passing a vote of no confidence? Likewise, does not the emphasis on the procedures for emergency legislation in Article 188 deflect attention from the far more crucial issue of the appropriate content of whatever measures are enacted? But from a structural perspective, all such issues must in any case be deemed subordinate to a more fundamental query. Baldly formulated, what we have to ask is whether, on the basis of past experience, there does indeed seem a reasonable prospect of increasing parliamentary supervision over military affairs. And if, as we shall argue, the answer is negative, then should not whatever enthusiasm for reform still remains in the legislature be directed into other activities?

Residual resistance in Israeli society to the adoption of a binding constitution is only one of the hurdles that have to be overcome before the reforms suggested by the IDI group can be adopted. Equally obstructive,

228 *Perspectives and prescriptions*

especially in the short term, is what appears to be an inherent reluctance on the part of the *knesset* itself to exercise the degree of oversight over military conduct that many observers deem advisable (e.g., Ya'ari 2004). Debates in Israel's parliament over all aspects of national security have, of course, been frequent and sometimes conducted with a passion befitting their importance. But once MKs have said their piece, and thereby perhaps salved their consciences, little further action has been taken. The historical catalog of practical measures initiated by the *knesset*, therefore, reads like a roll-call of negatives. As a body, the *knesset* has never taken any institutional steps to ensure that it might exercise a corporate supervisory role over IDF operations in the Territories; it has never once influenced the content of any of Israel's peace treaties; and its scrutiny of the defense budget, although in all fairness certainly less negligent now than was the case prior to the 1980s, remains only partial. Neither has the *knesset* ever come close to establishing anything like the post of Parliamentary Commissioner for the Armed Forces such as exists in Germany, where the civilian official of that title, who is elected to office by parliamentary vote, is required by Article 45b of the Basic Law passed in 1957 '…to safeguard basic rights of members of the Armed Forces and to assist the Bundestag in exercising parliamentary control over the Armed Forces'. Israel's parliamentarians have been quite content to leave such matters to the ISC or even to the IDF's own ombudsman.

Altogether, in fact, far from exhibiting any willingness to play a more active role in national security affairs, MKs seem anxious to divest themselves of some of the authority that they now possess. An outstanding example is provided by their attitude towards the custom whereby governments have since the 1970s requested parliamentary approval for international treaties, even though formal ratification remains an executive prerogative. A recent study by a group of scholars at the Hebrew University indicates that *knesset* involvement in treaty ratification, although thus limited, performs an important function since it enhances public debate over the efficacy of the norms in these documents (Broude and Noam 2008). Here too, nevertheless, recent *knesset* behavior demonstrates an unwillingness to strengthen the legislature's standing. Legislation passed in November 2010 stipulates that no peace treaty involving withdrawals from sovereign Israeli territory, including areas that have been annexed by previous governments (i.e., eastern Jerusalem and the Golan Heights) will be deemed ratified unless it is supported by a minimum of 80 MKs. Failure to attain that measure of support will require the submission of the proposed treaty to a national referendum. The undisguised purpose of the act, which passed after a long debate by 65–33 votes with 22 abstentions, was clearly to place restrictions on the executive's freedom of maneuver in current and future negotiations with both the Palestinians and the Syrians. Nevertheless, the choice of this particular method to attain that end seems to indicate an aversion on the part of most of the public's elected representatives to be burdened with possible responsibility for difficult decisions that, whichever the result, are bound to generate dissent in some quarters.

Similar criticisms can be leveled at the *knesset*'s Foreign Affairs and Defense Committee (FADC). Occasional indications that this forum might be prepared to play a more active role in national security affairs have not hitherto been translated into a practical program. The small group that, with not inconsiderable fanfare, the FADC established in 2004 in order 'to examine parliamentary supervision over the defense system and to study methods of improvement' turned out to be a rather tame affair. Chaired by Amnon Rubinstein (a professor of constitutional law who had in the past held several cabinet posts and had chaired the *knesset*'s Law and Legislation Committee, 1999–2003) the team tabled a tepid list of proposals – not one of which has hitherto been implemented or even formulated as a legislative measure (Bar-Or 2005). What is more, the FADC has never evinced any particular eagerness to exercise the powers that it has been granted in recent legislation. Article 12b of the GSS law of 2002, for instance, requires the head of the GSS to present a report on the agency's activities at least once every three months to the FADC sub-committee on intelligence and the secret services (which Article 6 recognizes as the parliamentary forum responsible for supervising GSS activity). Likewise, Article 64 of the Reserve Duty Law enacted in 2008 requires the IDF to submit for FADC approval proposals for the utilization of reservists on military duties. Thus far, however, the opportunities for parliamentary oversight thus provided have not been exploited. Invariably, the FADC and its sub-committees merely take note of the fact that the requirement of reporting has been fulfilled.

Given that attitude, attempts to compel the *knesset* to play a more active supervisory role in national security affairs seem forlorn, especially in times of emergency. Energy might more profitably be invested in encouraging MKs to do what they do best – enact legislation that lays down norms and standards of military conduct. Elsewhere, it might be noted, constitutional lawyers are arguing that the prime duty of legislatures is not to supervise the executive's implementation of law but to create the laws to which the executive is supposed to adhere.[10] A similar case can be posited with respect to the role of the *knesset* in the structural dimension of Israel's national security legal framework. In this sense, distinct parallels can be drawn with regards to the ways in which we propose both the *knesset* and the ISC should operate. Neither institution, we suggest, ought to focus on assuming supervisory roles of the everyday facets of national security affairs – a function that, as we shall shortly demonstrate, we believe can best be performed by other agencies. Rather, just as the principal task of the judiciary must be to apportion responsibilities amongst the arms of government, so the primary mission of the legislature ought to be to set down in legislation the standards in accordance with which those arms are to conduct themselves.

Of course, here too considerable prodding may be required, since the *knesset* has also evinced a marked reluctance to assume its legislative responsibilities. It took a virtual diktat on the part of the ISC to ensure the passage of the Service Deferral Law of 2002, which, by incorporating the proposals of the Tal Committee, itemized criteria for the granting of service exemptions to full-time *yeshivah* students. Likewise, only after considerable pressure from the attorney general did the *knesset* revise in 2002 the draft of the GSS law tabled in 1998, and thus establish rules of GSS conduct, other than with respect to interrogations, a topic still considered too sensitive to be included in the final version (Roter 2009:79–81). Finally, and most remarkably of all, only after reservists in the IDF had launched an extended public campaign, which produced a groundswell of support from other civilian groups, especially after the Second Lebanon War, did the *knesset* (which may also have feared another round of judicial pressure) in 2008 enact the Reserve Duty Law, which both restricts the number of days per year to which reservists can be summoned for duty and sets 40 as the age at which reservists are discharged from further service.

Individually, these are of course small steps, which in terms of substance still affect only the subsidiary levels of national security conduct. Nevertheless, we argue, they provide promising indications of the role that the *knesset* can play, and ought to do so. What is now required is a concerted effort to expand the legislative enterprise to other areas, of which undoubtedly the most necessary is a 'war crimes' act that would specifically implement the four Geneva conventions. The fact that legislation of that sort could, if properly packaged, improve Israel's image in the eyes of the international legal community must be counted a collateral gain. Its primary purpose would be more substantive, to clarify the circumstances under which, when required, criminal prosecutions could proceed.

The functional alternative – 'sentinels'

If the role of the ISC is to apportion national security functions amongst the arms of government and the mission of the *knesset* to set down in legislation the standards in accordance with which those arms are to conduct themselves, it remains to determine the forum or forums that ought to assume responsibility for ensuring that the representatives of the executive, and especially the armed forces, are indeed behaving in conformity with both judicial decisions and parliamentary legislation. We shall refer to those forums as 'sentinels', a term that we believe conveys the uniqueness of their status in the bureaucratic framework.[11] Their singularity, we suggest, derives from the bifurcate nature of the allegiances owed by their personnel. On the one hand, 'sentinels' are committed to preserving and advancing the institutional health of the government agency whose conduct they supervise and with which (in many cases) they may be professionally affiliated. At the same time, however, they also operate under a normative obligation to ensure that those agencies will perform their tasks in a manner that is correct as well as efficient.

As thus described, sentinels have always been a prominent feature of the Israeli bureaucratic framework. Indeed, some officials who perform sentinel functions, notably the attorney general and the accountant general, have become so powerful in some fields that they have often been accused of exceeding the correct boundaries of their commissions, especially over the past couple of decades when incumbents of both offices have fought tirelessly (and for the most part successfully) to eradicate blatant instances of corruption in high places. Instead of merely supervising agencies under their purview, they have been said to have attempted to control them and thereby undermine the policies of the responsible government minister (Gavison 1996; Zelicha 2008).

Where national security matters are concerned, the list of existing sentinels in Israel is especially lengthy and includes ad hoc commissions as well as standing agencies that have become almost permanent components of the bureaucratic scene. Within each of these categories, moreover, the spectrum can range over a wide assortment of models. One type of 'ad hoc sentinels', for instance, has traditionally consisted of committees of professionals, civilians as well as military personnel, appointed by the cabinet to table recommendations that might repair visible deficiencies in an area of national security concern in which they possess expertise. Ben-Gurion appreciated how such bodies could be utilized as mechanisms for triggering reform as early as 1962, when he instructed the Yadin-Sherf Commission to investigate the agencies responsible for the gathering and assessment of national security intelligence (above p. 64). A more recent model of the genre, and one that performed especially well, was the committee chaired by David Brodet, a former director-general of Israel's ministry of finance. Established by the Olmert government in 2007, the mandate of the Brodet Committee was to investigate Israel's defense budgeting, an area of national security concern thereto protected by a thick smokescreen of self-censorship. Shocked, albeit not altogether surprised, by its own revelations, the committee's report presented both a damning critique of the ways in which the IDF squandered many of its funds and detailed review of the steps needed to repair such distortions (*Brodet Report* 2007). Especially salient, within the context of the present discussion, were the recommendations designed to augment civilian oversight. *Inter alia*, the Brodet Report insists that all IDF financial estimates be subjected to a non-military audit based on unitary standards of measurement. Implicitly suggesting that both the finance and defense ministries are too tarred with the brush of collusion to carry out the task, the committee also recommends that it be entrusted to the NSS, which thus here too emerges as a linchpin in the new national security framework.

Much better known to the public at large is a second variety of 'ad hoc sentinels' in the national security sphere, which consists of national commissions of enquiry. The establishment of forums of this type was facilitated by the passage of the Commissions of Enquiry Law in 1968 (thereto bodies of that name had operated in accordance with the antiquated terms of an ordinance that dated back to the British mandate), which allows the government the right to decide on the establishment of the commission and to define its terms of reference but grants to the president of the ISC the authority to select the commissioners, whose chairperson must be a sitting or retired judge. This mechanism was put into operation as early as August 1969, when the Sussman Commission was charged with investigating the torching of the El Aksa mosque in Jerusalem by a Jewish extremist earlier that year. More famous, however, are the commissions established in the wake of more extensive national security failures, some of which were also far more consequential in terms of the material damage they inflicted on the state: the Agranat Commission 1973; the Kahan Commission 1982; the Landau Commission 1987; and the Winograd Commission 2006. In each case, members of these tribunals performed the role of sentinels by acting as both auditors of existing practices and advocates of remedies.

Other countries too have long employed commissions of enquiry for similar purposes, and continue to do so. Recent examples include the 'Somalia Commission' appointed by the government of Canada in order to investigate the misconduct of members of the Canadian Airborne Regiment at Belet Huen in south central Somalia in 1993; the enquiry conducted by the Dutch Institute for War Documentation into the responsibility of Netherlands forces for the Srebrenica massacre of 1995 in former Yugoslavia; and the Chilcot Inquiry established by the British government in order to consider the UK's involvement in Iraq from mid-2001 to July 2009. True, enquiries into the Abu Ghraib prison abuses that came to light in 2004 were restricted in the USA to entirely military tribunals, but in 2005 the European Court of Human Rights indicated its preference for resort to wider forums in cases of alleged violations of human rights.[12] Specifically, it ruled that national investigations would not be deemed adequate unless, in addition to being prompt and open to public scrutiny, they could also demonstrate the formal and practical independence of the investigators from the persons whose actions they were examining and the ability of the investigation to lead to effective remedies including, where appropriate, criminal investigations. Although ad hoc Israeli commissions of enquiry generally meet these criteria, as a type of sentinel this form of tribunal nevertheless remains open to several objections. The most general is that, by their very nature, commissions of enquiry impinge on parliamentary rule (Klagsbald 2001:351–8). After all, they exchange a democratic regime, which rests on oversight by elected representatives, for government by unelected bureaucrats. More specific is the charge that in any case commissions are prone to being 'hijacked' by military experts and will therefore essentially serve the interests of the military institution.

Classic administrative literature suggests that most attempts at regulation end up with the putative target of regulation imposing its will and views on the supposed 'regulator' (Stigler 1971; Moe 1995). That is exactly what occurred in 1984, when minister of defense Arens appointed an internal committee to investigate the deaths of two of the terrorists who had hijacked an Israeli bus (the 'route 300 affair'). It later transpired that one member of the commission leaked information to the GSS personnel who were about to be investigated, thereby enabling them to prepare versions of the events that misled the commission and resulted in a misinformed report. The chances of a similar outcome occurring where the IDF is concerned are especially high, principally because of the enormous knowledge gap that distinguishes the military framework in Israel from any of its possible civilian investigators (Michael 2006).

But even when that is not the case, commissions can suffer from a third defect, which is perhaps even more telling. Precisely because they are established in order to investigate a specific occurrence, they give rise to the suspicion that they are merely ploys used by governments in order to deflect political pressure and dampen public outcry in the hope that the memory of the national security failure which brought them into existence will have faded by the time the commission presents its report. Since they are thus established in bad faith, their utility is bound to be limited.

Some of the defects thus inherent in the establishment of one-time sentinels can be repaired by resort to more permanent external agencies. As far as the military is concerned, the most prominent is the state comptroller, a genuinely civilian appointment, who is elected by the *knesset* and is required to present the results of his investigations every year to the chairperson of that body. The State Comptroller Law, the first version of which dates to 1949, specifically authorizes incumbents of that office to investigate every ministry and official agency, including those associated with state security. Those powers are regularly exercised. Over the past decade alone, *State Comptroller Reports* have dealt with such topics as the military industries (2001:213–74); the GSS (2002:41–64); emergency fire services (2003:63–75); Bedouin troops in IDF service (2004:129–42); IDF treatment of underprivileged conscripts (2005:145–64); the advancement of women soldiers (2006:169–85); the IDF radio station (2007:541–59); and provisions for post-service employment of conscripts (2009:243–60).

But impressive though the state comptroller's activity thus is, that office too does not fully comply with the requirements of an effective sentinel of the national security framework.[13] Partly, this is because comptrollers lack the power to ensure that their recommendations are implemented, or to impose sanctions when subsequently discovering that they have been bypassed or ignored. More specifically, however, the fault lies with the methodology of their investigations. In areas of national security interest, as in other fields, state comptrollers invariably focus on whether the targets of enquiry are executing their functions efficiently. Their gauge therefore generally amounts to little more than cost-effectiveness. By comparison, questions of principle, of the sort that are more likely to concern the Supreme Court with regard to military conduct, and that ought also to fall within the remit of parliamentary review, often pass completely unnoticed. Especially prominent amongst the victims of this situation are the observance of humanitarian standards and respect for constitutional divisions of authority, neither of which have ever been discussed by a *State Comptroller Report.*

The various weaknesses that thus disqualify all of the agencies hitherto mentioned from genuinely fulfilling the function of national security 'sentinels' enhance the need to search for alternative bureaucratic candidates for that office. We suggest that two alternatives deserve to be considered possible role models.

The first alternative model is provided by 'National Humanitarian Law Committees' (NHLC's), which now exist in 93 countries. Although these bodies are not all identical, most are composed of government officials from the ministries of defense (and its equivalents), justice, and foreign affairs. In many cases, membership also includes representatives from other bodies involved in state security, such as the police services and intelligence gathering agencies. Less commonly, but not unusually, NHLC's also co-opt representatives of civil society and academics with relevant expertise in international humanitarian law (IHL). The functions of NHLC's vary from country to country, but frequently extend to: monitoring decisions taken by national security agencies, coordinating between different government agencies regarding the implementation of IHL, disseminating IHL material, proposing legislation that conforms with IHL, and reviewing international treaties and developments.

Another version of the same general idea can be found in the 'National Human Rights Institutions' (NHRIs), sometimes termed 'Commissions', which currently operate in more than 100 countries. Here too precise powers and functions vary from one instance to another. In many places, institutions of these names operate independently, and adjudicate complaints against the executive and its various agencies regarding violations of human rights. Even so, in Mexico, for instance, the armed forces are considered immune to such enquiries. Elsewhere, however, NHRIs have conducted more extensive investigations, that occasionally (as in the case of Uganda) have also extended to the security services. Overriding such differences are certain shared characteristics. What all NHRIs have in common, it has been noted, is that they are:

> statutory bodies and are usually state sponsored and state funded,set up either under an act of parliament, the constitution, or by decree with specific powers and a mandate to promote and protect human rights. Unlike NGOs, which are not appointed by the people or parliament, NHRIs, which vary considerably in composition and structure,

have a different status in the community and different tools at their disposal to hold the state and other bodies to account for violating human rights standards.

(Smith 2006)

In Israel, where neither a NHLC nor a NHRI has ever been established, much of this activity takes place informally, on the basis of communications between individual lawyers who work in the various relevant ministries. Even so, we suggest that much is to be gained from endowing those contacts with the sort of form and structure that an NHLC or a strong NHRI can provide. Unlike the ISC, an NHLC/NHRI will be capable of playing an umbrella role prior to the submission of complaints about an alleged violation of human rights. In that capacity, an NHLC/NHRI could coordinate IHL policy amongst all the various national security organizations, each of which is presently largely left to its own devices in this area, and hence render redundant many of the 'principled' petitions that are currently presented to the ISC and that trigger the undesirable phenomenon of judicial over-intrusion in military affairs. The co-option of external (i.e., non-governmental) experts might serve the additional purpose of endowing the NHLC/NHRI with a semi-investigative capacity that would shift the focus of supervisory enquiry from matters of administrative efficiency and corruption, such as are presently investigated by the state comptroller, to substantive issues relevant to executive compliance with humanitarian law.

Whereas an Israeli version of a NHLC/NHRI would have to be created *de novo*, that is not the case with respect to our second proposed alternative, which envisages a military agency that interacts closely with the civilian milieu, by which it is heavily influenced. In recent years, the IDF has in fact developed two separate prototypes of such frameworks: the 'conscience committees' (*va'adot matzpun*) for reservists; and the IDF's 'International Law Branch' (*DABLA*). Although assigned to deal with very different spheres of military activity, these two agencies share one major common characteristic. In addition to benefiting from the backing and material assistance given by the military bureaucracy, of which they constitute integral parts, both also maintain strong ties of association with their respective civilian environments. This combination of advantages, we argue, enables these two agencies to function as genuine sentinels in their separate spheres. It also justifies a slightly more extended examination of the ways in which they do so.

'Conscience committees' act as advisory commissions to the minister of defense, on whose behalf they vet applications from reservists who apply to be excused from military service on the grounds that they are pacifists. Such applications, once limited to a handful of Jehovah's Witnesses (Shelach 1978), grew to almost 1,000 per annum in the 1990s, in large part thanks to petitions presented by increasing numbers of youngsters who had spent extended post-service periods in eastern Asia, where they claimed to have developed a deep personal abhorrence of violence and militarism in any shape or form. Initially, the tribunals established in order to examine the veracity of those claims consisted entirely of IDF officers, whose understandable suspicion of potential 'draft dodgers' was reported to have introduced a negative bias into the proceedings. In *Ben Artzi v. Minister of Defense* (2002) the ISC suggested that the IDF would do well to deal with this problem, and to deflect criticism, by modifying the composition of the 'conscience committees'.

As from 2002, accordingly, standing orders have required that the tribunals also include at least one civilian, usually an academic who specializes in law, philosophy and/or the social sciences, whose task is to act as a 'watchdog' and ensure that the petitioners are receiving a fair hearing. Since the IDF does not release figures respecting discharges from service, it is impossible to calculate what effect the change in composition might have had on the grant of exemptions. Personal observation, however, indicates that the proceedings of the tribunals are certainly conducted with a degree of empathy uncharacteristic of most military settings. The civilian representative invariably plays the role of the barometer of the committee's adherence to standards of tolerance towards genuine pacifism that might otherwise not find expression.

Personnel attached to the *DABLA* units, whose mission statement is to provide their military colleagues and superiors with operational advice respecting the requirements of international law (see Chapter 6 p. 172) are even better placed to fulfill the function of sentinels. Primarily, this is because of the dual nature of their affiliations. In effect, they simultaneously belong to two professional communities: they are lawyers as well as soldiers. Like military physicians, *DABLA* lawyers too are prone to suffer from the 'role strain' induced by attempts to meet the occasionally divergent sets of occupational expectations.

A superficial and perhaps intuitive view might suggest that, confronted with such tensions, their priorities would be plain. The strict hierarchy and close supervision characteristic of military organizations would result in *DABLA* personnel acting primarily as soldiers. Only in a secondary sense would their behavior accord with the norms dictated by legal professionalism. That impression must largely be held responsible for the fact that members of the *DABLA* unit – even when not entirely disregarded – have often been denigrated (e.g., Feldman and Blau 2009). Considered as little more than apologists for military actions, for which it is their task to provide legal cover, they are not thought to have any material effect on IDF decisions.

Closer examination indicates that such depictions distort the picture. They exaggerate the validating role played by *DABLA* lawyers whilst also underplaying the way in which they sensitize IDF commanders to international law and thereby make them more respectful of its requirements.

Observation reveals that *DABLA* personnel in fact possess considerable independence from their nominal military superiors. Partly, this is because they are trained lawyers, and as such possess a body of knowledge not available to other officers. By virtue of their mastery of the law, they possess an advantage over the military commanders to whom they are attached when in the field and to whom they directly supply advice in an operational situation. True, final responsibility for whatever decision is ultimately taken must lie with the commander (Blum 2009). That, however, might be of little solace to a commander who lacks the professional knowledge required to question the advice that his lawyer is providing.

Of even greater importance are the advantages that accrue to *DABLA* personnel by virtue of their ability to enlist pressure groups to support their positions. They form part of an 'epistemic community' of human rights and humanitarian lawyers (Am. Cohen 2011). They participate in conferences on international law, they write law review articles on the subject, they study with professors, and sometimes they even teach courses in one or more aspect of this discipline at universities. One consequence of this situation is a heightened awareness on their part of the price that they will have to pay if they give their approval to military policies of dubious legality. They will be criticized, perhaps even ostracized, by other members of the legal fraternity. By the same token, however, they are secure in the knowledge that, should they decide to challenge military decisions on legal grounds, they can depend upon an extensive network of legal professionals to support their point of view. By comparison, military commanders are relatively isolated. They are conversant enough with recent judicial practice to realize that, should they not follow the dictates of international law (as expounded by *DABLA* personnel), they run the risk of finding their policies overruled by the ISC. And in the background there also lurks the threat, real or imagined, that international courts might apply to them the rule of universal jurisdiction.

We propose that efforts be made to buttress still further the contribution made by *DABLA* to IDF adherence to the norms of IHL. In part, the onus for that development lies with the military establishment, which controls the budgets that *DABLA* will require if it is to grow in size and provide its personnel with the facilities and time required to keep abreast of developments in IHL. At the same time, however, the ISC can make an additional contribution by explicitly enunciating a doctrine of deference to the legal branches of government agencies. This would not require it to give an automatic carte blanche to each and every *DABLA* decision. What we have in mind, rather, is a declaration of a disposition to adopt *DABLA*'s perspective, such as has been indicated in the USA. There, the Supreme Court in 1984 adopted what became known as the '*Chevron* doctrine', declaring that: 'If the statute is silent or ambiguous with respect to the specific question, the issue for the court is whether the agency's answer is based on a permissible construction of the statute.' In other words, in cases where the norm is unclear, the justices have announced their readiness to defer to whatever reasonable interpretation of the law may be given by the relevant administrative agency. We submit that the adoption of a similar standard by the ISC would materially strengthen the authority of *DABLA*, thus enhancing its ability to serve as a one of the sentinels whose existence we consider to be crucial to a reform of the functional dimension of the Israeli national security legal framework as a whole.

The temporal dimension

Thanks to the system of Defense (Emergency) Regulations (DERs) inherited from the British mandate, the temporal dimension of Israel's national security framework has never lacked legal regulatory form. Incorporated into Israeli law within four days of the establishment of the State, the DER's immediately established an emergency regime that, with only very minor adjustments, has formally remained in force ever since. As previous chapters in this book have repeatedly observed, however, whatever the possible justification for the original adoption of what is sometimes referred to as Israel's 'emergency constitution', its deficiencies have by now become too glaring to justify its continued perpetuation. The limitations that current Israeli law imposes on the duration of the exercise of emergency powers have been almost totally diluted by the almost ritual manner in which they are annually renewed by the *knesset*. Substantive restrictions, designed to define areas in which governments cannot derogate from right under any circumstances, have similarly been eroded by the inclusion in Article 12 of Basic Law: Human Dignity and Liberty of such open-ended phrases as 'proper purpose' and 'extent that is required'. Altogether, in fact, as matters stand, 'emergency' has become a portmanteaux term. It can be used – and has been used – to cover a multitude of national security situations and thus extended almost without hindrance. By the same token, it can be used – and, again, has been used – to sanction a multitude of executive actions that can infringe upon human rights.

By far the tidiest way to correct this situation is to introduce legislation that would both differentiate between diverse types of 'emergencies' and specify the prerogatives of the executive in each case. One possible prototype is provided by the constitution of the Netherlands, which provides for a two-tier distinction between 'a state of war' (Article 96) and 'a state of emergency' (Article 103). The first of these circumstances ('a state of war') implies the existence of an existential and immediate threat to the State. Hence, it clearly sanctions some form of 'extra-legal' activity (in Gross' terms), which could be taken by the government, for a circumscribed period of time, without recourse to the regular and time-consuming parliamentary channels. When a lower-level 'state of emergency' exists, by contrast, whatever curtailment of human rights might be necessary would require sanction via the normal legal processes (although it could also include an 'expedited route' should a specific issue be especially pressing but would still impose a time limit).

In the US context, Bruce Ackerman has proposed a variant on the same theme and posits the creation of what he calls a 'supermajoritarian escalator' (Ackerman 2004, 2006). Under this system, the president of the USA would be empowered to declare an emergency situation for a maximum period of two weeks. Extensions of that situation, however, would require the approval of ever-increasing congressional majorities: a simple majority for the first request for an extension of two to three months, and additional percentages thereafter. Within a year, the votes required would have reached 80 percent of the membership of both houses, a consensus that would surely foreclose sanction under any but the direst circumstances (and that Ackerman therefore considers the maximum required. Ackerman 2006:80).[14]

Some critics have taken Ackerman to task for his alleged willingness to trade human rights for national security even for a short period of time (Tribe and Gudridge 2004; Cole 2004). From the perspective of the present work, however, the failing of his proposal might lie less in its substance than in the tradition out of which it grows. Ackerman builds on a long history of American democracy which, as detailed as early as *The Federalist* no. 10 for instance, relies on institutional and party struggles to limit the power of government to curtail the rights of individuals. The US Congress can perhaps reasonably be expected to guillotine an executive declaration of emergency when it considers no such emergency exists and, by the same token, to act in consensus in support of the president when the emergency does indeed appear to be real. A review of *knesset* behavior inspires no confidence that such would also be the case in Israel. If anything, past experience indicates that Israeli legislatures have tended to declare an emergency even when no real emergency existed.

Those precedents clearly preclude a simplistic imposition of US models on the processes whereby emergency situations are handled in Israel. Even so, there remains a pressing need for a mechanism capable of supplementing parliamentary curbs on the executive's misuse of its prerogatives. We submit that the insertion of the ISC into the 'escalator' process can fulfill such a requirement. In practice, the system we envisage would distinguish between two stages in the chronology of sanction for an executive decision to declare the existence of a state of emergency. In the first instance (stage I) sanction would have to be obtained from the FADC of the *knesset*, which would be empowered to authorize the declaration for a set time period. Should the government subsequently wish to extend the state of emergency beyond the specified date (stage II), it would have to submit its request to the ISC, and, in the process, to specify the purposes to which it intends to put the emergency powers, if granted. Thus presented with an itemized agenda of future executive actions, justices would be able to consider the constitutional validity of whatever measures it is proposed to initiate through the continued exercise of emergency powers.

If adopted, this system too would by no means be unique. An extensive survey of new constitutions in post-Communist eastern Europe has demonstrated how commonly many countries now require 'constitutional courts' to review and affirm the constitutionality of laws and certain decrees before they can be enacted (Schwartz 2000). In this view, the growth of this practice and its spread eastwards is intimately connected to the development of human rights in western Europe subsequent to World War II and in eastern Europe after the implosion of the Soviet empire. Indeed, basic to the conception underlying the emergence of constitutional courts is the understanding that courts do not merely arbitrate disputes and dispense judgments. They also guard against the misuse of power. Awareness that courts might declare, in advance, one or more of its proposed measures to be unconstitutional, itself imposes restraints on possible executive infringements of human rights. The existence of 'constitutional courts' compels governments to submit justifications for their proposals convincing enough to show that the interests of state security do not arbitrarily override the liberties of individual citizens.

Attempts to introduce a similar system into Israel's national security framework will doubtless have to overcome several obstacles. In all likelihood, they will be resisted by the executive branch, which must be expected to insist on its continued need for autonomy where matters of national security are concerned. They will also probably be opposed by several MKs, and especially by those (such as representatives of ultra-orthodox parties) who are in any case critical of what they consider to be judicial 'over-activism'. But the primary impediment to reform might be a more fundamental feeling, shared by many in the judicial community itself, that the insertion of the ISC into an 'escalator' procedure for sanctioning emergency situations would contradict Israel's legal culture. Lawyers schooled in the common law tradition, which has been the principal influence on Israel's legal culture, are still far more likely to consider the entire notion of prior judicial approval for executive actions to be deeply anomalous, if not ludicrous. After all, the function conventionally attributed to courts by common law is to solve conflicts that are submitted for its adjudication after they have erupted. Judges are not expected to pass opinions on situations that, since they have not yet occurred, are still in the realm of the hypothetical and speculative.

We submit that, where the temporal dimension of Israel's national security framework is concerned, the traditional common law approach has outlived its utility. Indeed, it has resulted in a situation whereby the ISC over-performs at one level and under-performs at another. It over-performs when attempting to scrutinize – and sometimes micro-manage – the ways in which the security branches go about their business on a day-to-day basis. Indeed, we have argued, such practices have now reached a level of frequency and intensity that they threaten to undermine the professional autonomy of the military and security service and thus adversely affect their performance. On the other hand, however, the ISC underperforms in the sense that it refrains from laying down the guidelines and principles in accordance with which it expects the executive to act. Justice Aharon Barak did show his awareness of this fault when suggesting that courts ought to be considered 'partners' in the legislative process (Barak 2002:16; Barak 2006). It now behooves Israel's entire legal community – together, of course, with its national security establishment – to adopt that view and draw the necessary practical inferences.

Only the foolhardy would dare to try and predict how soon, and how effectively, Israel is likely to implement the reform agenda outlined in this chapter. As has always been the case in matters affecting the country's national security, the vagaries of personality are likely to play a pivotal role in determining both the substance of whatever changes might be set in motion and the pace of their movement. Even so, one of the central themes of this study is that, to judge by previous experience, much will also depend on the push and pull of a multitude of more fundamental influences, of which the most visible are underlying shifts in societal attitudes towards the use of force and transformations in the operational contexts of military action. Indeed, much of the history of Israel's national legal framework can be interpreted as an attempt to come to terms with the reverberations caused by periodic movements in the societal and strategic environments with which it constantly interacts.

Circumstances of such inherent volatility do not lend themselves to orderly and evolutionary realignment. On the contrary, and as has been seen, individual events and processes have exerted distinctive influences on each of the four dimensions of the national security framework. As a result, the reaction of the template as a whole has often assumed a distinctly disparate form. Whereas in some periods of time issues pertinent to the functional and hierarchical dimensions loomed large, in others the spatial and temporal dimensions have clamored more insistently for attention. Because there is no reason to expect this see-saw pattern to be any different in the future, reforms are likely to be implemented – if at all – in an uneven manner. Instead of unfolding in a steady and uniform manner, they will in all likelihood stumble forward (and back) in a series of fits and starts, the rhythm of which will be dictated by the unpredictable prominence and urgency of the individual dimension to which they relate.

Whether or not this pattern is entirely idiosyncratic, and hence unique to the Israeli national security framework, cannot at present be ascertained. Certainly, some elements in the ecology of that framework must be judged *sui generis*, and hence resistant to comparison with those of other countries. Even so, we suggest that the basic nature of the issues incorporated within each of the four dimensions of the framework that we have identified traverse geographical and political boundaries. In a world of increasing legal globalization, the study of how they have developed and changed in one society deserves to be considered relevant to others too.

Notes

1 Frameworks of analysis

1 One important exception is provided by the role played by King Carlos of Spain in suppressing an attempted military coup in February 1981. Particularly effective was his appearance on national television dressed in the uniform of the Captain General of the Armed Forces (*Capitán General de los Ejércitos*), when he denounced the insurgents and exhorted all Spaniards to abide by the constitution.
2 In recent years, such questions have become pertinent in even the most mature of democracies, especially since the terrorist attacks of 11 September 2001. In the USA, President Bush immediately (on September 14) issued proclamation 7463, declaring the existence of a state of emergency. Within a month, on 12 November, the British Home Secretary likewise declared the existence of a state of emergency, a move that allowed the government to release itself from the constraints imposed on it by the European Convention on Human Rights, and cleared a path for the passage of laws intended to extend dramatically the powers of the security services. Four years later, in response to Muslim riots in the streets of Paris, the President of France, Jacques Chirac, declared a state of emergency, thereby allowing police forces to impose a curfew, to conduct searches without a warrant, to place suspects under house arrest, and to prohibit public assembly.
3 The document specified three mechanisms: the President 'in every possible instance shall consult with Congress' before sending American troops into battle; the President must notify Congress within 48 hours of committing armed forces to military action; and unless explicitly excused from doing so, the President must terminate military intervention overseas within sixty days of reporting its occurrence to Congress.
4 However, in July 2008 the House of Commons defeated a motion to bring under its administration the Intelligence and Security Committee (established in 1994 in order to provide oversight of the secret services). The majority decided that the members of this committee would continue to be appointed directly by the prime minister, to whom they also report.

2 Cultural contexts

1 Babylonian Talmud (BT), tractate *Yoma* folio 85b, commentary on Exodus 31:6. In its original context, this ruling, attributed to a sage named Simeon ben Menasya, referred to the duty to violate the Sabbath in order to preserve human life. Subsequently, however, it was also applied to other transgressions.
2 Rabbi Natan, cited in *Mishnah* (the code compiled in third-century Palestine),

tractate *Berakhot* 9:5. Subsequent talmudic analysis deemed the biblical precedent for such actions to be the prophet Elijah's construction of an altar outside the precinct of the Jerusalem Temple (see I Kings chap. 18), a violation of a Divine prohibition that could only be justified by the urgency of the need to disprove the prophets of Baal (BT *Sanhedrin*, folio 90a).

3 Gross and Ni Aolain (2006:113–19) argue that the rabbinic sources indicate the adoption by their authors of what they term an 'extra-legal' approach to national emergencies, in consideration of which the rabbis advocated temporary suspensions of the *halakhah*. This seems to us to be a misconstruction, which is based on too limited a view of the entire *halakhic* enterprise. Unlike the Napoleonic Code, for instance, *halakhah* never constituted a set of norms that had at one point in time been codified and canonized. On the contrary, as is shown by Urbach (Urbach 1986), it was always regarded as a dynamic and ever evolving corpus, the development of which was facilitated by a range of techniques, such as *takanot* ('regulations') *gezerot* ('decrees') and *drashot* ('interpretations'). Thus, the resort to the tools of *hora'ot sha'ah* etc. did not imply that rabbis were working outside the *halakhah*. Rather, they were incorporating emergency measures into its application and, in the terms of the models developed by Gross and Ni Aolain, in fact adopting a legal strategy of 'accommodation'.

The only exception to that convention is supplied by the permission given to 'zealots' (*kana'im*) to slay any Israelite who performs an act of sexual intercourse with a gentile woman in public (e.g., Maimonides, *Laws of Forbidden Intercourse* 12:4–5) – an act of killing without trial that *halakhah* derives from the precedent described in the biblical book of Numbers (25:1–15) and that is sanctioned only when undertaken instinctively and without consultation or deliberation. However, it is noteworthy that this ruling, although certainly commensurate with the 'extra-legal' model posited by Gross and Ni Aolain, is so out of character that there exists not a single reference to its use in the entire storehouse of case law supplied by rabbinic correspondence (the 'responsa' literature) covering the past millennium and a half.

4 These differences might also be explained by the divergent purposes of the two works. Maimonides aimed to compile an all-embracing but nevertheless essentially theoretical work. Karo's objectives were far more practical. Hence, he felt it necessary to address as soon as possible the prerogatives that judges could assume, especially in the Diaspora, where their writ was not originally have supposed to run. We are grateful to Rabbi Yonatan Cohen for elucidating this point.

5 Surely the most exotic of exceptions was Ismail ibn Nagrela (993–1055/6). Known in Jewish sources as *Shemuel ha-Nagid* ('Samuel the Prince'), this vizier to the Muslim rulers of Grenada in Spain had the altogether unique distinction of being a Jewish commander of an Islamic army. He compounded that achievement by commemorating his forces' exploits in Hebrew verse, written in a style unmatched since the Psalms. See, e.g., 'The War with Yadir', translated in P. Cole 1996:49–51.

6 Hence their depiction as 'secular yeshivah students' (Almog 2000:18–72). Almog calculates that members of this sociological group never numbered more than 10 percent of the *Yishuv*, but they stamped their influence on the entire community.

7 The resilience of Israel's civil–military 'partnership' was for long a topos of political analysis. See, for instance, the introductions by both Moshe Lissak and Samuel Finer to the Hebrew translation of the latter's *The Man on Horseback: The Role of the Military in Politics* (Finer 1982).

3 Centralization, 1948–1963

1 This announcement created a legal tangle that it took weeks to unravel. Article 18 of the Law and Administration Ordinance, passed on 19 May 1948, had already authorized the government to establish armed forces for the protection of the state. By contrast, the IDF ordinance proclaimed by Ben-Gurion on 26 May was not ratified by his cabinet colleagues until five days later (Ostfeld 1994:104–6). Even then, it possessed no legal force, since the power to issue ordinances was a prerogative of the Provisional Council (the predecessor of the *Knesset*), which did not get around to doing so until 7 July (Bendor and Kremnitzer 2000:28–9). Ben-Gurion clearly considered all this bother worthwhile, and it is not hard to see why. Unlike Article 18 of the Law and Administration Ordinance, the IDF Ordinance specifically required all soldiers to swear allegiance to the State of Israel and its elected government (Article 3), expressly forbade the maintenance of all other militias (the *Palmach*, the *Etzel* and the *Lechi*; Article 4), and cemented Ben-Gurion's own authority by identifying the minister of defense as the person responsible for the Ordinance's implementation.
2 Some 20 percent of the 5,800 Jews killed in the course of the fighting in 1947–1949 were civilians, a proportion roughly equivalent to the UK war dead during World War II. Nevertheless, the fatalities that Israelis chose to commemorate were exclusively military (Sivan 1999).
3 The number of non-Jews resident in Israel in this period is notoriously difficult to calculate. The census taken in November 1948 categorized 70,000 Arabs as 'legal' residents. But it had not included Bedouins; neither had it encompassed areas subsequently conquered by or ceded to Israel. According to later government figures, 20,500 Arab 'infiltrators', who entered Israel between 1949 and 1953 (less than 5 percent of the total number of Palestinian refugees) were allowed to remain and were granted citizenship. Three thousand others, who lived outside Israel, were granted entry permits for humanitarian reasons. All told, in 1949 some 156,000 non-Jews, principally Arabs, lived in Israel, constituting almost one-quarter of the total population of the time (Morris 1987:297–8; Ozacky-Lazar 1998:347).
4 The latter also chaired 'The Central Security Committee', the body ultimately responsible for deciding how to implement government policies vis-à-vis Israel's Arab minority, the other members of which were the CO of the Military Administration, the CO of the Arab Unit in the GSS, and the head of the Office for Special Missions in the Police Force.
5 Tel-Aviv, especially, had experienced several air raids by Egyptian bombers in 1948, as a result of which, 133 civilians had been killed and scores more wounded. Fears of a repetition of such incidents were graphically expressed in a letter that Israel Rokach (the Mayor of Tel-Aviv) wrote to Ben-Gurion in January 1950 (Bichur 2003:131–2).
6 In one instance, the committee thwarted the government's wish to extend the military censorship to matters not related to security. In another, it prevented the extension of death penalty (restricted to acts of treason in time of active war) to murder committed by Arab infiltrators.
7 The ISC did on several occasions address the status of soldiers employed, on military orders, on civilian tasks, but it never asked whether the IDF had the authority to issue such orders (*Fichman* v. *Minister of Defense* [1951]). For later critical views see Zamir 1996:235–6; Tirosh 2004.
8 Although the outraged response of Galilee's colleagues in the military hierarchy compelled Ben-Gurion to recall him to service, he refused to re-instate the office of *RAMAH*. Instead, Galilee was to be Ben-Gurion's personal assistant. Shifris 2010:76–9.

9 Dayan's appointment to [CO] Southern Command [in 1949] revealed Ben-Gurion's tendencies to man senior military positions with people who were either loyal to Mapai or unaligned. Dayan, who had not made his mark in the War of Independence, now became Ben-Gurion's protégé and candidate for leadership from among the sabras. Allon, against his will, was shoved out of the military circle.

(Shapira 2008:296)

10 Thus, unprepared to take sole onus for opposing Dayan's proposal to launch a large scale attack against Egypt in November 1955, Ben-Gurion brought the matter to the cabinet, which turned it down by seven votes to six. Likewise, after the 1956 war, when he was aware that his agreement to succumb to USA pressure and withdraw all IDF forces from Sinai and the Gaza Strip would be unpopular, he in March 1957 submitted the issue to cabinet vote. In this case three ministers opposed the withdrawal (Baron 1992:72–3, 368).

11 Even so, the two ministers representing the (left-wing) *Mapam* party voted against the war, on the grounds that it served the interests of the Imperialist powers.

12 The immediate cause for the establishment of the commission was Ben-Gurion's complaint that the *Mosad*, headed by Isser Harel, had misjudged the degree of German involvement in Egypt's missile program. Deeper causes were also at work. Weaknesses in military intelligence had been revealed in 1960, when the IDF's Intelligence Branch had failed to detect Egyptian troop movements into Sinai, and suspicions of Russian infiltration into Israel's security services were rife in the wake of the arrest on charges of espionage on behalf of the USSR of Israel Ber, a close adviser to Ben-Gurion on security affairs. And above all else there hovered the shadow of 'the Lavon affair' (Kafkafi 1998:379–87).

4 Diffusion, 1963–1977

1 In both meetings, the core group consisted of Dayan (the newly appointed minister of defense), Eban (foreign minister), Allon (minister of labor), Yaakov Herzog (director-general of the prime minister's office) and Rabin. Discussion focused on whether or not Israel ought to continue to postpone taking military action in order to give the USA more time to find a diplomatic solution to the crisis. The fullest account of Israeli decision-making in the 'waiting period', based on unprecedented access to official Israeli archives, is Gluska 2007:131–256.

2 As Golan demonstrates (Golan 2003), during the war the diffusion of decision-making authority also extended to the IDF. CGS Elazar took most of his most important operational decisions in the course of 'informal' consultations with just five persons: his deputy, (Gen. Israel Tal), the CO of the Intelligence Branch (Gen. Eli Zeira), the CO Israel Air Force (Gen. Benny Peled) and two recently retired officers: Aharon Yariv (Zeira's long-term predecessor as CO Intelligence) and Rechavam Zeevi (former CO Central Command). Only after receiving the opinions of this body did Elazar refer to the full general staff. To complicate matters even further, soon after the outbreak of the war, Elazar also summoned back to active duty Chaim Bar-Lev, his predecessor as CGS, who was at the time minister for commerce and industry. The appointment triggered a minor constitutional crisis when prime minister Meir rejected justice minister Shapira's opinion that Bar-Lev had to resign his cabinet post for the duration of his renewed military service. Ultimately, Bar-Lev remained a minister and was appointed 'advisor' to the CGS. See Gai 1998:252.

3 The precise terms of reference were to investigate:

1 The intelligence information for the days preceding the Yom Kippur War on the enemy's moves and intentions to launch the war, the evaluation of this information, and the decisions taken by the responsible military and civil authorities in response thereto.
2 The general deployment of the IDF in case of war, its state of readiness during the days preceding the Yom Kippur War, and its operations up to the containment of the enemy.

(Agranat Commission, *Final Unclassified Report* 1975:10)

4 Only a handful of Bedouins inhabited the Sinai desert. Prior to 1967, the Golan Heights had contained a substantial population, but some 100,000 persons fled from the area during the course of the fighting. Of the few thousand who remained, the vast majority were Druze (Segev 2007:398).
5 Israel argued that the area was never recognized under international law as falling under the sovereignty of the Hashemite Kingdom of Transjordan. This was not an implausible claim (Rostow 1979). More problematic was the corollary, which claimed that therefore the Fourth Geneva Convention did not apply to this region. The problem is that Article 2 of that document states that it applies 'to all cases of declared war or of any other armed conflict which may arise between two or more of the high contracting parties, even if the state of war is not recognized by one of them.' Israel's response was that the second paragraph of Article 2 limits the application of the treaty to areas under the legal sovereignty of the parties (Blum 1968; 1971:85–8). However, this interpretation was expressly rejected by, among others, the International Court of Justice in its 2004 'Advisory Opinion: Legal Consequences of the Construction of a Wall in the Occupied Palestinian Territory.'
6 It seems that in 1967 the accepted legal position was that the Hague Regulations reflected customary international law, and that the Fourth Geneva Convention was merely conventional (Dinstein 1974:934). In *Oyeb* v. *Minister of Defense* (1979), the ISC acknowledged that both documents represent customary international law.
7 The violation was especially glaring in the 'Rafah Approach' case. Anyone who read newspapers (a population that certainly included the members of the ISC) could see that military necessity played no part in the eviction of the Bedouin from the area. The land was confiscated to build the first Israeli settlements in Sinai (Zertal and Eldar 2007:283–4).

5 Realignment, 1977–1995

1 Kretzmer 2002 provides by far the most comprehensive survey. Two subsequent reports by the Israeli human rights group, *Yesh Din* (*Yesh Din* 2007 and 2008), although focusing on the years after 1995 also provide much information on the evolution of Israeli control over the Territories.
2 Direct government ownership of the electronic media had ceased with the Israel Broadcasting Authority Act of 1965, which placed both radio and TV (the latter introduced into Israel in 1968) under a public authority. Even so, government influence remained paramount until the 1980s, when privately-funded radio and TV channels took to the air. A similar process took place in the printed media. During the 1980s, 16 party-owned newspapers were closed and the market was taken over by privately owned dailies.
3 In international terms the effects of Basic Law: Jerusalem were in fact entirely deleterious. It prompted the unanimous adoption in August 1980 of Security Council Resolution 478, which declared Basic Law: Jerusalem to be in violation

of international law and called upon all states to withdraw their embassies from the city. In consequence, not one foreign embassy is today located even in the western part of Jerusalem.

4 At the meeting held on the morning of 1 July, Rabin informed members of the FASC that his recommendation to the Cabinet would be to accede to a prisoner exchange, as demanded by the terrorists who had hijacked an Air France plane with almost 100 Israeli passengers on board. Three days later, the Cabinet decided to launch a rescue operation, a change of mind to which the FASC was not privy (Maoz 1981:689).

5 Two revelations had caused particular concern. One was the evidence made available in 1986, showing that GSS personnel had consistently lied with respect to the fate of two terrorists allegedly killed in action in 1984 but who had been photographed being taken into GSS custody. Another was the admission, made public in 1987, that the GSS had used torture in order to extract a confession from Izat Nafsu, a member of Israel's Circassian community and a former IDF officer, who had been accused of espionage.

6 Later cases reviewed by the ISC showed that the methods employed included deprivation of sleep, food and liquids, sitting the suspect on a very low chair with his hands tied behind his back, hooding his head for long hours and, in extreme cases, 'dangling' him several times (*Public Committee against Torture* v. *The Government of Israel* 1999).

7 For many years, the ISC and the government simply assumed as a procedural matter that the law of occupation applies. Only in *Jama'at Aschan Elmualamin* v. *IDF Commander in Judea and Samaria Region* (1982) did Justice Barak unequivocally rule that the regime of belligerent occupation was indeed the controlling regime in the Territories. Significantly, however, after the *Elon Moreh* case the ISC refused to offer an opinion on the legality of settlements all of which were henceforth built entirely on 'public' land (*Bargil* v. *The Government of Israel* 1994).

8 In this connection, note must be taken of an often-neglected comment made by Justice Witkon in a separate opinion appended to the *Elon Moreh* judgment. In Witkon's view, the minister of defense had submitted his affidavit in his capacity as a military expert rather than as a member of the Cabinet. Hence, Justice Witkon saw no necessary connection between the decision in *Dawikat* and the hierarchy issues of national security.

9 In several cases, it seems that all justices, with the exception of Justice M. Cheshin agreed that demolition of houses as a punishment to the family of the terrorist was not a form of collective punishment and thus did not contradict international law. See *Nazaal* v. *IDF Commander in Judea and Samaria* (1994) and *Ghanimat* v. *CO Central Command* (1997), Justice Cheshin dissenting. For the argument that house demolitions are not a legal form of punishment, see Dinstein 2000.

6 Legislation, 1995–2008

1 Neither of the Basic Laws passed in 1992 ('Dignity and Liberty' and 'Freedom of Occupation') specifically refer to the protection of equality, and in the mid-1990s there existed no agreement in the ISC regarding the right to equality as part of the right to human dignity. See Sommer 1997.

2 In *Smith and Grady* v. *UK* (1999) the European Court of Human Rights forced the UK to revise its policy of discharging homosexuals from the army. Similarly, in Germany, where for historical reasons women were exempt from military service except for medical services and military bands, it took a decision of the European Court of Justice to change this position. For a review of these and other cases, see Harries-Jenkins 2002.

3 The closest parallel is provided by the decision taken in 1989 by the Canadian Human Rights Tribunal, which after hearing a petition relevant to the issue ruled that: 'Full integration is to take place with all due speed, as a matter of principle and as a matter of practice, for both active and reserve forces' (Winslow and Dunn 2002:659). However, unlike the ISC, the CHR Tribunal is not part of the judicial branch. Established under Article 48.1 of the Canadian Human Rights Act (1977), it is an independent administrative body, funded directly by the Canadian parliament.
4 For example, when physical pressure was the only way of extracting from a terrorist held in custody knowledge (which he was known to possess) about when and where a specific bomb was timed to explode.
5 The first official presentation of that opinion was *First Statement of the Government of Israel to the Sharem el-Sheikh Fact-Finding Committee*, presented on 28 December 2000 (pp. 112–31). It subsequently appears in the State's response to *The Public Committee Against Torture* v. *The Government of Israel* (2006).
6 Several international bodies checked these claims. Even those prepared to accept that the IDF had violated international law during its Jenin operation, denied that a massacre had taken place. All in all, between 52 and 56 Palestinians (most of whom were combatants) lost their lives during the operation.
7 The notion of a 'separation/security fence' had first been mooted by the Rabin government as early as 1995. But the project did not begin to gain widespread support until public opinion was aroused by a spate of especially horrific suicide bombing attacks in major Israeli cities in 2001. Thereafter, however, progress on construction, largely funded by the ministry of defense, was for several years fairly rapid (Kershner 2005). Although far from complete, the fence now follows (albeit with several modifications) much of the old Green Line in northern Samaria and southern Judea, snakes around east Jerusalem, and encompasses various enclaves of Jewish settlements in the Territories that are situated adjacent to the central Sharon plain.
8 Of course, this claim is not exactly accurate. Amongst the cardinal legal issues disputed by the ICJ and the ISC were: the legality of the settlements (the ICJ declared them to be illegal, the ISC refused to decide); whether there is a 'proportionality' and 'necessity' defense attached to every violation of rights (the ISC thinks that violation can be justified by necessity, as long as the violations are proportional to the necessity; the ICJ seems to think that the only possible justifications for violations are if they are mentioned in the treaty). These and other aspects have been analyzed extensively, *inter alia* in volume 38 (2005) of *Israel Law Review* and volume 99 (2005) of the *American Journal of International Law*.
9 In *Zemach* v. *Minister of Defense* (1999), the ISC ruled that Basic Law: Human Dignity and Liberty outlawed the practice whereby detained soldiers could be held in custody for 96 hours (rather than 24). Symbolically, the case was important. Nevertheless, in terms of national security, the issue was marginal.
10 For instance, Article 18 of the GSS Law provides its employees with a degree of immunity to criminal proceedings far more extensive than that granted to other government employees (including soldiers). Likewise, this measure makes several provisions for political authorization of actions (such as wiretapping) and thereby diminishing the need for court authorizations. It also specifies that complaints against GSS employees will be investigated by the institution's own comptroller (Rotter 2010:73).

7 Diagnosis: Israel's hybrid national security legal framework

1 Following a highly critical State Comptroller Report on the inadequacies of Israel's civil defenses, published in April 2007, the government did decide later

that year to establish a National Emergency Authority. According to the official announcement, this body was to function as a 'coordinating staff agency for the minister of defense and to help him exercise overall authority for civil defense in times of emergency.' As Elran points out, however, this arrangement is still very vague (Elran 2011). It lacks many of the provisions for precise divisions of functions contained, for instance, in the Civil Contingencies Act passed by the UK parliament in 2004.
2 On average, Israeli cabinets contained 15 ministers in the 1950s and 19 in the 1960s. The number remained constant at about 25 in the subsequent three decades, but rose to thirty when Binyamin Netanyahu put together a coalition in March 2009.
3 This compilation is approved by each cabinet during the course of its first meeting, but its basic principles are usually not significantly changed from one government to another. The most recent version was approved by Netanyahu's Cabinet on 5 April 2009, and is available at: www.pmo.gov.il/PMO/Government/Documents/takanongov.htm
4 For example, *Bargil* v. *The Government of Israel* (1993). This is a somewhat bizarre argument, contradicted by the range of cases with obvious political overtones in which the ISC has since allowed itself to intervene. One can only surmise that the hesitancy evinced by the justices stems from their unwillingness to alienate two influential consistencies. One consists of large sectors of the Israeli public, likely to be deeply (perhaps irremediably) disaffected by a decision that the settlements are illegal. The other consists of international legal scholars, who are likely to react equally abrasively were the ISC to declare the settlements to be legal.
5 Benvenisti 1992 suggested that the rationale underlying the ISC's adoption of the 'dualist' doctrine where Israel's foreign relations were concerned was not exclusively legal. Altogether, he argued, justices hesitated to become involved in matters related to national security, lest by doing so they restrict and/or weaken the government's freedom of diplomatic negotiation vis-à-vis other nations. They far preferred to confer control over foreign relations on the executive, even at the price of excluding the *knesset* from this field altogether.
6 According to Kaplow 1992 the difference between rules and standards hinges on whether their content is determined before or after the behavior occurs.
7 In February 2005 a British judge issued a warrant for the arrest of Major-General (res.) Doron Almog, in order to investigate him for suspicions of war crimes during his service as CO Southern Command (which includes the Gaza Strip). Almog, who learned about the warrant when his plane landed at Heathrow airport, avoided arrest by not disembarking. Former Minister of Foreign Affairs Tzipi Livni cancelled her proposed trip to London in December 2009 when informed that a similar warrant had been issued against her with respect to her alleged involvement in war crimes allegedly committed during operation 'Cast Lead', the IDF incursion into the Gaza Strip, earlier that year.
8 At first sight, two ISC decisions might seem to contradict our contention that the ISC avoids separation of power issues. In *Rubinstein* v. *the Minister of Defense* (1998) the ISC required the *knesset* to legislate the draft deferments granted to ultra-orthodox students in religious seminaries; and in the *The Public Committee Against Torture* v. *Government of Israel* (1999) it likewise demanded legislative action in order to determine a balance between the preservation of basic human rights and the protection of national security. Interestingly, however, both decisions, quite apart from being isolated instances, may in fact never have been intended to serve as expressions of ISC opinion regarding the degree to which the executive and legislature ought to share national security decision-making responsibilities. On the contrary, it has been persuasively argued that *The Public*

Committee Against Torture decision has to be read as no more than a thinly veiled attempt on the part of the court to attain a specific outcome that it was itself reluctant to impose (in this case restrictions on the use of physical force; Reichman 2001). The decision in *Rubinstein* v. *the Minister of Defense* seems to have been drafted with similar objectives in mind. An attitude of mind that favored a 'business as usual' approach to national security matters can only have reinforced the tendency thus revealed to abstain from judicial pronouncements of a general nature and to defend civil liberties and the principle of equality by the application of the Court's authority on a piecemeal basis.

8 Prognosis: modes of reform

1 Mordechai Gur (CGS 1974–1978) was deputy minister of defense under Rabin (1992–1995) and Amnon Lipkin-Shahak (CGS 1995–1998) minister of tourism under Barak (1999–2001).
2 True, some members of Olmert's cabinet did possess vast experience of the management of Israel's national security. That was especially true of Shimon Peres, Binyamin Ben-Eliezer (who had been minister of defense, 2001–2002) and Shaul Mofaz (CGS 1998–2002 and minister of defense 2002–2006). But in matters relating to national security all were in 2006 sidelined. Peres was minister for the development of the Negev and the Galilee, Ben-Eliezer was minister of national infrastructures and Mofaz was minister of transport.
3 In its English-language publications and websites, this body proclaims itself to be a 'Council', thereby (it must be assumed) implying that it carries the weight of the US agency of the same name. In fact, however, the Hebrew title is *ha-mateh le-bitachon le'umi*, which literally translates as 'Staff'.
4 Information presently available indicates that the NSS was not consulted in any meaningful sense at any stage of the planning of the IDF operation mounted to intercept the Turkish flotilla or during its implementation. Moreover, since the prime minister was out of the country on the night of 31 May 2009, when the incident occurred, no one was likely to summon Dr. Arad for advice. Ehud Barak, the minister of defense, who was deputizing for Prime Minister Netanyahu, had an obvious bureaucratic interest in keeping control firmly within the bounds of his own ministry.
5 A telling indication of the importance attached to the position of military secretary to the prime minister is provided by the rank of the incumbent of the post. This has risen steadily from lieutenant-colonel (*segan aluf*) between 1948–1954 to colonel (*aluf mishneh*) between 1955–1968, to brigadier-general (*tat aluf*, a rank created after the Six Days War) 1968–1993 and to major-general (*aluf*) since 1993.
7 Report of speech by Ashkenazy in *Haaretz* (Hebrew daily, Tel-Aviv), 2 December 2009. Similar recommendations were proposed in 2003 by a commission established by the minister of defense under the chairmanship of General (res.) David Ivry, a former deputy CGS. Although the cabinet did not accept all of Ivry's recommendations, it did establish in December 2006 a Civic Service Authority, mandated to coordinate the activities already being undertaken by volunteers.
8 According to a report compiled in Strashnov's bureau (Yahav 1993:92), between December 1987 and February 1989 alone, the IDF's Military Police Investigative Department lodged complaints against 9,243 defendants. By 1992, furthermore, military courts had filed indictments against 241 individuals (54 officers, 183 regular troops, and four civilians employed by IDF), principally on charges of unlawful use of weapons; cruelty towards Palestinian civilians; and the theft or destruction of their property. 194 of the accused were eventually found guilty.

9 However, Finkelstein's was a 'personal' promotion and not granted to his successor, Avishai Mandelblitt, who continued to hold the lower rank of *tat aluf.*
10 For the controversy generated by the decision of the US Supreme Court to strike down a law which required governmental agencies to obtain congressional approval for the implementation of a specific law (the *Chadha* decision of 1983) see: Tribe 1984; Eskridge and Ferejohn (1992).
11 Legal literature, especially when concerned with corporate law, frequently refers to 'gatekeepers' (e.g., Coffee 2006). The prime functions of such agencies, however, are to filter access to an environment, and to ensure that illegal activities and persons are kept out. 'Sentinels', by contrast, also operate within the agency of which they are a part.
12 *Isayeva* v. *Russia; Yusupova* v. *Russia; Bazayeva* v. *Russia,* 57947/00; 57948/00; 57949/00, Council of Europe: European Court of Human Rights, 24 February 2005, available at: www.unhcr.org/refworld/docid/422340c44.html (accessed 14 November 2010). The specific topic under discussion was the death of several hundred Russian-Chechnya civilians during the armed conflict in that region.
13 Many of these limitations were highlighted in January 2011, when State Comptroller Lindenstrauss was asked to investigate allegations that the minister of defense's nominee for the post of the next CGS had contravened planning laws when constructing his private home and had lied when reporting to various tribunals that he had complied with instructions to return to public ownership land that he had taken for private use. Lindenstrauss was able only to investigate the facts of the case and present the attorney general with a summary of his findings (some of which were indeed critical of the nominee for CGS).
14 Some aspects of Ackerman's escalator are based on the provisions made in the constitution of the Republic of South Africa, which enables the National Assembly to declare a state of emergency for a period of 21 days, which can be extended for a further three months by a regular majority. Any further extension requires a 60 percent majority.

Bibliography

Primary sources

A: Official documents

British Mandatory Legislation (listed chronologically)

Palestine (Defence) Order in Council (1937)
Emergency Powers (Defence of the Colonies) Order in Council (1939)
Defense (Emergency) Regulations (1945)

Knesset laws (Basic) (listed chronologically)

Basic Law: The Government (1968)
Basic Law: The Government (1992)
Basic Law: The Government (2001)
Basic Law: The Military (1976)
Basic Law: Jerusalem, The Capital of Israel (1980)
Basic Law: The Judiciary (1984)
Basic Law: Human Dignity and Liberty (1992)

Knesset laws (regular) (listed chronologically)

Law and Administration Ordinance (1948)
IDF Ordinance (1948)
Prevention of Terrorism Ordinance (1948)
Defense Service (1949) (New Version – 1968)
Demobilized Soldiers (1949)
Shelters (1949)
State Comptroller (1949)
Absentees' Property (1950)
Families of Soldiers who Fell in Battle (Compensation and Rehabilitation) 1950
Military Cemeteries (1950)
Civil Defense (1951)
Reserve Soldiers (1952)
Land Acquisition (1953)
National Service (1953)

Military Justice (1955)
Remembrance Day for IDF Fallen (1963)
Planning and Construction (1965)
Commissions of Inquiry (1968)
Private Investigators and Security Services (1972)
Emergency (Powers) Detention (1979)
Golan Heights (1981)
Compensation of the Sinai Evacuees (1982).
Implementation of the Peace Agreement between Israel and Hashemite Kingdom of Transjordan (1995)
Implementation of the interim agreement between Israel and the PLO (1996)
The Government (2001)
Service Deferral ('Tal') (2002)
General Security Services (2002)
Citizenship and Entrance to Israel (Temporary Measures) (2003)
Criminal Procedure (2005)
Reserve Duty (2008)
National Security Staff (2008)

Commissions of enquiry (listed chronologically)

Agranat Commission (1975), published as *Doch Ha-Va'adah le-Cheker Iruyei Milkhemet Yom ha-Kippurim* ('[Unclassified] Report of the Commission of Inquiry into the Yom Kippur War'), Tel-Aviv: Yediot 1975.

Kahan Commission (1983), English version: *The Beirut Massacre*, Princeton: Karz-Cohl.

Landau Commission (1989), published as *Doch Va'adat ha-Chakirah le-Inyan Shitot ha-Chakirah shel Sherut ha-Bitachon ha-Kelali* ('Commission of Inquiry into the Methods of Investigation of the General Security Service Regarding Hostile Terrorist Activity'). Excerpted in English in: *Israel Law Review* 23:146–88.

Rubinstein Commission (2004), *Ha-va'adah ha-Tziburit Libchinat ha-Pikuach ha-Parliamentari al Ma'arechet ha-Bitachon ve-ha-Derakhim le-Shipuro* ('Report of the Public Commission for review of Parliamentary Control over the Security System'). Jerusalem: The Knesset.

Brodet Commission (2007), *Doch ha-Va'adah Libchinat Taktziv ha-Bitachon* ('Report on Defense Budgeting'), available at www.nsc.gov.il/NSCWeb/Docs/Brodet.pdf

Winograd Commission (2007/2008), *Doch ha-Va'adah Libdikat Eruyei ha-Ma'arakhah Bilevanon* (Report of the Committee into the Lebanon Campaign'), 'Partial' Report – March 2007; 'Final Report', January 2008, available at www.vaadatwino.org.il/reports.html.

Turkel Commission (partial report January 2011), English version: *Public Commission to Examine the Maritime Incident of May 31, 2010*, available at www.turkel-committee.com/content-107.html.

State Comptroller Reports

1987–2010, available at: www.mevaker.gov.il/serve/folderAdmin.asp?id=18&open tree=,2,

B: High court judgements – (listed chronologically)

Explanatory note: Decisions of the Israel Supreme Court are identified by their case number, which is assigned as soon as the petition is received and begin afresh each calendar year. Each case is categorized according to its procedural form. Thus: High Court of Justice cases are listed under 'HCJ'; criminal appeals under 'Crim. App.'; civil appeals as 'Civ. App.'; administrative appeals as 'Admin. App.', and cases referred for further discussion as 'FD'.

Decisions are officially published in *Piskey Din* ('Judgments'), shortened to 'PD', which is identified by the year of the decision, the volume number, section and page on which the judgment commences. These are published by the Nevo Publishing group, which also adds a synopsis of the case, and a list of sources. PD's are also available through the commercial legal services: *Takdin* (www.takdin.co.il) *NEVO* (www.nevo.co.il) and *PADOR* (www.pador.co.il).

Since PD usually appears only a few years after the issuance of the judgment itself, more recent judgments have to be located on the ISC's website (http://elyon1.court.gov.il/Files), where they can be located by their original case number. This website also includes translations to English of some of the judgments of the ISC.

HCJ 7/48 *Ahmed Showky Al-Karbutli* v. *Minister of Defence* (1949) PD 2:5.
HCJ 46/50 *Al Ayubi* v. *Minister of Defense* (1950) PD 4:222.
HCJ 83/50 *Fichman* v. *Minister of Defense* (1951) PD 4:724.
HCJ 73/53 *Kol Ha'Am* v. *Minister of the Interior* (1953) PD 7(2):871.
CrimApp 156/63 *Attorney General* v. *Ostreicher* (1963) PD 17(3):2088.
HCJ 39/64 *El-Ard Corp.* v. *Supervisor of the Northern District* (1964) PD 18(2):340.
HCJ 253/64 *Jaris* v. *Supervisor of the Haifa District* (1964) PD 18(4):673.
Election Appeal 1/64 *Yardor* v. *Chairman of the Central Elections Commission* (1965) PD 19(3):365.
HCJ 256/72 *Electricity Company for Jerusalem District* v. *Minister of Defense* (1972) PD 27(1):124.
HCJ 302/72 *Abu Chilu* v. *The Government of Israel* (1973) PD 27(2):172.
HCJ 390/79 *Dawikat* v. *The Government of Israel* (1979) PD 34(1):1.
HCJ 606/78 *Oyeb* v. *Minister of Defense* (1979) PD 33(2):113.
HCJ 320/80 *Kawasme* v. *Minister of Defense* (1980) PD 35(3):113.
HCJ 554/81 *Baransa* v. *CO Central Command* (1982) PD 36(4):247.
HCJ 69/81 *Abu Aita* v. *IDF Commander of Judea and Samaria Region* (1983) PD 37(2):197.
HCJ 393/82 *Jama'at Aschan Elmualamin* v. *IDF Commander Judea and Samaria Region* (1983) PD 37(4):785, 810.
HCJ 428/86 *Barzilai* v. *Government of Israel* (1986) PD 40(3):505.
H.C.J. 253/88 *Sajedia* v. *Minister of Defense* (1988) PD 42 (3):801.
HCJ 785/87 *Afu* v. *IDF Commander in the West Bank* (1988) PD 42(2):4.
HCJ 910/86 *Ressler* v. *Minister of Defense* (1988) PD 42(2):441.
HCJ 358/88 *Association for Civil Rights in Israel* v. *CO Central Command* (1989) PD 43(2):529.

HCJ 425/89 *Zuffan* v. *MAG* (1989) PD 43(4):718.
HCJ 680/88 *Schnitzer* v. *Chief Military Censor* (1989) PD 42 (4):617.
HCJ 168/91 *Morcos* v. *Minister of Defense* (1991) PD 45(1):467, 468–9.
HCJ 4481/91 *Bargil* v. *The Government of Israel* (1993) PD 47(4):210.
HCJ 5973/92 *The Association for Civil Rights in Israel* v. *Minister of Defense* (1993) PD 47(1):267.
HCJ 6026/94 *Nazaal* v. *IDF Commander in Judea and Samaria* (1994) PD 48(5):338, 346.
HCJ 4541/94 *Alice Miller* v. *Minister of Defense* (1995) PD 49(4):94.
Civ.App. 6821/93 *United Mizrachi Bank* v. *Migdal Cooperative Village* (1995) PD 49(4):221.
FDHCJ 3299/93 *Wichselbaum* v. *Minister of Defense* (1995) PD 49(2):195.
HCJ 5128/94 *Federman* v. *Minister of Police* (1995) PD 48(5):647.
HCJ 2006/97 *Ghanimat* v. *CO Central Command* (1997) PD 51(2):651.
HCJ 3267/97 *Rubinstein* v. *Minister of Defense* (1998) PD 52(5):481.
HCJ 1284/99 *Jane Doe* v. *Chief of General Staff* (1999) PD 53(2):62.
HCJ 5100/94 *The Public Committee Against Torture* v. *Government of Israel* (1999) PD 53(4):817.
HCJ 6055/95 *Zemach* v. *Minister of Defense* (1999) PD 56(1):981.
CrimFH 7048/97 *John Does* v. *Ministry of Defense* (2000) PD 53(1):721.
HCJ 5156/00 *Hillel Weiss* v. *Prime Minister Ehud Barak* (2001) PD 55(2):455.
HCJ 9070/00 *MK Limor Livnat* v. *MK Amnon Rubinstein Chairman of the Constitution, Law and Justice Committee of the Knesset* (2001) PD 55(4):800.
HCJ 1380/02 *Ben Artzi* v. *Minister of Defense* (2002) PD 56(4):476.
HCJ 2936/02 *Physicians for Human Rights* v. *IDF Commander in the West Bank* (2002) PD 56(3):3.
HCJ 2977/02 *Adalah* v. *IDF Commander in Judea and Samaria* (2002) PD 56(3):6.
HCJ 3022/02 *Canon (Law) and others* v. *IDF Commander of the West Bank* (2002) PD 56(3):9.
HCJ 3114/02 *MK Barake* v. *Minister of Defense* (2002) PD 56(3):11.
HCJ 3436/02 *Custodia Internazionale Di Terra Santa* v. *The Government of Israel* (2002) PD 56(3):22.
HCJ 3451/02 *Al-Madani* v. *Minister of Defense* (2002) PD 56(3):30.
HCJ 7015/02 *Ajuri* v. *IDF Commander in the West Bank* (2002) PD 56(6):352.
HCJ 8990/02 *Physicians for Human Rights* v. *CO Southern Command* (2003) PD 57(4):193.
HCJ 2056/04 *Beit Sourik Village Council* v. *The Government of Israel* (2004) PD 58(5):807.
HCJ 4764/04 *Physicians for Human Rights* v. *IDF Commander in Gaza* (2004) PD 58(5):385.
HCJ 1661/05 *Gaza Beach Regional Council* v. *The Knesset* (2005) PD 59(2):481.
HCJ 3799/02 *Adalah – The Legal Center for Arab Minority Rights in Israel* v. *OC Central Command* (2005) PD 60(3):67.
HCJ 6427/02 *The Movement for the Quality of Government and others* v. *the Knesset and others* (2005) PD 61(1):619.
HCJ 7957/04 *Mara'be* v. *The Government of Israel* (2005) PD 60(2):477.
HCJ 6893/05 *Levy* v. *The Government of Israel* (2005) PD 59(2):876.
HCJ 7455/05 *The Legal Forum for the Land of Israel* v. *the Government of Israel* (2005) PD 59(2):905.

HCJ 769/02 *The Public Committee Against Torture in Israel* v. *The Government of Israel* (2006).
HCJ 2732/05 *Azun Chairperson of Municipal Council* v. *IDF Commander in the West Bank* (2006).
HCJ 7052/03 *Adalah – The Legal Centre for Arab Minority Rights in Israel* v. *Minister of Interior* (2006).
HCJ 6204/06 *Dr. Yossi Beilin* v. *Prime Minister* (2006).
HCJ 5666/03 *Kav la-Oved* v. *National Labor Court* (2007).
AdminApp 2408/05 *Hoshaya* v. *The State of Israel – Ministry of Defense* (2007).
HCJ 9132/07 *Jaber Al Bassiouni Ahmed* v. *The Prime Minister* (2008).
HCJ 4258/08 *Gisha – Legal Center for Freedom of Movement* v. *Minister of Defense* (2008).
CrimApp 6659/06 *John Doe* v. *The State of Israel* (2008).
HCJ 8794/03 *Hass* v. *MAG* (2008).
HCJ 2150/07 *Abu Zafya* v. *Minister of Defense* (2009).
HCJ 201/09 *Physicians for Human Rights* v. *Government of Israel* (2009).
HCJ 8731/09 *Azam* v. *CO in the West Bank* (2009).
DACrim 8823/07 *John Doe* v. *The State of Israel* (2010).
HCJ 2690/09 *Yesh Din* v. *CO in the West Bank* (2010).
AdminApp 360/08 *Adam Teva va-Din* v. *Ministry of Defense* (2010).
HCJ 3091/99 *Association for Civil Rights in Israel* v. *The Knesset* (pending).

Secondary sources

Ackerman, Bruce (2004) 'The Emergency Constitution', *Yale Law Journal*, 113:1029–91.
—— (2006) *Before the Next Attack: Preserving Civil Liberties in an Age of Terrorism*, New Haven: Yale UP.
Allison, Graham and Zelikow, Philip (1999) *Essence of Decision: Explaining the Cuban Missile Crisis*, 2nd edition, New York: Longman.
Almog, Doron (2004) 'The West Bank Fence: a vital component in Israel's strategy of defense', *Policy Focus*, no. 47, Washington, DC: Washington Institute for Near East Policy.
Almog, Oz (2000) *The Sabra: The Creation of the New Jew*, Berkeley: University of California Press.
Aran, Gideon (1991) 'Jewish Zionist fundamentalism: the Bloc of the Faithful in Israel (Gush Emunim)', in: M.E. Marty and R. Scott Appleby (eds.), *Fundamentalisms Observed*, Chicago: University of Chicago Press, 265–344.
Arbel, Edna (2002) 'The State Attorneys in Times of Crisis' (Hebrew), *Mishpat ve-Tzava*, 16:37–92.
Arian, Asher (1995) *Security Threatened: Surveying Israeli Opinion on Peace and War*, Cambridge: CUP.
—— (1999) *Bitachon be-Tzel Iyum* ('Security Threatened: Surveying Israeli Opinion on Peace and War'), Tel-Aviv: JCSS.
Arieli, Shaul and Sfard, Michael (2008) *Choma u-Mechdal* ('The Wall of Folly'), Tel-Aviv: Yediot.
Azoulay, Ariella and Ophir, Adi (2008) *Mishtar Ze She'Eyno Echad* ('This Regime which is not One: Occupation and Democracy between the Sea and the River'), Tel-Aviv: Reisling.

Barak, Aharon (2002) 'Forward: A Judge on Judging: The Role of the Supreme Court in a Democracy', *Harvard Law Review*, 16:19–162.
—— (2006) *The Judge in a Democracy*, Princeton: PUP.
—— (2010) *Midatiyut be-Mishpat* ('Proportionality – Constitutional Rights and their Limitations'), Jerusalem: Nevo.
Barak-Erez, Daphna (ed.) (2002) *Tzavah, Chevrah u-Mishpat* ('Army, Society and Law'), Tel-Aviv: Ramot.
—— (ed.) (2007a) *Iyunim be-Mishpat Migdar ve-Feminism* ('Studies in Law, Gender and Feminism'), Kiryat Ono: Ono Academic College.
—— (2007b) 'On Women Pilots and Women Conscientious Objectors' (Hebrew), in: D. Barak-Erez (ed.), *Iyunim be-Mishpat Migdar ve-Feminism*, Kiryat Ono: Ono Academic College, 65–98.
Baron, Mordechai (1992) *Sha'arei Aza* ('The Gates of Gaza: Israel's Security and Foreign Policy, 1955–1957'), Tel-Aviv: Am Oved.
Bar-Or, Amir (2004) ' Supervision by Political Institutions over the Haganah and the IDF in it early years' (Hebrew) in: A. Kadish (ed.), *Milkhemet ha-Atzma'ut: Diyun Mehudash* ('The War of Independence: A Re-Assessment'), Tel-Aviv: Ministry of Defense, 741–7.
—— (2005) 'Supervision over the military – the FADC' (Hebrew), in: P. Gonosar (ed.), *Yahasei Gomlin* ('Civil–Military Relations'), Tel-Aviv: Ministry of Defense, 108–23.
Bar-Tal, Daniel (ed.) (1998) *Security Concerns: Insights from the Israeli Experience*, Stamford: JAI.
Bar Siman Tov, Yaacov (2001) 'Peace Policy as Domestic and Foreign Policy', in: S. Sofer (ed.), *Peacemaking in a Divided Society*, London: Cass, 27–54.
Barzilai, Gad (1996) *Wars, Internal Conflicts and Political Order: A Jewish Democracy in the Middle East*, Albany: SUNY.
—— (1999a) 'Center against Periphery: Politics and the Law of Prevention of Terrorist Acts' (Hebrew), *Pelilim*, 8:229–49.
—— (1999b) 'Courts as hegemonic institutions: The Israeli Supreme Court in a comparative perspective', *Israel Affairs*, 5:15–33.
—— (1999c) 'The Argument of 'National Security' in Politics and Jurisprudence', in: D. Bar-Tal (ed.), *Security Concerns – Insights from the Israeli Experience*, Stamford: JAI, 243–66.
Barzilai, Gad, Yuctman-Yaar, Efraim, and Segal Zeev (1994) 'The Deportation Case: The Rule and the Rule of Law' (Hebrew), *Pelilim*, 4:9–16
Bassiouni, M. Cherif (2008) *International Criminal Law*, 3rd edition, Leiden: Martinus Nijhoff.
Baumel, Yair (2002) 'The Military Administration and its Dismantlement, 1958–1968' (Hebrew), *Ha-Mizrach ha-Chadash*, 43:133–56.
Bavly, Dan (2002) *Chalomot Vehizdamnuyut SheHuchmetzu* ('Dreams and Missed Opportunities'), Jerusalem: Carmel.
Beckham, James (2007) *Comparative Legal Approaches to Homeland Security and Anti-Terrorism*, Aldershot: Ashgate.
Ben-Ami, Shlomo (2006) *Scars of war, wounds of peace. The Israeli–Arab Tragedy*, New York: OUP.
Bendor, Ariel and Kremnitzer, Mordechai (2000) *Hok Yesod: Ha-Tzarah* ('Basic Law: The Army'), Jerusalem: Sacher Institute.
Ben-Eliezer, Uri (1998) *The Making of Israeli Militarism*, Albany: SUNY.

258 Bibliography

Ben-Gurion, David (1955) *Tzavah u-Bitachon* ('Army and Security': [Collected speeches]), Tel-Aviv: Ma'arachot.
—— (1971) *Yihud ve-Yi'ud* ('Uniqueness and Mission' [collected speeches and articles]), Tel-Aviv: Am Oved.
Ben-Meir, Yehuda (1987) *Kabalat Hachlatot be-Sugyot Ha-Bitachon ha-Leumi* ('National Security Decision-Making'), Tel-Aviv: Hakibbutz Hameuchad.
—— (1992) 'The Home Front', in: J. Alpher (ed.), *War in the Gulf: The Implications for Israel,* Tel-Aviv: JCCS, 327–55.
—— (1995) *Civil-military relations in Israel,* New York: Columbia UP.
Ben-Meir, Yehuda and Bagno-Moldavsky, Olena (2010) *Vox Populi: Trends in Israeli Public Opinion on National Security 2004–2009,* Tel-Aviv: INSS.
Ben-Menahem, Hanina (1991) *Judicial Deviation in Talmudic Law,* London: Harwood.
Ben-Naftali, Orna and Michaeli, Keren (2004) '"Do Not Make a Scarecrow of the Law": A Legal Analysis of the Israeli Policy of Targeted Killings', *Cornell Journal of International Law,* 36:234–92.
Ben-Naftali, Orna and Zamir, Noam (2009) 'Whose Conduct Unbecoming?', *Journal of International Criminal Justice,* 7:155–75.
Benoliel, Daniel and Perry, Ronen (2010) 'Israel, Palestine and the ICC', *Michigan Journal of International Law,* 32:73–127.
Benvenisti, Eyal (1989) *Legal dualism: the absorption of the occupied territories into Israel,* Jerusalem: The Jerusalem Post.
—— (1992) 'Implications of Considerations of Security and Foreign Relations on the Application of Treaties in Israeli Law' (Hebrew), *Mishpatim,* 21:221–50.
—— (1993a) *The International Law of Occupation,* Princeton: PUP.
—— (1993b) 'Judicial Misgivings Regarding the Application of International Law: An Analysis of Attitudes of National Courts', *European Journal of International Law,* 4:159–83.
—— (1993c) 'Judicial Review of Deportation Orders' (Hebrew), *Mishpat u-Mimshal,* 1:441–70.
—— (2001) 'Judicially Sponsored Checks and Balances' (Hebrew), *Mishpatim,* 32:797–819.
—— (2008a) 'United We Stand: National Courts Reviewing Counter-Terrorism Measures', in: A. Bianchi and A. Keller (eds.), *Counterterrorism: Democracy's Challenge,* Oxford: Hart, 251–76.
—— (2008b) 'Reclaiming Democracy: The Strategic Use of Foreign and International Law by National Courts', *American Journal of International Law,* 102:241–74.
—— (2011) *The International Law of Occupation,* 2nd edition, Oxford: OUP.
Benvenisti, Eyal and Downs, George W. (2009) 'National Courts, Domestic Democracy, and the Evolution of International Law', *European Journal of International Law,* 20:59–72.
Benvenisti, Eyal and Zamir, Eyal (1993) *Admot Hayehudim Biyhuda Veshomron* ('The Legal Status of Lands Acquired by Israelis in the West Bank, Gaza Strip and East Jerusalem'). Jerusalem: Jerusalem Institute for Israel Studies.
Berkovitz, Nitza and Gordon, Neve (2008) 'The Political Economy of Transnational Regimes: The Case of Human Rights', *International Studies Quarterly,* 52:881–904.
Betts, Richard K. (2000) 'Is Strategy an Illusion?', *International* Security, 25:5–50.
Bialer, Uri (1991) 'Facts and Pacts: Ben-Gurion and Israel's International Orienta-

tion, 1948–1956,' in: R.W. Zweig (ed.), *David Ben-Gurion: Politics and Leadership in Israel*, London: Cass, 216–35.

Bichur, Avraham (2003) 'The Status of the Home Front in Israel's National Security Doctrine' (Hebrew), unpublished Ph.D. thesis, Bar-Ilan University, Ramat Gan.

Blum, Gabriella (2009) 'The Role of the Client: The President's Role in Government Lawyering', *Boston College Comparative and International Law Review*, 32:275–87.

Blum, Yehuda Zvi (1968) 'The Missing Reversioner, Reflections on the Status of Judea and Samaria', *Israel Law Review*, 3:279–301.

—— (1971) *Secure Boundaries and the Middle East Peace*, Jerusalem: Harry Sacher Institute.

Bowers, Paul (2003), *Parliament and the Use of Force*, available at www.parliament.uk/documents/upload/snia-01218.pdf.

Bracha, Baruch (1978) 'Restriction of Personal Freedom without Due Process of Law According to Defense (Emergency) Regulations 1945', *Israel Yearbook on Human Rights*, 8:296–323.

—— (1991) 'Judicial Review of Security Powers in Israel: A New Policy of the Courts', *Stanford Journal of International Law*, 28:39–102.

—— (2003) 'Checks and Balances in Protracted State of Emergency – the case of Israel' *Israel Yearbook on Human Rights*, 33:123–52.

Brecher, Michael (1972) *The Foreign Policy System of Israel: Setting, Images, Process*, London: OUP.

—— (1974) *Decisions in Israel's Foreign Policy*, London: OUP.

Broude, Tomer and Noam, Gilad (2008) 'Parliamentary Involvement in Treaty-Making Processes: Understanding the Knesset's Past Record and its Future Potential' (Hebrew), *Mishpat ve-Asakim*, 9:175–245.

Burk, James (2002) 'Theories of Democratic Civil–Military Relations', *Armed Forces & Society*, 29:7–29.

Caldwell, Dan and Williams, Robert E. (2006) *Seeking Security in an Insecure World*, Lanham: Rowman.

Caplan, Neil (1992) 'A Tale of Two Cities: The Rhodes and Lausanne Conferences 1949', *Journal of Palestine Studies*, 21:5–34.

—— (2001) '"Oom-Shmoom" Revisited: Israeli Attitudes towards the UN and the Great Powers, 1948–1960,' in: A. Ben-Zvi and A. Klieman (eds.), *Global Politics: Essays in Honour of David Vital*, London: Cass, 167–99.

Carter, Stephan (1984) 'The Constitutionality of the War Powers Resolution', *Virginia Law Review*, 70:101–34.

Cassese, Antonio (2008) *International Criminal Law*, 2nd edition, Oxford: OUP.

Coffee, John (2006) *Gatekeepers: The Professions and Corporate Governance*, Oxford: OUP.

Cohen, Amichai (2005) 'Administering the Territories: An Inquiry into the Application of International Humanitarian Law by the IDF in the Occupied Palestinian Territories'. *Israel Law Review*, 38:24–79.

—— (2007) 'Unequal Partnership? The Internalization of International Law into Israeli Law by the Israeli Supreme Court: The Case of the Territories', *Netanya Academic College Law Review*, 6:157–209.

—— (2008) 'Rules and Standards in the Implementation of International Humanitarian Law', *Israel Law Review*, 41:41–67.

—— (2011) 'Legal Operational Advice in the Israeli Defense Forces: The International Law Department and the Changing Nature of International Humanitarian Law', *The Connecticut Journal of International Law* (forthcoming).

Cohen, Amichai `and Shany, Yuval (2007) 'A development of modest proportions: The Application of the Principle of Proportionality in the Targeted Killing case', *Journal of International Criminal Law*, 5:310–21.

Cohen, Asher (2007) 'Non-Jewish Jews: Non-Halakhic Approaches to the Question of Joining the Jewish Collective', in: S.A. Cohen and B. Susser (eds.), *Ambivalent Jew: Charles Liebman in Memoriam*, New York: JTS, 157–72.

Cohen, Avner (1998) *Israel and the Bomb*, New York: Columbia U.P.

—— (2010) *The Worst-kept Secret: Israel's Bargain with the Bomb*, New York: Columbia U.P.

Cohen, Eliot (2000) 'Technology and Supreme Command', in: S.A. Cohen (ed.), *Democratic Societies and their Armed Forces: Israel in Comparative Context*, London: Cass, 89–105.

—— (2002) *Supreme Command: Soldiers, Statesmen and Leadership in Wartime*. New York: Free Press.

Cohen, Hillel (2000) *Nochachim Nifkadim* ('Present Absentees'), Jerusalem: Israel Institute for Israeli Arab Studies.

—— (2010) *Good Arabs: The Israeli Security Agencies and the Israeli Arabs, 1948–1967*, Berkeley: University of California Press.

Cohen, Samy (2009) *Tsahal à l'épreuve du terrorisme*, Paris: Le Seuil.

Cohen, Stuart A. (2000) 'Operational Limitations of Reserve Forces: The Lessons of the Yom Kippur War', in: P.R. Kumaraswamy (ed.), *Revisiting the Yom Kippur War*, London: Cass, 70–103.

—— (2003) 'Why do they quarrel? Civil–Military tensions in LIC situations', in: E. Inbar (ed.), *Democracies and Small Wars*, London: Cass, 21–40.

—— (2006) 'Changing Civil–Military Relations in Israel: Towards an Over-subordinate IDF?', *Israel Affairs*, 12:769–88.

—— (2008) *Israel and its Army: from collusion to confusion*, London: Routledge.

—— (ed.) (2009) *The New Citizen Armies: Israel's armed forces in comparative perspective*, London: Routledge.

Cohen-Eliya, Moshe (2005) 'The Formal and Substantive Meanings of Proportionality in the Supreme Court's Decision Regarding the Separation Fence', *Israel Law Review*, 38:262–91.

Cole, David (2004) 'The Priority of Morality: The Emergency Constitution's Blind Spot', *Yale Law Journal*, 113:1753–1800.

Cole, Peter (1996) *Selected Poems of Shemuel Hanagid*, Princeton: PUP.

Dandeker, Christopher (1994) 'New Times for the Military', *British Journal of Sociology*, 45:637–54.

Dayan, Moshe (1969) *Mapah Chadashah, Yachasim Hadashim* ('A New Map – Different Relations'), Tel Aviv: Ma'ariv.

—— (1981) *Breakthrough: A Personal Account of the Egypt–Israel Peace Negotiations*, New York: Knopf.

Delmas-Marty, Mireille (2006) 'Interactions between National and International Criminal Law in the Preliminary Phase of Trial at the ICC', *Journal of International Criminal Justice*, 2:4–5.

Dershowitz, Allan (1971) 'Preventive Detention of Citizens During National Emergency – A Comparison between Israel and the United States', *Israel Yearbook on Human Rights*, 1:295–321.

Dickinson, Laura A. (2010) 'Military Lawyers on the Battlefield: An Empirical Account of International Law Compliance', *American Journal of International Law*, 104:1–28.

Dinstein, Yoram (1974) 'The Judgment in the Rafah Approach case' (Hebrew), *Iyuney Mishpat*, 3:934–40.
—— (1978) 'The International Law of Belligerent Occupation and Human Rights'. *Israel Yearbook on Human Rights*, 8:104–43.
—— (1979) 'Settlement and Expulsion in the Occupied Territories' (Hebrew), *Iyuney Mishpat*, 7:188–94.
—— (1981) 'Expulsion of the Mayors from Judea' (Hebrew), *Iyuney Mishpat*, 8:158–71.
—— (1983) *Dinei Milkhamah* ('Laws of War'), Tel-Aviv: Schocken.
—— (1984) 'Value Added Tax in the Administered Territories' (Hebrew), *Iyuney Mishpat* 10:159–64.
—— (1988a) 'Deportations from Occupied Territories' (Hebrew), *Iyunei Mishpat*, 13:403–16.
—— (1988b) 'Family Unification in Occupied Territories' (Hebrew), *Iyuney Mishpat*, 13:221–9.
—— (1993) 'The Israel Supreme Court and the Law of Belligerent Occupation: Deportations', *Israel Yearbook on Human Rights*, 23:1–26.
—— (1995) 'The Israel Supreme Court and the Law of Belligerent Occupation: Article 43 of the Hague Regulations', *Israel Yearbook on Human Rights*, 25:1–20.
—— (2000) 'The Israel Supreme Court and the Law of Belligerent Occupation: Demolitions and Sealing Off of Houses', *Israel Yearbook on Human Rights*, 29:285–304.
—— (2005) *War, Aggression and Self Defense*, 4th edition, Cambridge: CUP.
Dloomy, Ariel (2005) 'The Israeli Refuseniks: 1982–2003', *Israel Affairs*, 11:695–716.
Doar, Yair (1992) *Lanu Ha-Magal Hu ha–Cherev* ('Our Sickle is our Sword'), Efal: Yad Tabenkin.
Don-Yehiyah, Eliezer (1993) 'Religion and Political Terror: Religious Jewry and Retaliation During the 1936–1939 "Arab Revolt"' (Hebrew), *Ha-Tziyonut*, 17:155–90.
Doron, Gideon and Lebel, Udi (2001) 'An Organization Defending Itself: The Military System Versus the Bereaved Parents' (Hebrew), *Plilim*, 9:369–412.
Dotan, Yoav (1999) 'Judicial Rhetoric, Government Lawyers and Human Rights: The Case of the Israeli High Court of Justice during the *Intifada*', *Law & Society Review*, 33:319–63.
Dror, Yehezkel (1989) *Estrategiah Rabati le-Yisrael* ('A Grand Strategy for Israel'), Jerusalem: Akadamon.
Drori, Zeev (2005) *Utopia in Uniform: The IDF and the Foundation of Israel*, London: Routledge.
Duffield, John S. (1999) 'Political Culture and State Behavior: Why Germany Confounds neo-Realism', *International Organization*, 53:764–804.
Eban, Abba (1992) *Personal Witness*, New York: Putnam.
Edelstein, David M. (2004) 'Occupational Hazards: Why Military Occupations Succeed or Fail', *International Security*, 24:49–91.
Ehrlich, Avishai (1987) 'Israel: Conflict, War and Social Change', in: C. Creighton and M. Shaw (eds.), *The Sociology of War and Peace*, London: Macmillan, 121–42.
Eilam, Yigal (1979) *Ha-Haganah* ('The Zionist Way to Power'), Tel-Aviv: Zmora.
Elazar, Daniel J. (1981) 'Covenant as the basis of the Jewish political tradition', in: D.J. Elazar (ed.), *Kinship and Consent*, Ramat Gan: Turtledove, 21–58.

Elon, Menachem (1994) *Jewish Law: History, Sources, Principles*, Philadelphia: Jewish Publication Society of America.
Elran, Meir (2011) 'The Rear Defense Law: Outlines of its Future Characteristics' (Hebrew), *Idkun Estrategie*, 13:45–54.
Elron, Zeev (2005) 'Remarks on Air Power and the Six-Day War', *Journal of Military History*, 69:811–20.
Ely, John Hart (1995) *War and Responsibility: Constitutional Lessons of Vietnam and its Aftermath*, Princeton: PUP.
Elyasuf, Yitzchak (1988) 'Legal questions relating to the involvement of the IDF in civilian labor disputes' (Hebrew), *Mishpat u-Tzavah*, 9:195–204.
Eskridge, William and Ferejohn, John (1992) 'The Article I section 7 Game', *Georgetown Law Journal*, 80:523–64.
Even, Shmuel (2007) 'Commissions of Investigation into the Israel Intelligence Community: Why the Similarity in their Recommendations?' (Hebrew), *Iyunim Be-Modi'in*, 1:25–48.
Even, Shmuel and Gross, Zvia (2008) 'Proposed Legislation on the IDF: Regulating Civil Military Relations in the Wake of the Second Lebanon War', *INSS Memorandum*. 93, Tel Aviv. INSS.
Fallon, Richard H. Jr. (1994) 'Reflections on the Hart and Wechsler Paradigm', *Vanderbilt Law Review*, 47:953–88.
Farber, Daniel A. and Frickey, Philip P. (1991) *Law and Public Choice: A Critical Introduction*, Chicago: University of Chicago Press.
Feaver, Peter D. (2003) *Armed Servants: Agency, Oversight and Civil-Military Relations*, Cambridge, Mass: Harvard University Press.
Feige, Michael (2003) *Shtei Mapot la-Gada* ('One Space, two places: Gush Emunim, Shalom Akhshav and the Construction of Israeli Space'), Jerusalem: Magnes.
Feldman, Yotam and Blau, Uri (2009) 'How IDF legal experts legitimized strikes involving Gaza civilians', *Ha'aretz* (Tel-Aviv Hebrew daily), January 22. www.haaretz.com/hasen/spages/1057648.html.
Finer, Samuel (1982) *Ha-ish al gav ha-Sus* ('The Man on Horseback: The Role of the Military in Politics'), Tel-Aviv: Maarachot.
Finkelstein, Menachem (2000) 'The Dilemma of the Military Judge-Advocate General', in: S.A. Cohen (ed.), *Democratic Societies and their Armed Forces: Israel in Comparative Context*, London: Cass, 175–83.
—— (2002) 'Law in Times of War' (Hebrew), *Mishpat ve-Tzava*, 16:15–34.
Fisher, Louis (1995) *Presidential War Power*, Kansas City: University of Kansas Press.
Foundation for Middle East Peace (2009) 'Comprehensive [Jewish] Settlement Population; www.fmep.org/settlement_info/settlement-info-and-tables/stats-data/comprehensive-settlement-population-1972–2006
Freilich, Charles D. (2006) 'National-Security Decision Making in Israel: Processes, Pathologies and Strength', *Middle East Journal*, 60:635–63.
Friedman, Menachem (1995) 'The Structural Foundation for Religio-Political Accommodation in Israel: Fallacy and Reality', in: I. Troen (ed.), *Israel: The First Decade of Independence*, Albany: SUNY, 51–82.
Friedman, Thomas L. (1989) *From Beirut to Jerusalem*, New York: Farrar Strauss Giroux.
Gai, Carmit (1998) *Bar-Lev* ('Bar-Lev-A Biography'), Tel-Aviv: Am Oved.
Gat, Azar and Merom, Gil (2010), 'Why Counterinsurgency Fails' in: A. Gat, *Victorious and Vulnerable: Why democracy won in the 20th century and how it is still imperiled*, Lanham: Rowman, 131–52.

Gavison, Ruth (1996) 'The Attorney General: A Critical Look at Some New Trends' (Hebrew), *Plilim*, 5:27–120.
—— (1997) 'The Constitutional Revolution: A Reality or a Self-Fulfilling Prophecy?' (Hebrew), *Mishpatim*, 28:21–147.
Gazit, Nir (2009) 'Social Agency, Spatial Practices, and Power: The Microfoundations of Fragmented Sovereignty in the Occupied Territories', *International Journal of Political and Cultural Sociology*, 22:83–103.
Gazit, Shlomo (2003) *Trapped Fools: Thirty Years of Israeli Policy in the Territories*, London: Cass.
Gelber, Yoav (2004) *Kommemiut ve-Naqba* ('Independence versus Naqba'), Or Yehuda: Kinneret.
Gewurz, Ilan G. (2000) 'Transition from Conflict: The Importance of Pre-Negotiations in the Oslo Peace Process', *Israel Affairs*, 6:177–99.
Gluska, Ami (2007) *The Israeli Military and the Origins of the 1967 War: Government, armed forces and defense policy 1963–1967*, London: Routledge.
Golan, Shimon (2003) 'Civil–Military Relations in Israel During the Yom Kippur War' (Hebrew), *Zemanim*, 84:4–17.
—— (2007) *Milkhamah be-shalosh Chazitot* ('A War on Three Fronts: Decision Making by the IDF High Command in the Six Days War'), Tel-Aviv: Ministry of Defense.
Golani, Mottie (1997) *Tiheyeh Mikhamah Ba-Kayitz* ('There Will be War Next Summer: The Road to the Sinai War, 1955–1956'), Tel-Aviv: Ministry of Defense.
—— (2000) 'Shall we go to war? And if we do, when? The genesis of the internal debate in Israel on the road to the Sinai war', *Israel Affairs*, 6:22–42.
—— (2001) 'Chief of Staff in Quest of War: Moshe Dayan Leads Israel into War', *Journal of Strategic Studies*, 24:49–70.
Gordon, Neve (2008) *Israel's Occupation*, Berkeley: University of California Press.
Gorenberg, Gershom (2006) *The Accidental Empire: Israel and the Birth of the Stellements 1967–1977*, New York: Holt.
Greenberg, Yitzchak (2001) *Am Lochem* ('The Israeli Reserves Army: Laying Down the Foundations 1949–1950'), Sde Boker: Ben-Gurion UP.
Gross, Emanuel (2006) *The Struggle of Democracy Against Terrorism: Lessons from the United States, United Kingdom and Israel*, Charlottsville: Virginia UP.
Gross, Oren (2003a) 'Providing for the Unexpected: Constitutional Emergency Provisions', *Israel Yearbook on Human Rights*, 33:13–43.
—— (2003b) 'Chaos and Rules: Should Responses to Violent Crises Always Be Constitutional?', *Yale Law Journal*, 112:1011–34.
Gross, Oren and Ni Alan, Fionnuala (2006) *Law in Times of Crisis: Emergency Powers in Theory and Practice*, Cambridge: CUP.
Guvrin, Pinchas (1976) *Tzav Keriyah Tashach* ('The Enlistment of the Yishuv – 1948'), Tel-Aviv: Ma'arachot.
Hadar, Zvi (1977) 'The operational authority of the CGS and the Minister of Defense vis-à-vis the IDF' (Hebrew), *Ha-Praklit*, 31:219–25.
Handel, Michael (1994) 'The Evolution of Israeli Strategy: The Psychology of Insecurity and the Quest for Absolute Security', in W. Murray, M. Knox and A. Bernstein (eds.), *The Making of Strategy: Rulers, States and War*, New York: CUP, 534–78.
Halperin, Morton and Clapp, Priscilla (2006) *Bureaucratic Politics and Foreign Policy*, 2nd edition, Washington, DC: Brookings.

Halperin-Kaddari, Ruth (2004) *Women in Israel: A State of Their Own*, Philadelphia: University of Pennsylvania Press.
Harel, Amos and Isacharoff, Avi (2004) *Ha-Milkhamah ha-Shevi'it* ('The Seventh War'), Tel-Aviv. Miskal.
Harries-Jenkins, Gwyn (2002) 'Women in Extended Roles in the Military: Legal Issues', *Current Sociology*, 50:745–69.
Hartman, David (2000) 'Forward', to M. Walzer (ed.), *The Jewish Political Tradition* vol. 1, New Haven: Yale UP, xiii–xv.
Hartman, Geoffrey (1997) *The Fateful Question of Culture*, New York: Columbia UP.
Head, Michael and Mann, Scott (2009) *Domestic Deployment of the Armed Forces: Military Powers, Law and Human Rights*, Aldershot: Ashgate.
Hermann, Charles (ed.) (1987) *New Directions in the Study of Foreign Policy*, London: Harper Collins.
Hilsman, Roger (1992) *The Politics of Policy Making in Defense and Foreign Affairs*. Englewood Cliffs, N.J.: Prentice Hall.
Hirsch, Moshe (2009) *Hasamchut Lichrot Amanot Bimdinat Yisrael* ('Treaty Making Power in Israel: A Critical Appraisal and Proposed Reform'). Jerusalem: Leonard Davis Institute.
Hodel, Sabina and Rauscher, Peter (2004) *Hofjuden und Landjuden: judische Leben in der Fruehen Neuzeit*, Berlin: Philo.
Hofnung, Menachem (1991) *Yisrael – Bitachon ha-Medinah* ('Israel – Security needs vs. the Rule of Law, 1948–1991'), Jerusalem: Nevo.
—— (1996) *Democracy, Law and National Security in Israel*, Aldershot: Dartmouth.
Hofnung, Menachem and Wienshall-Margel, Keren (2010) 'Terror Litigation and the Israeli High Court of Justice', *Journal of Empirical Legal Studies*, 7:634–63.
Holzman-Gazit, Yifat (2007) *Land Expropriation in Israel*, Aldershot: Ashgate.
Horowitz, Dan (1982) 'The IDF: A Civilianized Military in a Partially Militarized Society', in R. Kolkowitz and A. Korbonski (eds.), *Soldiers, Peasants and Bureaucrats*, London: Allen & Unwin, 77–105.
Horowitz, Dan and Lissak, Moshe (1978) *Origins of the Israeli Polity: Palestine under the Mandate*, Chicago: Chicago UP.
The Human Security Report (2005), Pt. 1 'The Changing Face of Violence', available at: www.hsrgroup.org/human-security-reports/2005/text.aspx
Huntington, Samuel (1957) *The Soldier and the State: The Theory and Practice of Civil-Military Relations*, New York: Vintage.
Hurwitz, Deena R. (2009) 'Universal Jurisdiction and the Dilemmas of International Criminal Justice: The Sabra and Shatila Case in Belgium', in: D.R. Hurwitz (ed.), *Human Rights Advocacy Stories*, Minnesota: Foundation, 267–314.
Inbar, Efraim (1999) *Rabin and Israel's National Security*, Washington, DC: Woodrow Wilson Center.
Inbar, Zvi (2005) *Moznayim ve-Cherev* ('The Scales of Justice and the Sword: The Foundations of Military Justice in Israel'), Tel-Aviv: Ma'arachot.
Issacharoff, Samuel and Pildes, Richard (2005) 'Between Civil Libertarianism and Executive Unilateralism: An Institutional Process Approach to Rights During Wartime', in: M. Tushnet (ed.), *The Constitution in Wartime: Beyond Alarmism and Complacency*, Durham: Duke UP, 161–97.
Israel Democracy Institute (2005) *Democracy By Consensus: Proposed by the IDI under the direction of Justice Meir Shamgar*, Jerusalem: IDI.

Izraeli, Dafna (1997) 'Gendering Military Service in the Israel Defense Forces', *Israel Social Science Research*, 12:129–66.
Jandoral, John W. (1999) 'War and Culture: A Neglected Relation', *Armed Forces & Society*, 25:541–56.
Johnston, Alastair Iain (1995a) 'Thinking About Strategic Culture', *International Security*, 19:32–64.
—— (1995b) *Cultural Realism: Strategic Culture and Grand Strategy in Chinese History*, Princeton: PUP.
Kadish, Alon and Kedar, Benzion (2006) *Me'atim mul rabim?* ('Few Against Many?'), Jerusalem: Magnes.
Kafkafi, Eyal (1998) *Pinchas Lavon* ('Pinchas Lavon – Anti-Messiah: A Biography'). Tel-Aviv: Am Oved.
Kaplow, Louis (1992) 'Rules Versus Standards: An Economic Analysis', *Duke Law Journal*, 42:557–629.
Kasher, Asa (2005) 'The Ethics of the Civil–Military Interface' (Hebrew), in. P. Gonosar (ed.), *Yahasei Gomlin* ('Civil–Military Relations'), Tel-Aviv: Ministry of Defense, 25–50.
Katz, Yossi (2007) *Lev va-Even* ('Heart and Stone: The Story of the Military Tombstone in Israel, 1948–2006'), Tel-Aviv: Ministry of Defense.
Katzenstein, Peter J. (1996) 'Alternative Perspectives on National Security' in P. Katzenstein (ed.), *The Culture of National Security: Norms and Identity in World Politics*, New York: Columbia UP, 3–17.
Kedar, Nir (2007) 'Jewish Republicanism', *Journal of Israeli History*, 26:179–99.
—— (2008) 'A Civilian Commander-on-Chief: Ben-Gurion's *Mamlakhti'ut*, the Army and the Law', *Israel Affairs*, 14:202–17.
—— (2009) *Mamlakhtiut* ('Ben Gurion's Concept of Citizenship'), Jerusalem: Yad Ben-Zvi.
Keller, Helen and Sweet, Alec Stone (2008) *A Europe of Rights: The Impact of the European Court of Human Rights on National Legal Systems*, Oxford: OUP.
Keren, Michael and Keren Shlomit (2010) *We Are Coming Unafraid. The Jewish Legions and the Promised Land in the First World War*, Lanham: Rowman.
Kershner, Isabel (2005) *Barrier: The Seam of the Israeli–Palestinian Conflict*, New York: Palgrave.
Kier, Elizabeth (2002) *Imagining War: French and British Military Doctrine Between the Wars*, Princeton: PUP.
Kimmerling, Baruch (1983) *Zionism and Territory: The Socio-Territorial Dimensions of Zionist Politics*, Berkeley: University of California Press.
—— (1993) 'Patterns of Militarism in Israel', *European Journal of Sociology*, 34:196–223.
—— (2001) *The Invention and Decline of Israeliness: State, Society and the Military*, Berkeley: University of California Press.
—— (2004) *Mehagrim* ('Immigrants, Settlers, Natives: The Israeli State and Society Between Cultural Pluralism and Cultural War'), Tel Aviv: Am Oved.
Kimmerling, Baruch and Migdal, Joel (2003) *Palestinians: The Making of a People*, Cambridge: Harvard UP.
King, Anthony (2006) 'The Post-Fordist Military', *Journal of Political and Military Sociology*, 34:359–74.
Klagsbald, Dori (2001) *Va'adot Chakira Mamlachtiyot* ('National Commissions of Inquiry'), Tel-Aviv: Nevo.

Klein, Yitzchak (1991) 'A Theory of Strategic Culture', *Comparative Strategy*, 10:3–23.
Klieman, Aaron S. (1990) *Israel & the World After 40 Years*, Washington, DC: Pergamon-Brassey's.
—— (2005) 'Israeli Negotiating Culture', in: T. Cofman Wittes (ed.), *How Israelis and Palestinians Negotiate*, Washington, DC: US Institute of Peace, 81–132.
—— (2008) '"Shtadlanut' as statecraft by the stateless', *Israel Journal of Foreign Affairs*, 2:99–113.
Klein, Avruch (1991), 'Jewish Fundamentalism in Israel' in: I. Lustick and B. Rubin (eds.), *Critical Essays on Israeli Society, Politics, and Culture*, Albany: SUNY, 129–43.
Kober, Avi (2009) *Israel's Wars of Attrition*, London: Routledge.
Koh, Harold (1990) *The National Security Constitution: Sharing Power After the Iran–Contra Affair*, New Haven: Yale UP.
—— (1996) 'Transnational Legal Process', *Nebraska Law Review*, 75:181–207.
—— (1997) 'Why Do Nations Obey International Law?' *Yale Law Journal*, 106:2599–2659.
—— (1998) 'Bringing International Law Home', *Houston Law Review* 35:623–81.
Kohn, Richard (2003) 'Using the Military at Home: Yesterday, Today and Tomorrow', *Chicago Journal of International Law*, 4:165–92.
Koren, Elina (1999) 'Criminalization of a Political Conflict. Crime amongst Arab citizens during the 1950s' (Hebrew), *Pelilim*, 8:157–91.
Kretzmer, David (1997) 'The Path to Judicial Review in Human Rights Cases: From *Bergman* and *Kol Ha'am* to *United Mizrahi Bank*' (Hebrew), *Mishpatim*, 28:359–85.
—— (2002) *The Occupation of Justice*, New York: SUNY.
Kuperman, Raanan (2001) 'The Impact of Internal Politics on Israel's Reprisal Policy during the 1950s', *Journal of Strategic Studies*, 24:1–28.
—— (2005) 'Who Should Authorize the IDF to Initiate a Military Operation?', *Israel Affairs*, 11:672–94.
Lahav, Penina (1981) 'American Influences on Israel's Jurisprudence of Free Speech', *Hastings Constitutional Law Quarterly*, 9:21–108.
—— (1997) *Judgment in Jerusalem: Chief Justice Simon Agranat and the Zionist Century*, Berkeley: University of California Press.
Lantis, Jeffrey S. (2002) 'Reflection and Reappraisal: Strategic Culture and National Security Policy,' *International Studies Review*, 4:87–113.
Laron, Michal (2002) *Mishpachot Yekarot* ('The Struggle of Bereaved Families over the Benefit System). Jerusalem: The Shain Center for Research in Social Sciences.
Lavi, Zvi (1987) 'The Editors' Council – Myth and Reality' (Hebrew), *Kesher*, 1:11–34.
Legro, Jeffrey W. (1996) 'Culture and Preferences in the International Co-operation Two-step', *American Political Science Review*, 90:118–37.
Lehman-Wilzig, Sam (1992) *Wildfire. Grassroots revolts in Israel in the post-Socialist era.* Albany: SUNY.
Leiter, Brian (1998) 'Rethinking Legal Realism: Towards a Naturalized Jurisprudence' *Texas Law Review*, 76:267–314.
Lempfrom, Arnon (ed.) (2002) *Levi Eshkol* ('Levi Eshkol – Selected Documents'), Jerusalem: Israel State Archives.
Levitzky, Naomi (2001) *Kvodo* ('Your Honor – Aharon Barak, A Biography'), Keter: Jerusalem.

—— (2006) *Ha-Elyonim* ('The Supremes: Inside the Supreme Court'), Tel-Aviv: Hakibbutz Hameuchad.

Lissak, Moshe (1967) 'Modernization and Role-Expansion of the Military in Developing Countries: A Comparative Analysis', *Comparative Studies in Society and History*, 9:233–55.

—— (1976) *Military Roles in Modernization: Civil-Military Relations in Thailand and Burma*, Beverly Hills: Sage.

—— (1983) 'Paradoxes of Israeli Civil–Military Relations: An Introduction', *Journal of Strategic Studies*, 6:1–12.

Luz, Ehud (1987) 'The Moral Price of Sovereignty: The Dispute About the Use of Military Power Within Zionism', *Modern Judaism*, 7:51–98.

MacKinnon, Catharine A. (1987) *Feminism Unmodified: Discourses on Life and Law*, Cambridge: Harvard UP.

Maimon, David (1993) *Ha-Terror Shenutzach* ('The Vincible Terror'), Tel Aviv: Steimatzky.

Makovsky, David (1996) *Making Peace with the PLO: The Rabin Government's Road to the Oslo Accord*, Boulder: Westview.

Maoz, Zeev (1981) 'The Decision to Raid Entebbe', *Journal of Conflict Resolution*, 25:677–708.

—— (2006) *Defending the Holy Land: A Critical Analysis of Israel's Security & Foreign Policy*, Ann Arbor: University of Michigan Press.

Mari, Mustafa (2005) 'The Israeli Disengagement from the Gaza Strip: An End of the Occupation?', *Yearbook of International Humanitarian Law*, 8:356–68.

Marks, Richard G. (1994) *The Image of Bar Kochba in Traditional Jewish Literature: False Messiah and National Hero*, Philadelphia: Pennsylvania State UP.

Martin, Susan and Warner, John (2005) 'Palestinian Refugees in Gaza', *Fordham International Law Journal*, 28:1457–78.

Martinez, Jenny C. (2006) 'Inherent Executive Powers: A Comparative Perspective', *Yale Law Journal*, 115:2480–2511.

Mashaw, Jerry L. (1997) *Greed, Chaos and Governance: Using Public Choice to Improve Public Law*, New Haven: Yale UP.

Mathews, Jessica (1989) 'Redefining Security', *Foreign Affairs*, 68:162–77.

Mautner, Menachem (1993) *Yeridat Haformalism ve-Aliyat Haarachim* ('The Decline of Formalism and the Rise of Values in Israeli Law'). Tel Aviv: Ma'agalei Da'at.

Medzini, Meron (2008) *Golda* ('Golda: A Political Biography'), Tel-Aviv: Chemed.

Meir, Golda (1975) *My Life*, Jerusalem: Steimatzky.

Merom, Gil (2003) *How Democracies Lose Small Wars: State, Society and the Failures of France in Algeria, Israel in Lebanon and the United States in Vietnam*, Cambridge: CUP.

Mersel, Yigal (2005) 'Judicial Review of Counter-Terrorism Measures: The Israeli Model for the Role of the Judiciary During the Terror Era', *NYU Journal of International Law and Policy*, 38:67–120.

Meydani, Asaf (2007) 'Security and Human Rights Policy: Israel and the Interrogation Case of 1999', *Contemporary Security Policy* 28:579–96.

Meydani, Asaf and Mizrachi, Shlomo (2006) 'The Politics and Strategies of Defending Human Rights: The Israeli Case', *Israel Law Review* 39:39–56.

Michael, Kobi (2006) 'Military Knowledge and Weak Civilian Control in the Reality of Low Intensity Conflict: The Israeli Case', *Israel Studies*, 12:28–52.

—— (2007) 'The Israel Defense Forces as an Epistemic Authority: An Intellectual Challenge in the Reality of the Israeli–Palestinian Conflict', *Journal of Strategic Studies*, 30:421–46.

—— (2008) *Bein Tzeva'iyut le-Medinaut be-Yisrael* ('Between Militarism and Statesmanship in Israel: The Influence of the Military on the Process of Change from War to Peace'), Tel-Aviv: Tel-Aviv UP.

Miller, Benjamin (2001) 'The Concept of Security: Should it be Redefined?', *The Journal of Strategic Studies*, 24:13–42.

Mizrahi, Shalom and Meydani, Asaf (2006) *Mediniyut tziburit – bein chevra lemishpat* ('Public Policy Between Society and Law'), Jerusalem: Carmel.

Moe, Terry M. (1997) 'The Positive Theory of Public Bureaucracy' in: D.C. Mueller(ed.), *Perspectives on Public Choice*, Cambridge: CUP, pp. 455–80.

Morris, Benny (1987) *The Birth of the Palestinian Refugee Problem, 1947–1949*, Cambridge: CUP.

—— (1993) *Israel's Border Wars 1949–1956*, Oxford: Clarendon Press.

—— (1999) *Righteous Victims: A History of the Zionist-Arab Conflict*, New York: Knopf.

Moskos, Charles (1998) 'The Post-modern Military', in: J. Burk (ed.), *The Adaptive Military: Armed Forces in a Turbulent World*, London: Transaction, 163–82.

Moskos, Charles, Williams, Jay and Segal, David (eds.), (2000), *The Postmodern Military: Armed Forces After the Cold War*, Oxford: OUP.

Nakdimon, Shlomo (1993) *Tamuz be-Lehavot* ('Tamuz in Flames'), Jerusalem: Idanim.

Naor, Aryeh (1986) 'The Israeli Cabinet in the Lebanon War', *Jerusalem Quarterly*, 39:3–16.

—— (2006) 'Civil–Military Relations and Strategic Goal Setting in the Six Day War', *Israel Affairs*, 12:395–411.

Navot, Suzie (2007) *The Constitutional Law of Israel*, The Hague: Kluwer Law International.

Negbi, Moshe (1981) *Kevalim shel Tzedek* ('Justice Under Occupation: The Israeli Supreme Court versus the Military Administration in the Occupied Territories'), Jerusalem, Cana.

—— (2005) 'The Rise and Fall of the Security Censorship in Israel' (Hebrew), in: U. Lebel (ed.), *Bitachon ve-Tikshoret* ('Security and Media'), Sede Boqer: Ben Gurion Research Institute, 183–99.

Nun, Eyal (1999) 'The Constitutional Limitations on the Army in Israel' (Hebrew), *Mishpat ve-Tzava*, 13:79–128.

—— (2002) 'The Constitutional limits on the Army in Israel – A suggestion for reform in Basic Law: the Army' (Hebrew). *Mishpat ve-Ttzava*, 16:161–201.

Oren, Amiram (2007) ' Shadow lands: the use of land resources for security needs in Israel', *Israel Studies*, 12:149–70.

—— (2009) *Shetachim Meguyasim* ('The Creation of Israeli Army Hegemony over the State's Land, 1948–1956'), Givatayim: Madaf.

Oren, Amiram and Newman, David (2006) 'Competing Land Uses: The Territorial Dimension of Civil–Military Relations in Israel', *Israel Affairs*, 12:561–77.

Oren, Amiram and Regev, Rafi (2008) *Eretz be-Kahki* ('Land in Uniform: Territory and Defense in Israel'), Jerusalem: Carmel.

Ostfeld, Zehava (1994) *Tzavah Nolad* ('An Army is Born'), Tel-Aviv: Ministry of Defense.

Ozacky-Lazar, Sarah (1998) 'Security and Israel's Arab Minority', in: D. Bar-Tal (ed.), *Security Concerns: Insights from the Israeli Experience*. Stamford: JAI, 347–70.

—— (2002) 'The Military Administration as an Apparatus of Control over Arab Citizens' (Hebrew), *Ha-Mizrach Ha-Chadash*, 43:103–32.

—— (2006) *Ha-Aravim ba-Asor ha-Rishon* ('The Arab Citizens in Israel: The First Decade') Tel-Aviv: Open University of Israel.

Pail, Meir (1987) *Hitpatchut Koach ha-Magen ha-Ivri* ('The Development of Jewish defense forces, 1907–1948'), Tel-Aviv: Ministry of Defense.

Paulus, Andreas L. (2002) 'Quo vadis Democratic Control? The Afghanistan Decision of the Bundestag and the Decision of the Federal Constitutional Court in the NATO Strategic Concept Case', *German Law Journal*, 3:1–15.

Pedahtzur, Reuven (1996) *Nitzachon ha-Mevuchah* ('The Triumph of Embarrassment: Israel and the Territories after the Six-Day War'), Tel-Aviv: Bitan.

Peleg, Samuel (2000) 'Peace now or later? Movement-countermovement dynamics and the Israeli political cleavage', *Studies in Conflict and Terrorism*, 23:235–54.

Perez, Oren and Rosenblum, Esther (2007) 'Chronicles of Planning Hegemony: The Special Status of the Defense Establishment in Planning Processes, 2001–2003' (Hebrew), *Mekhkarei Mishpat*, 23:371–431.

Peri, Yoram (1983) *Between Battles and Ballots: The Israeli Military in Politics*, Cambridge: CUP.

—— (1996) 'The Radical Social Scientists and Israeli Militarism', *Israel Studies*, 1:230–66.

—— (2000) 'The Media and the Military: From Collusion to Collision', in: S.A. Cohen (ed.), *Democratic Societies and their Armed Forces: Israel in Comparative Perspective*, London: Cass, 184–214.

—— (2005) 'The Political–Military Complex: The IDF Influence over Policy Towards the Palestinians since 1987', *Israel Affairs*, 11:324–44.

—— (2006) *Generals in the Cabinet Room: How the Military Shapes Israeli Policy*, Washington, DC, US Institute of Peace.

Perlmutter, Amos (1969) *Military and Politics in Israel: Nation-Building and Role Expansion*, London: Cass.

Posner Eric A. and Vermuele, Adrian (2007) *Terror in the Balance: Security, Liberty and the Courts*, New York: OUP.

Posner, Richard A. (2006) *Not a Suicide Pact: The Constitution in a Time of National Emergency*, New York: OUP.

—— (2007) 'Enlightened Despot', *The New Republic*, 23 April 2007, 53.

Presner, Todd Samuel (2007) *Muscular Judaism: the Jewish body and the politics of regeneration*, London: Routledge.

Rabinovich, Itamar (1998) *The Brink of Peace: The Israeli–Syrian Negotiations*, Princeton: PUP.

Ramsey, Michael D. (2002) 'Textualism and War Powers', *University of Chicago Law Review*, 69:1543–1637.

Ravitzky, Aviezer (1996) *Messianism, Zionism and Jewish Religious Radicalism*, Chicago: University of Chicago Press.

Reichman, Amnon (2001) 'When We Sit to Judge We Are Being Judged: The Israeli G.S.S. Case, Ex Parte Pinochet and Domestic/Global Deliberation', *Cardozo Journal of International and Comparative Law*, 9:41–103.

Report of the Conference on Parliamentary Oversight of the Security Sector (2010), Sarajevo; www.racviac.org/downloads/2010/SSR-09_report.pdf

Roberts, Adam (2002), 'The Laws of War in the War on Terror', *Israel Yearbook on Human Rights*, 32:193–246.

Roman, Peter J. and Tarr, David W. (2002) 'Military Professionalism and Policy-making: Is there a civil–military gap at the top? If so, does it matter?', in: P.D. Feaver and R.H. Kohn (eds.), *Soldiers and Civilians*, Cambridge: Harvard UP, 403–28.

Ronen, Yael (2010) 'ICC Jurisdiction over Acts Committed in the Gaza Strip: Article 12(3) of the ICC Statute and Non-State Entities', *Journal of International Criminal Justice*, 8:3–27.

Rosen, Stephen (1996) *Societies and Military Power*, Ithaca: Cornell UP.

Rostow, Eugene (1979) 'Palestinian Self-Determination, Possible Futures for the Unallocated Territories of the Palestinian Mandate', *Yale Studies in World Public Order*, 5:147–69.

Roter, Aryeh (2009) *Chok ha-Shabak* ('The GSS Law – Anatomy of Legislation'), Tel-Aviv: The National Security College.

Rubin, Edward L. (1996) 'The New Legal Process, The Synthesis of Discourse, and the Microanalysis of Institutions', *Harvard Law Review* 109:1393–1468.

Rubinstein, Amnon (1986) 'The Changing Status of the Territories From Trust to Legal Hybrid ' (Hebrew), *Iyuney Mishpat*, 11:439–56.

Rubinstein, Amnon and Medina, Barak (2006) *Mishpat ha-Chukati* ('The Constitutional Law of the State of Israel'), 6th edition, Tel-Aviv: Shoken.

Rubinstein, Elyakim (1997a) 'Basic Law: Human Dignity and Personal Freedom and Security Authorities' (Hebrew), *Iyuney Mishpat*, 21:21–61.

—— (1997b) 'Supreme Court Chief Justice Meir Shamgar: A Man of Law and His Times' (Hebrew), *Mechkarey Mishpat*, 14:97–125.

Rudman, Mara and Qupti, Mazen (1990) 'The Emergency Powers (Detention) Law: Israel Court's have a Mission – Should they Choose to Accept It?', *Columbia Human Rights Law Review*, 21:469–513.

Harold, Rudolph (1984) 'The Judicial Review of Administrative Detention Orders in Israel', *Israel Yearbook on Human Rights*, 14:148–81.

Saban, Ilan (1996) 'The impact of the Supreme Court on the Status of the Arabs in Israel' (Hebrew), *Mishpat u-Mimshal*, 3:541–69.

—— (2008) 'Law and the Arab-Palestinian Minority in the First Three Decades of the State: The Control Framework' (Hebrew), *Mechkarey Mishpat*, 24:565–637.

Sandhoff, Michelle, Wechsler Segal, Mady and Segal, David (2010) 'Gender Issues in the Transformation to an All-Volunteer Force: A Transnational Perspective', in: S.A. Cohen (ed.), *The New Citizen Armies: Israel in Comparative Perspective*, London: Routledge, 111–31.

Sandler, Shmuel (2007) 'Toward a theory of world Jewish politics and Jewish foreign policy', *Hebraic Political Studies*, 2:326–60.

Sapir, Gideon (2010) *Hamahapecha Hachukatit* ('The Constitutional Revolution in Israel – Past, Present and Future'), Tel-Aviv: Miskal.

Sarkesian, Sam C. and Connor, Robert E. (1999) *The US Military Profession into the Twenty-first Century*, London: Cass.

Sasson-Levy, Orna (2006) *Zehuyot Be-Madim* ('Identities in Uniform: Masculinities and Femininities in the Israeli Military'), Jerusalem: Magnes.

Savir, Uri (1998) *The Process*, New York: Random House.

Schabas, William (2010) *The International Criminal Court: A Commentary on the Rome Statute*, New York: OUP.

Schiff, Benjamin N. (2008) *Building the International Criminal Court*, Cambridge: CUP.

Schiff, Zeev and Yaari, Ehud (1986) *Israel's Lebanon War*. London: Unwin.
Schwartz, Herman (2000) *The Struggle for Constitutional Justice in Post – Communist Europe*, Chicago: University of Chicago Press.
Schwarzenberger, Georg (1968) *International Law as Applied by International Courts and Tribunals*, London, Stevens & Sons.
Segev Joshua (2008) 'Relief in the Interest of Justice: Two Models of an Unconventional Functional Authority' (Hebrew), *Kiryat Ha-Mishpat*, 7:63–114.
Segev, Tom (2007) *1967: Israel, the War and the Year that Transformed the Middle East*, New York: Metropolitan.
Seidman, Guy I. (1996) *Ha-Zechut le-Sharet be-Tzahal* ('The Right to Conscript and the Authority to Recruit'), Tel-Aviv. Perlstein.
Seidman, Guy I. and Nun, Eyal (2001) 'Women, The military and the Court: Israel at 2001', *Southern California Review of Law and Women Studies*, 11:91–150.
Shafir, Gershon and Peled, Yoav (2002) *Being Israeli: The Dynamics of Multiple Citizenship*, Cambridge: CUP.
Shai, Aharon (2002) 'The Fate of Abandoned Arab Villages in Israel on the eve of the Six Days War and Afterwards' (Hebrew), *Kathedra*, 105:151–70.
Shaked, Michal (2002) 'How Did Brigadier-General Galili Lose His Promotion?' (Hebrew), in: D. Barak-Erez (ed.), *Tzavah, Chevrah u-Mishpat*, Tel-Aviv: Ramot, 443–78.
Shamgar, Meir (1971) 'The Observance of International Law in the Administered Territories', *Israel Yearbook on Human Rights* 1:262–82.
—— (1982) 'Legal Concepts and Problems of the Israeli Military Government – The Initial Stage' in: M. Shamgar (ed.), *Military Government in the Territories Administered by Israel 1967–1980: The Legal Aspects*. Jerusalem: Harry Sacher Institute, pp. 13–60.
Shamir, Ronen (1990) ' Landmark Cases and the Reproduction of Legitimacy: The Case of Israel's High Court of Justice', *Law and Society*, 24:781–805.
Shany, Yuval (2005) 'Faraway, So Close: The Legal Status of Gaza After Israel's Disengagement', *Yearbook of International Humanitarian Law*, 8:369–83.
—— (2010) 'In Defense of a Functional Interpretation of Article 12(3) of the Rome Statute', *Journal of International Criminal Justice*, 8:329–43.
Shany, Yuval and Ben-Naftali, Orna (2004) 'Living in Denial: The Application of Human Rights in the Occupied Territories', *Israel Law Review*, 37:17–118.
Shapira, Anita (1984) *Berl: The Biography of a Socialist Zionist, 1887–1944*, Cambridge: CUP.
—— (1985) *Mipiturei ha-Rama ad Piruk ha-Palmach* ('The Army Controversy, 1948: Ben-Gurion's Struggle for Control'), Tel-Aviv: Hakibbutz Hameuchad.
—— (1992) *Land and Power: The Zionist Resort to Force, 1881–1948*, New York: OUP.
—— (2008) *Yigal Allon: Native Son*, Philadelphia: University of Pennsylvania Press.
Sharett, Moshe (1978) *Yoman Ishi*, vol. 5 ('Personal Diary'), Tel-Aviv: Ma'ariv.
Shavit, Yaakov (1983) *Havlagah o Teguvah?* ('Self-Restraint or Response?'), Ramat Gan: Bar-Ilan UP.
Sheffer, Gabriel (1996) *Moshe Sharett: Biography of a Political Moderate*, Oxford: OUP.
Shelach, Chaim (1978) 'Freedom of Religion and Conscience in Israeli Law' (Hebrew), unpublished Ph.D. thesis, Hebrew University of Jerusalem.
Shelef, Leon (1993) 'The Green Line is the Border of Judicial Activism: Queries about Supreme Court Judgments and the Territories' (Hebrew), *Iyuney Mishpat*, 17:757–809.

Shetreet, Shimon (1986) 'International Protection of Human Rights in Israeli Law', *Israeli Reports to the XII International Congress on Comparative Law*, 307–53.

—— (1984) 'A Contemporary Model of Emergency Detention Law: An Assessment of the Israeli Law', *Israel Yearbook on Human Rights*, 14:182–220.

—— (1988) 'The Scope of Judicial Review of National Security Considerations in Free Speech and Other Areas: The Israeli Perspective', *Israel Yearbook on Human Rights*, 18:35–48.

Shifris, Amos (2010) *Israel Galili* ('Israel Galili: A Man of Words and Deeds'), Tel-Aviv: Yad Tabenkin.

Shlaim, Avi (2000) *The Iron Wall: Israel and the Arab World*. New York: Norton.

Shoham, Uri (2002) 'The MAG and the Attorney General' (Hebrew), *Mishpat ve-Tzava*, 16:203–448

Simon, Dan (1994) 'The Demolition of Homes in the Israeli occupied Territories' *Yale Journal of International Law* 19:1–79.

Sivan, Emmanuel (1999) 'Private pain and public remembrance in Israel', in: J. Winter and E. Sivan (eds.), *War and Remembrance in the Twentieth Century*, Cambridge: CUP, 177–204.

Smith, Anne (2006). 'The Unique Position of National Human Rights Institutions: A Mixed Blessing?', *Human Rights Quarterly*, 28:904–50.

Sofer, Sasson (1998) *Zionism and the foundations of Israeli diplomacy*, Cambridge: CUP.

Sommer, Hillel (1986) 'Epur si Applica – The Geneva Convention (IV) and Israeli Law' (Hebrew), *Iyuney Mishpat*, 11:263–80.

—— (1997) 'The Non-Enumerated Rights: On the Scope of the Constitutional Revolution' (Hebrew), *Mishpatim*, 28:257–340.

Sommer, Udi (2010) 'A Strategic Court and National Security: Comparative Lessons from the Israeli Case, *Israel Studies Forum*, 25:54–80.

Sprinzak, Ehud (1993) 'Elite Illegalism in Israel', in: E. Sprinzak and L. Diamond (eds.), *Israeli Democracy Under Stress*, Boulder: Lynne Reiner, 173–98.

—— (2000) 'Israel's radical right and the countdown to the Rabin assassination', in: Y. Peri (ed.), *The Assassination of Yitzchak Rabin*, Stanford: California UP, 96–128.

Stigler, George (1971) 'The Theory of Economic Regulation', Bell *Journal of Economics and Management Science*, 2:3–21.

Stirk, Peter (2009) *The Politics of Military Occupation*, Edinburgh: Edinburgh UP.

Strashnov, Amnon (1994) *Tzedek Tachat Eish* ('Justice Under Fire: The Legal System During the Intifada'), Tel-Aviv: Yediot.

Tal, David (1998) *Tefisat ha-Bitachon ha-Shotef shel Yisrael* ('Israel's Concept of Current Security 1949–56'), Sde Boker: Ben-Gurion UP.

—— (2003) 'The 1948 War – Ben-Gurion's War' (Hebrew), *Iyunim Bitkumat Yisrael*, 13:115–38.

Teveth, Shabtai (1970) *Kilelat ha-Berachah* ('The Cursed Blessing'), Jerusalem: Shocken.

—— (1996) *Ben-Gurion's spy: the story of the political scandal that shaped modern Israel*, New York: Columbia UP.

Tirosh, Yair (2004) 'The Legal Framework for the Operation of the Military in Israel: Comparative Perspectives' (Hebrew), *Mishpat ve-Tzava*, 17:289–349.

Tribe, Laurence (1984) 'The Legislative Veto Decision: A Law by Any Other Name?, *Harvard Journal on Legislation*, 21:1–27.

Tribe, Laurence and Gudridge, Patrick (2004) 'The Anti-Emergency Constitution', *Yale Law Journal*, 113:1801–70.
Ullman, Richard (1983) 'Redefining Security', *International Security*, 8:129–51.
Urbach, Efraim Elimelech (1986) *The Halakhah: Its Sources and Development*, Givatayim: Masada.
Van Creveld, Martin (1998) *The Sword and the Olive: A Critical History of the Israel Defense Force*, New York: Public Affairs.
Vital, David (1971) *The survival of small states: studies in small power/great power conflict*, London: OUP.
Walzer, Clive (2007) 'Keeping Control of Terrorists Without Losing Control of Constitutionalism', Stanford Law Review, 59: 1395–1463.
Walzer, Michael (1974) 'Political Action: The Problem of Dirty Hands', in: M. Cohen (ed.), *War and Moral Responsibility*, Princeton: PUP, 62–82.
Waters, Christopher (2008) 'Is the Military Legally Encircled?', *Defence Studies*, 8:26–48.
Winslow, Donna and Dunn, Jason (2002) 'Women in the Canadian Forces: Between Legal and Social Integration', *Current Sociology*, 50:641–67.
Wolfers, Arnold (1962) 'National Security as an Ambiguous Symbol', in: A. Wolfers, *Discord and Collaboration: Essays on International Politics*, Baltimore: Johns Hopkins UP, 147–65.
Ya'ari, Aviezer (2004) *Ha-Pikuach Ha-Ezrachi Al Ha-Tzavah be-Yisrael* ('Civilian Control over the Military in Israel'), Tel-Aviv: Jaffee Center.
—— (2006) *Le-mi Meyaetzet ha-Moetzah?* ('Whom Does the Council Advise? A New Model for the National Security Council'), Tel-Aviv: Jaffee Center.
Yahav, Doron (ed.) (1993) *Israel, the 'Intifada' and the Rule of Law*, Tel-Aviv: Ministry of Defense.
Yaniv, Avner (1985) 'Deterrence and Defense in Israeli Strategy' (Hebrew), *Medinah, Mimshal ve-Yahbal*, 24:27–62.
—— (1994) *Politikah ve-Estrategiah be-Yisrael* ('Politics and Strategy in Israel). Tel-Aviv: Sifriyat Poalim.
Yesh Din (2007) 'Backyard Proceedings: The Implementation of Due Process Rights in the Military Courts in the Occupied Territories', available at: www.yesh-din.org/site/index.php?page=militarycourts3&lang=en
Yesh Din (2008) 'The Prohibited Zone: Israeli Planning Policy in the Palestinian Villages in Area C', available at: http://eng.bimkom.org/Index.asp?ArticleID=137&CategoryID=125&Page=1
Yoo, John C. (2002) 'War and the Constitutional Text', *University of Chicago Law Review*, 69:1639–84.
—— (2006) *War by Other Means: An Insider Account of the War on Terror*, New York: Atlantic Monthly.
Young, Ernest A. (2005) 'Institutional Settlement in a Globalizing Judicial System', *Duke Law Journal*, 54:1143–1261.
Zak, Moshe (1996) *Hussein Oseh Shalom* ('Hussein Makes Peace'), Ramat Gan: Bar-Ilan UP.
Zamir, Yitzchak (1996) *Ha-Samchut ha-Minhalit* ('Administrative Authority'), Jerusalem: Nevo.
Zemach, Ariel (2009) 'What Does Israel Owe Gaza?' (Hebrew), *Mishpat u-Mimshal*, 12:83–143.

Zelekha, Yaron (2008) *Ha-Gvardiya ha-Shchorah* ('The Black Guard'), Tel-Aviv: Kinneret.

Zertal, Idith and Eldar, Akiva (2007) *Lords of the Land: The War Over Israel's Settlements in the Occupied Territories 1967–2007*, New York: Nation Books.

Zilbershats, Yaffa (1995) 'The Adoption of International Law into Israeli Law: The Real is Ideal', *Israel Yearbook on Human Rights*, 25:243–80.

Zimerman, Ariel (1997) 'The GSS Law Proposal: A Comparative Analysis' (Hebrew), *IDI Policy Papers* 3, Jerusalem: The Israel Democracy Institute.

Index

Absentees' Property Law (1950) 56
Abu Aita v. *IDF Commander Judea and Samaria Region* (1983) 137, 194
Abu Chilu v. *The Government of Israel* (1973) 101–3, 247n7
Abu Zafya v. *Minister of Defense* (2009) 163
Ackerman, Bruce 239
'accommodation', as judicial strategy 178; failure to implement in Israel 182–92; *see also* Gross, Oren and Ni Aolain, Fionnuala
'activism', as judicial strategy 133–5; limitations of 193–8, 206–7; reasons for adoption of 204; *see also* justiciability
Adalah v. *IDF Commander in Judea and Samaria* (2002) 157
Adalah – The Legal Center for Arab Minority Rights in Israel v. *OC Central Command* (2005) 163
Adalah v. *Minister of Interior* (2006) 165–6
Adam Teva va-Din v. *Ministry of Defense* (2010) 195, 212
Afu v. *IDF Commander in the West Bank* (1988) 138
Agranat Commission (1973–1974) 129; established 84; recommendations 86; terms of reference 247n3
Agranat, Shimon 67; and judicial deference (1950) 134
Ahmed Showky Al-Karbutli v. *Minister of Defense* (1949) 67
Ajuri v. *IDF Commander of West Bank* (2002) 160, 194
Al Ayubi v. *Minister of Defense* (1950) 134
Alice Miller v. *Minister of Defense* (1995) 147–9
Allon, Yigal 73, 80–1, 83, 245n1
Al-Madani v. *Minister of Defense* (2002) 158
Arab minority in Israel: attitude of ISC towards (1950s) 67–8; control over (1948–1966) 55–6; population figures 58, 244n3; requisition of property 56–7, 60–1; *see also* military administration
Arad, Uzi 221

Arens, Moshe 127; *see also* foreign affairs and defense committee
armed forces: civilian supervision over 25–6
armistice agreements of 1949 51, 66
Ashkenazy, Gabi 223
Ashkenazy, Mottie 113
'assigned residence' 159–60; *see also Ajuri* v. *IDF Commander of West Bank*
Association for Civil Rights in Israel v. *CO Central Command* (1989) 138
Association for Civil Rights in Israel v. *The Knesset* (pending) 183, 194
Attorney General v. *Ostreicher*, (1963) 183
'attribution', as judicial strategy by ISC (1995–2008) 151–3
Azun Chairperson of Municipal Council v. *IDF Commander in the West Bank* (2006) 171–2

Bankovic v. *Belgium* (2001) 22
Barak, Aharon 2, 14, 17; *Ajuri* judgment 160; *Al-Madani* judgment 158; as attorney general 105; *Beit Sourik Village Council* judgment 160; as justice of ISC 133; and judicial 'activism' 132–3, 144; as Kahan commissioner 129; *Mara'be* judgment 162, 204; *Physicians for Human Rights* judgment 159; *Schnitzer* judgment 138–40; targeted killings judgment 162–3, 204
Barak, Ehud 1, 118; as prime minister 154, 214
Barak-Erez, Dafna 7
Baransa v. *CO Central Command* (1982) 139
Bargil v. *The Government of Israel* (1994) 247n7, 249n4
Bar-Lev, Chaim 81, 83, 246n2
Barzilai, Gad 47, 62, 111, 124, 132, 141, 209
Barzilai v. *The Government of Israel* (1986) 135
Basic Law: Freedom of Occupation 247n1

276 Index

Basic Law: Human Dignity and Liberty of the Person (1992) 182, 238, 247n1, 248n9
Basic Law: Jerusalem (1980) 121, 247n3
'basic' laws 11–12, 208
Basic Law: The Government (1968) 84–6, 186; amendments to (1992) 122–3, 196; proposals to reform 227–8; revised (2001) 182
Basic Law: The Judiciary (1984) 132
Basic Law: The Knesset (1958) 93
Basic Law: The Military (1976) 87, 186; deficiencies of 88–93, 186–7; ignored by Kahan commission 130; as implemented in 2006 215
Begin, Menachem 16, 78, 106; and first Lebanon war 119–20; and peace with Egypt 117
Beit Sourik Village Council v. *The Government of Israel* (2004) 160–1
Belgium: emergency regulations in 20
Ben Artzi v. *Minister of Defense* (2002) 236
Bendor Ariel and Kremnitzer Mordechai 187
Ben-Eliezer, Binyamin 250n2
Ben-Gurion, David 16; advocacy of 'military role expansion' 68–70; attitude towards judicial interference in national security 77; hegemony over Israel's defense establishment and policy 53–4, 71–2, 75–6; influence on national security legislation 62, 64–5; relationship with *Palmach* and *Haganah* 40, 53, 71; relationship with Sharett 52; and 'statism' (*mamalkhtiut*) 43; use of the cabinet 245n10
Ben-Meir, Yehuda 1, 46, 122
Benvenisti, Eyal 47, 137, 153, 249n5
Ber, Israel 245n12
'Bloody Sunday' 26
Bracha, Baruch 140
Brazil: national security council in 19; unitary system of command 19
Brecher, Michael 65
Brodet Committee (2007) 231
B'tselem 115–16
Burg, Yosef 117
Burk, James 28
'business as usual', assessment of 201–7; as judicial strategy after 1995 178, 192–8; reasons for choice of by Aharon Barak 198–201; *see also* Gross, Oren and Ni Aolain, Fionnuala

cabinet, constitutional position of: according to Basic Law: The Government 192, 196–7; according to Basic Law: The Military 87, 187, 189; and principle of collective responsibility 74, 81, 88, 91, 104, 217–21; *see also Yossi Beilin* v. *Prime Minister* (2006)
Camp David Accords (1979) 111, 117, 121, 123
Camp David Summit (2000) 154
Canon (Law) and others v. *IDF Commander of the West Bank* (2002) 157
Chief of General Staff (CGS), constitutional position of 222–3; according to Basic Law: The Military 87; according to *Dawikat* v. *Government of Israel* (1979) 89–90
Church of the Nativity, Bethlehem: IDF siege of (2002) 158
civic service in Israel 224, 250n7
Civil Defense Law (1951) 56, 63; amended (1997) 182–3
civil-military relations in Israel: in mandate period 40–1; post-1948 45–6
Cohen, Avner 75, 85
commissions of enquiry 26, 232; in Israel 128–32, 232; Rubinstein and Medina view of 132; weaknesses of 232–3; *see also* Agranat; Kahan; Landau; Winograd
'complimentarity' principle, applied to Israel 204
comptroller of the security establishment 224
'conscience committees' in IDF 235–6
conscription: enacted in Israel (1949) 63; exemptions from 92, 135, 223–4; proposals to reform 224; *see also* haredim; Defense Service Law (1949); National Service Law (1953)
'constitutional review', as judicial strategy: rarely adopted by ISC (1995–2008) 162–6
'constitutional revolution' in Israel 144
Criminal Procedure Law (2005), declared unconstitutional by ISC 164
Custodia Internazionale Di Terra Santa v. *The Government of Israel* (2002) 158

DABLA (IDF International Law Branch) 172–3; as candidate for 'sentinels' 236–8
Dawikat v. *Government of Israel* (1979) 89, 92, 111, 136–7, 159, 192, 193, 216, 247n8
Dayan, Moshe 245n9; as CGS 52, 73, 74; influence over policy in Territories 98–100; as minister of defense 80–3, 188
declaration of war: legal position with respect to in Israel 226–7; procedures 24; *see also Beilin* judgment (2006)
defense budget: scrutiny of 25
Defense Emergency Regulations (1945) 55–6, 61, 125–6, 182, 238; legality of

questioned in *Levy* v. *The Government of Israel* (2005) 194
Defense Service Law (1949) 63–4; amended (1950) 70
'delegation', as *knesset* strategy 169
Demobilized Soldiers Law (1949) 63
Denmark: supreme command in 19
deportations, of Hamas operatives 1–3; ISC approval of in general 138
Dinstein, Yoram 47
disengagement from Gaza (2006) 165, 215; ratified by *knesset* 184
Dori, Yaakov 90
Dotan, Yoav 140–1
Dror, Yehezkel 219

Eban, Abba 82, 83, 127
Editors' Council (*va'adat ha-orchim*) 68–9, 112–13
Egypt, disengagement agreements with (1974) 123; Israel peace treaty with (1979) 108, 117–18, 123
Ehrlich, Avishai 45
Eiland, Giora 215
Eitan, Refael 118, 136
El- Ard Corp. v. *Supervisor of the Northern District* (1965) 68
Elazar, Daniel 32
Elazar, David 81, 86, 90
Electricity Company for Jerusalem District v. *Minister of Defense* (1972) 195
Elon Moreh, *see Dawikat* v. *Government of Israel*
Emergency (Powers) Detention Law (1979) 125–6
emergency regulations: in Israel 34, 55, 124, 182, 194; in Jewish legal traditions 31–4; in the West 20–1, 226; possible modes of reform 239–40; *see also Association for Civil Rights in Israel* v. *The Knesset* (pending); Defense Emergency Regulations
'enforcement', as ISC policy after 1980s 137–8; between 1995–2008 146–51
Entebbe raid (1976) 126
Eshkol, Levi: policy with respect to Territories 94; relationship with Dayan 84–5; style of national security decision-making 79–80
European Court of Human Rights 26, 251n12
'extra legal action', as judicial strategy 178; as practiced by Ben-Gurion 180, 184; *see also* Gross, Oren and Ni Aolain, Fionnuala

'facilitation', as judicial strategy practiced by ISC (1995–2008) 156–9
Feaver, Peter 28
Federman v. *Minister of Police* (1995) 195

Fichman v. *Minister of Defense* (1951) 244n7
Finkelstein, Menachem 225
foreign affairs and defense committee (FADC) of the *knesset* 65, 126–7; and Civil Defense Law (1997) 183; role in declarations of war 128
Fourth Geneva Convention (1949) 2, 95, 99–101, 160; incorporated into Israeli law (1982) 101
France: constitutional council in 226; emergency regulations in 242n2; national security council in 19; unitary system of command 19
functional dimension of national security: as affected by *Barzilai* and *Ressler* judgments 134–5; as affected after 1967 by IDF administration of the Territories 96–7; in Basic Law: The Military (1974) 91–2; under Ben-Gurion 61–71; continuities in 186–9; defined 18, 24–7; ISC reticence with respect to 196–8; *knesset* influence over (1997–1995) 124–5; proposed reforms 211, 223–38; re-defined after 1995 110–13

Galilee, Yisrael 39, 71, 76, 83, 85–6, 98, 244n8,
Galili judgment, *see Jane Doe* v. *Chief of General Staff* (1999)
Gavison, Ruth144
Gaza Beach Regional Council v. *The Government of Israel* (2005) 137, 165; *see also* disengagement from Gaza (2006)
Gazit, Nir 185
Gazit, Shlomo 99
General Security Services Law (2002)169, 185, 229, 248n10
General Security Services (*shabak*) 58, 64, 91, 112–13; attitude of ISC towards 153; investigated by Landau Commission (1987) 131
German Federal Republic: deployment of armed forces 22–3, 226; supervision over armed forces 228; supreme command in 19
Ghanimat v.*CO Central Command* (1997) 247n9
Golan Heights Law (1981) 121
Gordon, Neve 194–5
Greenbaum Committee (1948) 72, 219
Gross, Oren and Ni Aolain, Fionnuala 20, 177–80
Grunis, Asher 166
Gulf War (1991) 109–10, 183
Gur, Mordechai 117, 250n1
Gush Emunim 113–14

Haganah 35–6; Ben-Gurion's relationship with 71; command in 39

278 Index

Hague Regulations of War 99–100
halakhah (traditional Jewish law) 32; emergency regulations in 243n3
Halevy, Efraim 215
Harel, Isser 245n12
Hass v. *MAG* (2008) 204
Herzl, Theodore 35
hierarchical dimension of national security: absent from discourse during mandate period 38; under Ben-Gurion 71–5; changes in consequent upon *Schnitzer* judgment (1989) 137–42; defined 18–21; dissolution of (1977–1995) 116–20, 122–4; judicial reticence with respect to 197–8; *knesset* role in (1977–1995) 125–8; proposed reforms in 210–11, 213–23; as regulated by Basic Law: The Military (1974) 87–91; weaknesses of 189–92
Hillel Weiss v. *Prime Minister Ehud Barak* (2001) 123, 198
Hizbollah 15, 150, 154, 183, 197, 215
Hofnung, Menachem 47, 126, 203
Holland: emergency declarations in 238; supreme command in 19–20
Holzman-Gazit, Yifat 56
Hoshaya v. *The State of Israel – Ministry of Defense* (2007) 195
house demolitions, ISC approve of as punishment 138, 247n9
Hungary: supreme command in 20
human rights: ISC's record respecting 140–1, 202–3
Huntington, Samuel 28, 205
Hussein, King 118

'illegalism' in Israeli culture 41–3
immigration into Israel: during 1950s 54; post-1980s 107, 212
incarcerations, ISC attitude towards 150–1
infringement of human rights by executive 20, 139, 195, 240
Inter-American Court of Human Rights 26
'internalization', of IHL by executive 170–3
International Criminal Court 26, 203
International Court of Justice (ICJ) 248n8; *Advisory Opinion – Legal Consequences of the Construction of a Wall in the Occupied Palestinian Territories* 161–2, 204
international humanitarian law (IHL): development of 159
international law of occupation 22, 99, 102–3, 136–7, 159, 185, 194, 198, 217, 247n7
internment, ISC approval of as punishment 138
'interpretation', as judicial strategy practiced by ISC (1995–2008) 146–51

'interpretative doctrine' re IHL, as applied by ISC 198
intifada: first 15, 109–10; impact on ISC attitudes towards IDF operations 155–6; second 154–6, 157
Ismail ibn Nagrela 243n5,
Israel: 'basic laws' in 11–12, 2008 *see* Basic Law; civil defense 248n1; civil–military relations 243n7; immigration 54, 60, 107, 114, 212; media 247n2; militarism 45; national culture 41–5; non-Jewish population in 1949 244n3; political changes 104–7; security concerns 14–15; size of cabinets 249n2; warfare 44–5
Israel Defense Force (IDF): 'conscience committees' 235–6; foundation of 54; gender issues 146–9; *haredi* (ultra-orthodox) non-service 92, 135, 151–3, 164; influence over formulation of national security policy 188–9; international law branch (*DABLA*) 172–3, 236–8; legal status with respect to land use 61, 195, 211–12; Ombudsman 224; operational doctrine 52; 'over-subordination' of 205–6; Rear Command 14; relocation of bases to the Negev 212; relationships with settlers 114–15; 'role contraction' 223–4; 'role expansion' 69–71; status in territories 97–8; societal status 11, 112–13
Israel Defense Force Law (proposed) 221–2
Israel Supreme Court (ISC): attitudes towards Arab minority in 1950s 67–8; attitude towards IHL 160–2, 198; Ben-Gurion's attitude towards 66, 76–7; changes in policies required 225–7, 240–1; deference to executive (1948–1963) 66–8; deficiencies of policies 201–7; and deportations in 1992 2–4; and draft deferments to *haredim* 151–2, 165; emergence of as a national security actor after 1969 101–4; human rights record 140–1, 202–3; judicial strategies (1995–2008) 145–173; and incarcerations 150–1; non-intervention since 1995 with respect to hierarchical and functional dimensions of national security 195–8; non-intervention since 1995 with respect to settlements and Territories 193–5; number of petitions to (1970–1994) 132; petitions by Palestinians to 133; role in national security (1977–1995) 132–42; and separation fence 160–2, 171–2; studies of 48; and targeted killings 162–3, 204
Issa v. *Turkey* (2004) 22–3

Jaber Al Bassiouni Ahmed v. *The Prime Minister* (2008) 195
Jama'at Aschan Elmualamin v. *IDF Commander Judea and Samaria Region* (1983) 137, 139, 163, 194, 247n7
Jane Doe v. *Chief of General Staff* (1999) ['Galili judgment'] 149–50
Japan: supreme command in post-1945 constitution 19
Jaris v. *Supervisor of the Haifa District* (1964) 68
Jenin, IDF operations in (2002) 157, 248n6
Jerusalem: Basic Law (1980) 121, 247n3; decisions re in 1967 94–5
Jewish political traditions 30–4, non-bellicosity of 34–6
Jewish soldiers in foreign armies 36
John Does v. *Ministry of Defense* (2000) 151
Jordan, Israel peace treaty with (1994) 108, ratified by *knesset* 144
judicial activism *see* 'activism' as judicial strategy
'justiciability', as legal doctrine 4, 157; not applied by ISC to Jewish settlements 193; as promoted by Aharon Barak 133–5, 144

Kahan Commission (1982–1983) 129–30
Karo, Joseph 34
Kav la-Oved v. *National Labor Court* (2007) 137
Kawasme v. *Minister of Defense* (1980) 138
Kfar Etzion 98
Kimmerling, Baruch 45
Klieman, Aaron 43
knesset: absence of influence over policy in the Territories 98–9; absence of influence over separation fence 184–5; foreign affairs and defense committee (FADC) 65, 126–7, 229; ratification of peace treaty with Jordan 144; responses to ISC activism (1995–2008) 167–9; role in national security legislation (1948–1963) 62–4, 66; (1963–1977) 91–2; (1977–1995) 120–2; role in ratification of international agreements 66, 123–4, 249n5; Service Deferral Law (2005) 164; weaknesses of 227–30, 239; *see also* foreign affairs and defense committee (FADC)
Koh, Harold 5, 170
Kol ha-Am v. *Minister of the Interior* (1955) 67, 146
Kook, Rabbi Zvi Yehuda 113–14
Kook v. *Minister of Defense* (1948) 67
Kretzmer, David 47, 101–2, 144, 203, 247n1,

Land Acquisition Law (1953) 56, 68

Landau commission (1987) 129
Lavon 'affair' (1954) 65, 245n12
Lavon, Pinchas 73
Law and Administration Ordinance (1948) 54–5, 244n1
Law for the Compensation of the Sinai Evacuees (1982) 121–2, 184
Law of Families of Soldiers who Fell in Battle (1950), amended 2001 167–8
Lebanon Wars: first (1982) 109–10, 115, 119–20; second (2006) 197, 215–20; *see also* Sabra and Shatilla; Winograd Commission
Labor Party 104, 106–7, 116, 121, 125, 127, 213
The Legal Forum for the Land of Israel v. *the Government of Israel* (2005) 196
'legal process' school 6, 210
Lehi 38, 62
Levy v. *The Government of Israel* (2005) 194
Likud Party 43, 104, 118, 123, 206
Lipkin-Shahak, Amnon 250n1
Lissak, Moshe 243n7

Maimonides 33, 35, 243 n4,
Maoz, Zeev 46
Mapai Party 94, 57, 75
Mara'be v. *The Government of Israel* (2005) 162, 204
Meir, Golda 91, 113; relationship with Dayan 84–5; style of national security decision making 82
Meir, Yehuda 139
Meydani, Asaf 7
mifkadah artzit (high command of the *Haganah*) 39
militarism in Israel 45
military administration 58–60, 65, 74, 97; *see also* Rozen Committee
military advocate general (MAG): ordered to prosecute by the ISC 139; relationship with attorney general 48; strengths and weaknesses 224–5
Military Cemeteries Law (1950) 57
Military Justice Law (1955) 63, 88
military 'role expansion' 69–71
military secretary to the prime minister 250n5
ministerial committee on defense and foreign affairs 74
ministerial committee on security affairs 191; establishment of 76; use by Eshkol 79, 81
minister of defense: constitutional position of according to Basic Law: The Military 87–9, 187, 189; constitutional position of according to *Dawikat* v. *Government of Israel* 89; Winograd Commission (2006) on 216–20
Mizrachi, Shlomo 7

MK Barake v. *Minister of Defense* (2002) 158
MK Livnat v. *Chairperson of the Constitution, Law and Justice Committee* (2001) 144
Mofaz, Shaul 223, 250n2
Morcos v. *Minister of Defense* (1991) 140, 146
Mosad 64, 91, 245n12; absence of legislation regarding 185
The Movement for the Quality of Government and others v. *the Knesset and others* (2005) 164

Nahal, establishment of 70
National Humanitarian Law Committees 234–5
National Human Rights Institutions 234–5
national security, changing definitions of 12–14; cultural influences on 28–9; dimensions of 17–19; public debates on in Israel 111–15, 211–12; suggested reforms to dimensions of 208–40; *see also* functional; hierarchical; spatial; temporal
national security committee of the cabinet 191
national security council (NSC) in Israel 214–15, 218–19
national security decision-making in Israel: criticism of procedures 191, 214–15; defined by Agranat Commission 84–5; dissent 117–18; IDF influence on 188–9; proposals to reform 72–3, 76; under Ben-Gurion 71–2; under Eshkol 80–1; under Meir 82–3
national security staff 192
National Security Staff Law (2008) 215, 220–1
National Service Law (1953) 63–4
NATO campaign in Serbia 22
Nazaal v. *IDF Commander in Judea and Samaria* (1994) 247n9
'neighbor practice' 163, 171; *see also Adalah – The Legal Center for Arab Minority Rights in Israel* v. *OC Central Command* (2005)
Netanyahu, Binyamin 123, 221
NGOs, numbers of in Israel (1987–2002) 156; petitions to ISC 156–9; *see also Association for Civil Rights in Israel* v. *CO Central Command* (1989); *Association for Civil Rights in Israel* v. *Minister of Defense* (1993); *Public Committee Against Torture* v. *Government of Israel* (1999); *Physicians for Human Rights* v. *IDF Commander in the West Bank* (2002); *Adalah* v. *IDF Commander in Judea and Samaria* (2002); *Canon (Law) and others* v. *IDF Commander of the West Bank* (2002); *Physicians for Human Rights* v. *CO Southern Command* (2003); *Physicians for Human Rights* v. *IDF Commander in Gaza* (2004); *Adalah – The Legal Center for Arab Minority Rights in Israel* v. *OC Central Command* (2005); *The Movement for the Quality of Government and others* v. *the Knesset and others* (2005); *The Legal Forum for the Land of Israel* v. *the Government of Israel* (2005); *The Public Committee Against Torture in Israel* v. *The Government of Israel* (2006); *Adalah – The Legal Centre for Arab Minority Rights in Israel* v. *Minister of Interior* (2006); *Gisha – Legal Center for Freedom of Movement* v. *Minister of Defense* (2008); *Physicians for Human Rights* v. *Government of Israel* (2009); *Yesh Din* v. *CO in the West Bank* (2010); *Adam Teva va-Din* v. *Ministry of Defense* (2010); *Association for Civil Rights in Israel* v. *The Knesset* (pending)
Northern Ireland, British policy towards 23
Nuclear program, Israeli 46, 143; Ben-Gurion's control over 75–6; in Eshkol–Dayan memorandum (1967) 85; Israeli attack on Iraqi reactor (1981) 118; in Meir–Dayan agreement (1969) 85
Nun, Eyal 186

Ofrah 97
Olmert, Ehud: criticized by Winograd Commission 190–1, 216–20
ombudsman, IDF 224
Ordinance for the Prevention of Terrorism (1985–1993) 124–5
Oren, Amiran 57
Osiraq (1981), Israeli attack on 118–19
Oslo accords (1993) 109, 118, 123, 125; (1995) 144
Oyeb v. *Minister of Defense* (1979) 247n6

Palestine authority, Israel agreements with (1993, 1994, 1995) 108; *see also* Oslo accords
Palmach: Ben-Gurion's relationship with 71; foundation of 38; relationship with civil authorities 40
Peres, Shimon 74–5, 97, 104, 114, 116, 118, 213–14, 250n2
Peretz, Amir: cricized by Winograd Commission 190–1, 216–20
Physicians for Human Rights v. *CO Southern Command* (2003) 194
Physicians for Human Rights v. *IDF Commander in Gaza* (2004) 158
Physicians for Human Rights v. *IDF Commander in the West Bank* (2002) 157
Planning and Construction Law (1965) 61, 195, 211

Poland: emergency regulations in 20
'political question' (judicial doctrine) 132, 134, 193, 202
Pollard affair (1986) 127
Posner, Eric 201
Posner, Richard 200
Prevention of Terrorism Ordinance (1948) 62
prime minister: role in national security decision making 87; Winograd Commission (2006) on 216–20
proportionality as legal principle 161
The Public Committee against Torture in Israel v. *The Government of Israel* (2006) 155, 162–3, 194, 248n5
The Public Committee against Torture v. *The Government of Israel* (1999) 153, 169, 247n6, 249n8

Rabin, Yitzchak 1, 213; as ambassador to USA 81, 83; as CGS 79; as prime minister (1974–7) 104–5, 114 (1992–1995) 124–5, 214
'Rafah Approach' case (1973) see: *Abu Chilu* v. *The Government of Israel*
'ratchet' claim, as advance by Aharon Barak 199–200
Reizner, Daniel 155
Remembrance Day of IDF Fallen Law (1963) 63
reprisal raids 73
Reserve Duty Law (2008) 168, 185, 229
Ressler v. *Minister of Defense* (1988) 135, 152, 192–3
Rozenbluтт, Pinchas 55
Rozen Committee (1959) 74
Rubinstein, Amnon 47, 152
Rubinstein v. *Minister of Defense* (1998) 152, 249n8

Sabra and Shatilla (1982) 115, 129
Sadat, Anwar 117
Sajedia v. *Minister of Defense* (1988) 138
Salech Shechade see targeted killings
Sapir, Gideon 201
Sapir, Pinchas 83
Schnitzer v. *Chief Military Censor* (1989) 113, 139; significance of 140, 146
Sebastia 114
security/separation fence 160–2, 171–2, 184–5, 248 n7; *see also Beit Sourik Village Council* v. *The Government of Israel*; *Mara'be* v. *The Government of Israel*
security zone, Israeli in southern Lebanon 92
Segev, Joshua 132
'sentinels': as agents of supervision over armed forces 230–1; types of 231–8
Service Deferral Law (2002) 164, 229
settlements (Jewish) in Territories 97–8, 107–8, 114; ISC attitude towards 193; *see also* Kfar Etzion Ofrah, Sebastia
Shalom Akhshav ('Peace Now') 115
Shamgar, Meir 2, 47, 95, 99, 101, 132
Shamir, Yitzchak 116, 118, 130
Sharett, Moshe: relationship with Ben-Gurion 53, 73–5
Sharon, Ariel 116, 119–20, 130, 131
Shelters Law (1949) 63
Sherf, Zeev 77
Shitrit, Bekhor 58
shtadlanut (intercession), tradition of 31
Sinai Campaign (1956) 65, 75–6
'situation of extraordinary emergency', declarations of 110
Six Days War (1967) 80; decision-making in 81–2, 246n1; *see also* Territories
South Africa, emergency regulations in 20
South Korea, national security council in 19
South Lebanese Army 109; absence of *knesset* control over 92
Spain, supreme command in 19
spatial dimension of national security: absent from Basic Law: The Military (1974) 93–5; as affected by *Dawikat* decision (1979) 136; as affected by *knesset* legislation (1977–1995) 121–2, 183–5; under Ben-Gurion 57–61; defined 18, 21–4; ISC attitude towards since 1980s 193–6; suggested reforms regarding 205, 211–13
Sprinzak, Ehud 41
Srebrenica 26
'standing doctrine', ISC policy respecting 134, 152, 156, 192, 202; *see also Barzilai* v. *The Government of Israel* (1986); *Ressler* v. *Minister of Defense* (1988)
state comptroller in Israel 84, 131, 212, 214; weaknesses of 233–4
State Comptroller Law (1949) 233
strategic culture 29–30, 44
'statism' (*mamalkhtiut*) 43
Strashnov, Amnon 225, 250n8

Tal Law *see* Service Deferral Law
Tal, Zvi 164
Tamir, Shemuel 15–16
targeted killings 162–3, 204; *see also The Public Committee Against Torture in Israel* v. *The Government of Israel* (2006)
temporal dimension of national security, affected by 2001 revision to Basic Law: The Government 182; as affected by *Dawikat* judgment (1979) 136–7; as affected after 1967 by military administration over the Territories 96–7; ambiguity of (1977–1995) 110–11; defined 18–19, 19–21; during Ben-Gurion era 54–7; ignored in Basic

Law: The Military (1974) 92–3; influence of Jewish traditions on 32–4; ISC attitudes towards after 1995 193–4; not affected by 1992 revision to Basic Law: The Government 124; proposed reforms 211, 238–41

Territories: as 'administered' regions 95–7; Arab population in 93; Dayan's policies towards 95; 'fragmented sovereignty' in 185, 212–13; government decisions respecting in 1967 94; IDF status in 97–8; ISC's definition of situation in after 2000 194, 212–13; Jewish settlers in 97–8, 107–8

Thailand, supreme command in 19

'ticking bomb' situation, discussed by ISC 153

tohar ha-neshek ('purity of arms') 36

'transference', as judicial strategy by ISC (1995–2008) 159–62

Turkel Commission (2010) 187

Turkey, national security council in 19; supreme command in 19

United Kingdom, anti-terror legislation 21, 242n2; supreme command in 19

United Mizrachi Bank v. *Migdal Cooperative Village* (1995) 144

United States of America, emergency regulations 21, 242n2; unitary system of command 19; use of Guantanamo Bay base 22; 'War on Terror' 23

universal jurisdiction, applied to Israelis 203–4, 249n7

Walzer, Michael 180

Weizmann, Ezer 81, 117–18, 136

'West Bank', legal status of 247n5; *see also* Territories

Wichselbaum v. *Minister of Defense* (1995) 150

Winograd Commission (2006) 187, 216–20

Wye Plantation agreement (1998) 123, 154

Ya'alon, Moshe 223

Yadin, Yigael 57, 73, 77, 85, 90, 118

Yamit, withdrawal from (1982) 184; *see also* Law for the Compensation of the Sinai Evacuees

Yardor v. *Chairman of the Central Elections Commission* (1965) 68

Yesh Din 247n1,

Yesh Din v. *IDF Commander in the West Bank* (2010) 198

yishuv (Jewish community in Mandate Palestine), militarism in 37

Yom Kippur War (1973), decision-making during 83–4, 246n2

Yossi Beilin v. *Prime Minister* (2006) 196

Zemach v. *Minister of Defense* (1999) 248n9

Zuffan v. *MAG* (1989) 139